Health and Safety

Redgrave Fife & Machin

Health and Safety

1995 Cumulative Supplement

John Hendy LLB, LLM, QC

of Gray's Inn

Michael Ford LLB, MA

of the Middle Temple, Barrister

BUTTERWORTHS
LONDON, DUBLIN, EDINBURGH
1995

United Kingdom	Butterworths a Division of Reed Elsevier (UK) Ltd, Halsbury House, 35 Chancery Lane, LONDON WC2A 1EL and 4 Hill Street, EDINBURGH EH2 3JZ
Australia	Butterworths, SYDNEY, MELBOURNE, BRISBANE, ADELAIDE, PERTH, CANBERRA and HOBART
Canada	Butterworths Canada Ltd, TORONTO and VANCOUVER
Ireland	Butterworth (Ireland) Ltd, DUBLIN
Malaysia	Malayan Law Journal Sdn Bhd, KUALA LUMPUR
New Zealand	Butterworths of New Zealand Ltd, WELLINGTON and AUCKLAND
Puerto Rico	Butterworth of Puerto Rico, Inc, SAN JUAN
Singapore	Reed Elsevier (Singapore) Pte Ltd, SINGAPORE
South Africa	Butterworths Publishers Pty Ltd, DURBAN
USA	Michie, CHARLOTTESVILLE, Virginia

Crown copyright material is reproduced with the permission of the Controller of Her Majesty's Stationery Office.

A CIP catalogue record for this book is available from the British Library.

ISBN 0 406 00561 3

Printed and bound in Great Britain by Clays Ltd, St Ives plc

Preface

This is the second annual supplement to the second edition of *Redgrave*. From size alone, it should be clear that a great deal of legislation has been passed in the intervening period. For ease of reference this Supplement contains the material included in the 1994 Supplement as well as new material.

Continuing the interventionist approach of the European Commission under Article 118A of the Treaty, new European Directives have been introduced since the last Supplement. These include the Protection of Young People at Work Directive (94/33/EC), which prohibits work by children except in certain specified activities and regulates the health and safety aspects of work of young people. Minimum health and safety standards for temporary and mobile construction sites, which fall outside the Workplace Directive (see Art. 1(2)(c)), are laid down in another Directive (92/57/EEC); this recognises the especially high levels of risk in the building industry, often a result of poor overall planning. We have corrected an earlier omission by including the Pregnant Workers Directive, which affords important legal protections to pregnant and breastfeeding women (not confined to health and safety).

The UK government is pursuing a different domestic policy, as illustrated in the Deregulation and Contracting Out Act 1994, which permits the repeal of health and safety regulations subject only to consultation with the Health and Safety Commission. Yet, at the same time and in tension with this goal, the Government has been obliged to enact regulations to comply with European Directives. The Construction (Design and Management) Regulations 1994 purport to implement the Temporary or Mobile Construction Sites Directive but exclude civil liability for most of the duties (reg. 21), a regrettable omission in the light of the serious hazards of building site work. The Control of Substances Hazardous to Health Regulations 1994, the Chemicals (Hazard Information and Packaging for Supply) Regulations 1994 and the Electrical Equipment (Safety) Regulations 1994 all owe their origin to Europe. These regulations, passed under the Health and Safety at Work etc. Act 1974, do give rise to civil liability (see s. 47(2)).

The government has not, however, introduced any legislation to implement the rights of worker participation on health and safety matters as required by the European Directives. Although new regulations have been introduced in the context of transfer of undertakings and collective redundancies, extending duties to consult to workplaces where no unions are recognised (see the Collective Redundancies and Transfer of Undertakings (Protection of Employment) (Amendment) Regulations 1995), the duties under health and safety regulations are still restricted to those workplaces where an employer chooses to recognise a union. This remains a glaring deficiency in implementation.

Finally, important cases have been decided over the last year. Two deserve special mention. In *R v Associated Octel* [1995] ICR 281, the Court of Appeal adapted a sensible approach to what is the "conduct of [an employer's] undertaking" under the

Health and Safety at Work etc. Act 1974, s. 3; the fact that activities were performed by independent contractors did not mean that they fell outside the section. In *R v British Steel plc* [1995] ICR 586 the same court rejected an argument that corporate employers were not criminally liable under s. 3 of the Act unless the "directing mind" of the company was involved, recognising that to hold otherwise "would drive a juggernaut through the legislative scheme" (per Steyn LJ). Both decisions, in rejecting rather technical defences, demonstrate a recognition of the public importance of protecting health and safety.

Once more we wish to express our great thanks to the staff at Butterworths for the enormous amount of work and time they have devoted to this Supplement. The usual attributions of responsibility apply.

John Hendy QC
Michael Ford
October 1995

Contents

TABLE OF STATUTES

References in this Table to *Statutes* are to Halsbury's Statutes of England (Fourth Edition) showing the volume and page at which the annotated text of the Act will be found.

ALPHABETICAL TABLE OF ORDERS AND REGULATIONS

References in **bold** type indicate where the Order or Regulations are set out in part or in full.

CHRONOLOGICAL TABLE OF ORDERS AND REGULATIONS

References in **bold** type indicate where the Order or Regulations are set out in part or in full.

PAGE

TABLE OF CASES

TABLE OF EUROPEAN
COMMUNITY LEGISLATION

References in **bold** type indicate where the Directive is set out in part or in full.

PART 1

NOTER UP

lxviii   **Add to end of second full paragraph.** In *R v Secretary of State for Employment, ex p NACODS* CO/2576/93 (16 December 1993, unreported) the Divisional Court held that the question of whether Regulations or ACOPS were in fact "designed to maintain or improve" health and safety standards was a matter for Parliament and one not susceptible to review by the Courts. It is submitted that the European Court of Justice is unlikely to be so respectful to Member States in relation to Art. 118a.

lxxi   **Delete last sentence of second paragraph and insert.** In *Griffin v South West Water Services Ltd* [1995] IRLR 15, HCJ, Blackburne J held that an injunction would not lie to enforce the obligation to consult under the Collective Redundancies Directive 75/129 even if that duty was directly effective (which he doubted). He held that United Kingdom law would not provide a remedy beyond that provided for in the implementing legislation (there, a payment of limited compensation). It is respectfully submitted that this decision is not consistent with the European authorities, and *Factortame* in particular (see p. lxxiii). His decision on remedies is of limited relevance to the obligation to consult workers or their representatives on health and safety matters, since no compensation is available for breach. But it clearly does have some bearing upon whether the provisions in the Directives on worker consultation are sufficiently certain to be directly effective (see note to pp. 315–316 post).

lxxii   **Add to end of third full paragraph.** Drawing upon these principles the Court held in *Emmott v Minister for Social Welfare and A-G:* C-208/90 [1993] ICR 8, [1991] IRLR 387 that Community law prevented a Member State from relying on national time limits to defeat a right based on an unimplemented directive. The case of *Johnson v Chief Adjudication Officer (No 2):* C-410/92 [1995] ICR 375, [1995] IRLR 157, however, illustrates a more cautious approach. The European Court of Justice ruled that Community law did not preclude the application, to a claim based on the direct effect of Directive 79/7, of a rule of national law which limited the period prior to the bringing of the claim in respect of which arrears of benefit were payable, even where that Directive had not been properly transposed within the prescribed period in the Member State concerned. The court decided that the national rule in the *Johnson* case was similar to that in *Steenhorst-Neerings v Bestuur van de Bedrijfvereniging voor Detailhandel, Ambachten en Huisvrouwen:* C-338/91 [1994] IRLR 244 in that, unlike *Emmott*, neither rule constituted a bar to bringing proceedings; rather both merely limited the time period for claiming arrears of benefit.

lxxxiii   **5. *Reasonably practicable; practicable.* Add to end of first paragraph.** In the context of s. 29(1) of the Factories Act 1961, foreseeability was not relevant in determining what was reasonably practicable. Whether the employee's place of work was safe was a question of fact: *Neil v Greater Glasgow Health Board* 1994 SCLR 673.

PAGE

PART 1 EUROPEAN DIRECTIVES

The Machinery Directive

29   Throughout the text, the term "EC mark" is replaced by "CE marking", by Council Directive 93/68/EEC (OJ No. L 220, 30.8.93 p. 1), art. 6.1.

32   **Article 1.** Amended by Council Directive 93/44/EEC (OJ No. L 175 19.7.93 p. 12), art. 1, as follows:

(i) the following subparagraph is added to para. 1:

"It shall also apply to safety components placed on the market separately.";

(ii) the following subparagraph is added to para. 2:

"For the purposes of this Directive, *safety components* means a component, provided that it is not interchangeable equipment, which the manufacturer or his authorized representative established in the Community places on the market to fulfil a safety function when in use and the failure or malfunctioning of which endangers the safety or health of exposed persons.";

(iii) in para. 3, the following indent is deleted;

"— lifting equipment designed and constructed for raising and/or moving persons with or without loads, except for industrial trucks with elevating operation position,";

(iv) the indent "—cableways for the public or private transposition of persons," is replaced by "—cableways, including funicular railways, for the public or private transportation of persons,"; and

(v) the following indents are added:

"— lifts which permanently serve specific levels of buildings and constructions, having a car moving between guides which are rigid and inclined at a angle of more than 15 degrees to the horizontal and designed for the transport of:
   — persons,
   — persons and goods,
   — goods alone if the car is accessible, that is to say, a person may enter it without difficulty, and fitted with controls situated inside the car or within reach of a person inside,
— means of transport of persons using rack and pinion rail mounted vehicles,
— mine winding gear,
— theatre elevators,
— construction site hoists intended for lifting persons or persons and goods."; and

(vi) para. 4 is replaced by the following:

"4. Where, for machinery or safety components, the risks referred to in this Directive are wholly or partly covered by specific Community directives, this Directive shall not apply, or shall cease to apply, in the case of such machinery or safety components and of such risks on the implementation of these specific Directives.".

33 **Article 2.** Replaced by Council Directive 93/44/EEC (OJ No. L175 19.7.93 p. 12), art. 1.2, as follows:

"Article 2

1. Member States shall take all appropriate measures to ensure that machinery or safety components covered by this Directive may be replaced on the market and put into service only if they do not endanger the health or safety of persons and, where appropriate, domestic animals or property, when properly installed and maintained and used for their intended purpose.

2. This Directive shall not affect Member States' entitlement to lay down, in due observance of the Treaty, such requirements as they may deem necessary to ensure that persons and in particular workers are protected when using the machinery or safety components in question, provided that this does not mean that the machinery or safety components are modified in a way not specified in the Directive.

3. At trade fairs, exhibitions, demonstrations, etc, Member States shall not prevent the showing of machinery or safety components which do not conform to the provisions of this Directive, provided that a visible sign clearly indicates that such machinery or safety components do not conform and that they are not for sale until they have been brought into conformity by the manufacturer or his authorized representative established in the Community. During demonstrations, adequate safety measures shall be taken to ensure the protection of persons.".

34 **Article 3.** Replaced by Council Directive 93/44/EEC (OJ No. L175 19.7.93 p. 12), art. 1.3, as follows:

"Article 3

Machinery and safety components covered by this Directive shall satisfy the essential health and safety requirements set out in Annex I.";

Article 4. Amended by Council Directive 93/44/EEC (OJ No. L175 19.7.93 p. 12), art. 1.4, as follows:

(i) para. 1 is replaced by the following:

"1. Member States shall not prohibit, restrict or impede the placing on the market and putting into service in their territory of machinery and safety components which comply with this Directive."; and (ii) the following paragraph is added:

"3. Member States may not prohibit, restrict or impede the placing on the market of safety components as defined in Article 1 (2) where they are accompanied by an EC declaration of conformity by the manufacturer or his authorized representative established in the Community as referred to in Annex II, point C.".

Article 5(1), (2). Replaced by Council Directive 93/44/EEC (OJ No. L175 19.7.93 p. 12), art. 1.5, as follows:

34

"1. Member States shall regard the following as conforming to all the provisions of this Directive, including the procedures for checking the conformity provided for in Chapter II:
— machinery bearing the CE marking and accompanied by the EC declaration of conformity referred to in Annex II.A.,
— safety components accompanied by the EC declaration of conformity referred to in Annex II.C.

In the absence of harmonized standards, Member States shall take any steps they deem necessary to bring to the attention of the parties concerned the existing national technical standards and specifications which are regarded as important or relevant to the proper implementation of the essential safety and health requirements in Annex I.

2. Where a national standard transposing a harmonized standard, the reference for which has been published in the *Official Journal of the European Communities,* covers one or more of the essential safety requirements, machinery or safety components constructed in accordance with this standard shall be presumed to comply with the relevant essential requirements.

Member States shall publish the references of national standards transposing harmonized standards.".

35   **Article 7.** Paras. 1, 3 are replaced by Council Directive 93/44/EEC (OJ No. L175 19.7.93 p. 12), art. 1.6, as follows:

"1. Where a Member State ascertains—
— that machinery bearing the CE marking,
    or
— safety components accompanied by the EC declaration of conformity,

used in accordance with their intended purpose are liable to endanger the safety of persons, and, where appropriate, domestic animals or property, it shall take all appropriate measures to withdraw such machinery or safety components from the market, to prohibit the placing on the market, putting into service or use thereof, or to restrict free movement thereof.

The Member States shall immediately inform the commission of any such measure, indicating the reason for its decision and, in particular, whether non-conformity is due to:

(a) failure to satisfy the essential requirements referred to in Article 3;
(b) incorrect application of the standards referred to in Article 5 (2);
(c) shortcomings in the standards referred to in Article 5 (2) themselves."

"3. Where:
— machinery which does not comply bears the CE marking,
— a safety component which does not comply is accompanied by an EC declaration of conformity,

the competent Member State shall take appropriate action against whomsoever has affixed the marking or drawn up the declaration and shall so inform the Commission and other Member States.".

36   **Article 8.** Para. 1 is replaced by Council Directive 93/44/EEC (OJ No. L175 19.7.93 p. 12), art. 1.7(a), as follows:

"1. The manufacturer or his authorized representative established in the Community must, in order to certify that machinery and safety components are in conformity with this Directive, draw up for all machinery or safety component manufactured an EC declaration of conformity based on the model given in Annex II, A or C as appropriate.

In addition, for machinery alone, the manufacturer or his authorized representatives established in the Community must affix to the machine the CE marking referred to in Article 10.".

Para. 4a is inserted by Council Directive 93/44/EEC (OJ No. L175 19.7.93 p. 12), art. 1.7(b), as follows:

"4a. Safety components shall be subject to the certification procedures applicable to machinery pursuant to paragraphs 2, 3 and 4. Furthermore, during EC type-examination, the notified body shall verify the suitability of the safety component for fulfilling the safety functions declared by the manufacturer.".

The fifth paragraph is replaced by the following text, by Council Directive 93/68/EEC (OJ No. L220, 30.8. 93 p. 1), art. 6.2:

"5. (a) Where the machinery is subject to other Directives concerning other aspects and which also provide for the affixing of the EC marking, the latter shall indicate that the machinery is also presumed to conform to the provisions of those other Directives.

(b) However, where one or more of these Directives allow the manufacturer, during a transitional period, to choose which arrangements to apply, the CE marking shall indicate conformity only to the Directives applied by the manufacturer, In this case, particulars of the Directives applied, as published in the *Official Journal of the European Communities*, must be given in the documents, notices or instructions required by the Directives and accompanying such machinery.".

Para. 6 is replaced by Council Directive 93/44/EEC (OJ No. L175 19.7.93 p. 12), art. 1.7(c), as follows:

"6. Where neither the manufacturer nor hid authorized representative established in the Community fulfils the obligations of the preceding paragraphs, these obligations shall fall to any person placing the machinery or safety component on the market in the Community. The same obligations shall apply to any person assembling machinery or pacts thereof or safety components of various origins or constructing machinery or safety components for his own use.".

Article 9. Para 1 is replaced by Council Directive 93/44/EEC (OJ No. L175 19.7.93 p. 12), art. 1.8, as follows:

> "1. Each Member State shall notify the Commission and the other Member States of the bodies responsible for carrying out the certification procedures referred to in Article 8. The Commission shall publish a list of those bodies in the *Official Journal of the European Communities* for information and shall ensure that the list is kept up to date.".

That paragraph is further replaced by the following text, by Council Directive 93/68/EEC (OJ No. L220, 30.8. 93 p. 1), art. 6.3:

> "1. Member States shall notify the Commission and the other Member States of the approved bodies which they have appointed to carry out the procedures referred to in Article 8 together with the specific tasks which these bodies have been appointed to carry out and the identification numbers assigned to them beforehand by the Commission.

> The Commission shall publish in the *Official Journal of the European Communities* a list of the notified bodies and their identification numbers and the tasks for which they have been notified. The Commission shall ensure that this list is kept up to date.".

Article 10. Amended by Council Directive 93/68/EEC (OJ No. L220, 30.1. 93 p. 1), art. 6.4–6, as follows:

The first paragraph is replaced by the following text:

> "1. The CE conformity marking shall consist of the initials 'CE'. The form of the marking to be used is shown in Annex III.".

The third paragraph is replaced by the following text:

> "3. The affixing of markings on the machinery which are likely to deceive third parties as to the meaning and form of the CE marking shall be prohibited. Any other marking may be affixed to the machinery provided that the visibility and legibility of the CE marking is not thereby reduced.".

The following paragraph is added as follows:

> "4. Without prejudice to Article 7:
> (a) where a Member State establishes that the CE marking has been affixed unduly, the manufacturer or his authorized representative established within the Community shall be obliged to make the product conform as regards the provisions concerning the CE marking and to end the infringement under the conditions imposed by the Member State;
> (b) where non-conformity continues, the Member State must take all appropriate measures to restrict or prohibit the placing on the market of the product in question or to ensure that it is withdrawn from the market in accordance with the procedures laid down in Article 7.".

PAGE

38 **Article 11.** Replaced by Council Directive 93/44/EEC (OJ No. L175 19.7.93 p. 12), art. 1.9, as follows:

"Article 11

Any decision taken pursuant to this Directive which restricts the placing on the market and putting into service of machinery or safety component shall state the exact grounds on which it is based. Such a decision shall be notified as soon as possible to the party concerned, who shall at the same time be informed of the legal remedies available to him under the laws in force in the Member State concerned and of the time limits to which such remedies are subject.".

39 **Annex I.** The Title is replaced by Council Directive 93/44/EEC (OJ No. L175 19.7.93 p. 12), art. 1.10(a)–(c), as follows:

"ESSENTIAL HEALTH AND SAFETY REQUIREMENTS RELATING TO THE DESIGN AND CONSTRUCTION OF MACHINERY AND SAFETY COMPONENTS"; and the following is inserted after the title:

"For the purposes of this Annex, 'machinery' means either 'machinery' or 'safety component' as defined in Article 1 (2)."; and the preliminary observations are supplemented by the following:

"3. The essential health and safety requirements have been grouped according to the hazards which they cover.

Machinery presents a series of hazards which may be indicated under more than one heading in this Annex.

The manufacturer is under an obligation to assess the hazards in order to identify all those which apply to his machine; he must then design and construct it taking account of his assessment.".

43 **Annex 1, section 1.2.4.** The last paragraph is replaced by Council Directive 93/44/EEC (OJ No. L175 19.7.93 p. 12), art. 1.10(d), as follows:

"Once active operation of the emergency stop control has ceased following a stop command, that command must be sustained by engagement of the emergency stop device until that engagement is specifically overridden; it must not be possible to engage the device without triggering a stop command; it must be possible to disengage the device only by an appropriate operation, and disengaging the device must not restart the machinery but only permit restarting.".

51 **Annex I, section 1.5.13.** The following sections are added after this section by Council Directive 93/44/EEC (OJ No. L175 19.7.93 p. 12), art. 1.10(e):

"1.5.14. Risk of being trapped in a machine
Machinery must be designed, constructed or fitted with a means of preventing an exposed person from being enclosed within it or, if that is impossible, with a means of summoning help.

51   **1.5.15. Risk of slipping, tripping or falling**

Parts of the machinery where persons are liable to move about or stand must be designed and constructed to prevent persons slipping, tripping or falling on or off these parts."

52   **Annex I, section 1.6.2.** The second paragraph is deleted by Council Directive 93/44/EEC (OJ No. L175 19.7.93 p. 12), art. 1.10(f).

54   **Annex I, section 1.7.3.** Amended by Council Directive 93/68/EEC (OJ No. L220, 30.8. 93 p. 1), art. 6.7, as follows.

The second indent is replaced by the following text:

"— the CE marking (see Annex III)"; and a fifth indent is added as follows:
"— the year of construction".

Annex 1, section 1.7.4(a). The first indent is replaced by Council Directive 93/44/EEC (OJ No. L175 19.7.93 p. 12), art. 1.10(g), as follows:

"— a repeat of the information with which the machinery is marked, except the serial number (see 1.7.3) together with any appropriate additional information to facilitate maintenance (e.g. addresses of the importer, repairers etc.),".

Annex 1, section 1.7.4(b). Replaced by Council Directive 93/44/EEC (OJ No. L175 19.7.93 p. 12), art. 1.10(h), as follows:

"The constructions must be drawn up in one of the Community languages by the manufacturer or his authorized representative established in the Community. On being put into service, all machinery must be accompanied by a translation of the instructions in the language or languages of the country in which the machinery is to be used and by the instructions in the original language. This translation must be done either by the manufacturer or his authorized representative established in the Community or by the person introducing the machinery into the language area in question.

By way of derogation from this requirement, the maintenance instructions for use by specialized personnel employed by the manufacturer or his authorized representative established in the Community may be drawn up in only one of the Community languages understood by that personnel.".

55   **Annex I, section 1.7.4(d).** Replaced by Council Directive 93/44/EEC (OJ No. L175 19.7.93 p. 12), art. 1.10(i), as follows:

"Any literature describing the machinery must not contradict the instructions as regards safety aspects. The technical documentation describing the machinery must give information regarding the airborne noise emissions referred to in (f) and, in the case of hand-

PAGE

55   held and/or hand-guided machinery, information regarding vibration as referred to in 2.2.".

56–57   **Annex I, section 2.** Amended by Council Directive 93/44/EEC (OJ No. L175 19.7.93 p. 12), art. 1.10(j), (k), as follows:

(i) the title is replaced by the following:

"ESSENTIAL HEALTH AND SAFETY REQUIREMENTS FOR CERTAIN CATEGORIES OF MACHINERY";

(ii) in Sections 2.1, 2.2 and 2.3, the following words are deleted:

"In addition to the essential health and safety requirements set out in 1 above,".

58   **Annex 1, section 3.** The first paragraph is replaced by Council Directive 93/44/EEC (OJ No. L175 19.7.93 p. 12), art. 10.1(l), as follows:

"Machinery presenting hazards due to mobility must be designed and constructed to meet the requirements set out below.".

67   **Annex I, section 4.** The first paragraph is replaced by Council Directive 93/44/EEC (OJ No. L175 19.7.93 p. 12), art. 1.10(m), as follows:

"Machinery presenting hazards due to lifting operations—mainly hazards of load falls and collisions or hazards of tipping caused by a lifting operation—must be designed and constructed to meet the requirements set out below.".

72   **Annex 1, section 4.2.3.** The following paragraph is added to that section by Council Directive 93/44/EEC (OJ No. L175 19.7.93 p. 12), art. 1.10(n), as follows:

"Machinery serving specific levels at which operators can gain access to the load platform in order to stack or secure the load must be designed and constructed to prevent uncontrolled movement of the load platform, in particular while being loaded or unloaded.".

75   **Annex I, section 5.** The title is replaced by Council Directive 93/44/EEC (OJ No. L175 19.7.93 p. 12), art. 1.10(o), as follows:

"ESSENTIAL HEALTH AND SAFETY REQUIREMENTS FOR MACHINERY INTENDED FOR UNDERGROUND WORK"; and the first paragraph is replaced as follows by art. 1.10(p):

"Machinery intended for underground work must be designed and constructed to meet the requirements set out below."

76   **Annex 1, section 6.** Added by Council Directive 93/44/EEC (OJ No. L175 19.7.93 p. 12), art. 1.10(q), Annex, as follows:

76   "6.   ESSENTIAL HEALTH AND SAFETY REQUIREMENTS TO OFFSET THE PARTICULAR HAZARDS DUE TO THE LIFTING OR MOVING OF PERSONS.

Machinery presenting hazards due to the lifting or moving of persons must be designed and constructed to meet the requirements set out below.

6.1.   General

6.1.1.   *Definition*

For the purposes of this Chapter, 'carrier' means the device by which persons are supported in order to be lifted, lowered or moved.

6.1.2.   *Mechanical strength*

The working coefficients defined in heading 4 are inadequate for machinery intended for the lifting or moving of persons and must, as a general rule, be doubled. The floor of the carrier must be designed and constructed to offer the space and strength corresponding to the maximum number of persons and the maximum working load set by the manufacturer.

6.1.3.   *Loading control for types of device moved by power other than human strength*

The requirements of 4.2.1.4 apply regardless of the maximum working load figure. This requirement does not apply to machinery in respect of which the manufacturer can demonstrate that there is no risk of overloading and/or overturning.

6.2.   Controls

6.2.1.   *Where safety requirements do not impose other solutions:*

The carrier must, as a general rule, be designed and constructed so that persons inside have means of controlling movements upwards and downwards and, if appropriate, of moving the carrier horizontally in relation to the machinery.

In operation, those controls must override the other devices controlling the same-movement, with the exception of the emergency stop devices.

The controls for these movement must be of the maintained command type, except in the case of machinery serving specific levels.

6.2.2.   If machinery for the lifting or moving of persons can be moved with the carrier in a position other than the rest position, it must be designed and constructed so that the person or persons in the carrier have the means of preventing hazards produced by the movement of the machinery.

6.2.3.   Machinery for the lifting or moving of persons must be designed, constructed or equipped so that excess speeds of the carrier do not cause hazards.

6.3.   Risks of persons falling from the carrier

6.3.1.   If the measures referred to in 1.1.15 are not adequate, carriers must be fitted with a sufficient number of anchorage points for the number of persons possibly using the carrier, strong enough for the attachment of personal protective equipment against the danger of falling.

6.3.2.   Any trapdoors in floors or ceilings or side doors must open in a direction which obviates any risk of falling should they open unexpectedly.

6.3.3.   Machinery for lifting or moving must be designed and constructed to ensure that the floor of the carrier does not tilt to an extend which creates a risk of the occupants falling, including when moving.

The floor of the carrier must be slip-resistant.

6.4.   Risks of the carrier falling or overturning

6.4.1.   Machinery for the lifting or moving of persons must be designed and constructed to prevent the carrier falling or overturning.

6.4.2.   Acceleration and braking of the carrier or carrying vehicle, under the control of the operator or triggered by a safety device and under the maximum load and speed conditions laid down by the manufacturer, must not cause any danger to exposed persons.

6.5.   Markings

Where necessary to ensure safety, the carrier must bear the relevant essential information.".

Annex II. The title of point A is replaced by Council Directive 93/44/EEC (OJ No. L175 19.7.93 p. 12), art. 1.11(a), as follows:

"**Contents of the EC declaration of conformity for machinery**", and the following point is added by art. 1.11(c):

"C. Contents of the EC declaration of conformity for safety components placed on the market separately.

The EC declaration of conformity must contain the following particulars:

— name and address of the manufacturer or his authorized representative established in the Community,
— description of the safety component,

— safety function fulfilled by the safety component, if not obvious from the description,
— where appropriate, the name and address of the notified body and the number of the EC type-examination certificate,
— where appropriate, the name and address of the notified body to which the file was forwarded in accordance with the first indent of Article 8 (2) (c),
— where appropriate, the name and address of the notified body which carried out the verification referred to in the second indent of Article 8 (2) (c),
— where appropriate, a reference to the harmonized standards,
— where appropriate, the name and address of the notified body which carried out the verification referred to in the second indent of Article 8 (2) (c),
— where appropriate, a reference to the harmonized standards,
— where appropriate, the national technical standards and specifications used,
— identification of the person empowered to sign on behalf of the manufacture or his authorized representative established in the Community.".

77   **Annex III.** Replaced by Council Directive 93/68/EEC (OJ No. L220, 30.8.93 p. 1), art. 6.8, as follows:

"ANNEX III

CE CONFORMITY MARKING

— The CE conformity marking shall consist of the initials "CE" taking the following form:

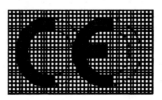

— If the CE marking is reduced or enlarged the proportions given in the above drawing must be respected.
— The various components of the CE marking must have substantially the same vertical dimension, which may not be less than 5mm. This minimum dimension may be waived for small-scale machinery.".

Annex IV. Amended by Council Directive 93/44/EEC (OJ No. L175 19.7.93 p. 12), art. 1.12(a)–(c), as follows:

(i) the title is replaced by the following:

"TYPES OF MACHINERY AND SAFETY COMPONENTS FOR WHICH THE PROCEDURE REFERRED TO IN ARTCLE 8 (2) (b) AND (c) MUST BE APPLIED";

(ii)   the following subtitle is inserted after the title:

"A. Machinery"; and

(iii)   section 1 is replaced by the following:

"1.   Circular saws (single or multi-blade) for working with wood and analogous materials or for working with meat and analogous materials.

1.1.   Sawing machines with fixed tool during operation, having a fixed bed with manual feed of the workpiece or with a demountable power feed.

1.2.   Sawing machines with fixed tool during operation, having a manually operated reciprocating saw-bench or carriage.

1.3.   Sawing machines with fixed tool during operation, having a built-in mechanical feed device for the workpieces, with manual loading and/or unloading.

1.4.   Sawing machines with movable tool during operation, with a mechanical feed device and manual loading and/or unloading.".

Annex IV, section 4. Replaced by Council Directive 93/44/EEC (OJ No. L175 19.7.93 p. 12), art. 1.12(d), as follows:

"4.   Band-saws with a fixed or mobile bed and band-saws with a mobile carriage, with manual loading and/or unloading, for working with wood and analogous materials or for working with meat and analogous materials.".

Annex IV, section 5. Replaced by Council Directive 93/44/EEC (OJ No. L175 19.7.93 p. 12), art. 1.12(e), as follows:

"5.   Combined machines of the types referred to in 1 to 4 and 7 for working with wood and analogous materials.".

Annex IV, section 7. Replaced by Council Directive 93/44/EEC (OJ No. L175 19.7.93 p. 12), art. 1.12(f), as follows:

"7. Hand-fed vertical spindle moulding machines for working with wood and analogous materials.".

Annex IV, section 15. The following are inserted after section 15 by Council Directive 93/44/EEC (OJ No. L175 19.7.93 p. 12), art. 1.12(g):

"16. Devices for the lifting of persons involving a risk 6f falling from a vertical height of more than three metres.

17. Machines for the manufacture of pyrotechnics.";

and the following section is added by art. 1.12(h):

78   **"B. Safety components**

1.   Electro-sensitive devices designed specifically to detect persons in order to ensure their safety (non-material barriers, sensor mats, electromagnetic detectors, etc).

2. Logic units which ensure the safety functions of bi-manual controls.

3. Automatic movable screens to protect the presses referred to in 9, 10 and 11.

4. Roll-over protection structures (ROPS).

5. Fallings-object protective structures (FOPS).".

Annex V. The following is added after the title by Council Directive 93/44/EEC (OJ No. L175 19.7.93 p. 12), art. 1.13:

"For the purposes of this Annex, 'machinery' means either 'machinery' or 'safety component' as defined in Article 1 (2).".

80   **Annex VI.** The following is added after the title by Council Directive 93/44/EEC (OJ No. L175 19.7.93 p. 12), art. 1.14:

"For the purposes of this Annex, 'machinery' means either 'machinery' or 'safety component' as defined in Article 1 (2).".

81   **Annex VII.** The following is added after the title by Council Directive 93/44/EEC (OJ No. L175 19.7.93 p. 12), art. 1.15:

"For the purposes of this Annex, 'machinery' means either 'machinery' or 'safety component' as defined in Article 1 (2).".

The Contained Use of Genetically Modified Organisms Directive

195   **Annex II.**   Replaced by Commission Directive 94/51/EEC (OJ No. L297, 18.11.94, p. 29), art. 1, Annex, as follows:

"ANNEX II

CRITERIA FOR CLASSIFYING GENETICALLY MODIFIED MICRO-ORGANISMS INTO GROUP I

A genetically modified micro-organism is classified as falling within Group I when all the following criteria are fulfilled:

   (i)   the recipient or parental micro-organism is unlikely to cause disease to humans, animals or plants;

   (ii) the nature of the vector and the insert is such that they do not endow the genetically modified micro-organism with a phenotype likely to cause disease to humans, animals or plants, or likely to cause adverse effects in the environment;

   (iii) the genetically modified micro-organism is unlikely to cause disease to humans, animals or plants and is unlikely to have adverse effects on the environment.".

PAGE

PART 2 THE PRINCIPAL LEGISLATION

The Health and Safety at Work etc Act 1974

Safety Representatives and Safety Committees Regulations 1977

310   **Add to end of note (g)** *Health and safety regulations.* (See also *R v Secretary of State for Employment, ex p NACODS* CO 2576/93 (16 December 1993, unreported) noted to p. lxviii ante.)

315–316   **Delete last paragraph and add to the end of** *General note.* In *EC Commission v United Kingdom:* C—383/92 [1994] ICR 664, [1994] IRLR 412 and *EC Commission v United Kingdom:* C—382/92 [1994] ICR 664, [1994] IRLR 392, the ECJ held that the Employment Protection Act 1975, s. 99, etc. and the Transfer of Undertakings (Protection of Employment) Regulations 1981, reg. 10, failed properly to transpose respectively Article 2 of the Directive on Collective Redundancies (75/129) and Article 6 of the Directive on Transfer of Undertakings (77/187) in that the English legislation provided that the workers representatives to whom information must be provided and with whom consultation must be carried out were restricted to the nominees of recognised unions. There was no warrant for excluding the obligation to inform and consult in cases where the employer has refused or terminated union recognition. It is submitted that the same reasoning must apply to the provisions concerning safety representatives. It is to be noted, however, that Directives 75/129 and 77/187 impose the obligation to inform and consult only worker representatives, whereas Directive 89/391 imposes the relevant obligations in respect of "workers and/or their representatives", as do the other "daughter" Directives. Nevertheless, the underlying aim of the Directive is to improve standards of health and safety (Art. 1), which may be inconsistent with an employer unilaterally refusing to consult with chosen representatives and consulting with the whole workforce instead.

Less clear, is whether the Directive itself gives rise to rights which are directly effective. In *Griffin v South West Water Services Ltd* [1995] IRLR 15, HCJ, Blackburne J refused a remedy for direct enforcement of the Collective Redundancies Directive (75/129). He held, obiter, that the Directive, in specifying that "workers' representatives means the workers' representatives provided for by the laws or practices of the Member States", was insufficiently precise. A similar phrase is found in the Framework Directive (89/391) at Art. 3 (c) and so direct enforcement would not be available here either. Blackburne J further held that United Kingdom law would not provide a remedy beyond that provided for in the implementing legislation (there, a payment of limited compensation). It is respectfully submitted that this decision is not consistent with the European authorities, and *Factortame* in particular (see p. lxxiii). His decision on remedies is of limited relevance to the obligation to consult workers or their representatives on health and safety matters, since no compensation is available for breach.

Employment Protection (Consolidation) Act 1978.

Sections 22B, 22C have effect as if the reference in s. 22B(1) of that Act to s. 22A included a reference to the Sunday Trading Act 1994, Sch. 4, para. 10, which reads as follows:

"10.—(1) Subject to sub-paragraphs (2) and (4) below, a protected or opted-out shop worker has the right not to be subjected to any detriment by any act, or any deliberate failure to act, by his employer done on the ground that the shop worker refused, or proposed to refuse, to do shop work on Sunday or on a particular Sunday.

(2) Sub-paragraph (1) above does not apply to anything done in relation to an opted-out shop worker on the ground that he refused, or proposed to refuse, to do shop work on any Sunday or Sundays falling before the end of the notice period.

(3) Subject to sub-paragraph (4) below, a shop worker has the right not to be subjected to any detriment by any act, or any deliberate failure to act, by his employer done on the ground that he gave, or proposed to give, an opting-out notice to his employer.

(4) Sub-paragraphs (1) and (3) above do not apply where the detriment in question amounts to dismissal.

(5) For the purposes of this paragraph a shop worker who does not work on Sunday or on a particular Sunday is not to be regarded as having been subjected to any detriment by—

(a) any failure to pay remuneration in respect of shop work on a Sunday which he has not done,

(b) any failure to provide him with any other benefit, where that failure results from the application, in relation to a Sunday on which the employee has not done shop work, of a contractual term under which the extent of that benefit varies according to the number of hours worked by the employee or the remuneration of the employee, or

(c) any failure to provide him with any work, remuneration or other benefit which by virtue of paragraph 14 or 15 below the employer is not obliged to provide.

(6) Where an employer offers to pay a sum specified in the offer to any one or more employees who are protected or opted-out shop workers or who, under their contracts of employment, are not obliged to do shop work on Sunday, if they agree to do shop work on Sunday or on a particular Sunday—

(a) an employee to whom the offer is not made is not to be regarded for the purposes of this paragraph as having been subjected to any detriment by any failure to make the offer to him or to pay him that sum, and

(b) an employee who does not accept the offer is not to be regarded for those purposes as having been subjected to any detriment by any failure to pay him that sum.".

321   **Section 3(2).** Modified in relation to an activity involving the consignment, storage or use of certain biological agents by the Control of Substances Hazardous to Health Regulations 1994, S.I. 1994 No. 3246, reg. 20, set out in Pt. 2 at p. 287 post.

322   **Add to end of *General note*.** The Court of Appeal in *R v Associated Octel Ltd* [1994] 4 All ER 1051, [1995] ICR 281 effectively overruled the reasoning of the Divisional Court in *RMC Roadstone v Jester* [1994] 4 All ER 1037, [1994] ICR 456 on control. The Court of Appeal said that control was only relevant to what was reasonably practicable; it did not affect the prior question of what was the 'conduct of the undertaking'.

Section 3(1) creates absolute criminal liability subject only to the defence of reasonable practicability. The Court of Appeal so held in *R v British Steel plc* [1995] ICR 586, [1995] IRLR 311 where a corporate employer was not able to avoid liability for an offence under the section on the basis that the company at 'directing mind' or senior management level was not involved in the offence, having taken all reasonable care to delegate supervision of the work in question. *Tesco v Nattrass* [1972] AC 153, [1971] 2 All ER 127 was distinguished on the basis that the Trade Descriptions Act 1968 contained a defence that the defendant had exercised all due diligence to avoid the commission of an offence. Section 3(1) contained no such defence and furthermore more stringent protection was required in the field of health and safety.

The Health and Safety Executive will thus be able to bring prosecutions without establishing whether particular employees were part of senior management or not. As a result companies will now need to assess whether there are any further measures they can to take to avert, so far as is reasonably practicable, risks to third parties arising from the actions of their employees.

Add to (*c*) *Undertaking*. In *R v Associated Octel Ltd* [1995] 4 All ER 1051, [1995] ICR 281, CA, it was held that the conduct of the undertaking in s. 3 included the repair and maintenance of plant which was necessary for the carrying on of business, whether done by employees of the employer or by independent contractors.

324   **Add to end of *General note*.** This section is capable of operating for the benefit and protection of children using play centres: see *Moualem v Carlisle City Council* (1994) 158 JP 1110.

325   **Section 5.** By the Environment Act 1995, ss. 2(1)(g), (h), (2)(c), 21(1)(g), (h), (2)(a), as from a day to be appointed, the functions of inspectors appointed under s. 19 in relation to improvement notices and prohibition notices under the Health and Safety at Work etc. Act 1974, Pt. I (ss. 1–54 and Schs. 1–3), are to be transferred to the Environment Agency or, in Welsh, Asiantaeth yr Amgylchedd ("the Agency") and the Scottish Environment Protection Agency ("SEPA") established under ss. 1, 20 of, Schs. 1, 6 to, the 1995 Act respectively, and the functions of the Secretary of State by virtue of his being, for the purposes of that Part, the authority

325   which is by any of the relevant statutory provisions made responsible for the enforcement of s. 5. By virtue of the transfer effected by ss. 2(2)(c), 21(2)(a), the Agency and the SEPA are to be regarded for the purposes of Pt. I of the 1974 Act as the authority which is, by any of the relevant statutory provisions, made responsible in relation to England and Wales or, as the case may be, Scotland for the enforcement of s. 5 (and, accordingly, as the enforcing authority in relation to that section); see s. 120(1) of, Sch. 22, para. 30(1), (2) to, the 1995 Act.

351   **Add at end of (b) *Regulations*.** See also ss. 1(2), 50 and *R v Secretary of State, ex p NACODS* CO/2576/93 (16 December 1993, unreported) on the limitations on making regulations.

The Health and Safety (Enforcing Authority) Regulations 1989

357   **Regulation 2(1).** The definition "dangerous substance" is revoked, and after the definitions "pleasure craft" and "railway" respectively there are inserted the following definitions, by the Carriage of Dangerous Goods by Road and Rail (Classification, Packaging and Labelling) Regulations 1994, S.I. 1994 No. 669, reg. 15(6), Sch. 5, paras. 1, 2:

> "'preparation dangerous for supply' has the meaning assigned to it by regulation 2(1) of the Chemicals (Hazard Information and Packaging) Regulations 1993 (S.I. 1993 No. 1746); and

> 'substance dangerous for supply' has the meaning assigned to it by regulation 2(1) of the Chemicals (Hazard Information and Packaging) Regulations 1993;".

In the definition "preparation dangerous for supply" as so inserted, the words "the Chemicals (Hazard Information and Packaging) Regulations 1993 (S.I. 1993 No. 1746)" are substituted by the words "the Chemicals (Hazard Information and Packaging for Supply) Regulations 1994 (S.I. 1994/3247)", and in the definition "substance dangerous for supply", as so inserted, the words "the Chemicals (Hazard Information and Packaging) Regulations 1993" are substituted by the words "the Chemicals (Hazard Information and Packaging for Supply) Regulations 1994" by the Chemicals (Hazard Information and Packaging for Supply) Regulations 1994, S.I. 1994 No. 3247, reg. 19(7).

361   **Schedule 1, para 1(c).** The word "safe" should read "sale". The words "dangerous substance" are substituted by the words "substance or preparation dangerous for supply" by the Carriage of Dangerous Goods by Road and Rail (Classification, Packaging and Labelling) Regulations 1994, S.I. 1994 No. 669, reg. 15(6), Sch. 5, paras. 1, 3.

362   **Schedule 2, para. 4.** Sub-para. (a)(i) is substituted by the Construction (Design and Management) Regulations 1994, S.I. 1994 No. 3140, reg. 24(4), as follows:

> "(i) regulation 7(1) of the Construction (Design and Management) Regulations 1994 (S.I. 1994/3140) (which requires projects

362   which include or are intended to include construction work to be notified to the Executive) applies to the project which includes the work; or".

                Section 19. By the Environment Act 1995, s. 120(1), Sch. 22, para. 30(1), (3), as from a day to be appointed, neither the Agency nor the SEPA have power to appoint inspectors under this section.

364   **Section 20(2)(l).** The words "any matters to things" in the second line should read "any matters or things".

366   **Section 21.** By the Environment Act 1995, s. 120(1), Sch. 22, para. 30(1), (3), as from a day to be appointed, this section and ss. 22, 23 are to have effect in relation to s. 5 as if the references in those sections to an inspector were references to the Agency or the SEPA.

                See further, in relation to an improvement notice served under s. 21, the Electrical Equipment (Safety) Regulations 1994, S.I. 1994 No. 3260, reg. 2(4), set out in Pt. 2 at p. 353 post.

                Section 22. See further, in relation to a prohibition notice served under this section, the Electrical Equipment (Safety) Regulations 1994, S.I. 1994 No. 3260, reg. 2(4), set out in Pt. 2 at p. 353 post.

370   **The Industrial Tribunals (Improvement and Prohibition Notices Appeals) Regulations 1974.** Revoked and replaced by S.I. 1993 No. 2687, Sch. 4, set out in Pt. 2 at pp. 230–241 post.

377   **Section 27.** Modified by the Environment Act 1995, s. 120(1), Sch. 22, para 30(1), (5), as from a day to be appointed, which reads as follows:

                "(5) Section 27 (obtaining of information by the Commission etc) shall have effect in relation to the appropriate new Agency, in its relevant capacity, as it has effect in relation to the Health and Safety Commission (and not as it has effect in relation to an enforcing authority), except that the consent of the Secretary of State shall not be required to the service by the appropriate new Agency of a notice under subsection (1) of that section; and, accordingly, where that section has effect by virtue of this sub-paragraph—

           (a) any reference in that section to the Commission shall be construed as a reference to the appropriate new Agency;

           (b) any reference to an enforcing authority shall be disregarded; and

           (c) in subsection (3) of that section, the words from "and also" onwards shall be disregarded.".

380   **Section 28.** In sub-s. (3), para. (c)(ii) is substituted as follows:

                "(ii) an officer of the National Rivers Authority or of a water undertaker, sewerage undertaker, water authority or water development board who is authorised by that Authority, undertaker, authority or board to receive it,";

in sub-s. (5)(b) the words from "local authority" to "or board" are substituted by the words "body which is a local authority, the National Rivers Authority, a water undertaker, a sewerage undertaker, a water authority, a river purification board or a water development board, the purposes of the body" by the Water Act 1989, s. 190, Sch. 25, para. 46; in sub-s. (6) the words "the Inner London Education Authority and" were repealed by the Education Reform Act 1988, s. 237, Sch. 13, Pt. I; and sub-s. (10) was added by the Norfolk and Suffolk Broads Act 1988, s. 21, Sch. 6, para. 13 as follows:

> "(10) For the purposes of this section the Broads Authority shall be treated as a local authority.".

In relation to Scotland only, in sub-s. (3)(c)(ii), as substituted as noted above, for the words "water authority or water development board who is authorised by that Authority, undertaker, authority or board" there are substituted the words "sewerage authority or water authority who is authorised by that authority or undertaker" and in sub-s. (5)(b), as amended as noted above, for the words "a water authority, a river purification board or a water development board" there are substituted the words "a sewerage authority, a water authority or a river purification board" by the Local Government etc. (Scotland) Act 1994, s. 180(1), Sch. 13, para. 93(1), (2), as from a day to be appointed.

Amended by the Environment Act 1995, s. 120(1), (3), Sch. 22, para. 30(1), (6), Sch. 24, as from a day to be appointed, as follows:

In sub-s. (3)(a) after the words "the Executive," there are inserted the words "the Environment Agency, the Scottish Environment Protection Agency,", sub-s. (3)(c)(iii) is repealed, in sub-s. (4) after the words "the Executive," in the first place where they occur, there are inserted the words "the Environment Agency, the Scottish Environment Protection Agency,", and in sub-s. (5)(a) after the words "of the Executive or" there are inserted the words "of the Environment Agency or of the Scottish Environment Protection Agency or".

In relation to England and Wales only, in sub-s. (3)(c)(ii), as substituted, the words "of the National Rivers Authority or" and the word "Authority," where it next occurs are repealed, and in sub-s. (5)(b) the words "the National Rivers Authority" are repealed.

In so far as this section applies to Scotland, sub-s. (3)(c)(ii), as so amended, is substituted as follows:

> "(ii) an officer of a water undertaker, sewerage undertaker, sewerage authority or water authority who is authorised by that authority to receive it;"; and

in sub-s. (5)(b), as so amended, for the words from the beginning to "in connection" there are substituted the words "in the case of information given to an officer of a body which is a local authority, a water undertaker, a sewerage undertaker, a sewerage authority or a water authority the purposes of the body in connection".

380   Sub-s. (10), as inserted as noted, is substituted by the Environment Act 1995, s. 78, Sch. 10, para. 12, as from a day to be appointed, as follows:

> "(10) The Broads Authority and every National Park authority shall be deemed to be local authorities for the purposes of this section.".

The Residuary Body for Wales established under the Local Government (Wales) Act 1994, s. 39, Sch. 13 is to be treated as a local authority for the purposes of this section; see para. 20(e) of Sch 13 to that Act.

382   **Section 33(1)(h).** This subsection should read as follows:

> "(h) intentionally to obstruct an inspector in the exercise or performance of his powers or duties or to obstruct a customs officer in the exercise of his powers under section 25A;".

384   **Health and Safety at Work etc. Act 1974.** In *Cleveland Structural Engineering Ltd v Hamilton* 1994 SLT 590 a company was charged with an offence under the Health and Safety at Work Act 1974, ss. 4(2) and 33(1). The complaint alleged a general failure to ensure the safety of employees together with particular failures. The court held that the company was guilty, on the basis of failures other than those set out, with the result that there was no specification of any particular respects in which the company could have been said to have been in breach of the Act. On appeal it was held that in making the deletions the court had acted to the detriment of the company as it had been convicted upon a basis which was not set out in the complaint, so depriving the company of the opportunity to object or of seeking relief against any prejudice that might result due to lack of notice in the complaint.

388   **Section 38.** After the words "except by an inspector or" there are inserted the words "the Environment Agency or" by the Environment Act 1995, s. 120(1), Sch. 22, para. 30(1), (7), as from a day to be appointed.

399   **Section 46(6).** *Service of notices.* It has been held that where there is a contravention of the 1974 Act by a person or limited company as occupier of premises, then notice can be served on them under s. 46(6). If the contravention is not as an occupier, but as an employer, that section cannot be invoked. The subsections of the 1974 Act, s 46 are permissive only and do not constitute a complete code of all the methods by which relevant notices may be served: *Health and Safety Executive v George Tancocks Garage (Exeter) Ltd* [1993] Crim LR 605.

402   **Section 48.** The Crown is no longer immune in respect of health service bodies and premises; see the National Health Service and Community Care Act 1990, s. 60.

404   **Section 52.** The definitions of "work" and "at work" are extended for the purposes of the Control of Substances Hazardous to Health Regulations 1994, S.I. 1994 No. 3246, reg. 19, set out in Pt. 2 at p. 287 post.

PAGE

404   **Add to end of (*b*) *Work*.** An employee ceased to be "at work" when under police caution: see *Thomson v Barbour* 1994 SCLR 485.

406   **Section 53(1).** In para. (a) of the definition "local authority", the words "and Wales" are repealed and after that paragraph there is inserted the following paragraph by the Local Government (Wales) Act 1994, ss. 22(3), 66(8), Sch. 9, para. 9, Sch. 18, as from a day to be appointed:

> "(aa)   in relation to Wales, a county council or a county borough council;".

In para. (b) of that definition the words from "regional" to "county council" are substituted by the words "council constituted under section 2 of the Local Government etc. (Scotland) Act 1994" by the Local Government etc. (Scotland) Act 1994, s. 180(1), Sch. 13, para. 93(1), (3), as from a day to be appointed.

407   **Add to (*g*) *Employee*.** For a discussion of the distinction between employees and independent contractors, see *Lane v Shire* [1995] IRLR 493.

412   **Section 60(1).** The words "Area Health Authority and each District Health Authority arranges for one of its officers who is" are substituted by the words "Health Authority arranges for" by the Health Authorities Act 1995, s. 2(1), Sch. 1, para. 99, as from 28 June 1995 in so far as is necessary for enabling the making of any regulations, orders, directions, schemes or appointments, and as from 1 April 1996 otherwise.

414   **Section 78(3).** Repealed by the Statute Law (Repeals) Act 1993, s. 1(1), Sch. 1, Pt. XVI.

415   **Section 78(8)(d).** Repealed by the Health Authorities Act 1995, s. 5(1), Sch. 3, as from 1 April 1996.

418   **Section 83.** Repealed by the Statute Law (Repeals) Act 1993, s. 1(1), Sch. 1, Pt. XVI.

420   **The Health and Safety at Work etc. Act 1974 (Application outside Great Britain) Order 1989.** Revoked and replaced by the Health and Safety at Work etc. Act 1974 (Application outside Great Britain) Order 1995, S.I. 1995 No. 263, reg. 1(2), set out in Pt. 2 at pp. 362–366 post.

431–   **Schedule 8.** Para. 3 is repealed by the Statute Law (Repeals) Act 1993,
432   s. 1(1), Sch. 1, Pt. XVI.

Schedules 9, 10. Repealed by the Statute Law (Repeals) Act 1993, s. 1(1), Sch. 1, Pt. XVI.

The Management of Health and Safety at Work Regulations 1992.

433   **Add to end of *General note*.** (See also *Griffin v South West Water Services Ltd* [1995] IRLR 15, HCJ, noted to pp. 315–316 ante.)

434   **Regulation 1(2).** By the Management of Health and Safety at Work (Amendment) Regulations 1994, S.I. 1994 No. 2865, reg. 2(1), (2), before the definition of "the assessment" there is added the following definition:

> "'the 1978 Act' means the Employment Protection (Consolidation) Act 1978;",

and after the definition of "fixed-term contract of employment" there are added the following definitions:

> "'given birth' means "delivered a living child or, after twenty-four weeks of pregnancy, a stillborn child"';
> 'maternity leave period' in relation to an employee is the period referred to in section 33(1) of the 1978 Act;
> 'new or expectant mother' means an employee who is pregnant; who has given birth within the previous six months; or who is breastfeeding;".

435   **Add (a) *General note.*** As to the duty to conduct a risk assessment, see eg *Barclays Bank plc v Fairclough Building Ltd (No 2)* (1995) Times, 15 February, CA, where it was held that any contractor who undertook work on materials containing asbestos was under a duty to find out about the risks from asbestos before undertaking the work.

441   **Regulations 13A–13C.** Inserted by the Management of Health and Safety at Work (Amendment) Regulations 1994, S.I. 1994 No. 2865, reg. 2(1), (3), as follows:

> "13A.—(1) Where—
> (a) the persons working in an undertaking include women of child-bearing age; and
> (b) the work is of a kind which could involve risk, by reason of her condition, to the health and safety of a new or expectant mother, or to that of her baby, from any processes or working conditions, or physical, biological or chemical agents, including those specified in Annexes I and II of Council Directive 92/85/EEC on the introduction of measures to encourage improvements in the safety and health at work of pregnant workers and workers who have recently given birth or are breastfeeding,
> the assessment required by regulation 3(1) shall also include an assessment of such risk.
>
> (2) Where, in the case of an individual employee, the taking of any other action the employer is required to take under the relevant statutory provisions would not avoid the risk referred to in paragraph (1) the employer shall, if it is reasonable to do so, and would avoid such risks, alter her working conditions or hours of work.
>
> (3) If it is not reasonable to alter the working conditions or hours of work, or if it would not avoid such risk, the employer shall, subject to section 46 of the 1978 Act, suspend the employee from work for so long as is necessary to avoid such risk.

(4) In paragraphs (1) to (3) references to risk, in relation to risk from any infectious or contagious disease, are references to a level of risk at work which is in addition to the level to which a new or expectant mother may be expected to be exposed outside the workplace.

13B. Where—

(a) a new or expectant mother works at night; and

(b) a certificate from a registered medical practitioner or a registered midwife shows that it is necessary for her health or safety that she should not be at work for any period of such work identified in the certificate

the employer shall, subject to section 46 of the 1978 Act, suspend her from work for so long as is necessary for her health or safety.

13C.—(1) Nothing in paragraph (2) or (3) of regulation 13A shall require the employer to take any action in relation to an employee until she has notified the employer in writing that she is pregnant, has given birth within the previous six months, or is breastfeeding.

(2) Nothing in paragraph (2) or (3) of regulation 13A or in regulation 13B shall require the employer to maintain action taken in relation to an employee—

(a) in a case—

　　(i) to which regulation 13A(2) or (3) relates; and

　　(ii) where the employee has notified her employer that she is pregnant,

where she has failed, within a reasonable time of being requested to do so in writing by her employer, to produce for the employer's inspection a certificate from a registered medical practitioner or a registered midwife showing that she is pregnant;

(b) once the employer knows that she is no longer a new or expectant mother; or

(c) if the employer cannot establish whether she remains a new or expectant mother.".

Regulation 14. After the word "obligations" there are inserted the words "other than those in regulations 13A to 13C," by the Management of Health and Safety at Work (Amendment) Regulations 1994, S.I. 1994 No. 2865, reg. 2(1), (4).

Regulation 15. Substituted by the Management of Health and Safety at Work (Amendment) Regulations 1994, S.I. 1994 No. 2865, reg. 2(1), (5), as follows:

"15.—(1) Breach of a duty imposed by these Regulations shall not confer a right of action in any civil proceedings.

(2) Paragraph (1) shall not apply to any duty imposed by these Regulations on an employer to the extent that it relates to risk referred to in regulation 13A(1) to an employee.".

PAGE

The Workplace (Health, Safety and Welfare) Regulations 1992.

443   **Add to end of** *General note.* (See also *Griffin v South West Water Services Ltd*[1995] IRLR 15, HCJ, noted to pp. 315–316 ante.)

444   **Regulation 2.** The following definitions are inserted before the definitions of "new workplace" and "traffic route" respectively by the Quarries Miscellaneous Health and Safety Provisions Regulations 1995, S.I. 1995 No. 2036, reg. 11, Sch. 3, as from 26 July 1998:

> "'mine' means a mine within the meaning of the Mines and Quarries Act 1954;" and
> "'quarry' means a quarry within the meaning of the Mines and Quarries Act 1954;".

445   **Regulation 3.** Para. (1)(c) is substituted, para. (1)(d) is revoked, and para. (5) is added by the Quarries Miscellaneous Health and Safety Provisions Regulations 1995, S.I. 1995 No. 2036, reg. 11, Sch. 3, as from 26 July 1998, as follows:

> "(c) a workplace located below ground at a mine.";
>
> "(5) As respects any workplace which is at a quarry or above ground at a mine regulation 12 shall only apply to a floor or traffic route which is located inside a building.".

452   **Add to end of (d)** *Reasonably practicable.* See *Disney v South Western Egg Products* (8 July 1993, unreported), CA: not reasonably practicable to sweep seeds up every time loaves were carried through a shop or to use trays to carry loaves in light of small amount of debris (see note to p. 2037 post; and see similarly *Graham v David A Hall Ltd* 1994 GWD 9–556, OH, noted to p. 1355 post). A purposive construction of "reasonably practicable" in reg. 12 might produce a different result under these Regulations.

PART 3 LEGISLATION OF GENERAL APPLICATION

The Employers' Liability (Compulsory Insurance) Act 1969

505   Modified by the Offshore Installations and Pipeline Works (Management and Administration) Regulations 1995, S.I. 1995 No. 738, reg. 21, set out in Pt. 2 at p. 374 post.

Add to end of *General note.* The Act does not give rise to civil liability for breach: see *Richardson v Pitt-Stanley* [1995] QB 123, [1995] 1 All ER 460.

506   **Section 3(2)(b).** The words "or Wales" are substituted by the words "the council of a county or county borough in Wales" by the Local Government (Wales) Act 1994, s. 66(6), Sch. 16, para. 37, as from a day to be appointed; the words from "a" where it thirdly appears to "in" where it secondly appears are substituted by the words "a council constituted under section 2 of the Local Government etc. (Scotland) Act 1994 in" and after the words "such council" there are inserted the words

506 "the Strathclyde Passenger Transport Authority" in relation to Scotland only, by the Local Government etc. (Scotland) Act 1994, s. 180(1), Sch. 13, para. 83, as from a day to be appointed; and after the words "the Broads Authority" there are inserted the words "a National Park authority" by the Environment Act 1995, s. 78, Sch. 10, para. 9, as from a day to be appointed.

The Control of Industrial Major Accident Hazards Regulations 1984

509 Modified by the Control of Industrial Major Accident Hazards (Amendment) Regulations 1994, S.I. 1994 No. 118, reg. 4, Schedule, at p. 240 post.

512 **Regulation 3(1)(e).** Revoked by the Control of Industrial Major Accident Hazards (Amendment) Regulations 1994, S.I. 1994 No. 118, reg. 3.

521 **Schedule 2, Pt. II.** After the words "assigned categories" there are inserted the words "of danger", and the words "regulation 5 of the Classification, Packaging and Labelling of Dangerous Substances Regulations 1984 (S.I. 1984/1244 amended by S.I. 1986/1922, S.I. 1988/766, S.I. 1989/2208 and S.I. 1990/1255)" are substituted by the words "regulation 5 of the Chemicals (Hazard Information and Packaging) Regulations (S.I. 1993 No. 1746) (which relates to the classification of substances and preparations dangerous for supply)" by the Chemicals (Hazard Information and Packaging) Regulations 1993, S.I. 1993 No. 1746, reg. 21(5).

For the words "the Chemicals (Hazard Information and Packaging) Regulations 1993 (S.I. 1993 No. 1746)", as so substituted, there are substituted the words "the Chemicals (Hazard Information and Packaging for Supply) Regulations 1994 (S.I. 1994/3247)" by the Chemicals (Hazard Information and Packaging for Supply) Regulations 1994, S.I. 1994 No. 3247, reg. 19(4).

The Health and Safety (First-Aid) Regulations 1981

534 **Regulation 7.** Paras. (c) and (g) are substituted by the Offshore Installations and Pipeline Works (First-Aid) Regulations 1989, S.I. 1989 No. 1689, reg. 8, as follows:

> "(c) where the Merchant Shipping (Medical Stores) Regulations 1986 apply;";
> "(g) where the Offshore Installations and Pipelines Works (First-Aid) Regulations 1989 apply.".

Para. (e) is revoked by the Management and Administration of Safety and Health at Mines Regulations 1993, S.I. 1993 No. 1897, reg. 44(1), (2)(a), in so far as it applies to mines and mining operations.

535 **Regulation 8.** Substituted by the Management and Administration of Safety and Health at Mines Regulations 1993, S.I. 1993 No. 1897, reg. 44(1)(b), in so far as it applies to mines and mining operations, as follows:

535   **"8. Application to mines.**

(1) Subject to paragraph (2), in their application to mines, regulations 3 and 4 shall have effect as if the owner of the mine were the employer and as if all persons for the time being employed at the mine were his employees.

(2) Paragraphs (3) and (4) of regulation 3 shall not apply in relation to mines.".

Regulation 10(3). Revoked by the Management and Administration of Safety and Health at Mines Regulations 1993, S.I. 1993 No. 1897, reg. 44(1, (2)(c), in so far as it applies to mines and mining operations.

The Reporting of Injuries, Diseases and Dangerous Occurrences Regulations 1985

546   **Add (a) *General note*.** Regulation 3(1)(b) extends to visitors, customers or other invitees on the premises: see *Woking Borough Council v BHS plc* (1994) 159 JP 427.

552   **Schedule 1, Pt. I.** Para. 14(2) is substituted by the Carriage of Dangerous Goods by Road and Rail (Classification, Packaging and Labelling) Regulations 1994, S.I. 1994 No. 669, reg. 15(2), as follows:

"(2) In this paragraph "dangerous substance" means any substance which falls within the definition of "dangerous goods" in regulation 2(1) of the Carriage of Dangerous Goods by Road and Rail (Classification, Packaging and Labelling) Regulations 1994 (S.I. 1994 No. 669) other than explosives or radioactive material.".

561   **Schedule 4, para. 1.** In the definition "appropriate person" in sub-para. (a) for the words "any official superior to a person appointed as a deputy" there are substituted the words "a person appointed to the management structure of the mine established in accordance with regulation 10(1) of the Management and Administration of Safety and Health at Mines Regulations 1993 (S.I. 1993 No. 1897)" by the Management and Administration of Safety and Health at Mines Regulations 1993, S.I. 1993 No. 1897, reg. 43(2), Sch. 6.

The Health and Safety (Training for Employment) Regulations 1990

569   **Regulation 2.** The definition "education establishment" should read "educational establishment".

The Health and Safety (Fees) Regulations 1992

570   Revoked and replaced by the Health and Safety (Fees) Regulations 1994, S.I. 1994 No. 397, reg. 16(2), Sch. 13. The 1994 Regulations are further revoked and replaced by the Health and Safety (Fees) Regulations 1995, S.I. 1995 No. 2646, reg. 17, Sch.14, set out in Pt. 2 at pp. 393–408 post.

PAGE

The Manual Handling Operations Regulations 1992

584   **Add to end of *General note*.** (See also *Griffin v South West Water Services Ltd*[1995] IRLR 15, HCJ, noted to pp. 315–316 ante.)

587   Leaving an employee to move a load so heavy as to be likely to cause an injury was a breach of s. 72 in *Brien v British Telecommunications plc* 1994 GWD 5–285, OH. In *Dickson v Lothian Health Board* 1994 GWD 7–419, OH it was held that an employer had failed to discharge the duty to provide a safe system of work when the training provided to nurses on how to lift patients was carried out in an atmosphere which was not conducive to the retention of the points raised and where investigation would have revealed the widespread use of dangerous lifting techniques among nurses. The conclusion is, it is submitted, entirely consistent with reg. 4(1)(b)(ii), especially when read in the light of the duty to provide training in the Management of Health and Safety at Work Regulations 1992, reg. 11. It should be contrasted with *Woolger v West Surrey and North East Hampshire Health Authority* (1993) 16 BMLR 120, where the Court of Appeal held that a hospital was not negligent in failing to warn a trained nurse against lifting patients with a method which caused her a back injury and *Forsyth v Lothian Regional Council* 1994 GWD 5–286, OH, in which an employer was held not to be operating an unsafe system of work where an employee injured himself lifting a 95 kg tamper box onto a lorry. The employer's workmen were all accustomed to heavy lifting and had, for over 25 years, lifted these boxes with a remarkable absence of injury; it was held that it could not be said that the employer ought to have adopted another system. It is submitted that a different result would have succeeded if they were able to demonstrate an alternative and reasonably practicable means of avoiding the need for the particular lifting (reg. 4(1)(a)) or if they could show that warnings or other steps to reduce the risk of injury were reasonable practicable (reg 4(1)(b)(ii)).

Add to end of *General note*. In *Colclough v Staffordshire County Council* [1994] CLY 208, it was held that an employer owed a duty at common law to warn a social worker of the risks of lifting clients.

PART 4 EQUIPMENT ETC

The Employer's Liability (Defective Equipment) Act 1969

706   **Section 1. (*a*) *Equipment*.** *Knowles v Liverpool City Council* [1993] ICR 21, [1993] IRLR 6, CA; affd [1993] 4 All ER 321, [1993] 1 WLR 1428, HL.

The Provision and Use of Work Equipment Regulations 1992

707   **Add to end of *General note*.** (See also *Griffin v South West Water Services Ltd*[1995] IRLR 15, HCJ, noted to pp. 315–316 ante.)

717   **Schedule 1, para. 1.** Substituted by the Electrical Equipment (Safety) Regulations 1994, S.I. 1994 No. 3260, reg. 2(2), as follows:

"1. Council Directive 73/23/EEC on the harmonization of the laws of Member States relating to electrical equipment designed for use within certain voltage limits (OJ No. L77, 26.3.1973, p. 29) as amended by Article 13 of Council Directive 93/68/EEC (OJ No. L220, 30.8.1993, p. 1.).".

Schedule 1, para. 25. Substituted by the Simple Pressure Vessels (Safety) (Amendment) Regulations 1994, S.I. 1994 No. 3098, reg. 7, as follows:

"25. Council Directive 87/404/EEC on the harmonisation of the laws of the member States relating to simple pressure vessels (OJ No. L220, 8.8.87, p. 48) as amended by Council Directive 90/488/EEC (OJ No. L270, 2.10.90, p. 25) and Article 2 of Council Directive 93/68/EEC (OJ No. L220, 30.8.93, p. 1).".

Schedule 1, para. 28. Substituted by the Electromagnetic Compatibility (Amendment) Regulations 1994, S.I. 1994 No. 3080, reg. 8(a), as follows:

"28. Council Directive 89/336/EEC on the approximation of the laws of the member States relating to electromagnetic compatibility (OJ No. L139, 23.5.89, p. 19); as amended by Council Directive 92/31/EEC (OJ No. L126, 12.5.92, p. 11) and Article 5 of Council Directive 93/68/EEC (OJ No. L220, 30.8.93, p. 1.).".

Schedule 1, para. 29. Substituted by the Supply of Machinery (Safety) (Amendment) Regulations 1994, S.I. 1994 No. 2063, reg. 5(a), as follows:

"29. Council Directive 89/392/EEC on the approximation of the laws of the Member States relating to machinery (OJ No L183, 29.6.1989, p. 9) as amended by Council Directive 91/368/EEC (OJ No L198, 22.7.1991, p. 16), Council Directive 93/44/EEC (OJ No L175, 19.7.1993, p. 12) and Article 6 of Council Directive 93/68/EEC (OJ No L220, 30.8.1993, p.1).".

Schedule 1, para. 31. By the Personal Protective Equipment (EC Directive) (Amendment) Regulations 1994, S.I. 1994 No. 2326, reg. 3(1), this paragraph shall have effect as if the reference to Council Directive 89/686/EEC were a reference to the Directive as amended by Commission Decision 93/95/EEC and Article 7 of Council Directive 93/68/EEC of 22nd July 1993.

Schedule 1, para. 34. Revoked by the Supply of Machinery (Safety) (Amendment) Regulations 1994, S.I. 1994 No. 2063, reg. 5(b).

Schedule 1, para. 35. Revoked by the Electromagnetic Compatibility (Amendment) Regulations 1994, S.I. 1994 No. 3080, reg. 8(b).

Schedule 1, para. 36. Added by the Medical Devices Regulations 1994, S.I. 1994 No. 3017, reg. 24, as follows:

718   "36. Council Directive 93/42/EEC concerning medical devices (OJ No. L169, 12.7.1993 p. 1).".

The Personal Protective Equipment at Work Regulations 1992
722   **Add to end of *General note*.** (See also *Griffin v South West Water Services Ltd* [1995] IRLR 15, HCJ, noted to pp. 315–316 ante.)

723   **Add (*a*) *General note* to 4. Provision of personal protective equipment.** It is unlikely that this Regulation requires foreseeability of injury; but, in any event, even a very slight risk to health and safety is likely to be foreseeable: see *Gerrard v Staffordshire Potteries* [1995] ICR 502, [1995] PIQR P169, CA.

727   **Schedule 1.** Substituted by the Medical Devices Regulations 1994, S.I. 1994 No. 3017, reg. 25, as follows:

"SCHEDULE 1

Regulation 4(3)(e)

RELEVANT COMMUNITY DIRECTIVE

1. Council Directive 89/686/EEC on the approximation of the laws of the member States relating to personal protective equipment (OJ No. L399, 30.12.89, p. 18).

2. Council Directive 93/42/EEC concerning medical devices (OJ No. L169, 12.7.93, p.1).".

By the Personal Protective Equipment (EC Directive) (Amendment) Regulations 1994, S.I. 1994 No. 2326, reg. 3(1), this Schedule shall have effect as if the reference to Council Directive 89/686/EEC were a reference to the Directive as amended by Council Directive 93/95/EEC and Article 7 of Council Directive 93/68/EEC of 22nd July 1993.

730   **Schedule 2, Pt. VIII.** Revoked by the Control of Substances Hazardous to Health Regulations 1994, S.I. 1994 No. 3246, reg. 18(1).

The Supply of Machinery (Safety) Regulations 1992
734   Amended by the Supply of Machinery (Safety) (Amendment) Regulations 1994, S.I. 1994 No. 2063, regs. 3, 4, Schs. 1, 2, as follows:

Except in respect of references to "Schedule 4 machinery", the words "or a relevant safety component", "or relevant safety component", "or a safety component" or "or safety component" are inserted, as the context may require, after the words "relevant machinery" or "machinery" wherever they occur in the definitions in reg. 2(2) of "EC type-examination certificate", "relevant essential health and safety requirements", "responsible person", "series manufacture", "supply", "technical file" and "technical specification", in regs. 6(1), 10(1)(a), 12 (except in paras. (1)(c)(ii), (d)), 13, 14, 15, 16, 18(4)(a), 20(1), (4), and 24(1) and, except for para. 6 thereof, in Sch. 6 (including the definition of "machinery for use at work" in para. 9 thereof).

Except in the case of regs. 4, 5, 7, 8, 9 and 34, and references to Schedule 4 machinery in the headings, after any reference to "machinery" or "relevant machinery" there are added the words "or safety components" or "or relevant safety components", as the context may require.

Except in the definition of "EC mark" in reg. 2(2), for the words "EC mark" wherever they occur there are substituted the words "CE marking".

Regulation 2(1). Substituted by the Supply of Machinery (Safety) (Amendment) Regulations 1994, S.I. 1994 No. 2063, reg. 4, Sch 2, para 1, as follows:

> "(1) In these Regulations, the "Machinery Directive" means Council Directive 89/392/EEC on the approximation of the laws of the Member States relating to machinery as amended by Council Directive 91/368/EEC, Council Directive 93/44/EEC and Article 6 of Council Directive 93/68/EEC.".

Regulation 2(2). Amended by the Supply of Machinery (Safety) (Amendment) Regulations 1994, S.I. 1994 No. 2063, regs. 3, 4, Sch. 1, Pt. II, para. 2, Sch. 2, para. 5, as follows:

(i) the definition "transposed harmonised standard" is substituted by the following:
> "'transposed harmonised standard' means a national standard of an EEA State which transposes a harmonised standard."

(ii) after the definition of business there is inserted the definition:
> "'CE marking' means a mark consisting of the symbol 'CE' set out in the form shown in Schedule 2A hereto:
> Provided that in respect of an item of machinery first supplied in the European Economic Area before 1st January 1997, a responsible person may, for the purposes of regulation 12(1)(d) below but without prejudice to the requirements as to proper affixation in regulation 25(1) below, elect to affix a mark in the form shown in Schedule 2 hereto, followed by the last two figures of the year in which it is affixed;";

(iii) the definition of "EC mark" is revoked;

(iv) after the definition of "relevant machinery" there is inserted the definition:
> "'relevant safety component' shall be construed in accordance with regulation 3(3) below;";

(v) in the definition of the word "safe", after the words "relevant machinery" in the first place where they occur there are inserted the words "or a relevant safety component" and in the second place where they occur there are inserted the words "or the relevant safety component", after the words "the machinery" there are inserted the words "or the safety component" and after the words "no risk (apart

734

from one reduced to a minimum)" there are inserted the words "of its endangering the health of or";

(vi) after the definition of "safe" there is inserted the definition:

"'safety component' means a component, provided that it is not interchangeable equipment, which is supplied separately to fulfil a safety function when in use and the failure or malfunctioning of which endangers the safety or health of exposed persons;"; and

(vii) for the definition of "Schedule 4 machinery" there is substituted:

"'Schedule 4 machinery' means—
(a) machinery which is specified in Annex IV of the Machinery Directive and listed under the heading of "A. Machinery" in Schedule 4 hereto; or
(b) safety components which are specified in Annex IV of the Machinery Directive and listed under the heading of "B. Safety Components" in Schedule 4 hereto;".

737   **Regulation 3.** The words "and relevant safety components" are added at the end of para. (1), and para. (3A) is added as follows, by the Supply of Machinery (Safety) (Amendment) Regulations 1994, S.I. 1994 No. 2063, reg. 4, Sch. 2, para. 6:

"(3) A relevant safety component is a safety component for machinery other than machinery to which regulation 5 or 10 below applies, unless that safety component is excluded from the scope of these Regulations pursuant to regulation 6, 7, 8 or 10(1)(a) below.".

Regulation 6(1). Substituted by the Supply of Machinery (Safety) (Amendment) Regulations 1994, S.I. 1994 No. 2063, reg. 3, Sch. 1, Pt. II, para. 2, as follows:

"(1) These Regulations do not apply to machinery which the supplier believes (with reasonable cause) will be put into service in a country outside the European Economic Area.".

Regulation 7. The words "Subject to regulation 7A below," are inserted at the beginning by the Supply of Machinery (Safety) (Amendment) Regulations 1994, S.I. 1994 No. 2063, reg. 4, Sch. 2, para. 7.

738   **Regulation 7A.** Inserted by the Supply of Machinery (Safety) (Amendment) Regulations 1994, S.I. 1994 No. 2063, reg. 4, Sch. 2, para. 8, as follows:

"7A.   Specific machinery or safety components first supplied or put into service before 1st January 1995

(1) These Regulations do not apply to any specific machinery or a safety component first supplied or put into service in the European Economic Area before 1st January 1995.

(2) For the purposes of this regulation, "specific machinery" means

lifting equipment designed and constructed for raising and/or moving persons with or without loads, except for industrial trucks with elevating operation position.".

Regulation 8(1). After the words "Subject to paragraph (2)" there are inserted the words "and regulation 8A below" by the Supply of Machinery (Safety) (Amendment) Regulations 1994, S.I. 1994 No. 2063, reg. 4, Sch. 2, para. 9.

Regulation 8A. Inserted by the Supply of Machinery (Safety) (Amendment) Regulations 1994, S.I. 1994 No. 2063, reg. 4, Sch. 2, para. 10, as follows:

"8A. Application of regulation 8 to safety components or machinery for the lifting or moving of persons

(1) The provisions of regulation 8 shall apply to a safety component.

(2) For the purposes of the application of regulation 8 to a safety component or machinery for lifting or moving persons, for the first date specified in paragraph (1) of that regulation there shall be substituted '31st December 1996' and for the date specified in paragraph 1(a) and (b) of that regulation there shall be substituted '14th June 1993'.".

Regulation 9(1). The words "and supplied with such plant" are added at the end of paras. (a), (b) by the Supply of Machinery (Safety) (Amendment) Regulations 1994, S.I. 1994 No. 2063, reg. 4, Sch. 2, para. 11.

739   **Regulation 11.** Substituted by the Supply of Machinery (Safety) (Amendment) Regulations 1994, S.I. 1994 No. 2063, reg. 4, Sch. 2, para. 12, as follows:

"(1) Subject to paragraph (4) below, no person who is a responsible person for the purposes of these Regulations shall supply relevant machinery or a relevant safety component unless the requirements of regulation 12 below are complied with in relation thereto.

(2) Subject to paragraph (4) below, it shall be the duty of any person who supplies relevant machinery or a relevant safety component, but who is not a person to whom paragraph (1) above applies, to ensure that that relevant machinery or relevant safety component is safe.

(3) Where a person—

(a) being the manufacturer of relevant machinery or a relevant safety component, himself puts that relevant machinery or relevant safety component into service in the course of a business; or

(b) having imported relevant machinery or a relevant safety component from a country or territory outside the European Economic Area, himself puts that relevant machinery or relevant safety component into service in the course of a business,

for the purposes of these Regulations that person shall be deemed to

739   have supplied that relevant machinery or relevant safety component to himself.

(4) The requirements of this regulation do not apply in relation to supply of relevant machinery or a relevant safety component which has previously been put into service in the Community or, on or after 1st January 1994, the European Economic Area.".

742   **Regulation 17.** Substituted by the Supply of Machinery (Safety) (Amendment) Regulations 1994, S.I. 1994 No. 2063, reg. 3, Sch. 1, Pt. II, para. 3, as follows:

"17. For the purposes of these Regulations, an approved body is a body responsible for carrying out functions relating to the conformity assessment procedures set out in Article 8 of the Machinery Directive and described in regulations 14 and 15 above which has been—

(a)   appointed as a United Kingdom approved body pursuant to regulation 18 below; or

(b)   appointed by an EEA State other than the United Kingdom.".

744   **Regulation 21.** By the Supply of Machinery (Safety) (Amendment) Regulations 1994, S.I. 1994 No. 2063, reg. 4, Sch. 2, para. 13, after the words "relevant machinery" in each place where they occur in paras. (1), (2) and (7), there are inserted the words "or the relevant safety component" and after the word "machinery" in each place where it occurs there are inserted the words "or the safety component", the word "and" at the end of para. (4)(b)(ii) is revoked, and para. (4)(b)(iv) is added, as follows:

"; and

(iv)   in the case of a safety component, that it is suitable for fulfilling the safety functions declared by the manufacturer".

745   **Regulation 22(2).** Except in sub-para. (c), after the words "relevant machinery" in each place where they occur there are inserted the words "or a relevant safety component" or "or the relevant safety component", as the context may require, and after the word "machinery" in each place it occurs there are inserted the words "or a safety component" or "or the safety component", as the context may require; and in sub-para. (c), after the words "machinery complies" there are added the words "or, in the case of a safety component, the safety function fulfilled by that safety component unless that safety function is obvious from the description of the safety component referred to in sub-paragraph (b) above" by the Supply of Machinery (Safety) (Amendment) Regulations 1994, S.I. 1994 No. 2063, reg. 4, Sch. 2, para. 14.

747   **Regulation 22(3).** By the Supply of Machinery (Safety) (Amendment) Regulations 1994, S.I. 1994 No. 2063, reg. 3, Sch. 1, Pt. I, para. 2, Pt. II, para. 4, for the words "An EEC declaration" there are substituted the words "An EC declaration", the word "and" at the end of sub-para. (a) is revoked, and sub-para. (c) is added, as follows:

747
         ", and

(c)   accompanied by a translation thereof in one of the official languages of the country in which the machinery is to be used in accordance with the requirements for the translation of the instructions as specified in sub-paragraph (a) above."

748
    Regulation 25. Para (1) is substituted by the Supply of Machinery (Safety) (Amendment) Regulations 1994, S.I. 1994 No. 2063, reg. 4, Sch. 2, para. 15, as follows:

"(1) For the purposes of these Regulations, the CE marking shall not be regarded as properly affixed to relevant machinery unless—

(a)   that machinery—
     (i)   satisfies the relevant health and safety requirements; and
     (ii) is safe; and

(b)   the responsible person who affixes the CE marking to the relevant machinery—
     (i)   has carried out the appropriate conformity assessment procedure and issued an EC declaration of conformity in respect thereof;
     (ii) affixes the said marking in a distinct, visible, legible and indelible manner; and
     (iii) in the case of relevant machinery which is the subject of Community Directives other than the Machinery Directive, which also provide for the affixing of the CE marking, has complied with the requirements of those other Directives in respect of that machinery:

Provided that—

(aa) where one or more of those other Community Directives permit the responsible person during a transitional period to apply the requirements of that Directive or its transitional arrangements, the CE marking on the relevant machinery shall only indicate conformity with those Directives which have been applied; and

(bb) in that event, the particulars (as published in the Official Journal of the European Communities) of the Directives which have been applied shall be given in the documents, notices or instructions required by those Directives and which must accompany that relevant machinery.";

para. (2) is revoked and para. (3) is substituted as follows:

"(3) No markings which—

(a)   are likely to deceive any person as regards the meaning and form of the CE marking; or

(b)   reduce the visibility or legibility of the CE marking,

shall be affixed to relevant machinery.".

749
    Regulation 26(1). After the word "affixed" there are inserted the words "or a relevant safety component which is accompanied by an EC declaration of conformity" and for the words "the relevant essential

health and safety requirements" there are substituted the words "all the provisions of the Machinery Directive" by the Supply of Machinery (Safety) (Amendment) Regulations 1994, S.I. 1994 No. 2063, reg. 4, Sch. 2, para. 17.

Regulation 28. Substituted by the Supply of Machinery (Safety) (Amendment) Regulations 1994, S.I. 1994 No. 2063, reg. 4, Sch. 2, para. 17, as follows:

"(1) Subject to paragraph (2) below, Schedule 6 shall have effect for the purposes of providing for the enforcement of these Regulations and for matters incidental thereto.

(2) Except in the case of relevant machinery which, in the opinion of an enforcement authority, is not safe, where an enforcement authority has reasonable grounds for suspecting that the CE marking has not been properly affixed to relevant machinery by the responsible person in accordance with regulation 25(1) above, it may give notice in writing to that person and, subject to paragraph (3) below, no action may be taken pursuant to Schedule 6 and no proceedings may be brought pursuant to regulation 29(a) below in respect of that machinery until such notice has been given and the responsible person to whom it has been given has failed to comply with its requirements.

(3) Notwithstanding paragraph (2) above, for the purpose of ascertaining whether or not the CE marking has been affixed in accordance with regulation 25(1) above, action may be taken pursuant to the following provisions as they are applied by Schedule 6—
(a) in Great Britain in relation to relevant machinery for use at work, section 20 of the Health and Safety at Work etc Act 1974;
(b) in Northern Ireland in relation to relevant machinery for use at work, Article 22 of the Health and Safety at Work (Northern Ireland) Order 1978; and
(c) in relation to relevant machinery as goods for private use and consumption, section 29 of the Consumer Protection Act 1987.

(4) Notice which is given under paragraph (2) above shall—
(a) state that the enforcement authority suspects that the CE marking has not been properly affixed to relevant machinery in accordance with regulation 25(1) above;
(b) specify the respect in which it is so suspected and give particulars thereof;
(c) require the responsible person—
   (i) to secure that any relevant machinery to which the notice relates conforms as regards the provisions concerning the proper affixation of the CE marking within such period as may be specified in the notice; or
   (ii) to provide evidence within that period, to the satisfaction of that enforcement authority, that the CE marking has been properly affixed; and

749

      (d) warn the responsible person that if the non-conformity continues (or if satisfactory evidence has not been provided) within the period specified in the notice, further action may be taken under the Regulations.".

750   **Regulation 29.** Para. (b) is revoked by the Supply of Machinery (Safety) (Amendment) Regulations 1994, S.I. 1994 No. 2063, reg. 4, Sch. 2, para. 18.

       Regulation 30(1). The words "or (b)" are revoked by the Supply of Machinery (Safety) (Amendment) Regulations 1994, S.I. 1994 No. 2063, reg. 4, Sch. 2, para. 19.

753   **Schedule 2A.** Inserted by the Supply of Machinery (Safety) (Amendment) Regulations 1994, S.I. 1994 No. 2063, reg. 4, Sch. 2, para. 20, as follows:

"SCHEDULE 2A

Regulation 2(2)

CE Conformity Marking

The CE conformity marking shall consist of the initials "CE" taking the following form:

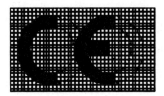

If the CE marking is reduced or enlarged the proportions given in the above drawing must be respected.

The various components of the CE marking must have substantially the same vertical dimension, which may not be less than 5 mm. This minimum dimension may be waived for small-scale machinery.".

754   **Schedule 3.** Amended by the Supply of Machinery (Safety) (Amendment) Regulations 1994, S.I. 1994 No. 2063, regs. 3, 4, Sch. 1, Pt. I, para. 3, Sch. 2, para. 21, as set out in relation to The Machinery Directive in Annex I at p. 39.

       Schedule 4. Substituted by the Supply of Machinery (Safety) (Amendment) Regulations 1994, S.I. 1994 No. 2063, reg. 3, Sch. 1 and set out in relation to The Machinery Directive in Annex IV at p. 77.

       Schedule 5. Substituted by the Supply of Machinery (Safety) (Amendment) Regulations 1994, S.I. 1994 No. 2063, reg. 4, Sch. 2, para. 23, as follows:

"SCHEDULE 5

Regulation 5

Excluded Machinery

Machinery whose only power source is directly applied manual effort unless it is a machine used for lifting or lowering loads.

Machinery for medical use used in direct contact with patients.

Special equipment for use in fairgrounds and/or amusement parks.

Steam boilers, tanks and pressure vessels.

Machinery specially designed or put into service for nuclear purposes which, in the event of failure, may result in an emission of radioactivity.

Radioactive sources forming part of a machine.

Firearms.

Storage tanks and pipelines for petrol, diesel fuel, inflammable liquids and dangerous substances.

Means of transport, that is vehicles and their trailers intended solely for transporting passengers by air or on road, rail or water networks, as well as means of transport in so far as such means are designed for transporting goods by air, on public road or rail networks or on water. Vehicles used in the mineral extraction industry shall not be excluded.

Seagoing vessels and mobile offshore units together with equipment on board such vessels or units.

Cableways, including funicular railways, for the public or private transportation of persons.

Agricultural and forestry tractors, as defined in Article 1(1) of Council Directive 74/150/EEC of 4th March 1974 on the approximation of the laws of member States relating to the type-approval of wheeled agricultural or forestry tractors, as last amended by Directive 88/297/EEC.

Machines specially designed and constructed for military or police purposes.

Lifts which permanently serve specific levels of buildings and constructions, having a car moving between guides which are rigid and inclined at an angle of more than 15 degrees to the horizontal and designed for the transport of:
— persons,
— persons and goods,
— goods alone if the car is accessible, that is to say, a person may enter it without difficulty, and fitted with controls situated inside the car or within reach of a person inside.

Means of transport of persons using rack and pinion rail mounted vehicles.

754   Mine winding gear.

Theatre elevators.

Construction site hoists intended for lifting persons or persons and goods.".

The Personal Protective Equipment (EC Directive) Regulations 1992

793   By the Personal Protective Equipment (EC Directive) (Amendment) Regulations 1994, S.I. 1994 No. 2326, reg. 3(1), these regulations shall have effect as if references to Council Directive 89/686/EEC were references to the Directive as amended by Council Directive 93/95/EEC and Article 7 of Council Directive 93/68/EEC of 22nd July 1993.

Throughout the text, the term "EC mark" is replaced by "CE marking", by the Personal Protective Equipment (EC Directive) (Amendment) Regulations 1994, S.I. 1994 No. 2326, reg. 3(2), Schedule, para. 1.

794   **Regulation 3(4).** The words "and no action" to the end are revoked by the Personal Protective Equipment (EC Directive) (Amendment) Regulations 1993, S.I. 1993 No. 3074, reg. 3.

798   **Schedule. Article 4.** The fist paragraph is replaced by the following text by the Personal Protective Equipment (EC Directive) (Amendment) Regulations 1994, S.I. 1994 No. 2326, reg. 3(2), Schedule, para. 2:

"1. Member States may not prohibit, restrict or hinder the placing on the market of PPE or PPE components which comply with the provisions of this Directive and which bear the CE marking attesting their conformity to all the provisions of this Directive, including the certification procedures in Chapter II.".

799   **Schedule. Article 5.** The following paragraph is added by the Personal Protective Equipment (EC Directive) (Amendment) Regulations 1994, S.I. 1994 No. 2326, reg. 3(2), Schedule, para. 3:

"6. (a) Where the PPE is subject to other Directives concerning other aspects and which also provide for the affixing of the CE marking, the latter shall indicate that the PPE is also presumed to conform to the provisions of the other Directives.

(b) However, where one or more of these Directives allow the manufacturer, during a transitional period, to choose which arrangements to apply, the CE marking shall indicate conformity to the provisions only of those Directives applied by the manufacturer. In this case, particulars of the Directives applied, as published in the Official Journal of the European Communities, must be given in the documents, notices or instructions required by the Directives and accompanying such PPE.".

801   **Schedule. Article 9.1.** Replaced by the Personal Protective Equipment (EC Directive) (Amendment) Regulations 1994, S.I. 1994 No. 2326, reg. 3(2), Schedule, para. 4, as follows:

> "1. Member States shall notify the Commission and the other Member States of the bodies which they have appointed to carry out the procedures referred to in Article 8 together with the specific tasks which these bodies have been appointed to carry out and the identification numbers assigned to them beforehand by the Commission.
>
> The Commission shall publish in the Official Journal of the European Communities a list of the notified bodies and their identification numbers and the tasks for which they have been notified. The Commission shall ensure that this list is kept up to date.".

805   **Schedule. Article 12.** The introductory sentence is replaced by the Personal Protective Equipment (EC Directive) (Amendment) Regulations 1994, S.I. 1994 No. 2326, reg. 3(2), Schedule, para. 4, as follows:

> "The EC declaration of conformity is the procedure whereby the manufacturer or his authorised representative established within the Contracting Parties:".

Schedule. Article 13. Replaced by the Personal Protective Equipment (EC Directive) (Amendment) Regulations 1994, S.I. 1994 No. 2326, reg. 3(2), Schedule, para. 6, as follows:

> *"Article 13*
>
> 1. The CE conformity marking shall consist of the initials "CE" in the form shown in the specimen in Annex IV. in the event of the involvement of a notified body in the production control phase as indicated in Article 11, its identification number shall be added.
>
> 2. The CE marking must be affixed to each piece of manufactured PPE so as to be visible, legible and indelible throughout the expected life of the PPE; however, if this is not possible in view of the characteristics of the product, the CE marking may be affixed to the packaging.
>
> 3. The affixing of markings on the PPE which are likely to deceive third parties as to the meaning and form of the CE marking shall be prohibited. Any other marking may be affixed to the PPE or its packaging provided that the visibility and legibility of the CE marking is not thereby reduced.
>
> 4. Without prejudice to Article 7:
> (a)   where a Member State establishes that the CE marking has been affixed unduly, the manufacturer or his authorised representative established within the Contracting Parties shall

805   be obliged to make the product conform as regards the provisions concerning the CE marking and to end the infringement under the conditions imposed by the Member State;

    (b) where non-conformity continues, the Member State must take all appropriate measures to restrict or prohibit the placing on the market of the product in question or to ensure that it is withdrawn from the market in accordance with the procedures laid down in Article 7.

808   **Annex II, section 1.4.** At the end there is added by the Personal Protective Equipment (EC Directive) (Amendment) Regulations 1994, S.I. 1994 No. 2326, reg. 3(2), Schedule, para. 7, as follows:

    "(h) where appropriate, the references of the Directives applied in accordance with Article 5(6)(b);

    (i) the name, address and identification number of the notified body involved in the design stage of the PPE.".

819   **Annex IV.** Replaced by the Personal Protective Equipment (EC Directive) (Amendment) Regulations 1994, S.I. 1994 No. 2326, reg. 3(2), Schedule, para. 8, as follows:

"ANNEX IV

CE CONFORMITY MARKING AND INFORMATION

— The CE conformity marking shall consist of the initials "CE" taking the following form

— If the CE marking is reduced or enlarged the proportions given in the above graduated drawing must be respected.

— The various components of the CE marking must have substantially the same vertical dimension, which may not be less than 5mm. This minimum dimension may be waived for small-scale PE.

Additional information

— The last two digits of the year in which the CE marking was affixed; this information is not required in the case of the PPE referred to in Article 8(3)."

PAGE

The Electrical Equipment for Explosive Atmospheres (Certification) Regulations 1990

845   **Regulation 2(1).** In the definition "Gassy Mines Directive" there are inserted at the end the words ", and as amended by Commission Directive No. 91/269/EEC (OJ No. L134, 29.5.91, p. 51)" by the Electrical Equipment for Explosive Atmospheres (Certification) (Amendment) (No. 2) Regulations 1991, S.I. 1991 No. 2826, reg. 2(2).

At the end of the definition of "the First Specific Directive" there are added the words "and as further adapted to technical progress by Commission Directive 94/26/EC"; and at the end of the definition of "the Gassy Mines Directive", as so amended, there are added the words "and as further adapted to technical progress by Commission Directive 94/44/EC" by the Electrical Equipment for Explosive Atmospheres (Certification) (Amendment) Regulations 1995, S.I. 1995 No. 1186, reg. 2(1), (2).

850   **Regulation 12.** Substituted by the Electrical Equipment for Explosive Atmospheres (Certification) (Amendment) Regulations 1995, S.I. 1995 No. 1186, reg. 2(1), (3), as follows:

"12. Transitional provisions

(1) Subject to paragraph (3) below, on or after the coming into force date of the Electrical Equipment for Explosive Atmospheres (Certification) (Amendment) Regulations 1995 (in this regulation referred to as "the effective date"), a manufacturer of electrical equipment may apply to a certification body (which has been appointed for the purpose set out in regulation 3(1)(a) of the unamended Regulations in respect of the electrical equipment for which the application is made) for a certificate of conformity attesting that the electrical equipment which is the subject of the application conforms to the harmonised standards prescribed for that equipment in the unamended Regulations; and in that case the provisions of the unamended Regulations, as appropriate, shall apply as if the application had been made under regulation 4 of those Regulations.

(2) Subject to paragraph (3) below, an application for a certificate of conformity made under regulation 4 or for review under regulation 7 of the unamended Regulations before the effective date shall continue to be dealt with under the unamended Regulations.

(3) No certificate of conformity shall be issued by a certification body under paragraph (1) or (2) above—
(a) in respect of electrical equipment to which the Framework Directive applies, after 29th February 1996; or
(b) in respect of electrical equipment to which the Gassy Mines Directive applies, after 31st December 1996.

(4) Subject to regulation 6 and without prejudice to paragraph (5) below, a certificate of conformity issued in accordance with the unamended Regulations—

850

(a) before 1st March 1996 in respect of electrical equipment to which the Framework Directive applies; or

(b) before 1st January 1997 in respect of electrical equipment to which the Gassy Mines Directive applies,

irrespective of whether such certificate was issued before, on or after the effective date, shall be regarded as in force for the purposes of regulation 11 (use of the distinctive Community mark) up to and including 30th June 2003.

(5) Subject to regulation 6, a certificate of conformity issued before 1st January 1993 in accordance with regulation 12 of the unamended Regulations applying the harmonised standards in force immediately before 31st December 1991 shall be regarded as in force for the purposes of regulation 11 up to and including 30th June 2003.

(6) In this regulation "the unamended Regulations" means these Regulations as in force immediately before the effective date.".

The Simple Pressure Vessels (Safety) Regulations 1991

862
Except in reg. 2(3), throughout the Regulation the term "CE marking" is substituted for the term "EC mark" wherever it occurs by virtue of the Simple Pressure Vessels (Safety) (Amendment) Regulations 1994, S.I. 1994 No. 3098, reg. 4(a).

Regulation 2. Amended by the Simple Pressure Vessels (Safety) (Amendment) Regulations 1994, S.I. 1994 No. 3098, regs. 3, 6(a), as follows:

(i) in para. (3), the word "Economic" in the definition of "the Community" and the definition of "property" is revoked, and the following definition is inserted before the definition of "the Commission":

"'the CE Marking Directive' means Council Directive 93/68/EEC;"; and

(ii) the following definition is substituted for the definition of "the Directive":

"'the Directive' means Council Directive 87/404/EEC on the harmonisation of the laws of the Member States relating to simple pressure vessels, as amended by—
(a) Council Directive 90/488/EEC; and
(b) Articles 2, 14.1 and 14.2 of the CE Marking Directive;";

(iii) para. (5) is substituted, and para. (6) is added, as follows:

"(5) A reference in these Regulations to a relevant national standard is a reference to a national standard of a member State, being a standard which transposes a harmonized standard the reference number of which has been published in the Official Journal of the European Communities pursuant to Article 5.1 of the Directive.

862

(6) In these Regulations, with respect to matters arising on or after 1st January 1994, a reference to the Community shall be read as a reference to the EEA, and a reference to a member State shall be read as a reference to an EEA State, and for the purposes of this paragraph—

(a) the "EEA" means the European Economic Area;

(b) an "EEA State" means a State which is a Contracting Party to the EEA Agreement, but until the EEA Agreement comes into force in relation to Liechtenstein does not include the State of Liechtenstein; and

(c) the "EEA Agreement" means the Agreement on the European Economic Area signed at Oporto on 2nd May 1992 as adjusted by the Protocol signed at Brussels on 17th March 1993.";

(iv) in para. (3) the definition of "EC mark" is revoked and paras. (7), (8) are added by the Simple Pressure Vessels (Safety) (Amendment) Regulations 1994, S.I. 1994 No. 3098, reg. 4(b), as follows:

"(7) In these Regulations, a reference to "the CE marking" or "the CE conformity marking" is a reference to a marking consisting of the initials "CE" in the form shown in the specimen in Schedule 2 to these Regulations; and Schedule 2 shall have effect for making provision in relation to the affixing of the said marking and other matters incidental thereto.

(8) In these Regulations, a reference to the identification number of an approved body is a reference to the identification number assigned to that body by the Commission pursuant to Article 9.1 of the Directive.".

863   **Regulation 3.** Para. (1) is substituted by the Simple Pressure Vessels (Safety) (Amendment) Regulations 1994, S.I. 1994 No. 3098, reg. 6(b), as follows:

"(1) Subject to paragraph (2) of this regulation, and regulation 6 below, these Regulations shall apply, and shall apply only, to vessels manufactured in series.".

864   **Regulation 4.** In paras. (1)(c) and (3)(b) the word "properly" is revoked and at the end of both paragraphs there are added the words ", and it complies in all other respects with that Schedule" by the Simple Pressure Vessels (Safety) (Amendment) Regulations 1994, S.I. 1994 No. 3098, reg. 4(c).

In para. (4) after the word "persons" there are inserted the words "or domestic animals" and at the end of para. (5), for the words from "The instructions must be" to the words "first taken into service." there is substituted the following by the Simple Pressure Vessels (Safety) (Amendment) Regulations 1994, S.I. 1994 No. 3098, reg. 6(c), (d):

"The language of the instructions shall be (without prejudice to the instructions being also in any other language) as follows—

(i) where the manufacturer believes (with reasonable cause) that the vessel is to be taken into service in a particular member State, in the official language or languages of that member State;

(ii) where (i) does not apply but the manufacturer believes (with reasonable cause) that the vessel is destined for a particular member State, in the official language or languages of that member State;

(iii) in any other case, in any official Community language.".

Regulation 5. Substituted by the Simple Pressure Vessels (Safety) (Amendment) Regulations 1994, S.I. 1994 No. 3098, reg. 4(d), as follows:

"5. Obligations of manufacturers, suppliers and importers

(1) Subject to the transitional and other exceptions in regulation 6 below, no person being—

(a) the manufacturer of a vessel;

(b) the manufacturer of a relevant assembly who imported the vessel incorporated therein from a country or territory outside the Community; or

(c) the person who imported a vessel (other than the person mentioned in sub-paragraph (b) above) or relevant assembly from such country or territory,

shall supply such vessel unless it complies with regulation 4 above or such relevant assembly as the case may be unless the vessel incorporated therein so complies.

(2) Subject to the same exceptions, no person shall, being the manufacturer of a vessel, himself take that vessel or a relevant assembly incorporating that vessel into service unless that vessel complies with regulation 4 above.

(3) Subject to the same exceptions, no person shall, having imported a vessel or a relevant assembly from a country or territory outside the Community, himself take that vessel or a relevant assembly incorporating that vessel, or the first mentioned relevant assembly into service unless that vessel or the vessel incorporated into the relevant assembly complies with regulation 4 above.

(4) Subject to the same exceptions, it shall be the duty of any person, not being a person mentioned in paragraph (1)(a) to (c) above, who supplies a vessel or relevant assembly to ensure that such vessel or relevant assembly as the case may be is safe.

(5) No markings which are likely to deceive any person as regards the meaning and form of the CE marking shall be affixed to a vessel.".

Regulation 6. Para. (2) is substituted, and para. (5) is added, by the Simple Pressure Vessels (Safety) (Amendment) Regulations 1994, S.I. 1994 No. 3098, reg. 6(e), as follows:

865

"(2) These Regulations also do not apply in the case of a vessel or a relevant assembly if the supplier believes (with reasonable cause) that it will be taken into service in a country outside the Community."

"(5) These Regulations do not apply to any vessel or relevant assembly which has previously been taken into service in the Community.".

868   **Regulation 11.** Para. (8) is added by the Simple Pressure Vessels (Safety) (Amendment) Regulations 1994, S.I. 1994 No. 3098, reg. 4(e), as follows:

"(8) Where a United Kingdom approved body withdraws a type-examination certificate, it shall so inform the Secretary of State, giving its reasons, with a view to this information being passed by him to the Commission and the other member States.".

869   **Regulation 12.** Substituted by the Simple Pressure Vessels (Safety) (Amendment) Regulations 1994, S.I. 1994 No. 3098, reg. 4(f), as follows, subject to transitional provisions in reg. 5 thereof, which provides that, in respect of vessels first supplied in the Community before 1 January 1997, and relevant assemblies incorporating vessels so supplied or, where the manufacturer of the relevant assemblies manufactured the vessels, relevant assemblies so supplied, the manufacturer or his authorised representative may elect to comply with the marking arrangements in force on 31 December 1994. If so, in order to demonstrate compliance with the marking arrangements in force on that date, the manufacturer or his authorised representative is to apply the 1991 Regulations as if the amendments made by reg. 4(f), (k) of the 1994 Regulations had not come into force.

"12. EC verification

(1) EC verification is the procedure whereby a manufacturer or his authorized representative established within the Community ensures and declares that the vessels which have been checked in accordance with paragraph (3) below are in conformity to the type described in the EC type-examination certificate or with the design and manufacturing schedule conforming with Schedule 3 of these Regulations having received a certificate of adequacy.

(2) The manufacturer shall take all the necessary measures for the manufacturing process to ensure that the vessels conform to the type described in the EC type-examination certificate or to the design and manufacturing schedule. The manufacturer or his authorized representative established within the Community shall affix the CE marking to each vessel and draw up a declaration of conformity.

(3) A United Kingdom approved body to which application is made for EC verification shall carry out the appropriate examinations and tests in order to check the conformity of the vessels with the requirements of the Directive by examination and testing of vessels in accordance with the following sub-paragraphs—

(a) the manufacturer shall present his vessels in the form of uniform batches and shall take all necessary measures in order that the manufacturing process ensures the uniformity of each batch produced;

(b) these batches shall be accompanied by the EC type-examination certificate, or, where the vessels are not manufactured in accordance with an approved prototype, by the design and manufacturing schedule; in the latter case the approved body shall, prior to EC verification, examine the schedule in order to certify its conformity;

(c) when a batch is examined, the approved body shall ensure that the vessels have been manufactured and checked in accordance with the design and manufacturing schedule and perform a hydrostatic test or a pneumatic test of equivalent effect on each vessel in the batch at a pressure Ph equal to 1.5 times the vessel's design pressure in order to check its soundness, and the following provisions shall apply, where appropriate, to such testing—

　　(i) a pneumatic test shall be subject to acceptance of the test safety procedures by the member State in which the test is performed;

　　(ii) the approved body shall carry out tests on test-pieces taken from a representative production test-piece or from a vessel, as the manufacturer chooses, in order to examine the weld quality; such tests shall be carried out on longitudinal welds, unless differing weld techniques are used for longitudinal and circular welds, in which case, the tests shall be repeated on the circular welds;

　　(iii) for vessels designed in accordance with the experimental method described in paragraph 9 of Part 2 of Schedule 1 to these Regulations these tests on test-pieces shall be replaced by a hydrostatic test on five vessels taken at random from each batch in order to check that they conform to the requirements of the said paragraph 9.

(4) In the case of accepted batches—

(a) the approved body shall affix, or cause to be affixed, its identification number to each recipient and draw up a written certificate of conformity relating to the tests carried out:

Provided that the manufacturer may, under the responsibility of the approved body, affix the latter's identification number during the manufacturing process;

(b) all recipients in the batch may be placed on the market except for those which have not successfully undergone a hydrostatic test or a pneumatic test.

(5) If a batch is rejected by an approved body carrying out examination and testing in accordance with this regulation in the United Kingdom, the approved body shall take appropriate measures to prevent the putting on the market of that batch and, in the event of frequent rejection of batches, the approved body may suspend the statistical verification.".

PAGE

871   **Regulation 14.** Paras. (1), (3), (4) are revoked and para. (2) is substituted by the Simple Pressure Vessels (Safety) (Amendment) Regulations 1994, S.I. 1994 No. 3098, reg. 4(g), as follows:

"(2) A manufacturer who has obtained an EC certificate of conformity may commence series manufacture and apply the CE marking to vessels which he declares to be in conformity—

(a) to the design and manufacturing schedule (submitted to the approved body pursuant to regulation 13(3)(b) above) on which a certificate of adequacy has been drawn up; or

(b) the relevant approved prototype.".

873   **Regulation 18.** Revoked by the Simple Pressure Vessels (Safety) (Amendment) Regulations 1994, S.I. 1994 No. 3098, reg. 4(h).

874   **Regulation 19.** Substituted by the Simple Pressure Vessels (Safety) (Amendment) Regulations 1994, S.I. 1994 No. 3098, reg. 4(i), as follows:

"19. Enforcement

(1) Subject to paragraph (2) below, Schedule 5 shall have effect for the purposes of providing for the enforcement of these Regulations and for matters incidental thereto.

(2) Except in the case of a vessel which, in the opinion of an enforcement authority, is not safe, where an enforcement authority has reasonable grounds for suspecting that the CE marking has not been properly affixed to a vessel, it may give notice in writing to the manufacturer of that vessel or his authorised representative established in the Community, as the case may be, and, subject to paragraph (3) below, no action may be taken pursuant to Schedule 5 to these Regulations, and no proceedings may be brought pursuant to regulation 20(1) below, in respect of that vessel until such notice has been given and the person to whom it is given has failed to comply with its requirements.

(3) Notwithstanding paragraph (2) above, for the purposes of ascertaining whether or not the CE marking has been properly affixed, action may be taken pursuant to the following provisions as they are applied by Schedule 5—

(a) in Great Britain in relation to vessels for use at work, section 20 of the Health and Safety at Work etc Act 1974;

(b) in Northern Ireland in relation to vessels for use at work, Article 22 of the Health and Safety at Work (Northern Ireland) Order 1978; and

(c) in relation to vessels as consumer goods, section 29 of the Consumer Protection Act 1987.

(4) Notice which is given under paragraph (2) above shall—

(a) state that the enforcement authority suspects that the CE marking has not been properly affixed to the vessel;

(b) specify the respect in which it is so suspected and give particulars thereof;

874 (c) require the person to whom the notice is given—

  (i) to secure that any vessel to which the notice relates conforms as regards the provisions concerning the proper affixation of the CE marking within such period as may be specified in the notice; or

  (ii) to provide evidence within that period, to the satisfaction of the enforcement authority, that the CE marking has been properly affixed; and

(d) warn that person that if the non-conformity continues after (or if satisfactory evidence has not been provided within) the period specified in the notice, further action may be taken under the Regulations.

(5) For the purposes of this regulation, the CE marking is properly affixed to a vessel if—

(a) it is affixed by the manufacturer or his authorized representative pursuant to regulation 12(2) above or by the manufacturer pursuant to regulation 14(2) above; and

(b) that vessel complies with the requirements of regulation 4 above which apply to it.".

Regulation 20(2). The words "regulation 14(3) or" are revoked by the Simple Pressure Vessels (Safety) (Amendment) Regulations 1994, S.I. 1994 No. 3098, reg. 4(j).

876 **Regulation 24.** Para. (1)(b) is substituted by the Simple Pressure Vessels (Safety) (Amendment) Regulations 1994, S.I. 1994 No. 3098, reg. 6(f), as follows:

"(b) taken into service,".

880 **Schedule 2.** Substituted by the Simple Pressure Vessels (Safety) (Amendment) Regulations 1994, S.I. 1994 No. 3098, reg. 4(k), subject to transitional provisions in reg. 5 thereof (see the note to reg. 12 at p. 869 ante), as follows:

"SCHEDULE 2

Regulations 2(7) and 4

THE CE MARKING AND OTHER INSCRIPTIONS

1. The CE conformity marking shall consist of the initials "CE" in the following form—

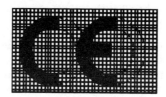

For the avoidance of doubt, it is hereby declared that the grid providing the background in the above graduated drawing is not part of the CE marking.

2.   If the CE marking is reduced or enlarged the proportions given in the above graduated drawing must be respected.

3.   The various components of the CE marking must have substantially the same vertical dimension, which may not be less than 5 mm.

4.   The CE marking, and the other inscriptions specified below, must be affixed in a visible, easily legible and indelible form, either to the vessel itself or to a data plate attached to the vessel in such a way that it cannot be removed.

5.   The CE marking shall be followed by the identification number of the approved body responsible for EC verifications or EC surveillance.

6.   The vessel or data plate must bear at least the following information—
— the maximum working pressure (PS in bar);
— the maximum working temperature (Tmax in °C);
— the minimum working temperature (Tmin in °C);
— the capacity of the vessel (V in litres);
— the name or mark of the manufacturer;
— the type and serial or batch identification of the vessel; and
— the last two digits of the year in which the CE marking was affixed.

Where the data plate is used, it must be so designed that it cannot be re-used and must include a vacant space to enable other information to be provided.

7.   Subject to paragraph 8 below, where a vessel is the subject of other Community Directives covering other aspects and which also provide for the affixing of the CE marking, such marking shall indicate that the vessel in question is also presumed to conform to those other Directives.

8.   Where one or more of the other Directives referred to in paragraph 7 above allow the manufacturer, during a transitional period, to choose which arrangements to apply, the CE marking shall indicate conformity only to the Directives applied by the manufacturer. In this case, particulars of the Directives applied, as published in the *Official Journal of the European Communities*, must be given in the documents, notices or instructions required by the Directives and accompanying such a vessel.

9.   It shall be presumed that a vessel which bears the CE marking complies with all the provisions of the Directive, including the conformity assessment procedures referred to in Chapter II thereof (being the means whereby safety clearance is obtained pursuant to

880   regulations 9 to 13 of these Regulations) unless there are reasonable grounds for suspecting that it does not so comply.

10.   Subject to the other provisions of these Regulations, any other marking may be affixed to the vessels or the data plate provided that he visibility and legibility of the CE marking is not thereby reduced.".

881   **Schedule 5.** Amended by the Simple Pressure Vessels (Safety) (Amendment) Regulations 1994, S.I. 1994 No. 3098, reg. 6(g), as follows:

   (i)   in the opening words of para. 1(b), after "21" there is inserted "22";

   (ii)   para. 1(b)(v), (vii) and (viii)(aa)(C) are revoked;

   (iii)   para. 1(b)(viii)(bb) is substituted as follows:

   "(bb)   subsection (1A) were omitted;
   (cc)   in subsection (2), the reference to paragraph (d) of subsection (1) were omitted;
   (dd)   subsection (2A) were omitted;";

   (iv)   para. 1(b)(viii)(cc) and (dd) are respectively relettered (ee) and (ff);

   (v)   in the opening words of para. 2(b), after "23" there is inserted "24";

   (vi)   para. 2(b)(v), (vii) and (viii)(aa)(C) are revoked;

   (vii)   para. 2(b)(viii)(bb) is substituted as follows:

   "(bb)   paragraph (1A) were omitted;
   (cc)   in paragraph (2), the reference to sub-paragraph (d) of paragraph (1) were omitted;
   (dd)   paragraph (2A) were omitted;"; and

   (viii)   para. 2(b)(viii)(cc), (dd) and (ee) are respectively relettered (ee), (ff) and (gg).

The Road Traffic (Carriage of Dangerous Substance in Packages etc) Regulations 1992

Amended by the Chemicals (Hazard Information and Packaging) Regulations 1993, S.I.1993 No. 1746, reg. 22, Sch. 11, Pt. I, paras 1, 2, and by the Carriage of Dangerous Goods by Road and Rail (Classification, Packaging and Labelling) Regulations 1994, S.I. 1994 No. 669, reg. 15(9), Sch. 6, as follows.

898   **Regulation 2.** In reg. 2(1), the following amendments are made

   (i)   the definition "1984 Regulations" is revoked;

   (ii)   after the definition "the 1992 Regulations" there is inserted the definition "'the 1993 Regulations' means the Chemicals (Hazard Information and Packaging) Regulations 1993 (S.I. 1993 No. 1746)", and that definition is substituted by the definition ""the 1994 Regulations" means the Carriage of Dangerous Goods by Road and Rail (Classification, Packaging and Labelling) Regulations 1994 (S.I. 1994 No. 669);";

898
    (iii) for the definition "approved list" there is substituted the definition "'approved carriage list' has the same meaning as in regulation 4(2) of the 1993 Regulations;", and for the words "regulation 4(2) of the 1993 Regulations" as so substituted there are substituted the words "regulation 4(1)(a) of the 1994 Regulations";

    (iv) for the definition "dangerous substance" there is substituted "'dangerous substance' means any substance which falls within the definition of "dangerous goods" in regulation 2(1) of the 1994 Regulations;";

    (v) in the definition "flammable gas" for the words "paragraph (2) or (4) of regulation 6 of the 1984 Regulations" there are substituted the words "paragraph (2), (3) or (5) of regulation 7 of the 1993 Regulations", and those words as so substituted are substituted by the words "regulation 5 of the 1994 Regulations";

    (vi) in the definition "flammable solid" for the words "paragraph (2) or (4) of regulation 6 of the 1984 Regulations" there are substituted the words "paragraph (2), (3) or (5) of regulation 7 of the 1993 Regulations", and those words as so substituted are substituted by the words "regulation 5 of the 1994 Regulations";

    (vii) in the definition "flash point" for the words "the 1984 Regulations" there are substituted the words "the 1993 Regulations", and the words "1993 Regulations" as so substituted are further substituted by the words "1994 Regulations";

    (viii) in the definition "organic peroxide" for the words "regulation 6(4) of the 1984 Regulations" there are substituted the words "regulation 7(5) of the 1993 Regulations", and those words as so substituted are substituted by the words "regulation 5 of the 1994 Regulations";

    (ix) in the definition "toxic gas" for the words "paragraph (2) or (4) of regulation 6 of the 1984 Regulations" there are substituted the words "paragraph (2), (3) or (5) of regulation 7 of the 1993 Regulations", and those words as so substituted are substituted by the words "regulation 5 of the 1994 Regulations".

In reg. 2(3), sub-para. (c) is substituted by the 1994 Regulations, as follows:

    "(c) the "packing group" of a dangerous substance shall have the same meaning as the definition of "packing group" in regulation 2(1) of the 1994 Regulations; and".

902
In reg. 3(1)(c)(v), the phrases "sub-paragraph (a) of" and "or any substance such as is specified in sub-paragraph (d) of that definition" are revoked.

In reg. 3(2) the following amendments are made:

    (i) in sub-para. (j), for the words "sub-paragraphs (c) to (i) of regulation 3(1) of the 1984 Regulations" there are substituted the words "sub-paragraphs (b) to (g) of regulation 3(1) of the 1993

902 Regulations", and those words as so substituted, are further substituted by the words "sub-paragraphs (k), (o) and (p) of regulation 3(1) of the 1994 Regulations";

(ii) in sub-para (l)(i), for the words "column 1 of Part 1A2 of the approved list" there are substituted the words "column 1 of Part 1 of approved carriage list", and the words "Part 1 of" as so substituted are further substituted by the words "of the";

(iii) in sub-para (l)(iv)(bb), for the words "regulation 13 of the 1984 Regulations" there are substituted the words "regulation 14 of the 1993 Regulations", and for those words as so substituted there are substituted the words "regulation 11 of the 1994 Regulations".

910 **Regulation 16(2)(b).** For the words "paragraph (2) or (4) of regulation 6 of the 1984 Regulations" there are substituted the words "paragraph (2), (3) or (5) of regulation 7 of the 1993 Regulations", and for those words as so substituted there are substituted the words "regulation 5 of the 1994 Regulations", and sub-para. (c) is revoked.

911 **Schedule.** Revoked by the Carriage of Dangerous Goods by Road and Rail (Classification, Packaging and Labelling) Regulations 1994, S.I. 1994 No. 669, reg. 15(9), Sch. 6, para. 9.

The Road Traffic (Training of Drivers of Vehicles Carrying Dangerous Goods) Regulations 1992.

916– These Regulations were amended by S.I. 1992 No. 1213, not S.I. 1992
917 No. 1312.

Regulation 1(3). The definition "approved list" is substituted by the following definition by the Chemicals (Hazard Information and Packaging) Regulations 1993, S.I. 1993 No. 1746, reg. 22, Sch. 11, Pt. III, paras. 1, 2(a):

> "'approved carriage list' has the same meaning as in regulation 4(2) of the Chemicals (Hazard Information and Packaging) Regulations 1993 (S.I. 1993 No. 1746);".

For the words "regulation 4(2) of the Chemicals (Hazard Information and Packaging) Regulations 1993 (S.I. 1993 No. 1746)" in the definition "approved carriage list", as substituted as noted above, there are substituted the words "regulation 4(1)(a) of the Carriage of Dangerous Goods by Road and Rail (Classification, Packaging and Labelling) Regulations 1994 (S.I. 1994 No. 669);", by the Carriage of Dangerous Goods by Road and Rail (Classification, Packaging and Labelling) Regulations 1994, S.I. 1994 No. 669, reg. 15(11), Sch. 8, paras. 1, 2(a).

In the definition "flash point", for the words "the Classification, Packaging and Labelling of Dangerous Substances Regulations 1984" there are substituted the words "the Chemicals (Hazard Information and Packaging) Regulations 1993", by the Chemicals (Hazard Information and Packaging) Regulations 1993, S.I. 1993 No. 1746; the words

916   "Chemicals (Hazard Information and Packaging) Regulations 1993", as so substituted, are further substituted by the words "Carriage of Dangerous Goods by Road and Rail (Classification, Packaging and Labelling) Regulations 1994" by the Carriage of Dangerous Goods by Road and Rail (Classification, Packaging and Labelling) Regulations 1994, S.I. 1994 No. 669, reg. 15(11), Sch. 8, paras. 1, 2(b).

919   **Regulation 2.** Amended by the Road Traffic (Training of Drivers of Vehicles Carrying Dangerous Goods) (Amendment) Regulations 1993, S.I. 1993 No. 1122, reg. 2(a), (b), as follows:

In para. (1)(a), after the word "substance" there are inserted the words "(whether or not it is also radioactive material) or any radioactive material which is not at the same time a dangerous substance", and after the words "Schedule 2" there are inserted the words "or, in the case of any radioactive material which is not also a dangerous substance, under the conditions set out in Schedules 1 to 4 to marginal 2704 of ADR".

In para. (3)(a), the words "or radioactive material" are inserted after the word "substance" where it first occurs, and the words "or the radioactive material" are inserted after the word "vapour"; and in sub-para. (b) after the word "substance" where it occurs first, second and third, there are inserted the words "or radioactive material" and the words "or the radioactive material" after the word "vapour".

922   **Regulation 4(1)(b).** The words "and where the load being carried includes a dangerous substance" are inserted after the "2(1)(a)" by the Road Traffic (Training of Drivers of Vehicles Carrying Dangerous Goods) (Amendment) Regulations 1993, S.I. 1993 No. 1122, reg. 2(c).

923   **Regulation 5.** Amended by the Health and Safety (Fees) Regulations 1994, S.I. 1994 No. 397, reg. 16(1)(a)–(d), as follows:

(i)   at the end of para. (2)(a), after the semi-colon, the word "and" is added;

(ii) at the end of para. (2)(b), the semi-colon is substituted by a full stop and the word "and" is revoked;

(iii) para. (2)(c) is revoked;

(iv) para. (5) is substituted as follows:

"(5) Each vocational training certificate issued in accordance with paragraph (1) shall be valid for a period of 5 years from the date of issue, but its validity may be extended for periods of up to 5 years by the Secretary of State where, within the period of 12 months which precede the expiry of the original certificate or any extension of it granted in accordance with this paragraph, the holder can show to the satisfaction of the Secretary of State that he has—

(a)   successfully completed a refresher course in the carriage of dangerous goods which has been approved by the Secretary of State; and

(b)   passed the examination referred to in paragraph (2)(b).".

924 **Regulation 8.** The words "5(2)(c) or (5)(b) or" are revoked by the Health and Safety (Fees) Regulations 1994, S.I. 1994 No. 397, reg. 16(1)(e).

927–
928 **Schedule 2, Pt. I.** Amended by the Road Traffic (Training of Drivers of Vehicles Carrying Dangerous Goods) (Amendment) Regulations 1993, S.I. 1993 No. 1122, reg. 2(d), as follows:

In the heading, the words "or radioactive material" are inserted after the word "substances", in sub-para.(d), a full-stop is substituted for the semi-colon and the word "or" at the end, and sub-para. (e) is revoked.

In sub-para. (d) for the words "dilute sulphuric acid" there are substituted the words "sulphuric acid, whether or not dilute", by the Carriage of Dangerous Goods by Road and Rail (Classification, Packaging and Labelling) Regulations 1994, S.I. 1994 No. 669, reg. 15(11), Sch. 8, paras. 1, 3(a).

928 **Schedule 2, Pt. II.** In sub-para. (e), for the words "sub-paragraphs (c) to (i) of regulation 3(1) of the Classification, Packaging and Labelling of Dangerous Substances Regulations 1984" there are substituted the words "sub-paragraphs (b) to (g) of regulation 3(1) of the Chemicals (Hazard Information and Packaging) Regulations 1993", by the Chemicals (Hazard Information and Packaging) Regulations 1993, S.I. 1993 No. 1746; for the words "(b) to (g) of regulation 3(1) of the Chemicals (Hazard Information and Packaging) Regulations 1993" as so substituted there are substituted the words "(k), (o) and (p) of regulation 3(1) of the Carriage of Dangerous Goods by Road and Rail (Classification, Packaging and Labelling) Regulations 1994", by the Carriage of Dangerous Goods by Road and Rail (Classification, Packaging and Labelling) Regulations 1994, S.I. 1994 No. 669, reg. 15(11), Sch. 8, paras. 1, 3(b).

The Health and Safety (Display Screen Equipment) Regulations 1992

931 **Add to end of *General note*.** (See also *Griffin v South West Water Services Ltd*[1995] IRLR 15, HCJ, noted to pp. 315–316 above.)

PART 5 SUBSTANCES, NOISE, RADIATION AND OTHER PHENOMENA

1005 **The Control of Substances Hazardous to Health Regulations 1988.** Revoked and replaced by the Control of Substances Hazardous to Health Regulations 1994, S.I. 1994 No. 3246, reg. 18(4), set out in Pt. 2 at pp. 277–303 post.

The Control of Asbestos at Work Regulations 1987

1042 It has been held that dry sweeping asbestos dust is capable of being a process to which the Asbestos Regulations 1969, S.I. 1969 No. 690, regs. 3(2) and 15(1)(a) apply: *Edgson v Vickers plc* [1994] ICR 510. The 1969 Regulations are now the Control of Asbestos at Work Regulations 1987, S.I. 1987 No. 2115.

1051   **Regulation 18(3)(a).** Substituted by the Carriage of Dangerous Goods by Road and Rail (Classification, Packaging and Labelling) Regulations 1994, S.I. 1994 No. 669, reg. 15(4)(a), as follows:

"(a) where the Carriage of Dangerous Goods by Road and Rail (Classification, Packaging and Labelling) Regulations 1994, S.I. 1994 No. 669) apply, in accordance with those Regulations;".

1053   **Schedule 2, para 1(1)(a).** The words "the Classification, Packaging and Labelling of Dangerous Substances Regulations 1984" are substituted by the words "the Chemicals (Hazard Information and Packaging) Regulations 1993 (S.I. 1993 No. 1746)" by the Chemicals (Hazard Information and Packaging) Regulations 1993, S.I. 1993 No. 1746, reg. 21(8); and the words "and the Carriage of Dangerous Goods by Road and Rail (Classification, Packaging and Labelling) Regulations 1994, S.I. 1994 No. 669)" are inserted after the words "S.I. 1993 No. 1746", as substituted as noted above, by the Carriage of Dangerous Goods by Road and Rail (Classification, Packaging and Labelling) Regulations 1994, S.I. 1994 No. 669, reg. 15(4)(b); and the words "the Chemicals (Hazard Information and Packaging) Regulations 1993 (S.I. 1993/1746)" as so substituted are further substituted by the words "the Chemicals (Hazard Information and Packaging for Supply) Regulations 1994 (S.I. 1994/3247)" by the Chemicals (Hazard Information and Packaging for Supply) Regulations 1994, S.I. 1994 No. 3247, reg. 19(6).

1060   **The Health and Safety (Dangerous Pathogens) Regulations 1981.** Revoked by the Control of Substances Hazardous to Health Regulations 1994, S.I. 1994 No. 3246, reg. 18(4).

1066   **The Genetic Manipulation Regulations 1989.** Revoked by the Genetically Modified Organisms (Contained Use) Regulations 1992, S.I. 1992 No. 3217, reg. 25.

The Genetically Modified Organisms (Contained Use) Regulations 1992

1082   **Regulation 22.** Revoked by the Health and Safety (Fees) Regulations 1995, S.I. 1995 No. 2646, reg. 17, Sch. 14.

The Electricity at Work Regulations 1989.

1099   **Regulation 14.** The word "so" should be inserted before the words "near any live conductor".

The Fire Precautions Act 1971

1150   **Section 40(10A).** Repealed by the Health Authorities Act 1995, s. 5(1), Sch. 3, as from 1 April 1996.

1151   **Section 43(1).** In para. (a) of the definition "local authority", the words "and Wales" are repealed and after that paragraph there is inserted the following paragraph by the Local Government (Wales) Act 1994, ss. 22(3), 66(8), Sch. 9, para. 8, Sch. 18, as from a day to be appointed:

"(aa) as respects Wales, the council of a county or county borough;".

1151   In para. (b) of that definition for the words "islands or district council" there are substituted the words "council for a local government area" by the Local Government etc (Scotland) Act 1994, s. 180(1), Sch. 13, para. 87, as from a day to be appointed.

The Fire Precautions (Sub-surface Railway Stations) Regulations 1989

1175   **Regulation 12.** In para. (1), the words "and (3)" are inserted after the words "regulations 4(1) and (3), 5(4) and (5), 6(1) and (3), 7(1), 8(2)", and the words ", subject to paragraph (1A)," are inserted after the words "they may", and para. (1A) is inserted by the Fire Precautions (Sub-surface Railway Stations) (Amendment) Regulations 1994, S.I. 1994 No. 2184, reg. 2, as follows, as from 1 January 1996:

> "(1A) A fire authority may not exercise their powers under paragraph (1) above in such a way that there would be in effect at the same time in respect of a particular station premises exemptions from requirements of regulation 5(4) or 6(1) and from requirements of regulation 5(4) or 6(1) and from requirements of regulation 8(3).".

The Highly Flammable Liquids and Liquefied Petroleum Gases Regulations 1972

1177   **Regulation 2.** The definition of "highly flammable liquid" is substituted for the following definition, and reg. 2(2A) is revoked, by the Chemicals (Hazard Information and Packaging) Regulations 1993, S.I. 1993 No. 1746, reg. 21(13), Sch. 10, Pt. II:

> "'highly flammable liquid' means any of the following, other than aqueous ammonia, liquefied flammable gas, and liquefied petroleum gas, that is to say, any liquid, liquid solution, emulsion or suspension which—
>
> (a)   when tested in accordance with Part III of Schedule 1 to the Chemicals (Hazard Information and Packaging) Regulations 1993 (S.I. 1993 No 1746) has a flash point (as defined in regulation 2(1) of those Regulations) of less than 32° Celsius except that for sub-paragraph (b) of paragraph 1 of that Part there shall be substituted the following sub-paragraph—
>
>> "(b)   by one of the non-equilibrium methods referred to in paragraph 4 except that when the flash point falls within the range 30° C to 34° C that flash point shall be confirmed by the use of like apparatus using the appropriate equilibrium method referred to in paragraph 3"; and
>
> (b)   when tested in the manner specified in Schedule 2 to these Regulations supports combustion".

In sub-para. (a) of the definition of "highly flammable liquid", as substituted as noted, for the words "the Chemicals (Hazard Information and Packaging) Regulations 1993 (S.I. 1993 No. 1746)" there are substituted the words "the Chemicals (Hazard Information and

1177   Packaging for Supply) Regulations 1994 (S.I. 1994/3247)" by the Chemicals (Hazard Information and Packaging for Supply) Regulations 1994, S.I. 1994 No. 3247, reg. 19(9), Sch. 8, Pt. II.

1179   **Regulation 6.** Where a substance or preparation dangerous for supply is required to be labelled in accordance with the Chemicals (Hazard Information and Packaging for Supply) Regulations 1994, S.I. 1994 No. 3247, and is so labelled, that labelling shall be deemed to satisfy the requirements of this regulation: see reg. 19(2)(b) set out in Pt. 2 at p. 319.

The Ionising Radiations Regulations 1985

1243   **Schedule 3.** The word "not" should appear after the word "shall" where it first appears.

PART 6 FACTORIES

The Factories Act 1961

1327   **Add to 5. *The absolute nature of the duty.*** In *Scott v Kelvin Concrete Ltd* 1993 SLT 935, OH, an employer had failed to take adequate precautions under s. 14 where an employee was injured while attempting to repair a hydraulically and pneumatically operated press which, though fenced with gates with interlock switches, should not have been operated while someone was within the hopper involved in carrying out a repair.

1335   **Add to *General note* after "DC".** See also *McMeechan v Uniroyal Engelbert Tyres* 1994 SLT (Sh Ct) 69, Sheriff's Court.

1352   **Section 26.** Certificate of Exemption No. 1 (F661) is no longer in force.

1355   **Add to *General note*.** In *Graham v David A Hall Ltd* 1994 GWD 9-556, OH, it was held that where the plaintiff's employers were aware of dangerous waste on a stairwell and provided a mat at the top of the stairs, which was changed every day and remained reasonably clean for at least an hour after it was changed, they were not liable where the plaintiff slipped and injured herself within an hour of the stairs being cleaned. The court stated that it was not reasonably practicable for the employer to do more than change the mat every hour, and also in view of the number of people employed it would have been impracticable to require the employer to provide a system of changing or cleaning footwear at the exit of each department. It is a matter of conjecture whether the result of this case would have been the same had the cause of action been reg. 9, 12 or 17 of the Workplace (Health, Safety and Welfare) Regulations 1992.

1357   **Section 29. Safe means of access and safe place of employment.** In *Houston v United Distillers Ltd* 1994 GWD 10-622, a warehouseman injured while stowing casks of whisky on racking had shown that the lack of space within the warehouse was a reasonably foreseeable cause of injury to people working there in a normal and reasonable manner. Hence there was a breach of s. 29

PAGE

1360   **Add to end of** (*c*) *Has ... to work.* Where access to scaffolding, although unapproved, was not effectively forbidden, that scaffolding was a place where an employee 'had to work': *Scott v EDC Pipework Services Ltd* 1995 SLT 561n, OH.

(*d*) *A place.* **Delete "but c.f. McFaulds" to end of sentence and add.** In *Gunion v Roche Products Ltd* 1995 SLT 38, (1994) Scotsman, 19 October 1994, OH, it was held that a forklift truck could be a place within the meaning of s. 29(1). In doubting the decision in *McFaulds v Reed Corrugated Cases Ltd* 1993 SLT 670n, the court held that there was nothing in the section to suggest that 'plant' and 'place' must be mutually exclusive.

1364–   **Section 31.** (*e*) *Exemptions.* Certificate of Exemption No. 3 (F664),
1365   Certificate of Exemption No. 4 (F672) and Certificate of Exemption No. 5 (F2052) are no longer in force.

1436   **Section 68.** (*g*) *Hygrometer records.* Form 48 is no longer in force.

1441   **Section 117(5)(b).** Repealed by the Trade Union Reform and Employment Rights Act 1993, s. 51, Sch. 10.

1443   **Section 119A(2)(a).** The words from ", under" to "the arrangements)" are substituted by the words "services are provided in pursuance of arrangements made, or a direction given, under section 10 of the Employment and Training Act 1973 in the area", by the Trade Union Reform and Employment Rights Act 1993, s. 49(2), Sch. 8, para. 1.

1454   **The Factories Act (Docks, Building and Engineering) Construction, etc) Modification Regulations 1938.** Reg. 2 only was revoked by S.I. 1989 No. 2169

1456   **Section 127.** Sub-ss. (6), (7) are repealed by the Construction (Design and Management) Regulations 1994, S.I. 1994 No. 3140, reg. 24(1).

1488–   **Add to** (*y*). In *Ballantyne v John Young and Co (Kelvinhaugh) Ltd* 1994
1489   GWD 13-852, OH, it was held that reg. 6(2) of the Construction (Working Places) Regulations 1966 did not apply to a tower in a cement plant, the construction of which was completed two months before the plaintiff suffered an accident. Further, at the time of the accident the tower was being used solely for the work of alteration of the plant and equipment and not for factory purposes, and although the plant had been put into operation abortively during the commissioning procedure this did not prevent the Factories Act 1961, s. 175(6) applying to exclude the application of the Act to the tower.

1489   **Section 176(1).** The definition "child" is substituted by the Education Act 1993, s. 307(1), Sch. 19, para. 36, as from a day to be appointed, as follows:

1489   "'child' means any person who is not over compulsory school age (construed in accordance with section 277 of the Education Act 1993) or over school age for the purposes of the Education (Scotland) Act 1946;".

The definition "magistrates' court" is repealed by the Statute Law (Repeals) Act 1993, s. 1(1), Sch. 1, Pt. XIV.

In the definition "parent", after the words "the Children Act 1989)", insert the words ", and includes, in relation to any child or young person, any person having direct benefit from his wages".

The definition "child", as so substituted, is further substituted as follows, and in the definition "parent" the words from "means" to "and includes" are substituted by the words "means a parent of a child or young person or any person who is not a parent of his but who has parental responsibility for him (within the meaning of the Children Act 1989) or who has parental responsibilities in relation to him (within the meaning of section 1(3) of the Children (Scotland) Act 1995), and includes", by the Children (Scotland) Act 1995, s. 105(4), Sch. 4, para. 10, as from a day to be appointed:

"'child' means any person who is not over—
(a) compulsory school age (construed in accordance with section 277 of the Education Act 1993); or
(b) school age (construed in accordance with section 31 of the Education (Scotland) Act 1980);".

In the definition of "district council" for the words from "Scotland," to the end there are substituted the words "Scotland, a council constituted under section 2 of the Local Government etc. (Scotland) Act 1994" by the Local Government etc. (Scotland) Act 1994, s. 180(1), Sch. 13, para. 55, as from a day to be appointed.

The definition "ship", "vessel", and "harbour" is substituted by the following definition by the Merchant Shipping Act 1995, s. 314(2), Sch. 13, para. 31, as from 1 January 1996:

"'ship' and 'vessel' have the same meaning as 'ship' in the Merchant Shipping Act 1995, and 'harbour' has the same meaning as in the Merchant Shipping Act 1995".

1491   **Section 176(5).** The words from "the provisions" to "expressly provided" are substituted by the words "section 119 of this Act shall not apply", by the Employment Act 1989, s. 29(3), Sch. 6, para. 6, as from a day to be appointed.

Section 176(8A). Inserted by the Local Government (Wales) Act 1994, s. 66(6), Sch. 16, para. 18, as from a day to be appointed, as follows:

"(8A) In the application of this Act in relation to Wales—
(a) any reference to a district council shall be construed as a reference to a county council or (as the case may be) county borough council; and

1491   (b)   any reference to the district of a district council shall be construed as a reference to a county or county borough." .

1496   **Section 178(1).** The Registration of Births, Deaths and Marriages (Fees) Order 1994, S.I. 1994 No. 3257 prescribed the fee payable for an extract of an entry in the birth register at £2.00.

1512   **The Abrasive Wheels Regulations 1970.** Certificate of Exemption No. 2 (F2354), Certificate of Exemption No. 6 (F2365) and Certificate of Exemption No. 9 (F2405)) are no longer in force.

1532   **The Clay Works (Welfare) Special Regulations 1948.** Form 1034 is no longer in force.

The Work in Compressed Air Special Regulations 1958.

1541   **Regulation 12(1).** The words "12 degrees" should read "27 degrees".

1548   Certificate of Exemption No. 1—Testing of Aircraft (F2075) is no longer in force.

1549   **The Cotton Cloth Factories Regulations 1929.** Form 321 is no longer in force.

The Dry Cleaning Special Regulations 1949

1571   **Regulation 2.** In the definition "Flash point" in reg. 2(2), for the words "Part IV of Schedule 1 to the Classification, Packaging and Labelling of Dangerous Substances Regulations 1984 S.I. 1984/1244" there are substituted the words "Part III of Schedule 1 to the Chemicals (Hazard Information and Packaging) Regulations 1993 (S.I. 1993 No 1746), except that for sub-paragraph (b) of paragraph 1 of that Part there shall be substituted the following sub-paragraph—

'(b) by one of the non-equilibrium methods referred to in paragraph 4 except that when the flash point falls within the range 30°C to 34°C that flash point shall be confirmed by the use of like apparatus using the appropriate equilibrium method referred to in paragraph 3.'";

and reg. 2(2A) is revoked by the Chemicals (Hazard Information and Packaging) Regulations 1993, S.I. 1993 No. 1746, reg. 21(13), Sch. 10, Pt. I.

In the definition of "Flash point", as amended as noted, for the words "the Chemicals (Hazard Information and Packaging) Regulations 1993 (S.I. 1993 No. 1746)" there are substituted the words "the Chemicals (Hazard Information and Packaging for Supply) Regulations 1994 (S.I. 1994/3247)" by the Chemicals (Hazard Information and Packaging for Supply) Regulations 1994, S.I. 1994 No. 3247, reg. 19(9), Sch. 8, Pt. II.

The Freight Containers (Safety Convention) Regulations 1984.

1587   **Regulation 7.** Para. (3) was revoked by the Health and Safety (Miscellaneous Fees) Regulations 1986, S.I. 1986 No. 392, reg. 10, Sch. 9.

PAGE

1607   **The Indiarubber Regulations 1922.** Form 983 is no longer in force.

1645   **The Non-Ferrous Metals (Melting and Founding) Regulations 1962.** Form 2118 is no longer in force.

The Shipbuilding and Ship-repairing Regulations 1960.

1676   **Regulation 3(2).** In the definition "Abel closed test" for the words "Part IV of Schedule 1 to the Classification, Packaging and Labelling of Dangerous Substances Regulations 1984 (S.I. 1984/1244)" there are substituted the words "Part III of Schedule 1 to the Chemicals (Hazard Information and Packaging) Regulations 1993 (S.I. 1993 No. 1746)" by the Chemicals (Hazard Information and Packaging) Regulations 1993, S.I. 1993 No. 1746, reg. 21(13), Sch. 10, Pt. II.

In the definition of "Abel closed test", as amended as noted, for the words "the Chemicals (Hazard Information and Packaging) Regulations 1993 (S.I. 1993 No. 1746)" there are substituted the words "the Chemicals (Hazard Information and Packaging for Supply) Regulations 1994 (S.I. 1994/3247)" by the Chemicals (Hazard Information and Packaging for Supply) Regulations 1994, S.I. 1994 No. 3247, reg. 19(9), Sch. 8, Pt. II.

1700   **Regulation 65(1).** The word "contained" should read "continued".

1708   Certificate of Exemption No. 3 (General) (F2194) is no longer in force.

The Factories (Testing of Aircraft Engines and Accessories) Special Regulations 1952

1722   Form 1021 is no longer in force. See now Certificate of Approval F2510.

1723   **Regulation 2(2).** In the definition "Petroleum-spirit" for the words "Part IV of Schedule 1 to the Classification, Packaging and Labelling of Dangerous Substances Regulations 1984 (S.I. 1984/1244) has a flash point" there are substituted the words "Part III of Schedule 1 to the Chemicals (Hazard Information and Packaging) Regulations 1993 (S.I. 1993 No 1746) has a flash point (as defined in regulation 2(1) of those Regulations)" by the Chemicals (Hazard Information and Packaging) Regulations 1993, S.I. 1993 No. 1746, reg. 21(13), Sch. 10, Pt. II.

In the definition of "Petroleum-spirit", as amended as noted, for the words "the Chemicals (Hazard Information and Packaging) Regulations 1993 (S.I. 1993 No. 1746)" there are substituted the words "the Chemicals (Hazard Information and Packaging for Supply) Regulations 1994 (S.I. 1994/3247)" by the Chemicals (Hazard Information and Packaging for Supply) Regulations 1994, S.I. 1994 No. 3247, reg. 19(9), Sch. 8, Pt. II.

The Woodworking Machines Regulations 1974

1738   **Add to *General note*.** An employee's duties under reg. 14(1)(a) only arise when his employers have provided a saw with a properly adjusted guard: *Arbuckle v AH McIntosh & Co Ltd* 1993 SLT 857n, OH.

PART 7 CONSTRUCTION

The Construction (General Provisions) Regulations 1961

1807   **Add to (e).** In *Morris v Breaveglen (t/a Anzac Construction Co)* [1993] ICR 766, [1993] IRLR 350, CA, the plaintiff, a building site worker, who was sub-contracted by the defendant, his employer, to work on the sub-contractor's building site injured himself whilst using a dumper truck. It was held that although the sub-contractor could instruct the plaintiff what to do and how to do it, the defendant remained liable under the contract of employment to fulfil his obligations to the plaintiff to take reasonable care to see that he was not exposed to unnecessary risk while at work. Accordingly, the defendant was in breach of his common law duty to the plaintiff by failing to provide him with proper instruction, by permitting him to use a dumper truck and by not ensuring the existence of a proper and safe system of work. Further, as the use of the dumper truck was within the scope of his employment, the defendant was in breach of his statutory obligation under regs. 32 and 37.

1809   **Regulations 5, 6.** Revoked by the Construction (Design and Management) Regulations 1994, S.I. 1994 No. 3140, reg. 24(2).

1814   **Add *General note* to reg. 14.** In *Blackman v CJ Pryor (Earth Moving Contractors) Ltd* (1994) Times, 5 July, QBD, it was held that reg. 14(2) only applies to plant or equipment situated at the top of an excavation pit and will not apply if it is situated at the bottom.

The Construction (Working Places) Regulations 1966

1856   **Regulation 3(b).** The words "or about to be performed" should appear after the words "act or operation performed".

1877   **Regulation 33.** The heading should read "Openings, corners, breaks, edges and open joisting".

PART 8 OFFICES, SHOPS AND RAILWAY PREMISES

The Offices, Shops and Railways Premises Act 1963

2019   **Section 7.** This section is repealed as from 1 January 1996.

2037   **Add to end of (e) *Reasonably practicable*.** In *Disney v South Western Egg Products* (8 July 1993, unreported), CA, it was held that there was no breach of s. 16 where an employee slipped on seeds in a bread shop. Owing to the inconvenience of sweeping seeds up every time loaves were carried through the shop, and the small amount of debris, it was held not to be reasonably practicable to avoid the accident. A different result might arise under the Workplace (Health, Safety and Welfare) Regulations 1992, reg. 12.

2068   **Section 84(2).** After the word "Namibia" there are inserted the words ", South Africa" by the South Africa Act 1995, s. 1, Schedule, para. 6.

2070   **Section 90(1).** The definitions "magistrates' court", "petty sessions area" and "police authority" are repealed by the Statute Law (Repeals) Act 1993, s. 1(1), Sch. 1, Pt. XIV.

PART 9 AGRICULTURE

The Agriculture (Safety, Health and Welfare Provisions) Act 1956

2118   **Section 24.** In sub-s. (1), in the definition "young person", for the words "for the purposes of the Education Act 1944" there are substituted the words "(construed in accordance with section 277 of the Education Act 1993)" by the Education Act 1993, s. 307(1), Sch. 19, para. 33, as from a day to be appointed.

2119   **Section 25.** That section reads as follows:

"25. Application to Scotland.

(1)   The provisions of this section shall have effect for the application of this Act to Scotland.

(2)   [*repealed*].

(3)   *For section three of this Act there shall be substituted the following section—*

"3.—(1) If it appears to the Health and Safety Executive that an agricultural unit in their district on which workers are employed in agriculture is without suitable and sufficient sanitary conveniences or washing facilities available for the use of workers so employed, the Executive shall, by notice served on the appropriate person, require him, within such time as may be specified in the notice, to execute such works or take such other steps for the purpose of providing the unit with suitable and sufficient sanitary conveniences or washing facilities, as the case may be, available for the use of workers employed thereon in agriculture as may be specified in the notice.

(2) In considering, for the purposes of this section, whether an agricultural unit is without suitable and sufficient sanitary conveniences or washing facilities available for the use of workers employed on the unit in agriculture, regard shall be had to the number and sex of the workers so employed, the location and duration of their work, and to all other relevant circumstances.

(3) The Health and Safety Executive shall not serve a notice under this section requiring the execution of works of the nature of fixed equipment unless they are satisfied that special circumstances exist which render requisite the execution of such works, and no such notice shall be of any effect unless it states that the Executive are so satisfied and what those circumstances are.

(4) For the purposes of this section the expression "appropriate person" means—

(a) in the case of a notice requiring the execution, on land being an agricultural holding, of works of the nature of fixed equipment, the landlord of the holding;

(b) in the case of a notice requiring the execution, on land in the occupation of the owner thereof, of works of the nature aforesaid, the owner of the land;

PAGE

2119

(c)   *in the case of a notice requiring the execution of works other than works of the nature of fixed equipment, or the taking of other steps, the occupier of the unit to which the notice relates.*

(5) Any person aggrieved by a notice under this section may appeal to the sheriff by giving notice of appeal within twenty-one days after the date of the service of the notice; and the sheriff may either confirm the notice or, if he is satisfied that the works required to be executed or the steps required to be taken are unnecessary or are unreasonable in character or extent, or are not reasonably practicable, or that the Health and Safety Executive have refused unreasonably to approve the execution of alternative works or the taking of alternative steps, or that for any other reason the notice should be disallowed or varied, may disallow the notice or may confirm the notice subject to such variation as he may specify and may make such order as to the expenses of the appeal as he may think equitable.

The decision of the sheriff shall be final and shall be binding on both the authority and on the person on whom the notice is served.

(6) Subject to the right of appeal conferred by the last foregoing subsection and to any order made by the sheriff on such appeal, a person on whom a notice is served under this section who fails to comply with the requirements of the notice shall be guilty of an offence."

(4)   Where by virtue of a notice served under section three of this Act any works of the nature of fixed equipment are required to be executed on any land being an agricultural holding, section 5(2), (3) and (5) of the Agricultural Holdings (Scotland) Act 1991 (liabilities of landlord and tenant of agricultural holding regarding fixed equipment) and section 10 of that Act (which empowers the landlord of a holding to enter thereon for the purpose of providing fixed equipment) shall apply in relation to such works as aforesaid as they apply in relation to fixed equipment within the meaning of that Act.

(5)   Where the landlord of an agricultural holding has executed thereon works of the nature of fixed equipment which are required to be executed as mentioned in the last foregoing subsection or has executed similar works at the request of, or in agreement with, the tenant, section 15 of the Agricultural Holdings (Scotland) Act 1991 (which provides for increases of rent in respect of improvements carried out by the landlord) shall have effect as if the works so executed were such an improvement as is mentioned in subsection (1) of that section.

(6)   *For section 5 there shall be substituted the following section—*

"(1) Any sanitary convenience and any washing facilities available for the use of workers employed on an agricultural unit in agriculture and any sanitary convenience provided in pursuance of regulations under section four of this Act shall be kept properly cleansed.

(2) In the event of a contravention of the provisions of this section in relation to a sanitary convenience provided in pursuance of regulations under the said section four, the employer by whom it was provided, and in any other case the occupier of the agricultural unit, shall be guilty of an offence".

2119   (7)–(9) [*repealed.*]

(10) In this Act the following expressions have the meanings hereby assigned to them respectively, that is to say—

"agricultural holding", "fixed equipment" and "landlord" have the like meanings as in the Agricultural Holdings (Scotland) Act 1991;

"owner" has the like meaning as in the Public Health (Scotland) Act 1897, and in the case of an agricultural unit occupied by a landholder within the meaning of the Small Landholders (Scotland) Acts 1886 to 1931, or a crofter within the meaning of the Crofters (Scotland) Act 1955, means the landholder or the crofter;

.....

"tort" means delict or quasi-delict;

"worker" means a person employed under a contract of service or apprenticeship or a person employed in accordance with the provisions of Part III of the Children and Young Persons (Scotland) Act 1937, and the Education (Exemptions) (Scotland) Act 1947, and "employer" and "employed" have corresponding meanings;

"young person" means a person who is over school age for the purposes of the Education (Scotland) Act 1946, but who has not attained the age of eighteen;

and subsection (1) of section twenty-four shall have effect as if the definition of "agricultural holding", "fixed equipment", "landlord", ... , "worker" and "young person" were omitted."

General note. Sub-ss. (3), (6) are repealed as from 1 January 1996 by the Workplace (Health, Safety and Welfare) Regulations 1992 for workplaces in existence on 31 December 1992. Those Regulations will apply to those workplaces from the former date. Workplaces coming into use after 31 December 1992 and modifications, extensions and conversions started after 31 December 1992 to existing workplaces must conform to those Regulations as soon as they come into use.

The Agriculture (Circular Saws) Regulations 1959

2124   **Schedule 1, Pt I, para. 4.** The words "vertical place" should read "vertical plane".

The Agriculture (Stationary Machinery) Regulations 1959

2152   **Schedule, Pt. II, para. 4(1).** The words "of every" should appear after the word "outlet".

PART 10 OFFSHORE AND DIVING

The Mineral Workings (Offshore Installations) Act 1971

2205   **Section 1.** Repealed by the Offshore Installations and Pipeline Works (Management and Administration) Regulations 1995, S.I. 1995 No. 738, reg. 22(1), Sch. 1, Pt. I.

2207   **Section 3(4).** The words "and of the installation manager, and of every person who, in relation to the installation, is a concession owner", the words "the installation manager and every person who, in relation to the installation, is a concession owner", where they next occur, and the word "each" are repealed by the Offshore Installations and Pipeline Works (Management and Administration) Regulations 1995, S.I. 1995 No. 738, reg. 22(1), Sch. 1, Pt. I.

Sections 4, 5. Repealed by the Offshore Installations and Pipeline Works (Management and Administration) Regulations 1995, S.I. 1995 No. 738, reg. 22(1), Sch. 1, Pt. I.

2211   **Section 9(3).** The words "section 4 or section 5" are repealed by the Offshore Installations and Pipeline Works (Management and Administration) Regulations 1995, S.I. 1995 No. 738, reg. 22(1), Sch. 1, Pt. I.

2212   **Section 11(5), (6).** Repealed by the Offshore Installations and Pipeline Works (Management and Administration) Regulations 1995, S.I. 1995 No. 738, reg. 22(1), Sch. 1, Pt. I.

Section 12(1). Before the definition of "controlled waters" there is inserted the following definition:

> "'the 1995 Regulations' means the Offshore Installations and Pipeline Works (Management and Administration) Regulations 1995;";

for the definitions of "controlled waters", of "installation manager", of "offshore installation" and of "owner" there are substituted the following definitions, respectively:

> "'controlled waters' means—
>
>> (a)   tidal waters and parts of the sea in or adjacent to Great Britain up to the seaward limits of territorial waters; and
>>
>> (b)   any area designated by order under section 1(7) of the Continental Shelf Act 1964;";

> "'installation manager' has the meaning given by regulation 2(1) of the 1995 Regulations;";
> "'offshore installation' has the same meaning as in regulation 3 of the 1995 Regulations;"; and
> "'owner', in relation to an offshore installation, means the person who is, in relation to the installation, the duty holder as defined by regulation 2(1) of the 1995 Regulations in relation to that installation;".

and the definitions of "designated area" and "foreign sector of the continental shelf" are revoked by the Offshore Installations and Pipeline Works (Management and Administration) Regulations 1995, S.I. 1995 No. 738, reg. 22, Sch. 1, Pts. I, II.

2213   **Section 12(2), (3).** Repealed by the Offshore Installations and Pipeline Works (Management and Administration) Regulations 1995, S.I. 1995 No. 738, reg. 22(1), Sch. 1, Pt. I.

2215   **The Offshore Installations (Registration) Regulations 1972.** Revoked by the Offshore Installations and Pipeline Works (Management and Administration) Regulations 1995, S.I. 1995 No. 738, reg. 23(1), Sch. 2, Pt. I.

2219   **The Offshore Installations (Managers) Regulations 1972.** Revoked by the Offshore Installations and Pipeline Works (Management and Administration) Regulations 1995, S.I. 1995 No. 738, reg. 23(1), Sch. 2, Pt. I.

The Offshore Installations (Inspectors and Casualties) Regulations 1973

2222   **Regulation 1(2).** The definition "manager" is revoked by the Offshore Installations and Pipeline Works (Management and Administration) Regulations 1995, S.I. 1995 No. 738, reg. 23(1), Sch. 2, Pt. I.

2224   **Regulation 5(1).** The words "or manager" are revoked by the Offshore Installations and Pipeline Works (Management and Administration) Regulations 1995, S.I. 1995 No. 738, reg. 23(1), Sch. 2, Pt. I.

2225   **Regulation 8(1).** Revoked by the Offshore Installations and Pipeline Works (Management and Administration) Regulations 1995, S.I. 1995 No. 738, reg. 23(1), Sch. 2, Pt. I.

2226   **Regulation 9(b).** Revoked by the Offshore Installations and Pipeline Works (Management and Administration) Regulations 1995, S.I. 1995 No. 738, reg. 23(1), Sch. 2, Pt. I.

2227   **Regulation 12(2).** In sub-para. (a) the words from "excluding therefrom" to the end and the words from "a reference" to "logbook and" are revoked by the Offshore Installations and Pipeline Works (Management and Administration) Regulations 1995, S.I. 1995 No. 738, reg. 23(1), Sch. 2, Pt. I.

The Offshore Installations (Operational Safety, Health and Welfare) Regulations 1976

2246   **Regulation 1(2).** The definition "installation manager" is revoked and the definition "responsible person" is substituted by the Offshore Installations and Pipeline Works (Management and Administration) Regulations 1995, S.I. 1995 No. 738, reg. 23(1), (3), Sch. 2, Pts. I, II, para. 1, as follows:

> "'responsible person' means a competent person authorised by or on behalf of the owner;".

2247   **Regulation 2(1).** Revoked by the Offshore Installations (Prevention of Fire and Explosion, and Emergency Response) Regulations 1995, S.I. 1995 No. 743, reg. 25, Schedule.

PAGE

2247   **Regulation 3.** Revoked by the Offshore Installations and Pipeline Works (Management and Administration) Regulations 1995, S.I. 1995 No. 738, reg. 23(1), Sch. 2, Pt. I.

Regulation 4(6). Revoked by the Offshore Installations (Prevention of Fire and Explosion, and Emergency Response) Regulations 1995, S.I. 1995 No. 743, reg. 25, Schedule.

2249   **Regulation 5.** In para. (3) the words "and 25(2)" and in para. (4) the words from "who shall read" to "logbook" are revoked by the Offshore Installations and Pipeline Works (Management and Administration) Regulations 1995, S.I. 1995 No. 738, reg. 23(1), Sch. 2, Pt. I.

2251   **Regulations 7–9.** Revoked by the Offshore Installations and Pipeline Works (Management and Administration) Regulations 1995, S.I. 1995 No. 738, reg. 23(1), Sch. 2, Pt. I.

2252   **Regulation 13.** The heading should read "Marking of lifting appliances and gear".

2254   **Regulations 16, 17(2), 18–26.** Revoked by the Offshore Installations and Pipeline Works (Management and Administration) Regulations 1995, S.I. 1995 No. 738, reg. 23(1), Sch. 2, Pt. I.

2259   **Regulation 29.** Revoked by the Offshore Installations and Pipeline Works (Management and Administration) Regulations 1995, S.I. 1995 No. 738, reg. 23(2), as from 20 June 1997.

Regulation 30. Revoked by the Offshore Installations and Pipeline Works (Management and Administration) Regulations 1995, S.I. 1995 No. 738, reg. 23(1), Sch. 2, Pt. I.

2260   **Regulation 32.** In para. (1) the words "the installation manager, and of" and the words "and of the concession owner," and paras. (3)–(7) are revoked by the Offshore Installations and Pipeline Works (Management and Administration) Regulations 1995, S.I. 1995 No. 738, reg. 23(1), Sch. 2, Pt. I.

2261   **Regulation 34(1).** The words "the installation manager, the concession owner and" and "each" are revoked by the Offshore Installations and Pipeline Works (Management and Administration) Regulations 1995, S.I. 1995 No. 738, reg. 23(1), Sch. 2, Pt. I.

2263   **Schedule 2.** Revoked by the Offshore Installations and Pipeline Works (Management and Administration) Regulations 1995, S.I. 1995 No. 738, reg. 23(1), Sch. 2, Pt. I.

2283   **The Offshore Installations (Emergency Procedures) Regulations 1976.** Revoked by the Offshore Installations (Prevention of Fire and Explosion, and Emergency Response) Regulations 1995, S.I. 1995 No. 743, reg. 25, Schedule.

PAGE

2289   **The Offshore Installations (Life-Saving Appliances) Regulations 1977.** Revoked by the Offshore Installations (Prevention of Fire and Explosion, and Emergency Response) Regulations 1995, S.I. 1995 No. 743, reg. 25, Schedule.

2295   **The Offshore Installations (Fire-Fighting Equipment) Regulations 1978.** Revoked by the Offshore Installations (Prevention of Fire and Explosion, and Emergency Response) Regulations 1995, S.I. 1995 No. 743, reg. 25, Schedule.

The Offshore Installations (Well Control) Regulations 1980

2303   **Regulation 1(2).** The definition of "installation manager" is revoked and the definition of "responsible person" is substituted by the Offshore Installations and Pipeline Works (Management and Administration) Regulations 1995, S.I. 1995 No. 738, reg. 23(1), (3), Sch. 2, Pts. I, II, para. 2, as follows:

> "'responsible person' means a competent person authorised by or on behalf of the owner;".

2304   **Regulation 3(1).** The words "the installation manager, the concession owner and" and the word "each" are revoked by the Offshore Installations and Pipeline Works (Management and Administration) Regulations 1995, S.I. 1995 No. 738, reg. 23(1), Sch. 2, Pt. I.

The Offshore Installations (Safety Representatives and Safety Committees) Regulations 1989

2305   *General note.* The last two lines of the first paragraph after the words "European Framework Directive (89/391)" should be amended to read as follows: "which requires consultation with safety representatives (whether a union is recognised or not) and/or consultation with workers" (on the discrepancy now see the entry to pp. 315–316 ante).

Regulation 2. Amended by the Offshore Installations and Pipeline Works (Management and Administration) Regulations 1995, S.I. 1995 No. 738, reg. 23(1), (3), Sch. 2, Pts. I, II, para. 5, as follows:

(i) the following definitions are inserted after the definitions of "the 1974 Act" and "appropriate languages" respectively:

> "'the 1995 Regulations' means the Offshore Installations and Pipeline Works (Management and Administration) Regulations 1995";
> "'duty holder' in relation to an offshore installation means the person who is the duty holder within the meaning of regulation 2(1) of the 1995 Regulations for the purpose of those Regulations";

(ii) the definition of "installation logbook" is revoked; and

(iii) the definition of "installation manager" is revoked and replaced as follows:

2305   "'installation manager' has the meaning given by regulation 2(1) of the 1995 Regulations;".

2306   **Regulation 3.** Substituted by the Offshore Installations and Pipeline Works (Management and Administration) Regulations 1995, S.I. 1995 No. 738, reg. 23(3), Sch. 2, Pt. II, para. 6, as follows:

"3. These Regulations shall apply to an offshore installation at a working station in controlled waters which normally has persons on board.".

2308   **Regulation 11.** For the words "installation owner" where they twice occur there are substituted the words "duty holder" by the Offshore Installations and Pipeline Works (Management and Administration) Regulations 1995, S.I. 1995 No. 738, reg. 23(3), Sch. 2, Pt. II, para. 7.

2309   **Regulation 13(b).** The words "the installation manager shall record those facts in the installation logbook and" are revoked by the Offshore Installations and Pipeline Works (Management and Administration) Regulations 1995, S.I. 1995 No. 738, reg. 23(1), Sch. 2, Pt. I.

2310   **Regulation 17.** For the words "installation owner" wherever they occur, there are substituted the words "duty holder" by the Offshore Installations and Pipeline Works (Management and Administration) Regulations 1995, S.I. 1995 No. 738, reg. 23(3), Sch. 2, Pt. II, para. 7.

2312   **Regulation 19.** For the words "owner of an offshore installation" there are substituted the words "duty holder in relation to an offshore installation" by the Offshore Installations and Pipeline Works (Management and Administration) Regulations 1995, S.I. 1995 No. 738, reg. 23(3), Sch. 2, Pt. II, para. 8.

Regulation 20(1). For the words "installation owner" there are substituted the words "duty holder" by the Offshore Installations and Pipeline Works (Management and Administration) Regulations 1995, S.I. 1995 No. 738, reg. 23(3), Sch. 2, Pt. II, para. 7.

2313   **Regulation 22.** For the word "employers" in para. (1)(c) there are substituted the words "duty holder" and for the words "installation owner" in para. (1)(h), there are substituted the words "duty holder" by the Offshore Installations and Pipeline Works (Management and Administration) Regulations 1995, S.I. 1995 No. 738, reg. 23(3), Sch. 2, Pt. II, paras. 7, 9.

Regulation 23. Substituted by the Offshore Installations and Pipeline Works (Management and Administration) Regulations 1995, S.I. 1995 No. 738, reg. 23(3), Sch. 2, Pt. II, para. 10, as follows:

"**23. Duties of installation operators and owners, and employers**

(1) The provisions of this regulation shall apply to every offshore installation served by a safety committee.

2313

(2) It shall be the duty of the duty holder—

(a) to facilitate the exercise by the committee of its functions and by the safety representatives of their functions and powers in respect of the installation under these Regulations, and for that purpose to make available the necessary accommodation, facilities for communication and office equipment supplies;

(b) to consult safety representatives with a view to the making and maintenance of arrangements which will enable them and the workforce to co-operate effectively in promoting and developing measures to ensure the health and safety of persons working on or from the installation, and in checking the effectiveness of such arrangements; and

(c) without prejudice to sub-paragraph (b) above, to consult safety representatives in good time with regard to—

  (i) the preparation of a safety case relating to the installation under the Offshore Installations (Safety Case) Regulations 1992;

  (ii) the introduction to the installation of any measure which may substantially affect the health and safety of the workforce; and

  (iii) the health and safety consequences for the workforce of the introduction (including the planning thereof) to the installation of new technologies;

(3) It shall be the duty of the duty holder and any employer of members of a workforce to consult safety representatives in good time with regard to—

(a) any health and safety information he is required to provide to members of a workforce by or under the relevant statutory provisions; and

(b) the planning and organisation of any health and safety training he is to provide to members of a workforce by or under the relevant statutory provisions.

(4) It shall be the duty of every employer of members of a workforce to consult safety representatives in good time with regard to his arrangements for appointing persons in accordance with regulation 6(1) of the Management of Health and Safety at Work Regulations 1992".

In reg. 23(2)(c), as so substituted, the word "and" after para. (ii) is revoked, and para. (iv) is added, by the Offshore Installations (Prevention of Fire and Explosion, and Emergency Response) Regulations 1995, S.I. 1995 No. 743, reg. 23, as follows:

"and (iv) the arrangements for the appointment of persons referred to in regulation 6(1) of the Offshore Installations (Prevention of Fire and Explosion, and Emergency Response) Regulations 1995.".

2314 **Regulations 24, 25.** For the words "installation owner" wherever they occur, there are substituted the words "duty holder" by the Offshore

2314   Installations and Pipeline Works (Management and Administration) Regulations 1995, S.I. 1995 No. 738, reg. 23(3), Sch. 2, Pt. II, para. 7.

2315   **Regulation 27.** Substituted by the Offshore Installations and Pipeline Works (Management and Administration) Regulations 1995, S.I. 1995 No. 738, reg. 23(3), Sch. 2, Pt. II, para. 11, as follows:

> **"27. Training**
>
> It shall be the duty of the duty holder to ensure that—
> (a) a safety representative for the installation is provided with such training in aspects of the functions of a safety representative as are reasonable in all the circumstances; and
> (b) any costs associated with such training, including travel and subsistence costs, are not borne by the safety representative.".

Regulation 28(1). For the words "installation owner" there are substituted the words "duty holder" by the Offshore Installations and Pipeline Works (Management and Administration) Regulations 1995, S.I. 1995 No. 738, reg. 23(3), Sch. 2, Pt. II, para. 7.

The Offshore Installations (Emergency Pipe-line Valve) Regulations 1989

2316   **Regulation 2.** Amended by the Offshore Installations and Pipeline Works (Management and Administration) Regulations 1995, S.I. 1995 No. 738, reg. 23(1), (3), Sch. 2, Pts. I, II, para. 12, as follows:

> (i) the following definition is inserted before the definition of "associated installation":
>
> "'the 1995 Regulations' means the Offshore Installations and Pipeline Works (Management and Administration) Regulations 1995";
>
> (ii) the definitions of "controlled waters" and of "manager" are revoked; and
>
> (iii) the following definitions are substituted for the definitions of "installation manager", "offshore installation" and "owner" respectively:
>
> "'installation manager' means, in relation to an associated installation, the person appointed for the purposes of regulation 6(1)(a) of the 1995 Regulations who is for the time being in charge of it";
> "'offshore installation' means an installation within the meaning of regulation 3 of the 1995 Regulations other than an installation which is—
> (a) used exclusively for flaring, or
> (b) used exclusively for the loading of substances into vessels or for their reception and storage prior to such loading and which normally has no persons on board"; and
> "'owner', in relation to—

2316

    (a) an offshore installation, means the person who is, in relation to the installation, the duty holder as defined by regulation 2(1) of the 1995 Regulations in relation to that installation; and

    (b) a pipeline in respect of which no person has been designated as its owner in pursuance of section 33(3) of the 1975 Act, means the person in whom the pipeline is vested;".

The Offshore Installations and Pipeline Works (First-Aid) Regulations 1989

2321   **Regulation 2.** Amended by the Offshore Installations and Pipeline Works (Management and Administration) Regulations 1995, S.I. 1995 No. 738, reg. 23(1), (3), Sch. 2, Pts. I, II, para. 13, as follows:

  (i) the definition of "the 1971 Act" is revoked;

  (ii) the following definition is inserted after the definition of "the 1989 Order":

    "'the 1995 Regulations' means the Offshore Installations and Pipeline Works (Management and Administration) Regulations 1995;";

  (iii) the following definition is substituted for the definition of "offshore installation":

    "'offshore installation' has the same meaning as in regulation 3 of the 1995 Regulations"; and

  (iv) paras. (a), (c) are substituted in the definition of "person in control" as follows:

    "(a) in relation to an offshore installation, the person who is the duty holder as defined by regulation 2(1) of the 1995 Regulations for the purposes of those Regulations;";

    "(c) in relation to an activity in connection with an offshore installation—

      (i) the person who is, in relation to the installation, the duty holder as defined by regulation 2(1) of the 1995 Regulations for the purposes of those Regulations; and

      (ii) the employer of persons engaged in that activity;".

2333   **The Offshore Safety (Protection Against Victimisation) Act 1992.** Repealed by the Trade Union Reform and Employment Rights Act 1993, s. 51, Sch. 10

The Offshore Installations (Safety Case) Regulations 1992

2336   **Regulation 2(1).** Amended by the Offshore Installations and Pipeline Works (Management and Administration) Regulations 1995, S.I. 1995 No. 738, reg. 23(3), Sch. 2, Pt. II, para. 14(a), as follows:

2336

(i) the following definitions are substituted for the definitions of "the 1971 Act", "the 1989 Order", "concession owner" and "installation" respectively:

"'the 1995 Regulations' means the Offshore Installations and Pipeline Works (Management and Administration) Regulations 1995;";

"'the 1995 Order' means the Health and Safety at Work etc Act 1974 (Application outside Great Britain) Order 1995";

"'concession owner' in relation to an installation has the same meaning as in regulation 2(1) of the 1995 Regulations";

"'installation' means an offshore installation within the meaning of regulation 3 of the 1995 Regulations"; and

(ii) para. (a) of the definition of "owner" is substituted as follows:

"(a) a mobile installation means the person who controls the operation of the installation".

Regulation 2(5). For the words from "carrying" to the end there are substituted the words "using the installation for any of the purposes described in regulation 3(1) of the 1995 Regulations" by the Offshore Installations and Pipeline Works (Management and Administration) Regulations 1995, S.I. 1995 No. 738, reg. 23(3), Sch. 2, Pt. II, para. 14(b).

Regulation 2(8). For the words "article 4(1)(b) of the 1989 Order" there are substituted the words "sub-paragraph (b) of paragraph (1) of article 4 of the 1995 Order, other than an activity specified in paragraph (i) or (ii) of that sub-paragraph" by the Offshore Installations and Pipeline Works (Management and Administration) Regulations 1995, S.I. 1995 No. 738, reg. 23(3), Sch. 2, Pt. II, para. 14(c).

2340 **Regulation 8(1A).** Added by the Offshore Installations (Prevention of Fire and Explosion, and Emergency Response) Regulations 1995, S.I. 1995 No. 743, reg. 24, as follows:

"(1A) The particulars required by paragraph (1) shall include a summary of the record kept pursuant to regulation 5(3) of the Offshore Installations (Prevention of Fire and Explosion, and Emergency Response) Regulations 1995".

2343 **Regulation 14(2).** The word "and" after sub-para. (f) is revoked, and after sub-para. (g) there is added the following sub-paragraph, by the Offshore Installations and Pipeline Works (Management and Administration) Regulations 1995, S.I. 1995 No. 738, reg. 23(3), Sch. 2, Pt. II, para. 15:

"and (h) the manager of the first-mentioned installation".

2347 **Schedule 3, para. 1.** After the word "name" there are added the words "and address" by the Offshore Installations and Pipeline Works (Management and Administration) Regulations 1995, S.I. 1995 No. 738, reg. 23(3), Sch. 2, Pt. II, para. 16.

PAGE

The Diving Operations at Work Regulations 1981

2353   **Regulation 2(1).** The definition "owner" is added after the definition of "offshore installation" by the Offshore Installations and Pipeline Works (Management and Administration) Regulations 1995, S.I. 1995 No. 738, reg. 23(3), Sch. 2, Pt. II, para. 3, as follows:

> "'owner', in relation to an offshore installation, means the person who is, in relation to the installation, the duty holder as defined by regulation 2(1) of the Offshore Installations and Pipeline Works (Management and Administration) Regulations 1995 in relation to that installation;".

2355   **Regulation 4(1)(b).** Para. (ii) is revoked by the Offshore Installations and Pipeline Works (Management and Administration) Regulations 1995, S.I. 1995 No. 738, reg. 23(1), Sch. 2, Pt. I.

2357   **Regulation 5(4)(b).** The following para. is substituted for paras. (i), (ii) by the Offshore Installations and Pipeline Works (Management and Administration) Regulations 1995, S.I. 1995 No. 738, reg. 23(3), Sch. 2, Pt. II, para. 4:

> "(i) from or in connection with an offshore installation, the owner".

2378–
2400   **Certificate of Exemption No. DOW 2/88**

The Health and Safety Executive in exercise of the powers conferred on it by Regulation 14 of the Diving Operations at Work Regulations 1981 and being satisfied that the health and safety of persons who are likely to be affected by the exemption will not be prejudiced in consequence of it hereby exempts diving operations:—

(a) which are primarily for the purposes of scientific research, and are carried out by scientific research workers who dive from time to time in the course of their work using self-contained underwater breathing apparatus (SCUBA), and

(b) in which no person at work dives at a greater depth than 50 metres nor does his routine decompression time exceed 20 minutes, and

(c) which are carried out by, or on behalf of, or under the auspices of a national or government research institute, a university, a museum or other similar organisation, and

(d) where a full diving team comprising persons with duties under the Regulations is not available,

from Regulations 5(1)(a), 5(3), 6, 7(1)(a), 7(2), 7(3)(b), 8, 9(4) and 10 as may be necessary for each diving operation and subject to the following conditions in relation to each diving operation:—

1.   That this certificate shall come into force on 14 November 1988 and shall remain in force until revoked in writing by an authorised person.

2.   That every person diving at work ensures that—

(a) when he is diving there is a person on the surface in immediate control of the operation;

(b) there is another person (ie in addition to the person required under sub-paragraph (a) above) available to render assistance in an emergency, that other person being either on the surface in immediate readiness to dive or in the water in a position to render assistance, except that this condition shall not apply where the diving operation is to be carried on in water which is not more than 1.5 metres deep;

(c) this diving operation is carried on in accordance with the conditions laid down in the current edition of the Code of Practice for Scientific Diving issued by the Underwater Association subject to the amendment of diver qualifications in accordance with Condition 3 below;

(d) he should not go or remain underwater or in a compression chamber, as the case may be, either if he is unfit or should some other reason not do so and in such case should inform the person on the surface in immediate control of the operation.

3. That every person diving at work who does not have a certificate issued under Regulations 10 or 15 has qualified as a British Sub-Aqua Club Advanced Diver, a Scottish Sub-Aqua Club 2nd Class Diver, or has obtained a 3 star qualification from Confederation Mondiale des Activités Subaquatiques and is adequately trained and competent to dive safely.

4. That where a diving contractor has not appointed a diving supervisor for a diving operation, the diving contractor shall, so far as is reasonably practicable, ensure that the diving operation is carried out in accordance with the diving rules and shall—

(a) ensure that the plant and equipment is not used unless Regulation 13(1)(c) and (d) have been complied with;

(b) make available to each member of the diving team a copy of the part or parts of the diving rules relevant to that member;

(c) ensure that an accurate record of the matters specified in Schedule 2 to the Regulations is entered in the diving operations log book provided under Regulation 6(1)(c), and shall sign the entries at the conclusion of the diving operation;

(d) countersign the entries relating to the diving operations in the diver's log book of each diver who took part in that operation.

5. That every person diving at work in the course of scientific research shall record in his log book the matters set out in Schedule 3 to the Regulations and shall sign each entry on every day on which he takes part in a diving operation.

6. This Certificate of Exemption replaces the certificate numbered DOW/1/86 dated 27 August 1986 which is revoked.

PART 2
SUPPLEMENTARY TEXTS

THE FISHING VESSELS DIRECTIVE

General note. This Directive must be implemented in the UK by 23 November 1995 (Art. 13 (1)). As well as general provisions on the safety of workers on fishing vessels, it contains specific requirements for new fishing vessels (as defined in Art. 2 (b)) and existing vessels: see Arts. 4 and 5.

COUNCIL DIRECTIVE 93/103/EC

of 23 November 1993

concerning the minimum safety and health requirements for work on board fishing vessels (thirteenth individual Directive within the meaning of Article 16 (1) of Directive 89/391/EEC)

THE COUNCIL OF THE EUROPEAN UNION,

Having regard to the Treaty establishing the European Community, and in particular Article 118a thereof,

Having regard to the proposal from the Commission drawn up after consultation with the Advisory Committee on Safety, Hygiene and Health Protection at Work,

In cooperation with the European Parliament,

Having regard to the opinion of the Economic and Social Committee,

Whereas, in its resolution of 21 December 1987 on safety, hygiene and health at work, the Council noted the Commission's intention of submitting to it minimum requirements concerning the organization of the safety and health of workers at work;

Whereas occupational safety and health measures should be introduced as part of the various Community measures for the fisheries sector;

Whereas compliance with the minimum requirements for ensuring a better level of safety and health on board fishing vessels is essential to ensure the safety and health of the workers concerned;

Whereas, because of the specific and particularly difficult working and living conditions on board fishing vessels, the incidence of fatal accidents among workers engaged in sea fishing is very high;

Whereas, on 15 April 1988, the European Parliament adopted a resolution recognizing the importance of the preventive aspects of safety at work on board fishing vessels;

Whereas, for the safety and health of the workers concerned, prominence should be given to locating fishing vessels in an emergency, particularly through the use of new technologies;

Whereas this Directive is an individual Directive within the meaning of Article 16 (1) of Council Directive 89/391/EEC of 12 June 1989 on the introduction of measures to encourage improvements in the safety and health of workers at work; whereas, therefore, the provisions thereof are fully applicable to work on board fishing vessels, without prejudice to more stringent and/or specific provisions contained in this Directive;

Whereas the individual Directives already adopted in the field of safety and health at work apply, unless otherwise specified, to sea fishing; whereas, therefore, it may in some cases be necessary to specify the particular characteristics of this activity in order to ensure that the individual Directives are applied in the best way;

Whereas Council Directive 92/29/EEC of 31 March 1992 on the minimum safety and health requirements for improved medical treatment on board vessels is applicable in full to the sea fishing industry;

Whereas this Directive constitutes concrete progress towards the achievement of the social dimension of the internal market,

HAS ADOPTED THIS DIRECTIVE:

Article 1

Object

1.   This Directive, which is the thirteenth individual Directive within the meaning of Article 16 (1) of Directive 89/391/EEC, lays down minimum safety and health requirements applicable to work on board the vessels defined in Article 2.

2.   The provisions of Directive 89/391/EEC are fully applicable to the field referred to in paragraph 1, without prejudice to more stringent and/or specific provisions contained in this Directive.

Article 2

Definitions

For the purposes of this Directive, the following terms shall have the meanings hereby assigned to them:
(a)   *fishing vessel*: any vessel flying the flag of a Member State or registered under the plenary jurisdiction of a Member State used for commercial purposes either for catching or catching and processing fish or other living resources from the sea;
(b)   *new fishing vessel*: a fishing vessel with a length between perpendiculars of 15 metres or over and for which, on or after the date specified in the first subparagraph of Article 13 (1):
    (i)   the building or major conversion contract is placed; or
    (ii)   the building or major conversion contract has been placed before the date specified in the first subparagraph of Article 13 (1) and which is delivered three or more years after that date; or
    (iii)   in the absence of a building contract:
       — the keel is laid, or
       — construction identifiable with a specific vessel begins, or
       — assembly has commenced, comprising at least 50 tonnes or 1% of the estimated mass of all structural material, whichever is the lesser;
(c)   *existing fishing vessel*: any fishing vessel with a length between perpendiculars of 18 metres or over and which is not a new fishing vessel;
(d)   *vessel*: any new or existing fishing vessel;
(e)   *worker*: any person carrying out an occupation on board a vessel, including trainees and apprentices but excluding shore personnel carrying out work on board a vessel at the quayside and port pilots;

(f) *owner:* the registered owner of a vessel, unless that vessel has been chartered by demise or is managed, either wholly or in part, by a natural or legal person other than the registered owner under the terms of a management agreement; in that case, the owner shall be construed as the demise charterer or natural or legal person managing the vessel, as appropriate;

(g) *skipper:* the worker who, in accordance with national legislation and/or practice, commands the vessel or has responsibility for it.

Article 3

General provisions

1. Member States shall take the measures necessary to see that:

(a) owners ensure that their vessels are used without endangering the safety and health of workers, in particular in foreseeable meterological conditions, without prejudice to the skipper's responsibility;

(b) account is taken of any hazards faced by the rest of the workers when Article 8 (4) of Directive 89/391/EEC is applied;

(c) any occurrences at sea which affect or could affect the safety and health of the workers on board are described in a detailed report to be forwarded to the relevant competent authorities and are recorded carefully and in detail in the ship's log, where the national regulations or legislation in force require such a log to be kept on the type of vessel in question or, in the absence of such a log, in a document required for the purpose.

2. Member States shall take the measures necessary to ensure that, as regards compliance with this Directive, vessels are subject to regular checks by authorities specifically empowered to carry out such checks.

Certain checks concerning compliance with this Directive may be carried out at sea.

Article 4

New fishing vessels

New fishing vessels must comply with the minimum safety and health requirements laid down in Annex I at the latest by the date referred to in the first subparagraph of Article 13 (1).

Article 5

Existing fishing vessels

Existing fishing vessels must comply with the minimum safety and health requirements laid down in Annex II within seven years of the date referred to in the first subparagraph of Article 13 (1).

Article 6

Extensive repairs, conversions and alterations

Where vessels undergo extensive repairs, conversions and alterations on or after the date specified in the first subparagraph of Article 13 (1), such extensive repairs, conversions and alterations must comply with the relevant minimum requirements laid down in Annex I.

Article 7

Equipment and maintenance

1.   For the protection of the safety and health of workers, Member States shall take the measures necessary to ensure that, without prejudice to the skipper's responsibility, owners:

(a)   ensure that the vessels and their fittings and equipment, particularly those referred to in Annexes I and II, are technically maintained, and that any defects found which are likely to affect the safety and health of workers are rectified as quickly as possible;

(b)   take measures to ensure that the vessels and all fittings and equipment are cleaned regularly in order to maintain an appropriate standard of hygiene;

(c)   keep on board the vessel an adequate quantity of suitable emergency and survival equipment in good working order;

(d)   take account of the minimum safety and health requirements concerning life-saving and survival equipment given in Annex III;

(e)   without prejudice to the provisions of Council Directive 89/656/EEC of 30 November 1989 on the minimum health and safety requirements for the use by workers of personal protective equipment at the workplace (third individual Directive within the meaning of Article 16 (1) of Directive 89/391/EEC), take account of the personal protective equipment specifications given in Annex IV to this Directive.

2.   Member States shall take all necessary measures to ensure that, for the protection of the safety and health of workers, the owner supplies the skipper with the means needed to enable him to fulfil the obligations imposed upon him by this Directive.

Article 8

Information for workers

1.   Without prejudice to the provisions of Article 10 of Directive 89/391/EEC, workers and/or their representatives shall be informed of all measures to be taken regarding safety and health on board vessels.

2.   The information must be comprehensible to the workers concerned.

Article 9

Training of workers

1.   Without prejudice to Article 12 of Directive 89/391/EEC, workers shall be given suitable training, in particular in the form of precise, comprehensible instructions, on safety and health on board vessels and on accident prevention in particular.

2.   The training referred to in paragraph 1 shall cover in particular fire fighting, the use of life-saving and survival equipment and, for the workers concerned, the use of fishing gear and hauling equipment and the use of various types of signs including hand signals.

Such training shall be subject to the necessary updating where this is required by changes in the activities on board.

Article 10

Detailed training of persons likely to command a vessel

Without prejudice to Article 5 (3) of Directive 92/29/EEC, any person likely to command a vessel shall be given detailed training on:

(a) the prevention of occupational illness and accidents on board and the steps to be taken in event of accident;

(b) stability and maintenance of the vessel under all foreseeable conditions of loading and during fishing operations;

(c) radio navigation and communication, including procedures.

Article 11

Consultation and participation of workers

The consultation of workers and/or their representatives and their participation in discussions on the matters covered by this Directive and its Annexes shall take place in accordance with Article 11 of Directive 89/391/EEC.

Article 12

Adaptation of the Annexes

Purely technical adaptations of the Annexes to take account of:

— the adoption of directives in the field of technical harmonization and standardization concerning certain aspects of safety and health on board vessels, and/or

— technical progress, changes in the international regulations or specifications and new findings in the field of safety and health on board vessels,

shall be adopted in accordance with the procedure laid down in Article 17 of Directive 89/391/EEC.

Article 13

Final provisions

1. Member States shall bring into force the laws, regulations and administrative provisions necessary to comply with this Directive by 23 November 1995. They shall forthwith inform the Commission thereof.

When Member States adopt these measures, they shall contain a reference to this Directive or shall be accompanied by such reference on the occasion of their official publication. The methods of making such a reference shall be laid down by the Member States.

2. Member States shall communicate to the Commission the texts of the provisions of national law which they have already adopted or adopt in the field covered by this Directive.

3. Member States shall report to the Commission every four years on the practical implementation of the provisions of this Directive, indicating the points of view of employers and workers.

The Commission shall inform the European Parliament, the Council, the Economic and Social Committee and the Advisory Committee on Safety, Hygiene and Health Protection at Work thereof.

4.   The Commission shall periodically submit to the European Parliament, the Council and the Economic and Social Committee a report on the implementation of this Directive, taking into account paragraphs 1, 2 and 3.

Article 14

This Directive is addressed to the Member States.

Done at Brussels, 23 November 1993.

For the Council

The President

M SMET

─────────────

ANNEX I

MINIMUM SAFETY AND HEALTH REQUIREMENTS FOR NEW FISHING VESSELS

(Articles 4, 6 and 7 (1) (a))

Preliminary note

The obligations laid down in this Annex apply whenever required by the features of the workplace, the activity, the circumstances or a risk on board a new fishing vessel.

1.   Seaworthiness and stability

1.1.   The vessel must be maintained in a seaworthy condition and be properly equipped appropriate to its purpose and use.

1.2.   Information on the vessel's stability must be available on board and must be accessible to the men on watch.

1.3.   All vessels must be sufficiently stable when intact in the conditions of service for which they are intended.

The skipper must take the precautionary measures necessary to maintain adequate stability of the vessel.

Instructions supplied concerning the vessel's stability must be strictly observed.

2.   Mechanical and electrical installations

2.1.   Electrical installations must be designed and constructed so as not to present any danger and so as to ensure:

— protection for the crew and vessel from electrical hazards,
— the proper functioning of all equipment necessary to maintain the vessel in normal operational and living conditions without recourse to an emergency power supply,

— the operation of electrical equipment essential for safety in all emergencies.

2.2. An emergency electrical power source must be provided.

Except in open vessels, it must be located outside the engine room and must, in all cases, be so arranged as to ensure in the event of fire or other failure of the main electrical installation, simultaneous functioning for at least three hours of:
— the internal communication system, fire detectors and emergency signals,
— the navigation lights and emergency lighting,
— the radio installation,
— the emergency electrical fire pump where present.

If the emergency electrical power source is an accumulator battery and the main electrical power source fails, the accumulator battery must be automatically connected to the emergency electrical switchboard and supply power for an uninterrupted period of three hours to the systems referred to in the first, second and third indents of the second subparagraph.

The main electrical switchboard and the emergency switchboard must, to the extent possible, be installed in such a way that they cannot be exposed simultaneously to water or fire.

2.3. Switchboards should be clearly marked; fuse boxes and fuse holders should be checked at regular intervals to ensure that the correct rating of fuse is being used.

2.4. Compartments housing electrical storage batteries must be adequately ventilated.

2.5. Electronic aids to navigation should be tested frequently and well maintained.

2.6. All equipment used in hoisting should be tested and examined at regular intervals.

2.7. All parts of hauling gear, hoisting gear and related equipment should be maintained in good repair and working order.

2.8. Where refrigeration plants and compressed air systems are installed they should be well maintained and examined at regular intervals.

2.9. Cooking and domestic appliances using heavy gases should be used only in well ventilated spaces and care should be taken to avoid any dangerous accumulation of gas.

Cylinders containing flammable and other dangerous gases should be clearly marked as to their contents and stowed on open decks.

All valves, pressure regulators and pipes leading from the cylinders should be protected against damage.

3. **Radio installation**

The radio installation must permit contact at all times with at least one coastal or land-based station, taking into account the normal conditions for propagation of radio waves.

4.   Emergency routes and exits

4.1.   Routes and exits which can be used as emergency routes and exits must be unobstructed and easily accessible at all times and lead out as directly as possible to the open deck or to a safe area and thence to the survival craft so that workers can evacuate their workstations or living areas quickly and as safely as possible.

4.2.   The number, distribution and dimensions of the routes and exits which can be used as emergency routes and exits must depend on the use, equipment and dimensions of workplaces and living areas and on the maximum potential number of persons present.

Exits which can be used as emergency exits and which are closed must be immediately and readily operable in an emergency by any worker or by rescue teams.

4.3.   Emergency doors and other emergency exits must be adequately weatherproof and watertight for their location and particular function.

Emergency doors and other emergency exits must be as fire-resistant as the bulkheads.

4.4   Emergency routes and exits must be indicated by signs in accordance with national provisions transposing Directive 92/58/EEC.

Such signs must be placed at appropriate points and be made to last.

4.5.   Escape routes and facilities and emergency exits requiring illumination must be provided with emergency lighting of adequate intensity in case the lighting fails.

5.   Fire detection and fire fighting

5.1.   Depending on the dimensions and use of the vessel, the equipment it contains, the physical and chemical properties of the substances present and the maximum potential number of persons present, living quarters and enclosed workplaces, including the engine-room and the fish hold if necessary, must be equipped with appropriate fire-fighting equipment and, as necessary, with fire detectors and alarm systems.

5.2.   Fire-fighting equipment must always be kept in its proper location, maintained in good working order, and be available for immediate use.

Workers must be familiar with the locations of fire-fighting equipment, the way it works and how it should be used.

The presence of extinguishers and other portable fire-fighting equipment must always be checked before the vessel gets under way.

5.3.   Manually-operated fire-fighting equipment must be easily accessible and simple to use and must be indicated by signs in accordance with the national provisions transposing Directive 92/58/EEC.

Such signs must be placed at appropriate points and be made to last.

5.4. Fire-detection and alarm systems should be regularly tested and well maintained.

5.5. Fire-fighting drills shall be carried out at regular intervals.

6. Ventilation of enclosed workplaces

Steps must be taken to see that there is sufficient fresh air in enclosed workplaces, having regard to the working methods used and the physical demands placed on the workers.

If a mechanical ventilation system is used, it must be maintained in good condition.

7. Temperature of working areas

7.1. The temperature in working areas must be adequate for the human body during the hours of working, having regard to the work methods used, the physical demands placed on the workers and the actual or potential weather conditions in the area in which the vessel operates.

7.2. The temperature in living quarters, sanitary facilities, canteens and first-aid rooms must, where those areas exist, be appropriate to the particular purpose of such areas.

8. Natural and artificial lighting of workplaces

8.1. Workplaces must as far as possible receive sufficient natural light and be equipped with artificial lighting suitable for the fishing operations in hand, without placing workers' safety and health in danger or jeopardizing other vessels.

8.2. Installations for the lighting of working areas, stairs, ladders and passageways must be placed in such a way that the type of lighting provided poses no risk of accident to workers and no hindrance to the navigation of the vessel.

8.3. Workplaces in which workers are especially exposed to risks in the event of failure of artificial lighting must be provided with emergency lighting of adequate intensity.

8.4. Emergency lighting must be maintained in an efficient operating condition and be tested at regular intervals.

9. Decks, bulkheads and deckheads

9.1. Spaces accessible to workers must be non-slip or anti-slip or be provided with devices to prevent falls and kept free of obstacles as far as possible.

9.2. Workplaces containing workstations must be adequately soundproofed and insulated, bearing in mind the type of tasks involved and the physical activity of workers.

9.3. The surface of decks, bulkheads and deckheads in working areas must be such that they can be cleaned or refurbished to an appropriate standard of hygiene.

10.   Doors

10.1.   Means should be provided so that doors can at all times be operated from the inside without special equipment.

The doors must be operable from either side when workplaces are in use.

10.2.   Doors, and in particular sliding doors, where such have to be used, must function as safely as possible for the workers, especially in adverse weather and sea conditions.

11.   Traffic routes — danger areas

11.1.   Passageways, trunks, the outer part of deckhouses and all traffic routes in general must be equipped with guard rails, grab rails and lifelines or other means of ensuring the safety of workers in the course of activities on board.

11.2.   If there is a risk that workers may fall through openings in the deck, or from one deck to another, adequate protection should be provided wherever possible.

Where guard rails provide such protection, they must be at least one metre high.

11.3.   Access to installations above the deck for operations or maintenance purposes must be such as to ensure workers' safety.

Guard rails or similar protective devices of appropriate height must be provided to prevent falls.

11.4.   Bulwarks or other means provided to prevent persons falling overboard must be maintained in an efficient condition.

Bulwarks must be fitted with freeing ports or other similar devices to enable water to drain away quickly.

11.5.   On stern trawlers with ramps, the upper part of the ramp must be fitted with a gate or other means of securing it of the same height as the bulwarks or other adjacent means, to protect workers from the risk of falling into the ramp.

This gate or other device must be easily opened and closed, preferably by remote control, and must be open only for casting the net or for hauling it in.

12.   Layout of workstations

12.1.   Working areas must be kept clear and, as far as possible, be protected from the sea and provide adequate protection for workers against falling on the vessel or falling overboard.

Handling areas must be sufficiently spacious, in terms of both height and surface area.

12.2.   If the engines are controlled from the engine room, they must be controlled from a separate area, soundproofed and insulated from the engine room *per se* and accessible without entering the latter.

The navigating bridge is considered to be an area that meets the requirements of the first subparagraph.

12.3.   The controls for the hauling gear must be installed in an area sufficiently large to enable operators to work unhindered.

The hauling gear must also have appropriate safety devices for emergencies, including emergency stop facilities.

12.4.   The hauling gear operator must have an adequate view of the hauling gear and the workers at work.

If the hauling gear is controlled from the bridge, the operator should also have a clear view of the workers at work, either directly or via any other suitable medium.

12.5.   A reliable communications system must be used between the bridge and the working deck.

12.6.   A sharp look out should always be maintained and the crew warned of the imminent danger of heavy oncoming seas during fishing operations or when other work is being done on deck.

12.7.   Contact with bare ropes and warps and with moving parts of the equipment must be minimized by installing protective devices.

12.8.   Controls must be installed for moving masses, particularly on trawlers:
— devices to immobilize the otter boards,
— devices to control the swinging motion of the codend.

13.   Living quarters

13.1.   The location, structure, soundproofing, means of insulation and layout of the workers' living quarters and facilities, where these exist, and means of access thereto should be such as to provide adequate protection against weather and sea, vibration, noise and unpleasant odours from other parts of the vessel likely to disturb the workers during their period of rest. Where the design, dimensions and/or purpose of the vessel allow, the workers' living quarters must be located so as to minimize the effects of motion and acceleration.

Appropriate measures should be taken as far as possible to protect non-smokers from discomfort caused by tobacco smoke.

13.2.   The workers' living quarters should be properly ventilated to ensure a constant supply of fresh air and prevent condensation.

Appropriate lighting must be provided in the living quarters, with:
— adequate normal general lighting,
— reduced general lighting to avoid disturbing workers who are resting, and
— local lighting in each berth.

13.3.   The galley and mess, where these exist, should be of adequate size, well lit and ventilated and easy to clean.

Refrigerators or other low-temperature food-storage equipment must be provided.

14.   **Sanitary facilities**

14.1.   On vessels with living quarters, shower facilities with hot and cold running water, wash-basins and toilets must be properly equipped and installed and the respective areas must be properly ventilated.

14.2.   Every worker must have the use of a place where he can keep his clothes.

15.   **First aid**

On all vessels first-aid equipment must be available which fulfils the requirements in Annex II to Directive 92/29/EEC.

16.   **Accommodation ladders and gangways**

An accommodation ladder, gangway or other similar equipment providing an appropriate, safe means of boarding the vessel must be available.

17.   **Noise**

All appropriate technical measures must be taken to reduce the noise level at workplaces and in the living quarters as far as possible, taking into account the size of the vessel.

ANNEX II

MINIMUM SAFETY AND HEALTH REQUIREMENTS FOR EXISTING FISHING VESSELS

(Articles 5 and 7 (1) (a))

Preliminary note

The obligations laid down in this Annex apply, in so far as the structural characteristics of the existing fishing vessel permit, whenever required by the features of the workplace, the activity, the circumstances or a risk on board an existing fishing vessel.

1.   **Seaworthiness and stability**

1.1.   The vessel must be maintained in a seaworthy condition and be properly equipped appropriate to its purpose and use.

1.2.   Where it exists, information on the vessel's stability must be available on board and must be accessible to the men on watch.

1.3.   All vessels must be sufficiently stable when intact in the conditions of service for which they are intended.

The skipper must take the necessary precautionary measures in order to maintain adequate stability of the vessel.

Instructions supplied concerning the vessel's stability must be strictly observed.

2.   Mechanical and electrical installations

2.1.   Electrical installations must be designed and constructed so as not to present any danger and so as to ensure:
— protection for the crew and vessel from electrical risks,
— the proper functioning of all equipment necessary to maintain the vessel in normal operational and living conditions without recourse to an emergency power supply,
— the operation of electrical equipment essential for safety in all emergencies.

2.2.   An emergency electrical power source must be provided.

Except in open vessels, the emergency electrical power source must be located outside the engine room and in all cases be so arranged as to ensure, in the event of fire or other failure of the main electrical installation, simultaneous functioning for at least three hours of:
— the internal communication system, fire detectors and emergency signals,
— the navigation lights and emergency lighting,
— the radio installation,
— the emergency electrical fire pump where present.

If the emergency electrical power source is an accumulator battery and the main electrical power source fails, the accumulator battery must be automatically connected to the emergency electrical switchboard and supply power for an uninterrupted period of three hours to the systems referred to in the first, second and third indents of the second subparagraph.

The main electrical switchboard and the emergency switchboard must, to the extent possible, be installed in such a way that they cannot be exposed simultaneously to water or fire.

2.3.   Switchboards should be clearly marked; fuse boxes and fuse holders should be checked at regular intervals to ensure that the correct rating of fuse is being used.

2.4.   Compartments housing electrical storage batteries must be adequately ventilated.

2.5.   Electronic aids to navigation should be tested frequently and well maintained.

2.6.   All equipment used in hoisting should be tested and examined at regular intervals.

2.7.   All parts of hauling gear, hoisting gear and related equipment should be maintained in good repair and working order.

2.8.   Where refrigeration plants and compressed air systems are installed, they should be well maintained and examined at regular intervals.

2.9.   Cooking and domestic appliances using heavy gases should be used only in well ventilated spaces and care should be taken to avoid any dangerous accumulation of gas.

Cylinders containing flammable and other dangerous gases should be clearly marked as to their contents and stowed on open decks.

All valves, pressure regulators and pipes leading from the cylinders should be protected against damage.

3.   **Radio installation**

The radio installation must permit contact at all times with at least one coastal or land-based station, taking into account the normal conditions for propagation of radio waves.

4.   **Emergency routes and exits**

4.1.   Routes and exits which can be used as emergency routes and exits must be unobstructed and easily accessible at all times and lead out as directly as possible to the open deck or to a safe area and thence to the survival craft so that workers can evacuate their workstations or living areas quickly and as safely as possible.

4.2.   The number, distribution and dimensions of the routes and exits which can be used as emergency routes and exits must depend on the use, equipment and dimensions of workplaces and living areas and on the maximum potential number of persons present.

Exits which can be used as emergency exits and which are closed must be immediately and readily operable in an emergency by any worker or by rescue teams.

4.3.   Emergency routes and exits must be indicated by signs in accordance with national provisions transposing Directive 92/58/EEC.

Such signs must be placed at appropriate points and be made to last.

4.4.   Escape routes and facilities and emergency exits requiring illumination must be provided with emergency lighting of adequate intensity in case the lighting fails.

5.   **Fire detection and fire fighting**

5.1.   Depending on the dimensions and use of the vessel, the equipment it contains, the physical and chemical properties of the substances present and the maximum potential number of persons present, living quarters and enclosed workplaces, including the engine-room and the fish hold if necessary, must be equipped with appropriate fire-fighting equipment and, as necessary, with fire detectors and alarm systems.

5.2.   Fire-fighting equipment must always be kept in its proper location, maintained in good working order, and be available for immediate use.

Workers must be familiar with the location of fire-fighting equipment, the way it works and how it should be used.

The presence of extinguishers and other portable fire-fighting equipment must always be checked before the vessel gets under way.

5.3.   Manually-operated fire-fighting equipment must be easily accessible and simple to use and must be indicated by signs in accordance with the national provisions transposing Directive 92/58/EEC.

Such signs must be placed at appropriate points and be made to last.

5.4.   Fire-detection and alarm systems should be regularly tested and well maintained.

5.5   Fire-fighting drills shall be carried out at regular intervals.

6.   Ventilation of enclosed workplaces

Steps must be taken to see that there is sufficient fresh air in enclosed workplaces, having regard to the working methods used and the physical demands placed on the workers.

If a mechanical ventilation system is used, it must be maintained in good condition.

7.   Temperature of working areas

7.1.   The temperature in working areas must be adequate for the human body during the hours of working, having regard to the work methods used, the physical demands placed on the workers and the actual or potential weather conditions in the area in which the vessel operates.

7.2.   The temperature in living quarters, sanitary facilities, canteens and first-aid rooms must, where those areas exist, be appropriate to the particular purpose of such areas.

8.   Natural and artificial lighting of workplaces

8.1.   Workplaces must as far as possible receive sufficient natural light and be equipped with artificial lighting suitable for the operations in hand, without placing workers safety and health in danger or jeopardizing the navigation of other vessels.

8.2.   Lighting installations in working areas, stairs, ladders and passageways must be placed in such a way that the type of lighting envisaged poses no risk of accident to workers and no hindrance to the navigation of the vessel.

8.3.   Workplaces in which workers are especially exposed to risks in the event of failure of artificial lighting must be provided with emergency lighting of adequate intensity.

8.4.   Emergency lighting must be maintained in an efficient operating condition and be tested at regular intervals.

9.   Decks, bulkheads and deckheads

9.1.   Spaces accessible to workers must be non-slip or anti-slip or be provided with devices to prevent falls and kept free of obstacles as far as possible.

9.2.   Workplaces containing workstations must, in so far as possible, be adequately soundproofed and insulated, bearing in mind the type of tasks involved and the physical activity of workers.

9.3.   The surface of decks, bulkheads and deckheads in working areas must be such that they can be cleaned or refurbished to an appropriate standard of hygiene.

10.   Doors

10.1.   Means should be provided so that doors can at all times be operated from the inside without special equipment.

The doors must be operable from either side when workplaces are in use.

10.2.   Doors and in particular sliding doors, where such have to be used, must function as safely as possible for the workers, especially in adverse weather and sea conditions.

11.   Traffic routes — danger areas

11.1.   Passageways, trunks, the outer part of deckhouses and all traffic routes in general must be equipped with guard rails, grab rails and lifelines or other means of ensuring the safety of workers in the course of activities on board.

11.2.   If there is a risk that workers may fall through openings in the deck, or from one deck to another, adequate protection should be provided wherever possible.

11.3.   Access to installations above the deck for operation or maintenance purposes must be such as to ensure workers' safety.

Guard rails or similar protective devices of appropriate height must be provided to prevent falls.

11.4.   Bulwarks or other means provided to prevent persons falling overboard must be maintained in an efficient condition.

Bulwarks must be fitted with freeing ports or other similar devices to enable water to drain away quickly.

11.5.   On stern trawlers with ramps, the ramp must be fitted with a gate or other means of securing it of the same height as the bulwarks or other adjacent means, to protect workers from the risk of falling into the ramp.

This gate or other device must be easily opened and closed and must be open only for casting the net or for hauling it in.

12.   Layout of workstations

12.1.   Working areas must be kept clear and, as far as possible, be protected from the sea and provide adequate protection for workers against falling on the vessel or falling overboard.

Handling areas must be sufficiently spacious, in terms of both height and surface area.

12.2.   If the engines are controlled from the engine room, they must be controlled from a separate area, soundproofed and insulated from the engine room *per se* and accessible without passing through the latter.

The navigating bridge is considered to be an area that meets the requirements of the first subparagraph.

12.3.   The controls for the hauling gear must be installed in an area sufficiently large to enable operators to work unhindered.

The hauling gear must also have appropriate safety devices for emergencies, including emergency stop facilities.

12.4.   The hauling gear operator must have an adequate view of the hauling gear and the workers at work.

If the hauling gear is controlled from the bridge, the operator should also have a clear view of the workers at work, either directly or via any other suitable medium.

12.5.   A reliable communications system must be used between the bridge and the working deck.

12.6.   A sharp look out should always be maintained and the crew warned of the imminent danger of heavy oncoming seas during fishing operations or when other work is being done on deck.

12.7.   Contact with bare ropes and warps and with moving parts of the equipment must be minimized by installing protective devices.

12.8.   Controls must be installed for moving masses, particularly on trawlers:
— devices to immobilize the otter boards,
— devices to control the swinging motion of the codend.

13.   Living quarters

13.1.   The workers' living quarters, where they exist, must be such as to minimize noise, vibration, the effects of motion and acceleration, and unpleasant odours from other parts of the vessel.

Appropriate lighting must be installed in the living quarters.

13.2.   The galley and mess, where they exist, should be of adequate size, adequately lit and ventilated and easy to clean.

Refrigerators or other low-temperature food-storage equipment must be provided.

14.   Sanitary facilities

On vessels with living quarters, toilets, wash-basins and, if possible, a shower must be installed and the respective areas must be properly ventilated.

15.   First aid

On all vessels first-aid equipment must be available which fulfils the requirements in Annex II to Directive 92/29/EEC.

16.   Accommodation ladders and gangways

An accommodation ladder, gangway or other similar equipment providing an appropriate, safe means of boarding the vessel must be available.

ANNEX III

MINIMUM SAFETY AND HEALTH REQUIREMENTS FOR CONCERNING LIFE-SAVING AND SURVIVAL EQUIPMENT

(Article 7 (1) (d))

Preliminary note

The obligations laid down in this Annex apply wherever required by the features of the workplace, the activity, the circumstances or a risk on board a vessel.

1.   Vessels must carry adequate life-saving and survival equipment, including adequate means of recovering workers from the water, and radio rescue, in particular an emergency position-indicating radio beacon with a hydrostatic release mechanism, taking account of the number of persons on board and the area in which the vessel is operating.

2.   All items of life-saving and survival equipment must be kept in their proper locations, maintained in good working order and be available for immediate use.

      They must be checked by the workers before the vessel leaves port and during the voyage.

3.   The life-saving and survival equipment must be inspected at regular intervals.

4.   All workers must receive proper training and appropriate instructions in anticipation of an emergency.

5.   If the length of the vessel exceeds 45 metres or if five or more workers are carried, a muster list must be provided with clear instructions for each worker which must be followed in case of emergency.

6.   Musters of workers for survival drill should be carried out each month in port and/or at sea.

      These drills must ensure that the workers thoroughly understand and are exercised in the duties which they have to perform with respect to the handling and operation of all life-saving and survival equipment.

      Workers must be trained in the setting up and operation of the portable radio equipment, where carried.

———————

ANNEX IV

MINIMUM SAFETY AND HEALTH REQUIREMENTS CONCERNING PERSONAL PROTECTIVE EQUIPMENT

(Article 7 (1) (e))

Preliminary note

The obligations laid down in this Annex apply whenever required by the features of the workplace, the activity, the circumstances or a risk on board a vessel.

1.   Where risks to the safety and health of workers cannot be prevented or sufficiently limited by collective or technical means of protection, they must be provided with personal protective equipment.

2.   Personal protective equipment in the form of clothing or worn over clothing must be in bright colours, contrasting with the marine environment and clearly visible.

THE EXPLOSIVE ATMOSPHERE DIRECTIVE

General note. This Directive must be implemented in the UK by 1 March 1996, the necessary regulations etc having been promulgated by 1 September 1995 (Art. 15 (1)). The Directive will replace earlier Directives on the same subject matter on 1 July 2003 (Art. 14 (1) and (2)). It applies to equipment and protective systems intended for use in potentially explosive atmospheres (Art. 1). Member States are under a general duty to ensure the safety of such equipment and systems (Art. 2 (1); and see also Art. 7). More specific requirements are laid down by Art. 3 and Annex II.

DIRECTIVE 94/9/EC OF THE EUROPEAN PARLIAMENT AND THE COUNCIL

of 23 March 1994

on the approximation of the laws of the Member States concerning equipment and protective systems intended for use in potentially explosive atmospheres

THE EUROPEAN PARLIAMENT AND THE COUNCIL OF THE EUROPEAN UNION,

Having regard to the Treaty establishing the European Community, and in particular Article 100a thereof,

Having regard to the proposal from the Commission,

Having regard to the opinion of the Economic and Social Committee,

Acting in accordance with the procedure referred to in Article 189b of the Treaty establishing the European Community,

Whereas it is the duty of Member States to protect, on their territory, the safety and health of persons and, where appropriate, domestic animals and property and, in particular, that of workers, especially against the hazards resulting from the use of equipment and systems providing protection against potentially explosive atmospheres;

Whereas mandatory provisions within the Member States determine the level of safety to be achieved by protective equipment and systems intended for use in potentially explosive atmospheres; whereas these are generally electrical and non-electrical specifications having an effect on the design and structure of equipment which can be used in potentially explosive atmospheres;

Whereas the requirements to be met by such equipment differ from one Member State to another in respect of their extent and differing inspection procedures; whereas these differences are, therefore, likely to raise barriers to trade within the Community;

Whereas harmonization of national legislation is the only way in which to remove these barriers to free trade; whereas this objective cannot be satisfactorily achieved by the individual Member States; whereas this Directive merely lays down the requirements vital to freedom of movement for the equipment to which it applies;

Whereas the regulations intended to remove technical barriers to trade are required to follow the new approach provided for in the Council resolution of 7 May 1985, which requires a definition of the essential requirements regarding safety and other requirements of society without reducing existing, justified levels of protection within the Member States; whereas that resolution provides that a very large number of products be covered by a single Directive in order to avoid frequent amendments and the proliferation of Directives;

Whereas the existing Directives on the approximation of the laws of the Member States to electrical equipment for use in potentially explosive atmospheres have made positive steps towards protection against explosions via measures linked with the structure of the equipment at issue and which have helped to remove barriers to trade in this area; whereas, in parallel, a revision and expansion of the existing Directives is necessary since, more particularly, in an overall context, action must be taken to guard against the potential hazards arising from such equipment. This implies in particular that measures intended to guarantee effective protection of users and third parties must already be contemplated at the design and manufacturing states;

Whereas the form taken by the hazard, the protective measures and the test methods are often very similar, if not identical, for both mining and surface equipment; whereas it is, therefore, absolutely necessary to cover by a single Directive protective equipment and systems falling within both groups;

Whereas the two groups of equipment referred to above are used in a large number of commercial and industrial sectors and possess considerable economic significance;

Whereas compliance with the basic safety and health requirements is essential in order to ensure the safety of protective equipment and systems; whereas those requirements have been subdivided into general and additional requirements which must be met by protective equipment and systems; whereas, in particular, the additional requirements are intended to take account of existing or potential hazards; whereas protective equipment and systems will, therefore, embody at least one of those requirements where this is necessary for their proper functioning or is to apply to their intended use; whereas the notion of intended use is of prime importance for the explosion-proofing of protective equipment and systems; whereas it is essential that manufacturers supply full information; whereas specific, clear marking of said equipment, stating its use in a potentially explosive atmosphere, is also necessary;

Whereas the intention is to prepare a Directive on operations in potentially explosive atmospheres which is based on Article 118a; whereas that additional Directive will, in particular, aim at explosion hazards which derive from a given use and/or types and methods of installation;

Whereas compliance with essential health and safety requirements is imperative if the safety of equipment is to be ensured; whereas judgment will have to be exercised in the implementation of those requirements in order to take account of both the technology obtaining at the time of manufacture and overriding technical and economic requirements;

Whereas, therefore, this Directive sets out essential requirements only; whereas, in order to facilitate the task of proving compliance with the essential requirements, harmonized European standards are necessary, more especially with regard to the non-electrical aspects of protection against explosions—standards relating to the design, manufacture and testing of equipment, compliance with which enables a product to be presumed to meet such essential requirements; whereas harmonized European standards are drawn up by private bodies and must retain their non-mandatory status; whereas, for this purpose, the European Committee for Standardization (CEN) and the European Committee for Electrotechnical Standardization (Cenelec) are recognized as the bodies competent to adopt harmonized standards which follow the general guidelines for cooperation between the Commission and those two bodies, signed on 13 November 1984; whereas, for the purposes of this Directive, a harmonized standard is a technical specification (European Standard or harmonization document) adopted by one or other of those bodies, or by both, at the prompting of the Commission pursuant to Council Directive 83/189/EEC of the 28 March 1983 providing for a procedure governing the provision of information on technical standards and regulations and pursuant to the general guidelines referred to above;

Whereas the legislative framework should be improved in order to ensure that employers and workers make an effective and appropriate contribution towards the standardization process; whereas this should be completed by the time this Directive is implemented;

Whereas, in view of the nature of the risks involved in the use of equipment in potentially explosive atmospheres it is necessary to establish procedures applying to the assessment of compliance with the basic requirements of the Directives; whereas these procedures must be devised in the light of the level of risk which may be inherent in equipment and/or against which systems must protect the immediate environment; whereas, therefore, each category of equipment conformity must be supplemented by an adequate procedure or a choice between several equivalent procedures; whereas the procedures adopted comply fully with Council Decision 93/465/EEC of 22 July 1993 concerning the modules for the various phases of the conformity assessment procedures which are intended to be used in the technical harmonization Directives;

Whereas the Council has provided for the affixing of the CE marking by either the manufacturer or his authorized representative within the Community; whereas that marking means that the product complies with all the basic requirements and assessment procedures provided for by the Community law applying to that product;

Whereas it is appropriate that the Member States, as provided for by Article 100a of the Treaty, may take temporary measures to limit or prohibit the placing on the market and the use of equipment and protective systems in cases where they present a particular risk to the safety of persons and, where appropriate, domestic animals or property, provided that the measures are subject to a Community control procedure;

Whereas the recipients of any decision taken as part of this Directive must be aware of the reasons behind that decision and the means of appeal open to them;

Whereas, on 18 December 1985, the Council adopted a framework Directive on electrical equipment for use in potentially explosive atmospheres (76/117/EEC) and, on 15 February 1982, a Directive concerning electrical equipment for use in potentially explosive atmospheres in mines susceptible to fire damp (82/130/EEC); whereas, from the outset of harmonization work, the conversion into total harmonization of the optional and partial harmonization on which these Directives are based had been contemplated; whereas this Directive fully covers the scope of the abovementioned Directives and whereas, therefore, these Directives must be repealed;

Whereas the internal market incorporates an area without internal frontiers within which the free movement of goods, persons, services and capital is assured;

Whereas it is necessary to provide for a transitional arrangement enabling equipment manufactured in compliance with the national regulations in force at the date of adoption of this Directive to be marketed and placed in service,

HAVE ADOPTED THIS DIRECTIVE:

CHAPTER I

Scope, placing on the market and freedom of movement

Article 1

1.   This Directive applies to equipment and protective systems intended for use in potentially explosive atmospheres.

2.   Safety devices, controlling devices and regulating devices intended for use outside potentially explosive atmospheres but required for or contributing to the safe functioning of equipment and protective systems with respect to the risks of explosion are also covered by the scope of this Directive.

3.   For the purposes of this Directive, the following definitions shall apply:

Equipment and protective systems intended for use in potentially explosive atmospheres

(a)   "Equipment" means machines, apparatus, fixed or mobile devices, control components and instrumentation thereof and detection or prevention systems which, separately or jointly, are intended for the generation, transfer, storage, measurement, control and conversion of energy for the processing of material and which are capable of causing an explosion through their own potential sources of ignition.

(b)   "Protective systems" means design units which are intended to halt incipient explosions immediately and/or to limit the effective range of explosion flames and explosion pressures. Protective systems may be integrated into equipment or separately placed on the market for use as autonomous systems.

(c)   "Components" means any item essential to the safe functioning of equipment and protective systems but with no autonomous function.

Explosive atmospheres

Mixture with air, under atmospheric conditions, of flammable substances in the form of gases, vapours, mists or dusts in which, after ignition has occurred, combustion spreads to the entire unburned mixture.

Potentially explosive atmosphere

An atmosphere which could become explosive due to local and operational conditions.

Equipment groups and categories

Equipment group I applies to equipment intended for use in underground parts of mines, and to those parts of surface installations of such mines, liable to be endangered by firedamp and/or combustible dust.

Equipment group II applies to equipment intended for use in other places liable to be endangered by explosive atmospheres.

The categories of equipment defining the required levels of protection are described in Annex I.

Equipment and protective systems may be designed for a particular explosive atmosphere. In this case, they must be marked accordingly.

Intended use

The use of equipment, protective systems, and devices referred to in Article 1 (2) in accordance with the equipment group and category and with all the information supplied by the manufacturer which is required for the safe functioning of equipment, protective systems and devices.

4.   The following are excluded from the scope of this Directive:
— medical devices intended for use in a medical environment,
— equipment and protective systems where the explosion hazard results exclusively from the presence of explosive substances or unstable chemical substances,
— equipment intended for use in domestic and non-commercial environments where potentially explosive atmospheres may only rarely be created, solely as a result of the accidental leakage of fuel gas,
— personal protective equipment covered by Directive 89/686/EEC,
— seagoing vessels and mobile offshore units together with equipment on board such vessels or units,
— means of transport, ie vehicles and their trailers intended solely for transporting passengers by air or by road, rail or water networks, as well as means of transport in so far as such means are designed for transporting goods by air, by public road or rail networks or by water. Vehicles intended for use in a potentially explosive atmosphere shall not be excluded,
— the equipment covered by Article 223 (1) (b) of the Treaty.

Article 2

1.   Member States shall take all appropriate measures to ensure that the equipment, protective systems and devices referred to in Article 1 (2) to which this Directive applies may be placed on the market and put into service only if, when properly installed and maintained and used for their intended purpose, they do not endanger the health and safety of persons and, where appropriate, domestic animals or property.

2.   The provisions of this Directive shall not affect Member States' entitlement to lay down, in due observance of the provisions of the Treaty, such requirements as they may deem necessary to ensure that persons and, in particular, workers are protected when using the equipment, protective systems, and devices referred to in Article 1 (2) in question provided that this does not mean that such equipment, protective systems, or devices are modified in a way not specified in the Directive.

3.   At trade fairs, exhibitions, demonstrations, etc, Member States shall not prevent the showing of equipment, protective systems, or the devices referred to in Article 1 (2) which do not conform to the provisions of this Directive, provided that a visible sign clearly indicates that such equipment, protective systems, and devices referred to in Article 1 (2) do not conform and that they are not for sale until they have been brought into conformity by the manufacturer or his authorized representative established in the Community. During demonstrations, adequate safety measures shall be taken to ensure the protection of persons.

Article 3

Equipment, protective systems, and the devices referred to in Article 1 (2) to which this Directive applies must meet the essential health and safety requirements set out in Annex II which apply to them, account being taken of their intended use.

Article 4

1.   Member States shall not prohibit, restrict or impede the placing on the market and putting into service in their territory of equipment, protective systems, or devices referred to in Article 1 (2) which comply with this Directive.

2.   Member States shall not prohibit, restrict or impede the placing on the market of components which, accompanied by a certificate of conformity as referred to in Article 8 (3), are intended to be incorporated into equipment or protective systems within the meaning of this Directive.

Article 5

1.   Member States shall regard as conforming to all the provisions of this Directive, including the relevant conformity assessment procedures laid down in chapter II:
— equipment, protective systems, and devices referred to in Article 1 (2) accompanied by the EC declaration of conformity referred to in Annex X and bearing the CE marking provided for in Article 10,
— the components referred to in Article 4 (2), accompanied by the certificate of conformity referred to in Article 8 (3).

In the absence of harmonized standards, Member States shall take any steps which they deem necessary to bring to the attention of the parties concerned the existing national technical standards and specifications regarded as important or relevant to the proper implementation of the essential health and safety requirements in Annex II.

2.   Where a national standard transposing a harmonized standard, the reference for which has been published in the *Official Journal of the European Communities*, covers one or more of the essential health and safety requirements, the equipment, protective system, device referred to in Article 1 (2), or the component referred to in Article 4 (2), constructed in accordance with that standard shall be presumed to comply with the relevant essential health and safety requirements.

Member States shall publish the references of national standards transposing harmonized standards.

3.   Member States shall ensure that appropriate measures are taken to enable the social partners to influence the process of preparing and monitoring the harmonized standards at national level.

Article 6

1.   Where a Member State or the Commission considers that the harmonized standards referred to in Article 5 (2) do not entirely satisfy the relevant essential health and safety requirements referred to in Article 3, the Commission or the Member State concerned shall bring the matter before the Committee set up under Directive 83/189/EEC, hereinafter referred to as "the Committee", giving reasons therefor. The Committee shall deliver an opinion without delay.

Upon receipt of the Committee's opinion, the Commission shall inform the Member States whether or not it is necessary to withdraw those standards from the published information referred to in Article 5 (2).

2.   The Commission may adopt any appropriate measure with a view to ensuring the practical application in a uniform manner of this Directive in accordance with the procedure laid down in paragraph 3.

3.   The Commission shall be assisted by a Standing Committee, consisting of representatives appointed by the Member States and chaired by a representative of the Commission.

The Standing Committee shall draw up its own rules of procedure.

The representative of the Commission shall submit to the Committee a draft of the measures to be taken. The Committee shall deliver its opinion on the draft, within a time limit which the chairman may lay down according to the urgency of the matter, if necessary by taking a vote.

The opinion shall be recorded in the minutes; in addition, each Member State shall have the right to ask to have its position recorded in the minutes.

The Commission shall take the utmost account of the opinion delivered by the committee. It shall inform the committee of the manner in which its opinion has been taken into account.

4.   The Standing Committee may furthermore examine any question relating to the application of this Directive and raised by its chairman either on the latter's initiative, or at the request of a Member State.

Article 7

1.   Where a Member State ascertains that equipment, protective systems or devices referred to in Article 1 (2) bearing the CE conformity marking and used in accordance with their intended use are liable to endanger the safety of persons and, where appropriate, domestic animals or property, it shall take all appropriate measures to withdraw such equipment or protective systems from the market, to prohibit the placing on the market, putting into service or use thereof, or to restrict free movement thereof.

The Member State shall immediately inform the Commission of any such measure, indicating the reasons for its decision and, in particular, whether non-conformity is due to:

(a)   failure to satisfy the essential requirements referred to in Article 3;
(b)   incorrect application of the standards referred to in Article 5 (2);
(c)   shortcomings in the standards referred to in Article 5 (2).

2.   The Commission shall enter into consultation with the parties concerned without delay. Where the Commission considers, after this consultation, that the measure is justified, it shall immediately so inform the Member State which took the initiative and the other Member States. Where the Commission considers, after this consultation, that the action is unjustified, it shall immediately so inform the Member State which took the initiative and the manufacturer or his authorized representative established within the Community. Where the decision referred to in paragraph 1 is based on a shortcoming in the standards and where the Member State at the origin of the decision maintains its position, the Commission shall immediately inform the Committee in order to initiate the procedures referred to in Article 6 (1).

3.   Where equipment or a protective system which does not comply bears the CE conformity marking, the competent Member State shall take appropriate action against the person(s) having affixed the marking and shall so inform the Commission and the other Member States.

4.   The Commission shall ensure that the Member States are kept informed of the progress and outcome of this procedure.

CHAPTER II

Conformity assessment procedures

Article 8

1.   The procedures for assessing the conformity of equipment, including where necessary the devices referred protective systems or devices referred to in Article 1 (2), shall be as follows:

(a)   *equipment-group I and II, equipment-category M 1 and 1*
  The manufacturer or his authorized representative established in the Community must, in order to affix the CE marking, follow the CE type-examination procedure (referred to in Annex III), in conjunction with:
  — the procedure relating to production quality assurance (referred to in Annex IV), or
  — the procedure relating to product verification (referred to in Annex V);

(b)   *equipment-group I and II, equipment-category M 2 and 2*
  (i)   In the case of internal combustion engines and electrical equipment in these groups and categories, the manufacturer or his authorized representative established in the Community shall, in order to affix the CE mark, follow the EC-type examination procedure (referred to in Annex III), in conjunction with:
    — the procedure relating to conformity to type referred to in Annex VI, or
    — the procedure relating to product quality assurance referred to in Annex VII;
  (ii)   in the case of other equipment in these groups and categories, the manufacturer or his authorized representative established in the Community must, in order to affix the CE mark, follow the procedure relating to internal control of production (referred to in Annex VIII)
    and
  communicate the dossier provided for in Annex VIII, paragraph 3, to a notified body, which shall acknowledge receipt of it as soon as possible and shall retain it.

(c)   *equipment-group II, equipment-category 3*
  The manufacturer or his authorized representative established in the Community must, in order to affix the CE marking, follow the procedure relating to internal control of production referred to in Annex VIII;

(d)   *equipment-groups I and II*
  In addition to the procedures referred to in paragraph 1(a), (b) and (c), the manufacturer or his authorized representative established in the Community may also, in order to affix the CE marking, follow the procedure relating to CE unit verification (referred to in Annex IX).

2.   The provisions of 1(a) or 1(d) above shall be used for conformity assessment of autonomous protective systems.

3.   The procedures referred to in paragraph 1 shall be applied in respect of components as referred to in Article 4 (2), with the exception of the affixing of the CE marking. A certificate shall be issued by the manufacturer or his authorized representative established in the Community, declaring the conformity of the

components with the provisions of this Directive which apply to them and stating their characteristics and how they must be incorporated into equipment or protective systems to assist compliance with the essential requirements applicable to finished equipment or protective systems.

4.   In addition, the manufacturer or his authorized representative established in the Community may, in order to affix the CE marking, follow the procedure relating to internal control of production (referred to in Annex VIII) with regard to the safety aspects referred to in point 1.2.7 of Annex II.

5.   Notwithstanding the previous paragraphs, the competent authorities may, on a duly justified request, authorize the placing on the market and putting into service on the territory of the Member State concerned of the equipment, protective systems and individual devices referred to in Article 1 (2) in respect of which the procedures referred to in the previous paragraphs have not been applied and the use of which is in the interests of protection.

6.   Documents and correspondence relating to the procedures referred to in the abovementioned paragraphs shall be drawn up in one of the official languages of the Member States in which those procedures are being applied or in a language accepted by the notified body.

7.   (a)   Where the equipment and protective systems are subject to other Community Directives covering other aspects which also provide for the affixing of the CE marking referred to in Article 10, that marking shall indicate that the equipment and protective systems are also presumed to conform with the provisions of those other Directives.

   (b)   However, where one or more of those Directives allow the manufacturer, during a transitional period, to choose which arrangements to apply, the CE marking shall indicate conformity only with the Directives applied by the manufacturer. In this case, particulars of the said Directives, as published in the *Official Journal of the European Communities*, must be given in the documents, notices or instructions required by the Directives and accompanying the equipment and protective systems.

Article 9

1.   Member States shall notify the Commission and the other Member States of the bodies which they have appointed to carry out the procedures referred to in Article 8, together with the specific tasks which these bodies have been appointed to carry out and the identification numbers assigned to them beforehand by the Commission.

The Commission shall publish in the *Official Journal of the European Communities* a list of the notified bodies, with their identification numbers and the tasks for which they have been notified. The Commission shall ensure that this list is kept up to date.

2.   Member States shall apply the criteria laid down in Annex XI in assessing the bodies to be indicated in such notification. Bodies meeting the assessment criteria laid down in the relative harmonized standards shall be presumed to fulfil those criteria.

3.   A Member State which has approved a body must withdraw its notification if it finds that the body no longer meets the criteria referred to in Annex XI. It shall immediately inform the Commission and the other Member States accordingly.

CHAPTER III

CE conformity marking

Article 10

1.   The CE conformity marking shall consist of the initials "CE". The form of the marking to be used is shown in Annex X. The CE marking shall be followed by the identification number of the notified body where such body is involved in the production control stage.

2.   The CE marking shall be affixed distinctly, visibly, legibly and indelibly to equipment and protective systems, supplementary to the provisions of point 1.0.5. of Annex II.

3.   The affixing of markings on the equipment or protective systems which are likely to deceive third parties as to the meaning and form of the CE marking shall be prohibited. Any other marking may be affixed to the equipment or protective systems, provided that the visibility and legibility of the CE marking is not thereby reduced.

Article 11

Without prejudice to Article 7:
(a)   where a Member State establishes that the CE marking has been incorrectly affixed, the manufacturer or his authorized representative established within the Community shall be obliged to make the product conform as regards the provisions concerning the CE marking and to end the infringement under the conditions imposed by the Member State;
(b)   in the event of continuing non-conformity, the Member State must take all appropriate measures to restrict or prohibit the placing on the market of the product in question or to ensure that it is withdrawn from the market in accordance with the procedures laid down in Article 7.

CHAPTER IV

Final provisions

Article 12

Any decision taken pursuant to this Directive which restricts or prohibits the placing on the market and/or the putting into service or requires the withdrawal from the market of equipment, a protective system, or a device referred to in Article 1 (2) shall state the exact grounds on which it is based. Such a decision shall be notified forthwith to the party concerned, who shall at the same time be informed of the legal remedies available to him under the laws in force in the Member State concerned and of the time limits to which such remedies are subject.

Article 13

Member States shall ensure that all the parties involved in the application of the Directive are bound to observe confidentiality in respect of all information obtained in the performance of carrying out their tasks. This does not affect the obligations of the Member States and of the notified bodies regarding reciprocal information and the dissemination of warnings.

Article 14

1.   Directive 76/117/EEC, Directive 79/196/EEC and Directive 82/130/EEC shall be repealed as from 1 July 2003.

2.   EC certificates of conformity to the harmonized standards obtained in accordance with the procedures laid down in the Directives referred to in paragraph 1 shall continue to be valid until 30 June 2003 unless they expire before that date. Their validity shall continue to be limited to the harmonized standards indicated in the aforementioned Directives.

3.   Member States shall take the necessary action to ensure that the notified bodies which are responsible pursuant to Article 8 (1) to (4) for the assessment of the conformity of electrical equipment placed on the market before 1 July 2003 take account of the results of tests and verifications already carried out under the Directives referred to in paragraph 1.

Article 15

1.   Member States shall adopt and publish the laws, regulations and administrative provisions necessary to comply with this Directive before 1 September 1995. They shall forthwith inform the Commission thereof.

The Member States shall apply these measures with effect from 1 March 1996.

When Member States adopt the measures referred to in the first subparagraph, they shall contain a reference to this Directive or shall be accompanied by such reference at the time of their official publication. The methods of making such reference shall be laid down by Member States.

2.   However, Member States shall allow the placing on the market and the putting into service of equipment and protective systems conforming with the national regulations in force in their territory at the date of adoption of this Directive for the period until 30 June 2003.

Article 16

This Directive is addressed to the Member States.

Done at Brussels, 23 March 1994.

<table>
<tr><td>*For the European Parliament*</td><td>*For the Council*</td></tr>
<tr><td>*The President*</td><td>*The President*</td></tr>
<tr><td>E. KLEPSCH</td><td>TH. PANGALOS</td></tr>
</table>

ANNEX I

CRITERIA DETERMINING THE CLASSIFICATION OF EQUIPMENT-GROUPS INTO CATEGORIES

1. **Equipment-group I**

   (a) Category M 1 comprises equipment designed and, where necessary, equipped with additional special means of protection to be capable of functioning in conformity with the operational parameters established by the manufacturer and ensuring a very high level of protection.

   Equipment in this category is intended for use in underground parts of mines as well as those parts of surface installations of such mines endangered by firedamp and/or combustible dust.

   Equipment in this category is required to remain functional, even in the event of rare incidents relating to equipment, with an explosive atmosphere present, and is characterized by means of protection such that:
   — either, in the event of failure of one means of protection, at least an independent second means provides the requisite level of protection,
   — or the requisite level of protection is assured in the event of two faults occurring independently of each other.

   Equipment in this category must comply with the supplementary requirements referred to in Annex II, 2.0.1.

   (b) Category M 2 comprises equipment designed to be capable of functioning in conformity with the operational parameters established by the manufacturer and ensuring a high level of protection.

   Equipment in this category is intended for use in underground parts of mines as well as those parts of surface installations of such mines likely to be endangered by firedamp and/or combustible dust.

   This equipment is intended to be de-energized in the event of an explosive atmosphere.

   The means of protection relating to equipment in this category assure the requisite level of protection during normal operation and also in the case of more severe operating conditions, in particular those arising from rough handling and changing environmental conditions.

   Equipment in this category must comply with the supplementary requirements referred to in Annex II, 2.0.2.

2. **Equipment-group II**

   (a) Category 1 comprises equipment designed to be capable of functioning in conformity with the operational parameters established by the manufacturer and ensuring a very high level of protection.

   Equipment in this category is intended for use in areas in which explosive atmospheres caused by mixtures of air and gases, vapours or mists or by air/dust mixtures are present continuously, for long periods or frequently.

Equipment in this category must ensure the requisite level of protection, even in the event of rare incidents relating to equipment, and is characterized by means of protection such that:
— either, in the event of failure of one means of protection, at least an independent second means provides the requisite level of protection,
— or the requisite level of protection is assured in the event of two faults occurring independently of each other.

Equipment in this category must comply with the supplementary requirements referred to in Annex II, 2.1.

(b) Category 2 comprises equipment designed to be capable of functioning in conformity with the operational parameters established by the manufacturer and of ensuring a high level of protection.

Equipment in this category is intended for use in areas in which explosive atmospheres caused by gases, vapours, mists or air/dust mixtures are likely to occur.

The means of protection relating to equipment in this category ensure the requisite level of protection, even in the event of frequently occurring disturbances or equipment faults which normally have to be taken into account.

Equipment in this category must comply with the supplementary requirements referred to in Annex II, 2.2.

(c) Category 3 comprises equipment designed to be capable of functioning in conformity with the operating parameters established by the manufacturer and ensuring a normal level of protection.

Equipment in this category is intended for use in areas in which explosive atmospheres caused by gases, vapours, mists, or air/dust mixtures are unlikely to occur or, if they do occur, are likely to do so only infrequently and for a short period only.

Equipment in this category ensures the requisite level of protection during normal operation.

Equipment in this category must comply with the supplementary requirements referred to in Annex II, 2.3.

ANNEX II

ESSENTIAL HEALTH AND SAFETY REQUIREMENTS RELATING TO THE DESIGN AND CONSTRUCTION OF EQUIPMENT AND PROTECTIVE SYSTEMS INTENDED FOR USE IN POTENTIALLY EXPLOSIVE ATMOSPHERES

Preliminary observations

A.   Technological knowledge, which can change rapidly, must be taken into account as far as possible and be utilized immediately.

B.   For the devices referred to in Article 1 (2), the essential requirements shall apply only in so far as they are necessary for the safe and reliable functioning and operation of those devices with respect to the risks of explosion.

1. COMMON REQUIREMENTS FOR EQUIPMENT AND PROTECTIVE SYSTEMS

1.0.   General requirements

1.0.1. *Principles of integrated explosion safety*

Equipment and protective systems intended for use in potentially explosive atmospheres must be designed from the point of view of integrated explosion safety.

In this connection, the manufacturer must take measures:
— above all, if possible, to prevent the formation of explosive atmospheres which may be produced or released by equipment and by protective systems themselves,
— to prevent the ignition of explosive atmospheres, taking into account the nature of every electrical and non-electrical source of ignition,
— should an explosion nevertheless occur which could directly or indirectly endanger persons and, as the case may be, domestic animals or property, to halt it immediately and/or to limit the range of explosion flames and explosion pressures to a sufficient level of safety.

1.0.2. Equipment and protective systems must be designed and manufactured after due analysis of possible operating faults in order as far as possible to preclude dangerous situations.

Any misuse which can reasonably be anticipated must be taken into account.

1.0.3. *Special checking and maintenance conditions*

Equipment and protective systems subject to special checking and maintenance conditions must be designed and constructed with such conditions in mind.

1.0.4. *Surrounding area conditions*

Equipment and protective systems must be so designed and constructed as to be capable of coping with actual or foreseeable surrounding area conditions.

1.0.5. *Marking*

All equipment and protective systems must be marked legibly and indelibly with the following minimum particulars:
— name and address of the manufacturer,
— CE marking (see Annex X, point A),
— designation of series or type,
— serial number, if any,
— year of construction,
— the specific marking of explosion protection ⟨Ex⟩ followed by the symbol of the equipment group and category,
— for equipment-group II, the letter "G" (concerning explosive atmospheres caused by gases, vapours or mists),
and/or
— the letter "D" (concerning explosive atmospheres caused by dust).
Furthermore, where necessary, they must also be marked with all information essential to their safe use.

1.0.6.   *Instructions*

    (a) All equipment and protective systems must be accompanied by instructions, including at least the following particulars:
— a recapitulation of the information with which the equipment or protective system is marked, except for the serial number (see 1.0.5.), together with any appropriate additional information to facilitate maintenance (eg address of the importer, repairer, etc);
— instructions for safe:
    — putting into service,
    — use,
    — assembling and dismantling,
    — maintenance (servicing and emergency repair),
    — installation,
    — adjustment;
— where necessary, an indication of the danger areas in front of pressure-relief devices;
— where necessary, training instructions;
— details which allow a decision to be taken beyond any doubt as to whether an item of equipment in a specific category or a protective system can be used safely in the intended area under the expected operating conditions;
— electrical and pressure parameters, maximum surface temperatures and other limit values;
— where necessary, special conditions of use, including particulars of possible misuse which experience has shown might occur;
— where necessary, the essential characteristics of tools which may be fitted to the equipment or protective system.

    (b) The instructions must be drawn up in one of the Community languages by the manufacturer or his authorized representative established in the Community.

On being put into service, all equipment and protective systems must be accompanied by a translation of the instructions in the language or languages of the country in which the equipment or protective system is to be used and by the instructions in the original language.

This translation must be made by either the manufacturer or his authorized representative established in the Community or the person introducing the equipment or protective system into the language area in question.

By way of derogation from this requirement, the maintenance instructions for use by the specialist personnel employed by the manufacturer or his authorized representative established in the Community may be drawn up in a single Community language understood by that personnel.

    (c) The instructions must contain the drawings and diagrams necessary for the putting into service, maintenance, inspection, checking of correct operation and, where appropriate, repair of the equipment or protective system, together with all useful instructions, in particular with regard to safety.

    (d) Literature describing the equipment or protective system must not contradict the instructions with regard to safety aspects.

1.1.   Selection of materials

1.1.1.   The materials used for the construction of equipment and protective systems must not trigger off an explosion, taking into account foreseeable operational stresses.

1.1.2.   Within the limits of the operating conditions laid down by the manufacturer, it must not be possible for a reaction to take place between the materials used and the constituents of the potentially explosive atmosphere which could impair explosion protection.

1.1.3.   Materials must be so selected that predictable changes in their characteristics and their compatibility in combination with other materials will not lead to a reduction in the protection afforded; in particular, due account must be taken of the material's corrosion and wear resistance, electrical conductivity, impact strength, ageing resistance and the effects of temperature variations.

1.2.   Design and Construction

1.2.1.   Equipment and protective systems must be designed and constructed with due regard to technological knowledge of explosion protection so that they can be safely operated throughout their foreseeable lifetime.

1.2.2.   Components to be incorporated into or used as replacements in equipment and protective systems must be so designed and constructed that they function safely for their intended purpose of explosion protection when they are installed in accordance with the manufacturer's instructions.

1.2.3.   *Enclosed structures and prevention of leaks*

Equipment which may release flammable gases or dusts must wherever possible employ enclosed structures only.

If equipment contains openings or non-tight joints, these must as far as possible be designed in such a way that developing gases or dusts cannot give rise to explosive atmospheres outside the equipment.

Points where materials are introduced or drawn off must, as far as possible, be designed and equipped so as to limit escapes of flammable materials during filling or draining.

1.2.4.   *Dust deposits*

Equipment and protective systems which are intended to be used in areas exposed to dust must be so designed that deposit dust on their surfaces is not ignited.

In general, dust deposits must be limited where possible. Equipment and protective systems must be easily cleanable.

The surface temperatures of equipment parts must be kept well below the glow temperature of the deposit dust.

The thickness of deposit dust must be taken into consideration and, if appropriate, means must be taken to limit the temperature in order to prevent a heat build up.

1.2.5.   *Additional means of protection*

Equipment and protective systems which may be exposed to certain types of external stresses must be equipped, where necessary, with additional means of protection.

Equipment must withstand relevant stresses, without adverse effect on explosion protection.

1.2.6.   *Safe opening*

If equipment and protective systems are in a housing or a locked container forming part of the explosion protection itself, it must be possible to open such housing or container only with a special tool or by means of appropriate protection measures.

1.2.7.   *Protection against other hazards*

Equipment and protective systems must be so designed and manufactured as to:
(a)   avoid physical injury or other harm which might be caused by direct or indirect contact;
(b)   assure that surface temperatures of accessible parts or radiation which would cause a danger, are not produced;
(c)   eliminate non-electrical dangers which are revealed by experience;
(d)   assure that foreseeable conditions of overload shall not give rise to dangerous situations.

Where, for equipment and protective systems, the risks referred to in this paragraph are wholly or partly covered by other Community Directives, this Directive shall not apply or shall cease to apply in the case of such equipment and protective systems and of such risks upon application of those specific Directives.

1.2.8.   *Overloading of equipment*

Dangerous overloading of equipment must be prevented at the design stage by means of integrated measurement, regulation and control devices, such as over-current cut-off switches, temperature limiters, differential pressure switches, flowmeters, time-lag relays, overspeed monitors and/or similar types of monitoring devices.

1.2.9.   *Flameproof enclosure systems*

If parts which can ignite an explosive atmosphere are placed in an enclosure, measures must be taken to ensure that the enclosure withstands the pressure developed during an internal explosion of an explosive mixture and prevents the transmission of the explosion to the explosive atmosphere surrounding the enclosure.

1.3.   Potential ignition sources

1.3.1.   *Hazards arising from different ignition sources*

Potential ignition sources such as sparks, flames, electric arcs, high surface temperatures, acoustic energy, optical radiation, electromagnetic waves and other ignition sources must not occur.

1.3.2. *Hazards arising from static electricity*

Electrostatic charges capable of resulting in dangerous discharges must be prevented by means of appropriate measures.

1.3.3. *Hazards arising from stray electric and leakage currents*

Stray electric and leakage currents in conductive equipment parts which could result in, for example, the occurrence of dangerous corrosion, overheating of surfaces or sparks capable of provoking an ignition must be prevented.

1.3.4. *Hazards arising from overheating*

Overheating caused by friction or impacts occurring, for example, between materials and parts in contact with each other while rotating or through the intrusion of foreign bodies must, as far as possible, be prevented at the design stage.

1.3.5. *Hazards arising from pressure compensation operations*

Equipment and protective systems must be so designed or fitted with integrated measuring, control and regulation devices that pressure compensations arising from them do not generate shock waves or compressions which may cause ignition.

1.4. Hazards arising from external effects

1.4.1. Equipment and protective systems must be so designed and constructed as to be capable of performing their intended function in full safety, even in changing environmental conditions and in the presence of extraneous voltages, humidity, vibrations, contamination and other external effects, taking into account the limits of the operating conditions established by the manufacturer.

1.4.2. Equipment parts used must be appropriate to the intended mechanical and thermal stresses and capable of withstanding attack by existing or foreseeable aggressive substances.

1.5. Requirements in respect of safety-related devices

1.5.1. Safety devices must function independently of any measurement or control devices required for operation.

As far as possible, failure of a safety device must be detected sufficiently rapidly by appropriate technical means to ensure that there is only very little likelihood that dangerous situations will occur.

For electrical circuits the fail-safe principle is to be applied in general.

Safety-related switching must in general directly actuate the relevant control devices without intermediate software command.

1.5.2. In the event of a safety device failure, equipment and/or protective systems shall, wherever possible, be secured.

1.5.3. Emergency stop controls of safety devices must, as far as possible, be fitted with restart lockouts. A new start command may take effect on normal operation only after the restart lockouts have been intentionally reset.

1.5.4.   *Control and display units*

Where control and display units are used, they must be designed in accordance with ergonomic principles in order to achieve the highest possible level of operating safety with regard to the risk of explosion.

1.5.5.   *Requirements in respect of devices with a measuring function for explosion protection.*

In so far as they relate to equipment used in explosive atmospheres, devices with a measuring function must be designed and constructed so that they can cope with foreseeable operating requirements and special conditions of use.

1.5.6.   Where necessary, it must be possible to check the reading accuracy and serviceability of devices with a measuring function.

1.5.7.   The design of devices with a measuring function must incorporate a safety factor which ensures that the alarm threshold lies far enough outside the explosion and/or ignition limits of the atmospheres to be registered, taking into account, in particular, the operating conditions of the installation and possible aberrations in the measuring system.

1.5.8.   *Risks arising from software*

In the design of software-controlled equipment, protective systems and safety devices, special account must be taken of the risks arising from faults in the programme.

1.6.   Integration of safety requirements relating to the system

1.6.1.   Manual override must be possible in order to shut down the equipment and protective systems incorporated within automatic processes which deviate from the intended operating conditions, provided that this does not compromise safety.

1.6.2.   When the emergency shutdown system is actuated, accumulated energy must be dispersed as quickly and as safely as possible or isolated so that it no longer constitutes a hazard.

This does not apply to electrochemically-stored energy.

1.6.3.   *Hazards arising from power failure*

Where equipment and protective systems can give rise to a spread of additional risks in the event of a power failure, it must be possible to maintain them in a safe state of operation independently of the rest of the installation.

1.6.4.   *Hazards arising from connections*

Equipment and protective systems must be fitted with suitable cable and conduit entries.

When equipment and protective systems are intended for use in combination with other equipment and protective systems, the interface must be safe.

1.6.5.   *Placing of warning devices as parts of equipment*

Where equipment or protective systems are fitted with detection or alarm devices for monitoring the occurrence of explosive atmospheres, the necessary instructions must be provided to enable them to be provided at the appropriate places.

2.   SUPPLEMENTARY REQUIREMENTS IN RESPECT OF EQUIPMENT

2.0.   Requirements applicable to equipment in category M of equipment-group I

2.0.1.   *Requirements applicable to equipment in category M I of equipment-group I*

2.0.1.1.   Equipment must be so designed and constructed that sources of ignition do not become active, even in the event of rare incidents relating to equipment.

Equipment must be equipped with means of protection such that:
— either, in the event of failure of one means of protection, at least an independent second means provides the requisite level of protection,
— or, the requisite level of protection is ensured in the event of two faults occurring independently of each other.

Where necessary, this equipment must be equipped with additional special means of protection.

It must remain functional with an explosive atmosphere present.

2.0.1.2.   Where necessary, equipment must be so constructed that no dust can penetrate it.

2.0.1.3.   The surface temperatures of equipment parts must be kept clearly below the ignition temperature of the foreseeable air/dust mixtures in order to prevent the ignition of suspended dust.

2.0.1.4.   Equipment must be so designed that the opening of equipment parts which may be sources of ignition is possible only under non-active or intrinsically safe conditions. Where it is not possible to render equipment non-active, the manufacturer must affix a warning label to the opening part of the equipment.

If necessary, equipment must be fitted with appropriate additional interlocking systems.

2.0.2.   *Requirements applicable to equipment in category M 2 of equipment-group I*

2.0.2.1.   Equipment must be equipped with means of protection ensuring that sources of ignition do not become active during normal operation, even under more severe operating conditions, in particular those arising from rough handling and changing environmental conditions.

The equipment is intended to be de-energized in the event of an explosive atmosphere.

2.0.2.2.   Equipment must be so designed that the opening of equipment parts which may be sources of ignition is possible only under non-active conditions or via appropriate interlocking systems. Where it is not possible to render equipment non-active, the manufacturer must affix a warning label to the opening part of the equipment.

2.0.2.3.   The requirements regarding explosion hazards arising from dust applicable to category M 1 must be applied.

2.1.   Requirements applicable to equipment in category 1 of equipment-group II

2.1.1.   *Explosive atmospheres caused by gases, vapours or hazes*

2.1.1.1.   Equipment must be so designed and constructed that sources of ignition do not become active, even in event of rare incidents relating to equipment.

It must be equipped with means of protection such that:
— either, in the event of failure of one means of protection, at least an independent second means provides the requisite level of protection,
— or, the requisite level of protection is ensured in the event of two faults occurring independently of each other.

2.1.1.2.   For equipment with surfaces which may heat up, measures must be taken to ensure that the stated maximum surface temperatures are not exceeded even in the most unfavourable circumstances.

Temperature rises caused by heat build-ups and chemical reactions must also be taken into account.

2.1.1.3.   Equipment must be so designed that the opening of equipment parts which might be sources of ignition is possible only under non-active or intrinsically safe conditions. Where it is not possible to render equipment non-active, the manufacturer must affix a warning label to the opening part of the equipment.

If necessary, equipment must be fitted with appropriate additional interlocking systems.

2.1.2.   *Explosive atmospheres caused by air/dust mixtures*

2.1.2.1.   Equipment must be so designed and constructed that ignition of air/dust mixtures does not occur even in the event of rare incidents relating to equipment.

It must be equipped with means of protection such that
— either, in the event of failure of one means of protection, at least an independent second means provides the requisite level of protection,
— or, the requisite level of protection is ensured in the event of two faults occurring independently of each other.

2.1.2.2.   Where necessary, equipment must be so designed that dust can enter or escape from the equipment only at specifically designated points.

This requirement must also be met by cable entries and connecting pieces.

2.1.2.3. The surface temperatures of equipment parts must be kept well below the ignition temperature of the foreseeable air/dust mixtures in order to prevent the ignition of suspended dust.

2.1.2.4. With regard to the safe opening of equipment parts, requirement 2.1.1.3 applies.

2.2. Requirements for category 2 of equipment-group II

2.2.1. *Explosive atmospheres caused by gases, vapours or mists*

2.2.1.1. Equipment must be so designed and constructed as to prevent ignition sources arising, even in the event of frequently occurring disturbances or equipment operating faults, which normally have to be taken into account.

2.2.1.2. Equipment parts must be so designed and constructed that their stated surface temperatures are not exceeded, even in the case of risks arising from abnormal situations anticipated by the manufacturer.

2.2.1.3. Equipment must be so designed that the opening of equipment parts which might be sources of ignition is possible only under non-active conditions or via appropriate interlocking systems. Where it is not possible to render equipment non-active, the manufacturer must affix a warning label to the opening part of the equipment.

2.2.2. *Explosive atmospheres caused by air/dust mixtures*

2.2.2.1. Equipment must be designed and constructed so that ignition of air/dust mixtures is prevented, even in the event of frequently occurring disturbances or equipment operating faults which normally have to be taken into account.

2.2.2.2. With regard to surface temperatures, requirement 2.1.2.3 applies.

2.2.2.3. With regard to protection against dust, requirement 2.1.2.2 applies.

2.2.2.4. With regard to the safe opening of equipment parts, requirement 2.2.1.3 applies.

2.3. Requirements applicable to equipment in category 3 of equipment-group II

2.3.1. *Explosive atmospheres caused by gases, vapours or mists*

2.3.1.1. Equipment must be so designed and constructed as to prevent foreseeable ignition sources which can occur during normal operation.

2.3.1.2. Surface temperatures must not exceed the stated maximum surface temperatures under intended operating conditions. Higher temperatures in exceptional circumstances may be allowed only if the manufacturer adopts special additional protective measures.

2.3.2. *Explosive atmospheres caused by air/dust mixtures*

2.3.2.1. Equipment must be so designed and constructed that air/dust mixtures cannot be ignited by foreseeable ignition sources likely to exist during normal operation.

2.3.2.2. With regard to surface temperatures, requirement 2.1.2.3 applies.

2.3.2.3. Equipment, including cable entries and connecting pieces, must be so constructed that, taking into account the size of its particles, dust can neither develop explosive mixtures with air nor form dangerous accumulations inside the equipment.

3. SUPPLEMENTARY REQUIREMENTS IN RESPECT OF PROTECTIVE SYSTEMS

3.0. General requirements

3.0.1. Protective systems must be dimensioned in such a way as to reduce the effects of an explosion to a sufficient level of safety.

3.0.2. Protective systems must be designed and capable of being positional in such a way that explosions are prevented from spreading through dangerous chain reactions or flashover and incipient explosions do not become detonations.

3.0.3. In the event of a power failure, protective systems must retain their capacity to function for a period sufficient to avoid a dangerous situation.

3.0.4. Protective systems must not fail due to outside interference.

3.1. Planning and design

3.1.1. *Characteristics of materials*

With regard to the characteristics of materials, the maximum pressure and temperature to be taken into consideration at the planning stage are the expected pressure during an explosion occurring under extreme operating conditions and the anticipated heating effect of the flame.

3.1.2. Protective systems designed to resist or contain explosions must be capable of withstanding the shock wave produced without losing system integrity.

3.1.3. Accessories connected to protective systems must be capable of withstanding the expected maximum explosion pressure without losing their capacity to function.

3.1.4. The reactions caused by pressure in peripheral equipment and connected pipe-work must be taken into consideration in the planning and design of protective systems.

3.1.5. *Pressure-relief systems*

If it is likely that stresses on protective systems will exceed their structural strength, provision must be made in the design for suitable pressure-relief devices which do not endanger persons in the vicinity.

3.1.6. *Explosion suppression systems*

Explosion suppression systems must be so planned and designed that they react to an incipient explosion at the earliest possible stage in the event of an incident and counteract it to best effect, which due regard to the maximum rate of pressure increase and the maximum explosion pressure.

3.1.7.　*Explosion decoupling systems*

Decoupling systems intended to disconnect specific equipment as swiftly as possible in the event of incipient explosions by means of appropriate devices must be planned and designed so as to remain proof against the transmission of internal ignition and to retain their mechanical strength under operating conditions.

3.1.8.　Protective systems must be capable of being integrated into a circuit with a suitable alarm threshold so that, if necessary, there is cessation of product feed and output and shutdown of equipment parts which can no longer function safely.

ANNEX III

MODULE EC-TYPE EXAMINATION

1.　This module describes that part of the procedure by which a notified body ascertains and attests that a specimen representative of the production envisaged meets the relevant applicable provisions of the Directive.

2.　The application for the EC-type examination shall be lodged by the manufacturer or his authorized representative established within the Community with a notified body of his choice.

The application shall include:
— the name and address of the manufacturer and, if the application is lodged by the authorized representative, his name and address in addition;
— a written declaration that the same application has not been lodged with any other notified body;
— the technical documentation, as described in point 3.

The applicant shall place at the disposal of the notified body a specimen representative of the production envisaged and hereinafter called "type". The notified body may request further specimens if needed for carrying out the test programme.

3.　The technical documentation shall enable the conformity of the product with the requirements of the Directive to be assessed. It shall, to the extent necessary for such assessment, cover the design, manufacture and operation of the product and shall to that extent contain:
— a general type-description;
— design and manufacturing drawings and layouts of components, sub-assemblies, circuits, etc.;
— descriptions and explanations necessary for the understanding of said drawings and layouts and the operation of the product;
— a list of the standards referred to in Article 5, applied in full or in part, and descriptions of the solutions adopted to meet the essential requirements of the Directive where the standards referred to in Article 5 have not been applied;

— results of design calculations made, examinations carried out, etc;
— test reports.

4.   The notified body shall:

4.1.   examine the technical documentation, verify that the type has been manufactured in conformity with the technical documentation and identify the elements which have been designed in accordance with the relevant provisions of the standards referred to in Article 5, as well as the components which have been designed without applying the relevant provisions of those standards;

4.2.   perform or have performed the appropriate examinations and necessary tests to check whether the solutions adopted by the manufacturer meet the essential requirements of the Directive where the standards referred to in Article 5 have not ben applied;

4.3.   perform or have performed the appropriate examinations and necessary tests to check whether these have actually been applied, where the manufacturer has chosen to apply the relevant standards;

4.4   agree with the applicant the location where the examinations and necessary tests shall be carried out.

5.   Where the type meets the provisions of the Directive, the notified body shall issue an EC-type-examination certificate to the applicant. The certificate shall contain the name and address of the manufacturer, conclusions of the examination and the necessary data for identification of the approved type.

        A list of the relevant parts of the technical documentation shall be annexed to the certificate and a copy kept by the notified body.

        If the manufacturer or his authorized representative established in the Community is denied a type certification, the notified body shall provide detailed reasons for such denial.

        Provision shall be made for an appeals procedure.

6.   The applicant shall inform the notified body which holds the technical documentation concerning the EC-type-examination certificate of all modifications to the approved equipment or protective system which must receive further approval where such changes may effect conformity with the essential requirements or with the prescribed conditions for use of the product. This further approval is given in the form of an addition to the original EC-type-examination certificate.

7.   Each notified body shall communicate to the other notified bodies the relevant information concerning the EC-type-examination certificates and additions issued and withdrawn.

8.   The other notified bodies may receive copies of the EC-type-examination certificates and/or their additions. The annexes to the certificates shall be kept at the disposal of the other notified bodies.

9.   The manufacturer or his authorized representative established in the Community shall keep with the technical documentation copies of EC-type-examination certificates and their additions for a period ending at least 10 years after the last equipment or protective system was manufactured.

Where neither the manufacturer nor his authorized representative is established within the Community, the obligation to keep the technical documentation available shall be the responsibility of the person who places the product on the Community market.

ANNEX IV

MODULE: PRODUCTION QUALITY ASSURANCE

1.   This module describes the procedure whereby the manufacturer who satisfies the obligations of point 2 ensures and declares that the products concerned are in conformity with the type as described in the EC-type-examination certificate and satisfy the requirements of the Directive which apply to them. The manufacturer, or his authorized representative established in the Community, shall affix the CE marking to each piece of equipment and draw up a written declaration of conformity. The CE marking shall be accompanied by the identification number of the notified body responsible for EC monitoring, as specified in Section 4.

2.   The manufacturer shall operate an approved quality system for production, final equipment inspection and testing as specified in Section 3 and shall be subject to monitoring as specified in Section 4.

3.   Quality system

3.1.   The manufacturer shall lodge an application for assessment of his quality system with a notified body of his choice, for the equipment concerned.

The application shall include:
— all relevant information for the product category envisaged;
— the documentation concerning the quality system;
— technical documentation on the approved type and a copy of the EC-type-examination certificate.

3.2.   The quality system shall ensure compliance of the equipment with the type as described in the EC-type-examination certificate and with the requirements of the Directive which apply to them.

All the elements, requirements and provisions adopted by the manufacturer shall be documented in a systematic and orderly manner in the form of written policies, procedures and instructions. The quality system documentation must permit a consistent interpretation of quality programmes, plans, manuals and records.

It shall contain, in particular, an adequate description of
— the quality objectives and the organizational structure, responsibilities and powers of the management with regard to equipment quality;
— the manufacturing, quality control and quality assurance techniques, processes and systematic actions which will be used;

- the examinations and tests which will be carried out before, during and after manufacture and the frequency with which they will be carried out;
- the quality records, such as inspection reports and test data, calibration data, reports on the qualifications of the personnel concerned, etc.;
- the means to monitor the achievement of the required equipment quality and the effective operation of the quality system.

3.3.   The notified body shall assess the quality system to determine whether it satisfies the requirements referred to in Section 3.2. It shall presume conformity with these requirements in respect of quality systems which implement the relevant harmonized standard. The auditing team shall have at least one member with experience of evaluation in the equipment technology concerned. The evaluation procedure shall include an inspection visit to the manufacturer's premises. The decision shall be notified to the manufacturer. The notification shall contain the conclusions of the examination and the reasoned assessment decision.

3.4.   The manufacturer shall undertake to fulfil the obligations arising out of the quality system as approved and to uphold the system so that it remains adequate and efficient.

The manufacturer or his authorized representative shall inform the notified body which has approved the quality system of any intended updating of the quality system.

The notified body shall evaluate the modifications proposed and decide whether the amended quality system will still satisfy the requirements referred to in Section 3.2 or whether a re-assessment is required.

It shall notify its decision to the manufacturer. The notification shall contain the conclusions of the examination and the reasoned assessment decision.

4.   Surveillance under the responsibility of the notified body

4.1.   The purpose of surveillance is to make sure that the manufacturer duly fulfils the obligations arising out of the approved quality system.

4.2.   The manufacturer shall, for inspection purposes, allow the notified body access to the manufacture, inspection, testing and storage premises and shall provide it with all necessary information, in particular
- the quality system documentation
- the quality records, such as inspection reports and text data, calibration data, reports on the qualifications of the personnel concerned, etc.

4.3.   The notified body shall periodically carry out audits to ensure that the manufacturer maintains and applies the quality system and shall provide an audit report to the manufacturer.

4.4.   Furthermore, the notified body may pay unexpected visits to the manufacturer. During such visits, the notified body may carry out tests, or arrange for tests to be carried out, to check that the quality system is functioning correctly, if necessary. The notified body shall provide the manufacturer with a visit report and, if a test has taken place, with a test report.

5.   The manufacturer shall, for a period ending at least 10 years after the last piece of equipment was manufactured, keep at the disposal of the national authorities:
        — the documentation referred to in the second indent of Section 3.1;
        — the updating referred to in the second paragraph of Section 3.4;
        — the decisions and reports from the notified body which are referred to in Section 3.4, last paragraph, Section 4.3 and Section 4.4.

6.   Each notified body shall apprise the other notified bodies of the relevant information concerning the quality system approvals issued and withdrawn.

ANNEX V

MODULE: PRODUCT VERIFICATION

1.   This module describes the procedure whereby a manufacturer or his authorized representative established within the Community checks and attests that the equipment subject to the provisions of point 3 are in conformity with the type as described in the EC-type-examination certificate and satisfy the relevant requirements of the Directive.

2.   The manufacturer shall take all measures necessary to ensure that the manufacturing process guarantees conformity of the equipment with the type as described in the EC-type-examination certificate and with the requirements of the Directive which apply to them. The manufacturer or his authorized representative established in the Community shall affix the CE marking to each piece of equipment and shall draw up a declaration of conformity.

3.   The notified body shall carry out the appropriate examinations and tests in order to check the conformity of the equipment, protective system or device referred to in Article 1 (2), with the relevant requirements of the Directive, by examining and testing every product as specified in Section 4.

        The manufacturer or his authorized representative shall keep a copy of the declaration of conformity for a period ending at least 10 years after the last piece of equipment was manufactured.

4.   **Verification by examination and testing of each piece of equipment**

4.1.   All equipment shall be individually examined and appropriate tests as set out in the relevant standard(s) referred to in Article 5 or equipment tests shall be carried out in order to verify their conformity with the type as described in the EC-type-examination certificate and the relevant requirements of the Directive.

4.2.   The notified body shall affix or have affixed its identification number to each approved item of equipment and shall draw up a written certificate of conformity relating to the tests carried out.

4.3.   The manufacturer or his authorized representative shall ensure that he is able to supply the notified body's certificates of conformity on request.

ANNEX VI

MODULE: CONFORMITY TO TYPE

1.   This module describes that part of the procedure whereby the manufacturer or his authorized representative established within the Community ensures and declares that the equipment in question is in conformity with the type as described in the EC-type-examination certificate and satisfy the requirements of the Directive applicable to them. The manufacturer or his authorized representative established within the Community shall affix the CE marking to each piece of equipment and draw up a written declaration of conformity.

2.   The manufacturer shall take all measures necessary to ensure that the manufacturing process assures compliance of the manufactured equipment or protective systems with the type as described in the EC-type-examination certificate and with the relevant requirements of the Directive.

3.   The manufacturer or his authorized representative shall keep a copy of the declaration of conformity for a period ending at least 10 years after the last piece of equipment was manufactured. Where neither the manufacturer nor his authorized representative is established within the Community, the obligation to keep the technical documentation available shall be the responsibility of the person who places the equipment or protective system on the Community market.

For each piece of equipment manufactured, tests relating to the anti-explosive protection aspects of the product shall be carried out by the manufacturer or on his behalf. The tests shall be carried out under the responsibility of a notified body, chosen by the manufacturer.

On the responsibility of the notified body, the manufacturer shall affix the former's identification number during the manufacturing process.

ANNEX VII

MODULE: PRODUCT QUALITY ASSURANCE

1. This module describes the procedure whereby the manufacturer who satisfies the obligations of Section 2 ensures and declares that the equipment is in conformity with the type as described in the EC-type-examination certificate. The manufacturer or his authorized representative established within the Community shall affix the CE marking to each product and draw up a written declaration of conformity. The CE marking shall be accompanied by the identification number of the notified body responsible for surveillance as specified in Section 4.

2. The manufacturer shall operate an approved quality system for the final inspection and testing of equipment as specified in Section 3 below and shall be subject to surveillance as specified in Section 4 below.

3.   Quality system

3.1.   The manufacturer shall lodge an application for assessment of his quality system for the equipment and protective systems, with a notified body of his choice.

The application shall include:
— all relevant information for the product category envisaged;
— documentation on the quality system;
— technical documentation on the approved type and a copy of the EC-type-examination certificate.

3.2.   Under the quality system, each piece of equipment shall be examined and appropriate tests as set out in the relevant standard(s) referred to in Article 5 or equivalent tests shall be carried out in order to ensure its conformity with the relevant requirements of the Directive. All the elements, requirements and provisions adopted by the manufacturer shall be documented in a systematic and orderly manner in the form of written policies, procedures and instruments. This quality system documentation must permit a consistent interpretation of the quality programmes, plans, manuals and records.

It shall contain, in particular, an adequate description of:
— the quality objectives and the organizational structure, responsibilities and powers of the management with regard to product quality;
— the examinations and tests which will be carried out after manufacture;
— the means to monitor the effective operation of the quality system;
— quality records, such as inspection reports and test data, calibration data, reports on the qualifications of the personnel concerned, etc.

3.3.   The notified body shall assess the quality system to determine whether it satisfies the requirements referred to in Section 3.2. It shall presume conformity with these requirements in respect of quality systems which implement the relevant harmonized standard.

The auditing team shall have at least one member experienced as an assessor in the product technology concerned. The assessment procedure shall include an assessment visit to the manufacturer's premises.

The decision shall be notified to the manufacturer. The notification shall contain the conclusions of the examination and the reasoned assessment decision.

3.4.   The manufacturer shall undertake to discharge the obligations arising from the quality system as approved and to maintain it in an appropriate and efficient manner.

The manufacturer or his authorized representative shall inform the notified body which has approved the quality system of any intended updating of the quality system.

The notified body shall evaluate the modifications proposed and decide whether the modified quality system will still satisfy the requirements referred to in Section 3.2 or whether a re-assessment is required.

It shall notify its decision to the manufacturer. The notification shall contain the conclusions of the examination and the reasoned assessment decision.

4.   Surveillance under the responsibility of the notified body

4.1.   The purpose of surveillance is to ensure that the manufacturer duly fulfils the obligations arising out of the approved quality system.

4.2.   The manufacturer shall for inspection purposes allow the notified body access to the inspection, testing and storage premises and shall provide it with all necessary information, in particular:
— quality system documentation;
— technical documentation;
— quality records, such as inspection reports and test data, calibration data, reports on the qualifications of the personnel concerned, etc.

4.3.   The notified body shall periodically carry out audits to ensure that the manufacturer maintains and applies the quality system and shall provide an audit report to the manufacturer.

4.4.   Furthermore, the notified body may pay unexpected visits to the manufacturer. At the time of such visits, the notified body may carry out tests or arrange for tests to be carried out in order to check the proper functioning of the quality system, where necessary; it shall provide the manufacturer with a visit report and, if a test has been carried out, with a test report.

5.   The manufacturer shall, for a period ending at least 10 years after the last piece of equipment was manufactured, keep at the disposal of the national authorities:
— the documentation referred to in the third indent of Section 3.1;
— the updating referred to in the second paragraph of Section 3.4;
— the decisions and reports from the notified body which are referred to in Section 3.4, last paragraph, Section 4.3 and Section 4.4.

6.   Each notified body shall forward to the other notified bodies the relevant information concerning the quality system approvals issued and withdrawn.

———————

ANNEX VIII

MODULE: INTERNAL CONTROL OF PRODUCTION

1.   This module describes the procedure whereby the manufacturer or his authorized representative established within the Community, who carries out the obligations laid down in Section 2, ensures and declares that the equipment satisfy the requirements of the Directive applicable to it. The manufacturer or his authorized representative established within the Community shall affix the CE marking to each piece of equipment and draw up a written declaration of conformity.

2.   The manufacturer shall establish the technical documentation described in Section 3 and he or his authorized representative established within the Community shall keep it at the disposal of the relevant national authorities for inspection purposes for a period ending at least 10 years after the last piece of equipment was manufactured.

   Where neither the manufacturer nor his authorized representative is established within the Community, the obligation to keep the technical documentation available shall be the responsibility of the person who places the equipment on the Community market.

3.   Technical documentation shall enable the conformity of the equipment with the relevant requirements of the Directive to be assessed. It shall, to the extent necessary for such assessment, cover the design, manufacture and operation of the product. It shall contain:
   — a general description of the equipment,
   — conceptual design and manufacturing drawings and schemes of components, sub-assemblies, circuits, etc,
   — descriptions and explanations necessary for the understanding of said drawings and schemes and the operation of the equipment,
   — a list of the standards applied in full or in part, and descriptions of the solutions adopted to meet the safety aspects of the Directive where the standards have not been applied,
   — results of design calculations made, examinations carried out, etc,
   — test reports.

4.   The manufacturer or his authorized representative shall keep a copy of the declaration of conformity with the technical documentation.

5.   The manufacturer shall take all measures necessary to ensure that the manufacturing process guarantees compliance of the manufactured equipment with the technical documentation referred to in Section 2 and with the requirements of the Directive applicable to such equipment.

ANNEX IX

MODULE: UNIT VERIFICATION

1. This module describes the procedure whereby the manufacturer ensures and declares that the equipment or protective system which has been issued with the certificate referred to in Section 2 conforms to the requirements of the Directive which are applicable to it. The manufacturer or his authorized representative in the Community shall affix the CE marking to the equipment or protective system and draw up a declaration of conformity.

2. The notified body shall examine the individual equipment or protective system and carry out the appropriate tests as set out in the relevant standard(s) referred to in Article 5, or equivalent tests, to ensure its conformity with the relevant requirements of the Directive.

    The notified body shall affix, or cause to be affixed, its identification number on the approved equipment or protective system and shall draw up a certificate of conformity concerning the tests carried out.

3. The aim of the technical documentation is to enable conformity with the requirements of the Directive to be assessed and the design, manufacture and operation of the equipment or protective system to be understood.

    The documentation shall contain:
    — a general description of the product;
    — conceptual design and manufacturing drawings and layouts of components, sub-assemblies, circuits, etc.;
    — descriptions and explanations necessary for the understanding of said drawings and layouts and the operation of the equipment or protective system;
    — a list of the standards referred to in Article 5, applied in full or in part, and descriptions of the solutions adopted to meet the essential requirements of the Directive where the standards referred to in Article 5 have not been applied;
    — results of design calculations made, examinations carried out, etc.;
    — test reports.

ANNEX X

A.   CE Marking

The CE conformity marking shall consist of the initials "CE" taking the following form:

If the marking is reduced or enlarged, the proportions given in the above graduated drawing must be respected.

The various components of the CE marking must have substantially the same vertical dimension, which may not be less than 5 mm.

This minimum dimension may be waived for small-scale equipment, protective systems or devices referred to in Article 1 (2).

B. **Content of the EC declaration of conformity**

The EC declaration of conformity must contain the following elements:
— the name or identification mark and the address of the manufacturer or his authorized representative established within the Community;
— a description of the equipment, protective system, or device referred to in Article 1 (2);
— all relevant provisions fulfilled by the equipment, protective system, or device referred to in Article 1 (2);
— where appropriate, the name, identification number and address of the notified body and the number of the EC-type-examination certificate;
— where appropriate, reference to the harmonized standards;
— where appropriate, the standards and technical specifications which have been used;
— where appropriate, references to other Community Directives which have been applied;
— identification of the signatory who has been empowered to enter into commitments on behalf of the manufacturer or his authorized representative established within the Community.

ANNEX XI

MAXIMUM CRITERIA TO BE TAKEN INTO ACCOUNT BY MEMBER STATES FOR THE NOTIFICATION OF BODIES

1. The body, its director and the staff responsible for carrying out the verification tests shall not be the designer manufacturer, supplier or installer of equipment, protective systems, or devices referred to in Article 1 (2) which they inspect, nor the authorized representative of any of these parties. They shall become involved neither directly nor as authorized representatives in the design, construction, marketing or maintenance of the equipment, protective systems or devices referred to in Article 1 (2) in question. This does not preclude the possibility of exchanges of technical information between the manufacturer and the body.

2. The body and its inspection staff shall carry out the verification tests with the highest degree of professional integrity and technical competence and shall be free from all pressures and inducements, particularly financial, which may influence their judgement or the results of the inspection, especially from persons or groups of persons with an interest in the result of verifications.

3. The body shall have at its disposal the necessary staff and possess the necessary facilities to enable it to perform properly the administrative and technical tasks connected with verification; it shall also have access to the equipment required for special verification.

4. The staff responsible for inspection shall have:
   — sound technical and professional training;
   — satisfactory knowledge of the requirements of the tests which they carry out and adequate experience of such tests
   — the ability to draw up the certificates, records and reports required to authenticate the performance of the tests.

5. The impartiality of inspection staff shall be guaranteed. Their remuneration shall not depend on the number of tests carried out or on the results of such tests.

6. The body shall take out liability insurance unless its liability is assumed by the State in accordance with national law or the Member State itself is directly responsible for the tests.

7. The staff of the body shall be bound to observe professional secrecy with regard to all information gained in carrying out its tasks (except *vis-a-vis* the competent administrative authorities of the State in which its activities are carried out) under this Directive or any provision of national law giving effect to it.

―――――――――

THE IONIZING RADIATION DIRECTIVE

General note. This Directive was implemented in the UK by the Ionising Radiations (Outside Workers) Regulations 1993 (S.I. 1993 No. 2379) at p. 219 post. The Directive extends the protection of Directive 80/836 to workers who perform any activity in a controlled area (see Art. 2). Even if only temporarily employed, they are to be given broadly the same protections as permanent employees (Art. 4). Duties are imposed on both the person responsible for the controlled area (Art. 6) and "outside undertakings" (Art. 5).

COUNCIL DIRECTIVE

of 4 December 1990

on the operational protection of outside workers exposed to the risk of ionizing radiation during their activities in controlled areas

(90/641/Euratom)

THE COUNCIL OF THE EUROPEAN COMMUNITIES,

Having regard to the Treaty establishing the European Atomic Energy Community, and in particular Articles 31 and 32 thereof,

Having regard to the proposal from the Commission, submitted following consultation with a group of persons appointed by the Scientific and Technical Committee from among scientific experts in the Member States, as laid down in Article 31 of the Treaty,

Having regard to the opinion of the European Parliament,

Having regard to the opinion of the Economic and Social Committee,

Whereas, Article 2 (b) of the Treaty provides that the Community shall establish uniform safety standards to protect the health of workers and of the general public and ensure that they are applied in accordance with the procedures laid down in Chapter III of Title II of the Treaty;

Whereas, on 2 February 1959, the Council adopted Directives laying down the basic standards for the protection of the health of workers and of the general public against the dangers arising from ionizing radiations, as amended by Directives 80/836/Euratom and 84/467/Euratom;

Whereas Title VI of Directive 80/836/Euratom lays down the fundamental principles governing operational protection of exposed workers;

Whereas Article 40 (1) of that Directive provides that each Member State shall take all necessary measures to ensure the effective protection of exposed workers;

Whereas Article 20 and 23 of that Directive establish a classification of areas of work and categories of exposed workers according to the level of exposure;

Whereas the workers performing activities in a controlled area within the meaning of the said Articles 20 and 23 can belong to the personnel of the operator or be outside workers;

Whereas Article 3 of Directive 80/836/Euratom concerning the activities referred to in Article 2 of that Directive provides that they should be reported or subject to prior authorization in cases decided upon by each Member State;

Whereas outside workers are liable to be exposed to ionizing radiation in several controlled areas in succession in one and the same Member State or in different Member States; whereas these specific working conditions require an appropriate radiological monitoring system;

Whereas any radiological monitoring system for outside workers must provide protection equivalent to that offered the operator's established workers, by means of common provisions;

Whereas, pending the introduction of a uniform Community-wide system, account should also be taken of the radiological monitoring systems for outside workers which may exist in the Member States;

Whereas, to optimize the protection of outside workers, it is necessary to define clearly the obligations of outside undertakings and operators, without prejudice to the contribution that outside workers themselves have to make to their own protection;

Whereas the system for the radiological protection of outside workers also applies as far as practicable to the case of a self-employed worker with the status of outside undertaking,

HAS ADOPTED THIS DIRECTIVE:

TITLE I

Purpose and definitions

Article 1

The purpose of this Directive is to supplement Directive 80/836/Euratom thereby optimizing at Community level operational protection arrangements for outside workers performing activities in controlled areas.

Article 2

For the purposes of this Directive:
— "controlled area" means any area subject to special rules for the purposes of protection against ionizing radiation and to which access is controlled, as specified in Article 20 of Directive 80/836/Euratom;
— "operator" means any natural or legal person who under national law, is responsible for a controlled area in which an activity required to be reported under Article 3 of Directive 80/836/Euratom is carried on;
— "outside undertaking" means any natural or legal person, other than the operator, including members of his staff, performing an activity of any sort in a controlled area;

— "outside worker" means any worker of category A, as defined in Article 23 of Directive 80/836/Euratom, performing activities of any sort in a controlled area, whether employed temporarily or permanently by an outside undertaking, including trainees, apprentices and students within the meaning of Article 10 of that Directive, or whether he provides services as a self- employed worker;

— "radiological monitoring system" means measures to apply the arrangements set out in Directive 80/836/Euratom, and in particular in Title VI thereof, during the activities of outside workers.

— "activities carried out by a worker" means any service or services provided by an outside worker in a controlled area for which an operator is responsible.

TITLE II

Obligations of Member States' competent authorities

Article 3

Each Member State shall make the performance of the activities referred to in Article 2 of Directive 30/836/Euratom by outside undertakings subject to reporting or prior authorization as laid down in accordance with Title II of the aforementioned Directive, in particular Article 3 thereof.

Article 4

1.   Each Member State shall ensure that the radiological monitoring system affords outside workers equivalent protection to that for workers employed on a permanent basis by the operator.

2.   Pending the establishment, at Community level, of a uniform system for the radiological protection of outside workers, such as a computer network, recourse shall be had:
(a)   on a transitional basis, in accordance with the common provisions set out in Annex I, to
      — a centralized national network, or
      — the issuing of an individual radiological monitoring document to every outside worker, in which case the common provisions of Annex II shall also apply;
(b)   in the case of cross-frontier outside workers, and until the date of establishment of a system within the meaning of paragraph 2, to the individual document referred to in (a).

TITLE III

Obligations of outside undertakings and operators

Article 5

Outside undertakings shall, either directly or through contractual agreements with the operators, ensure the radiological protection of their workers in accordance with the relevant provisions of Titles III to VI of Directive 80/836/Euratom, and in particular:
(a)   ensure compliance with the general principles and the limitation of doses referred to in Articles 6 to 11 thereof;
(b)   provide the information and training in the field of radiation protection referred to in Article 24 thereof;

(c) guarantee that their workers are subject to assessment of exposure and medical surveillance under the conditions laid down in Articles 26 and 28 to 38 thereof;

(d) ensure that the radiological data of the individual exposure monitoring of each of their workers within the meaning of Annex I, part II to this Directive are kept up to date in the networks and individual documents referred to in Article 4 (2).

Article 6

1. The operator of a controlled area in which outside workers perform activities shall be responsible, either directly or through contractual agreements, for the operational aspects of their radiological protection which are directly related to the nature of the controlled area and of the activities.

2. In particular, for each outside worker performing activities in a controlled area, the operator must:

(a) check that the worker concerned has been passed as medically fit for the activities to be assigned to him;

(b) ensure that, in addition to the basic training in radiation protection referred to in Article 5 (l) (b), he has received specific training in connection with the characteristics of both the controlled area and the activities;

(c) ensure that he has been issued with the necessary personal protective equipment;

(d) also ensure that he receives individual exposure monitoring appropriate to the nature of the activities, and any operational dosimetric monitoring that may be necessary;

(e) ensure compliance with the general principles and limitation of doses referred to in Articles 6 to 11 of Directive 80/836/Euratom;

(f) ensure or take all appropriate steps to ensure that after every activity the radiological data of individual exposure monitoring of each outside worker within the meaning of Annex I, Part III, are recorded.

TITLE IV

Obligations of outside workers

Article 7

Every outside worker shall be obliged to make his own contribution as far as practicable towards the protection that the radiological monitoring system referred to in Article 4 is intended to afford him.

TITLE V

Final Provisions

Article 8

1. Member States shall bring into force not later than 31 December 1993, the laws, regulations and administrative provisions necessary to comply with this Directive. They shall forthwith inform the Commission thereof.

2. When Member States adopt the measures referred to in paragraph 1, they shall contain a reference to this Directive or shall be accompanied by such reference on the occasion of their official publication. The methods of making such a reference shall be laid down by the Member States.

3.   Member States shall communicate to the Commission the main provisions of domestic law which they adopt in the field governed by this Directive.

Article 9

This Directive is addressed to the Member States.

Done at Brussels, 4 December 1990.

For the Council

The President

G DE MICHELIS

_____

ANNEX I

PROVISIONS COMMON TO THE NETWORKS AND INDIVIDUAL DOCUMENTS REFERRED TO IN ARTICLE 4 (2)

PART I

1.   Any radiological monitoring system of the Member States for outside workers must comprise the following three sections:
— particulars concerning the outside workers' identity;
— particulars to be supplied before the start of any activity;
— particulars to be supplied after the end of any activity.

2.   The competent authorities of the Member States shall take the measures necessary to prevent any forgery or misuse of, or illegal tampering with, the radiological monitoring system.

3.   Data on the outside worker's identity must also include the worker's sex and date of birth.

PART II

Before the start of any activity, the data to be supplied via the radiological monitoring system to the operator or his approved medical practitioner by the outside undertaking or an authority empowered to that end must be as follows:
— the name and address of the outside undertaking;
— the medical classification of the outside worker in accordance with Article 35 of Directive 80/836/Euratom;
— the date of the last periodic health review;
— the results of the outside worker's individual exposure monitoring.

PART III

The data which the operator must record or have recorded by the authority

empowered to that end in the radiological monitoring system after the end of any activity must be as follows:
— the period covered by the activity;
— an estimate of any effective dose received by the outside worker;
— in the event of non-uniform exposure, an estimate of the dose-equivalent in the different parts of the body;
— in the event of internal contamination, an estimate of the activity taken in or the committed dose.

———————

ANNEX II

PROVISIONS ADDITIONAL TO THOSE OF ANNEX I CONCERNING THE INDIVIDUAL RADIOLOGICAL MONITORING DOCUMENT

1.   The individual radiological monitoring document issued by the Member States' competent authorities for outside workers shall be a non-transferable document.

2.   Pursuant to Annex I, Part 1(2), individual documents shall be issued by the Member States' competent authorities, which shall give each individual document an identification number.

———————

THE WORKING TIME DIRECTIVE

General note. Passed under Art. 118a of the Treaty, this Directive seeks to regulate the organisation of work (Art. 13), as well as ensuring that workers have both daily and weekly rest breaks (Arts. 3–5), and setting a maximum *average* weekly working time of 48 hours (Art. 6). Further protections apply to night workers. Not satisfied with the permitted derogations (see Art. 17), the UK government has stated that it will challenge the Directives as being *ultra vires* Art. 118a, because it is not concerned with health and safety. Subject to further permissible relaxations of the minimum standards, the Directive should be implemented by 23 November 1996 (Art. 18). No regulations are likely to be introduced in the UK until the European Court of Justice has ruled on the UK appeal.

Two cases relating to EEC Council Regulations 3820/85 and 3821/85 on Drivers' Hours may give guidance as to how the European Court of Justice will approach terms in the Working Time Directive. In *Criminal Proceedings against Michielsen and Geybels Transport Service NV* C–394/92 [1995] IRLR 171, the Court clarified the meaning of the terms 'daily working period' and 'period of work': the 'daily working period' was the whole working day, including breaks between work (cf 'working day' in Art. 4). In *Prime v Hosking* [1995] IRLR 143, [1995] RTR 189, it was held by the Divisional Court that time spent working for an employer after finishing driving was part of driver's 'daily working period'.

COUNCIL DIRECTIVE

of 23 November 1993

concerning certain aspects of the organization of working time

(93/104/EC)

THE COUNCIL OF THE EUROPEAN UNION,

Having regard to the Treaty establishing the European Community, and in particular Article 118a thereof,

Having regard to the proposal from the Commission,

In cooperation with the European Parliament,

Having regard to the opinion of the Economic and Social Committee,

Whereas Article 118a of the Treaty provides that the Council shall adopt, by means of directives, minimum requirements for encouraging improvements, especially in the working environment, to ensure a better level of protection of the safety and health of workers;

Whereas, under the terms of that Article, those directives are to avoid imposing administrative, financial and legal constraints in a way which would hold back the creation and development of small and medium-sized undertakings;

Whereas the provisions of Council Directive 89/391/EEC of 12 June 1989 on the introduction of measures to encourage improvements in the safety and health of workers at work are fully applicable to the areas covered by this Directive without prejudice to more stringent and/or specific provisions contained therein;

Whereas the Community Charter of the Fundamental Social Rights of Workers, adopted at the meeting of the European Council held at Strasbourg on 9 December 1989 by the Heads of State or of Government of 11 Member States, and in particular points 7, first subparagraph, 8 and 19, first subparagraph, thereof, declared that:

> "7. The completion of the internal market must lead to an improvement in the living and working conditions of workers in the European Community. This process must result from an approximation of these conditions while the improvement is being maintained, as regards in particular the duration and organization of working time and forms of employment other than open-ended contracts, such as fixed-term contracts, part-time working, temporary work and seasonal work.
>
> 8.   Every worker in the European Community shall have a right to a weekly rest period and to annual paid leave, the duration of which must be progressively harmonized in accordance with national practices.
>
> 19. Every worker must enjoy satisfactory health and safety conditions in his working environment. Appropriate measures must be taken in order to achieve further harmonization of conditions in this area while maintaining the improvements made."

Whereas the improvement of workers' safety, hygiene and health at work is an objective which should not be subordinated to purely economic considerations;

Whereas this Directive is a practical contribution towards creating the social dimension of the internal market;

Whereas laying down minimum requirements with regard to the organization of working time is likely to improve the working conditions of workers in the Community;

Whereas, in order to ensure the safety and health of Community workers, the latter must be granted minimum daily, weekly and annual periods of rest and adequate breaks; whereas it is also necessary in this context to place a maximum limit on weekly working hours;

Whereas account should be taken of the principles of the International Labour Organization with regard to the organization of working time, including those relating to night work;

Whereas, with respect to the weekly rest period, due account should be taken of the diversity of cultural, ethnic, religious and other factors in the Member States;

whereas, in particular, it is ultimately for each Member State to decide whether Sunday should be included in the weekly-rest period, and if so to what extent;

Whereas research has shown that the human body is more sensitive at night to environmental disturbances and also to certain burdensome forms of work organization and that long periods of night work can be detrimental to the health of workers and can endanger safety at the workplace;

Whereas there is a need to limit the duration of periods of night work, including overtime, and to provide for employers who regularly use night workers to bring this information to the attention of the competent authorities if they so request;

Whereas it is important that night workers should be entitled to a free health assessment prior to their assignment and thereafter at regular intervals and that whenever possible they should be transferred to day work for which they are suited if they suffer from health problems;

Whereas the situation of night and shift workers requires that the level of safety and health protection should be adapted to the nature of their work and that the organization and functioning of protection and prevention services and resources should be efficient;

Whereas specific working conditions may have detrimental effects on the safety and health of workers; whereas the organization of work according to a certain pattern must take account of the general principle of adapting work to the worker;

Whereas, given the specific nature of the work concerned, it may be necessary to adopt separate measures with regard to the organization of working time in certain sectors or activities which are excluded from the scope of this Directive;

Whereas, in view of the question likely to be raised by the organization of working time within an undertaking, it appears desirable to provide for flexibility in the application of certain provisions of this Directive, whilst ensuring compliance with the principles of protecting the safety and health of workers;

Whereas it is necessary to provide that certain provisions may be subject to derogations implemented, according to the case, by the Member States or the two sides of industry; whereas, as a general rule, in the event of a derogation, the workers concerned must be given equivalent compensatory rest periods,

HAS ADOPTED THIS DIRECTIVE:

SECTION I

SCOPE AND DEFINITIONS

Article 1

Purpose and scope

1.   This Directive lays down minimum safety and health requirements for the organization of working time.

2.   This Directive applies to:
(a)   minimum periods of daily rest, weekly rest and annual leave, to breaks and maximum weekly working time; and
(b)   certain aspects of night work, shift work and patterns of work.

3.   This Directive shall apply to all sectors of activity, both public and private, within the meaning of Article 2 of Directive 89/391/EEC, without prejudice to Article 17 of this Directive, with the exception of air, rail, road, sea, inland waterway and lake transport, sea fishing, other work at sea and the activities of doctors in training;

4.   The provisions of Directive 89/391/EEC are fully applicable to the matters referred to in paragraph 2, without prejudice to more stringent and/or specific provisions contained in this Directive.

Article 2

Definitions

For the purposes of this Directive, the following definitions shall apply:

1.   *working time* shall mean any period during which the worker is working, at the employer's disposal and carrying out his activity or duties, in accordance with national laws and/or practice;

2.   *rest period* shall mean any period which is not working time;

3.   *night time* shall mean any period of not less than seven hours, as defined by national law, and which must include in any case the period between midnight and 5 am.

4.   *night worker* shall mean:
(a)   on the one hand, any worker, who, during night time, works at least three hours of his daily working time as a normal course; and
(b)   on the other hand, any worker who is likely during night time to work a certain proportion of his annual working time, as defined at the choice of the Member State concerned:
    (i)   by national legislation, following consultation with the two sides of industry; or
    (ii) by collective agreements or agreements concluded between the two sides of industry at national or regional level;

5.   *shift work* shall mean any method of organizing work in shifts whereby workers succeed each other at the same work stations according to a certain pattern, including a rotating pattern, and which may be continuous or discontinuous, entailing the need for workers to work at different times over a given period of days or weeks;

6.   *shift worker* shall mean any worker whose work schedule is part of shift work.

SECTION II

MINIMUM REST PERIODS—OTHER ASPECTS OF THE ORGANIZATION OF WORKING TIME

Article 3

Daily rest

Member States shall take the measures necessary to ensure that every worker is entitled to a minimum daily rest period of 11 consecutive hours per 24-hour period.

Article 4

Breaks

Member States shall take the measures necessary to ensure that, where the working day is longer than six hours, every worker is entitled to a rest break, the details of which, including duration and the terms on which it is granted, shall be laid down in collective agreements or agreements between the two sides of industry or, failing that, by national legislation.

Article 5

Weekly rest period

Member States shall take the measures necessary to ensure that, per each seven-day period, every worker is entitled to a minimum uninterrupted rest period of 24 hours' plus the 11 hours daily rest referred to in Article 3.

The minimum rest period referred to in the first subparagraph shall in principle include Sunday.

If objective, technical or work organization conditions so justify, a minimum rest period of 24 hours may be applied.

Article 6

Maximum weekly working time

Member States shall take the measures necessary to ensure that, in keeping with the need to protect the safety and health of workers:
1. the period of weekly working time is limited by means of laws, regulations or administrative provisions or by collective agreements or agreements between the two sides of industry;
2. the average working time for each seven-day period, including overtime, does not exceed 48 hours.

Article 7

Annual leave

1.   Member States shall take the measures necessary to ensure that every worker is entitled to paid annual leave of at least four weeks in accordance with the conditions for entitlement to, and granting of, such leave laid down by national legislation and/or practice.

2.   The minimum period of paid annual leave may not be replaced by an allowance in lieu, except where the employment relationship is terminated.

SECTION III

NIGHT WORK—SHIFT WORK—PATTERNS OF WORK

Article 8

Length of night work

Member States shall take the measures necessary to ensure that:
1. normal hours of work for night workers do not exceed an average of eight hours in any 24-hour period;
2. night workers whose work involves special hazards or heavy physical or mental strain do not work more than eight hours in any period of 24 hours during which they perform night work.

For the purposes of the aforementioned, work involving special hazards or heavy physical or mental strain shall be defined by national legislation and/or practice or by collective agreements or agreements concluded between the two sides of industry, taking account of the specific effects and hazards of night work.

Article 9

Health assessment and transfer of night workers to day work

1.   Member States shall take the measures necessary to ensure that:
(a) night workers are entitled to a free health assessment before their assignment and thereafter at regular intervals;
(b) night workers suffering from health problems recognized as being connected with the fact that they perform night work are transferred whenever possible to day work to which they are suited.

2.   The free health assessment referred to in paragraph 1 (a) must comply with medical confidentiality.

3.   The free health assessment referred to in paragraph 1 (a) may be conducted within the national health system.

Article 10

Guarantees for night-time working

Member States may make the work of certain categories of night workers subject to certain guarantees, under conditions laid down by national legislation and/or practice, in the case of workers who incur risks to their safety or health linked to night-time working.

Article 11

Notification of regular use of night workers

Member States shall take the measures necessary to ensure that an employer who regularly uses night workers brings this information to the attention of the competent authorities if they so request.

Article 12

Safety and health protection

Member States shall take the measures necessary to ensure that:
1.   night workers and shift workers have safety and health protection appropriate to the nature of their work;
2.   appropriate protection and prevention services or facilities with regard to the safety and health of night workers and shift workers are equivalent to those applicable to other workers and are available at all times.

Article 13

Pattern of work

Member States shall take the measures necessary to ensure that an employer who intends to organize work according to a certain pattern takes account of the general principle of adapting work to the worker, with a view, in particular, to alleviating monotonous work and work at a predetermined work-rate, depending on the type of activity, and of safety and health requirements, especially as regards breaks during working time.

SECTION IV

MISCELLANEOUS PROVISIONS

Article 14

More specific Community provisions

The provisions of this Directive shall not apply where other Community instruments contain more specific requirements concerning certain occupations or occupational activities.

Article 15

More favourable provisions

This Directive shall not affect Member States' right to apply or introduce laws, regulations or administrative provisions more favourable to the protection of the safety and health of workers or to facilitate or permit the application of collective agreements or agreements concluded between the two sides of industry which are more favourable to the protection of the safety and health of workers.

Article 16

Reference periods

Member States may lay down:
1. for the application of Article 5 (weekly rest period), a reference period not exceeding 14 days;
2. for the application of Article 6 (maximum weekly working time), a reference period not exceeding four months.
   The periods of paid annual leave, granted in accordance with Article 7, and the periods of sick leave shall not be included or shall be neutral in the calculation of the average;
3. for the application of Article 8 (length of night work), a reference period defined after consultation of the two sides of industry or by collective agreements or agreements concluded between the two sides of industry at national or regional level.
   If the minimum weekly rest period of 24 hours required by Article 5 falls within that reference period, it shall not be included in the calculation of the average.

Article 17

Derogations

1. With due regard for the general principles of the protection of the safety and health of workers, Member States may derogate from Article 3, 4, 5, 6, 8 or 16 when, on account of the specific characteristics of the activity concerned, the duration of the working time is not measured and/or predetermined or can be determined by the workers themselves, and particularly in the case of:
(a) managing executives or other persons with autonomous decision-taking powers;
(b) family workers; or
(c) workers officiating at religious ceremonies in churches and religious communities.

2. Derogations may be adopted by means of laws, regulations or administrative provisions or by means of collective agreements or agreements between the two sides of industry provided that the workers concerned are afforded equivalent periods of compensatory rest or that, in exceptional cases in which it is not possible, for objective reasons, to grant such equivalent periods of compensatory rest, the workers concerned are afforded appropriate protection:

2.1. from Articles 3, 4, 5, 8 and 16:
(a) in the case of activities where the worker's place of work and his place of residence are distant from one another or where the worker's different places of work are distant from one another;
(b) in the case of security and surveillance activities requiring a permanent presence in order to protect property and persons, particularly security guards and caretakers or security firms;

(c)   in the case of activities involving the need for continuity of service or production, particularly:
  (i)   services relating to the reception, treatment and/or care provided by hospitals or similar establishments, residential institutions and prisons;
  (ii)   dock or airport workers;
  (iii)   press, radio, television, cinematographic production, postal and telecommunications services, ambulance, fire and civil protection services;
  (iv)   gas, water and electricity production, transmission and distribution, household refuse collection and incineration plants;
  (v)   industries in which work cannot be interrupted on technical grounds;
  (vi)   research and development activities;
  (vii)   agriculture;
(d)   where there is a foreseeable surge of activity, particularly in:
  (i)   agriculture;
  (ii)   tourism;
  (iii)   postal services;

2.2. from Articles 3, 4, 5, 8 and 16:
(a)   in the circumstances described in Article 5 (4) of Directive 89/391/EEC;
(b)   in cases of accident or imminent risk of accident;

2.3. from Articles 3 and 5:
(a)   in the case of shift work activities, each time the worker changes shift and cannot take daily and/or weekly rest periods between the end of one shift and the start of the next one;
(b)   in the case of activities involving periods of work split up over the day, particularly those of cleaning staff.

3.   Derogations may be made from Articles 3, 4, 5, 8 and 16 by means of collective agreements or agreements concluded between the two sides of industry at national or regional level or, in conformity with the rules laid down by them, by means of collective agreements or agreements concluded between the two sides of industry at a lower level.

Member States in which there is no statutory system ensuring the conclusion of collective agreements or agreements concluded between the two sides of industry at national or regional level, on the matters covered by this Directive, or those Member States in which there is a specific legislative framework for this purpose and within the limits thereof, may, in accordance with national legislation and/or practice, allow derogations from Articles 3, 4, 5, 8 and 16 by way of collective agreements or agreements concluded between the two sides of industry at the appropriate collective level.

The derogations provided for in the first and second subparagraphs shall be allowed on condition that equivalent compensating rest periods are granted to the workers concerned or, in exceptional cases where it is not possible for objective reasons to grant such periods, the workers concerned are afforded appropriate protection.

Member States may lay down rules:
—   for the application of this paragraph by the two sides of industry, and
—   for the extension of the provisions of collective agreements or agreements concluded in conformity with this paragraph to other workers in accordance with national legislation and/or practice.

4. The option to derogate from point 2 of Article 16, provided in paragraph 2, points 2.1. and 2.2. and in paragraph 3 of this Article, may not result in the establishment of a reference period exceeding fix months.

However, Member States shall have the option, subject to compliance with the general principles relating to the protection of the safety and health of workers, of allowing, for objective or technical reasons or reasons concerning the organization of work, collective agreements or agreements concluded between the two sides of industry to set reference periods in no event exceeding 12 months.

Before the expiry of a period of seven years from the date referred to in Article 18 (1) (a), the Council shall, on the basis of a Commission proposal accompanied by an appraisal report, re-examine the provisions of this paragraph and decide what action to take.

Article 18

Final provisions

1. (a) Member States shall adopt the laws, regulations and administrative provisions necessary to comply with this Directive by 23 November 1996, or shall ensure by that date that the two sides of industry establish the necessary measures by agreement, with Member States being obliged to take any necessary steps to enable them to guarantee at all times that the provisions laid down by this Directive are fulfilled.

   (b) (i) However, a Member State shall have the option not to apply Article 6, while respecting the general principles of the protection of the safety and health of workers, and provided it takes the necessary measures to ensure that:
   — no employer requires a worker to work more than 48 hours over a seven-day period, calculated as an average for the reference period referred to in point 2 of Article 16, unless he has first obtained the worker's agreement to perform such work,
   — no worker is subjected to any detriment by his employer because he is not willing to give his agreement to perform such work,
   — the employer keeps up-to-date records of all workers who carry out such work,
   — the records are placed at the disposal of the competent authorities, which may, for reasons connected with the safety and/or health of workers, prohibit or restrict the possibility of exceeding the maximum weekly working hours,
   — the employer provides the competent authorities at their request with information on cases in which agreement has been given by workers to perform work exceeding 48 hours over a period of seven days, calculated as an average for the reference period referred to in point 2 of Article 16.
   Before the expiry of a period of seven years from the date referred to in (a), the Council shall, on the basis of a Commission proposal accompanied by an appraisal report, re-examine the provisions of this point (i) and decide on what action to take.

   (ii) Similarly, Member States shall have the option, as regards the application of Article 7, of making use of a transitional period of not more than three years from the date referred to in (a), provided that during that transitional period:

- every worker receives three weeks' paid annual leave in accordance with the conditions for the entitlement to, and granting of, such leave laid down by national legislation and/or practice, and
- the three-week period of paid annual leave may not be replaced by an allowance in lieu, except where the employment relationship is terminated.

(c)   Member states shall forthwith inform the Commission thereof.

2.   When Member States adopt the measures referred to in paragraph 1, they shall contain a reference to this Directive or shall be accompanied by such reference on the occasion of their official publication. The methods of making such a reference shall be laid down by the Member states.

3.   Without prejudice to the right of Member States to develop, in the light of changing circumstances, different legislative, regulatory or contractual provisions in the field of working time, as long as the minimum requirements provided for in this Directive are complied with, implementation of this Directive shall not constitute valid grounds for reducing the general level of protection afforded to workers.

4.   Member States shall communicate to the Commission the texts of the provisions of national law already adopted or being adopted in the field governed by this Directive.

5.   Member States shall report to the Commission every five years on the practical implementation of the provisions of this Directive, indicating the viewpoints of the two sides of industry.

The Commission shall inform the European Parliament, the Council, the Economic and Social Committee and the Advisory Committee on Safety, Hygiene and Health Protection at Work thereof.

6.   Every five years the Commission shall submit to the European Parliament, the Council and the Economic and Social Committee a report on the application of this Directive taking into account paragraphs 1, 2, 3, 4 and 5.

Article 19

This Directive is addressed to the Member States.

Done at Brussels, 23 November 1993.

For the Council

The President

M. SMET

THE PROTECTION OF YOUNG PEOPLE AT WORK DIRECTIVE

General note. This Directive should be implemented in the UK by 22 June 1996, although the implementation of Arts. 8 (1) (b), (2), 9 (1) (b), (2) may be delayed for up to four years (Art. 17).

COUNCIL DIRECTIVE 94/33/EC

of 22 June 1994

on the protection of young people at work

THE COUNCIL OF THE EUROPEAN UNION,

Having regard to the Treaty establishing the European Community, and in particular Article 118a thereof,

Having regard to the proposal from the Commission,

Having regard to the opinion of the Economic and Social Committee,

Acting in accordance with the procedure referred to in Article 189c of the Treaty,

Whereas Article 118a of the Treaty provides that the Council shall adopt, by means of directives, minimum requirements to encourage improvements, especially in the working environment, as regards the health and safety of workers;

Whereas, under that Article, such directives must avoid imposing administrative, financial and legal constraints in a way which would hold back the creation and development of small and medium-sized undertakings;

Whereas points 20 and 22 of the Community Charter of the Fundamental Social Rights of Workers, adopted by the European Council in Strasbourg on 9 December 1989, state that:

> "20. Without prejudice to such rules as may be more favourable to young people, in particular those ensuring their preparation for work through vocational training, and subject to derogations limited to certain light work, the minimum employment age must not be lower than the minimum school-leaving age and, in any case, not lower than 15 years;
>
> 22. Appropriate measures must be taken to adjust labour regulations applicable to young workers so that their specific development and vocational training and access to employment needs are met.
>
> The duration of work must, in particular, be limited—without it being possible to circumvent this limitation through recourse to overtime—and night work prohibited in the case of workers of under eighteen years of age, save in the case of certain jobs laid down in national legislation or regulations.";

Whereas account should be taken of the principles of the International Labour

Organization regarding the protection of young people at work, including those relating to the minimum age for access to employment or work;

Whereas, in this Resolution on child labour, the European Parliament summarized the various aspects of work by young people and stressed its effects on their health, safety and physical and intellectual development, and pointed to the need to adopt a Directive harmonizing national legislation in the field;

Whereas Article 15 of Council Directive 89/391/EEC of 12 June 1989 on the introduction of measures to encourage improvements in the safety and health of workers at work provides that particularly sensitive risk groups must be protected against the dangers which specifically affect them;

Whereas children and adolescents must be considered specific risk groups, and measures must be taken with regard to their safety and health;

Whereas the vulnerability of children calls for Member States to prohibit their employment and ensure that the minimum working or employment age is not lower than the minimum age at which compulsory schooling as imposed by national law ends or 15 years in any event; whereas derogations from the prohibition on child labour may be admitted only in special cases and under the conditions stipulated in this Directive; whereas, under no circumstances, may such derogations be detrimental to regular school attendance or prevent children benefiting fully from their education;

Whereas, in view of the nature of the transition from childhood to adult life, work by adolescents should be strictly regulated and protected;

Whereas every employer should guarantee young people working conditions appropriate to their age;

Whereas employers should implement the measures necessary to protect the safety and health of young people on the basis on an assessment of work-related hazards to the young;

Whereas Member States should protect young people against any specific risks arising from their lack of experience, absence of awareness of existing or potential risks, or from their immaturity;

Whereas Member States should therefore prohibit the employment of young people for the work specified by this Directive;

Whereas the adoption of specific minimal requirements in respect of the organization of working time is likely to improve working conditions for young people;

Whereas the maximum working time of young people should be strictly limited and night work by young people should be prohibited, with the exception of certain jobs specified by national legislation or rules;

Whereas Member States should take the appropriate measures to ensure that the working time of adolescents receiving school education does not adversely affect their ability to benefit from that education;

Whereas time spent on training by young persons working under a theoretical and/or practical combined work/training scheme or an in-plant work-experience should be counted as working time;

Whereas, in order to ensure the safety and health of young people, the latter should be granted minimum daily, weekly and annual periods of rest and adequate breaks;

Whereas, with respect to the weekly rest period, due account should be taken of the diversity of cultural ethnic, religious and other factors prevailing in the Member States; whereas in particular, it is ultimately for each Member State to decide whether Sunday should be included in the weekly rest period, and if so to what extent;

Whereas appropriate work experience may contribute to the aim of preparing young people for adult working and social life, provided it is ensured that any harm to their safety, health and development is avoided;

Whereas, although derogations from the bans and limitations imposed by this Directive would appear indispensable for certain activities or particular situations, applications thereof must not prejudice the principles underlying the established protection system;

Whereas this Directive constitutes a tangible step towards developing the social dimension of the internal market;

Whereas the application in practice of the system of protection laid down by this Directive will require that Member States implement a system of effective and proportionate measures;

Whereas the implementation of some provisions of this Directive poses particular problems for one Member State with regard to its system of protection for young people at work; whereas that Member State should therefore be allowed to refrain from implementing the relevant provisions for a suitable period,

HAS ADOPTED THIS DIRECTIVE:

SECTION I

Article 1

Purpose

1. Member States shall take the necessary measures to prohibit work by children.

They shall ensure, under the conditions laid down by this Directive, that the minimum working or employment age is not lower than the minimum age at which compulsory full-time schooling as imposed by national law ends or 15 years in any event.

2. Member States ensure that work by adolescents is strictly regulated and protected under the conditions laid down in this Directive.

3. Member States shall ensure in general that employers guarantee that young people have working conditions which suit their age.

They shall ensure that young people are protected against economic exploitation and against any work likely to harm their safety, health or physical, mental, moral or social development or to jeopardize their education.

Article 2

Scope

1. This Directive shall apply to any person under 18 years of age having an employment contract or an employment relationship defined by the law in force in a Member State and/or governed by the law in force in a Member State.

2.   Member States may make legislative or regulatory provision for this Directive not to apply, within the limits and under the conditions which they set by legislative or regulatory provision, to occasional work or short-term work involving:
(a)   domestic service in a private household, or
(b)   work regarded as not being harmful, damaging or dangerous to young people in a family undertaking.

Article 3

Definitions

For the purposes of this Directive:
(a)   "young person" shall mean any person under 18 years of age referred to in Article 2 (1);
(b)   "child" shall mean any young person of less than 15 years of age or who is still subject to compulsory full-time schooling under national law;
(c)   "adolescent" shall mean any young person of at least 15 years of age but less than 18 years of age who is no longer subject to compulsory full-time schooling under national law;
(d)   "light work" shall mean all work which, on account of the inherent nature of the tasks which it involves and the particular conditions under which they are performed:
    (i)   is not likely to be harmful to the safety, health or development of children, and
    (ii)   is not such as to be harmful to their attendance at school, their participation in vocational guidance or training programmes approved by the competent authority or their capacity to benefit from the instruction received;
(e)   "working time" shall mean any period during which the young person is at work, at the employer's disposal and carrying out his activity or duties in accordance with national legislation and/or practice;
(f)   "rest period" shall mean any period which is not working time.

Article 4

Prohibition of work by children

1.   Member States shall adopt the measures necessary to prohibit work by children.

2.   Taking into account the objectives set out in Article 1, Member States may make legislative or regulatory provision for the prohibition of work by children not to apply to:
(a)   children pursuing the activities set out in Article 5;
(b)   children of at least 14 years of age working under a combined work/training scheme or an in-plant work-experience scheme, provided that such work is done in accordance with the conditions laid down by the competent authority;
(c)   children of at least 14 years of age performing light work other than that covered by Article 5; light work other than that covered by Article 5 may, however, be performed by children of 13 years of age for a limited number of hours per week in the case of categories of work determined by national legislation.

3.   Member States that make use of the opinion referred to in paragraph 2 (c) shall determine, subject to the provisions of this Directive, the working conditions relating to the light work in question.

Article 5

Cultural or similar activities

1.   The employment of children for the purposes of performance in cultural, artistic, sports or advertising activities shall be subject to prior authorization to be given by the competent authority in individual cases.

2.   Member States shall by legislative or regulatory provision lay down the working conditions for children in the cases referred to in paragraph 1 and the details of the prior authorization procedure, on condition that the activities:
(i)   are not likely to be harmful to the safety, health or development of children, and
(ii) are not such as to be harmful to their attendance at school, their participation in vocational guidance or training programmes approved by the competent authority or their capacity to benefit from the instruction received.

3.   By way of derogation from the procedure laid down in paragraph 1, in the case of children of at least 13 years of age, Member States may authorize, by legislative or regulatory provision, in accordance with conditions which they shall determine, the employment of children for the purposes of performance in cultural, artistic, sports or advertising activities.

4.   The Member States which have a specific authorization system for modelling agencies with regard to the activities of children may retain that system.

SECTION II

Article 6

General obligations on employers

1.   Without prejudice to Article 4 (1), the employer shall adopt the measures necessary to protect the safety and health of young people, taking particular account of the specific risks referred to in Article 7 (1).

2.   The employer shall implement the measures provided for in paragraph 1 on the basis of an assessment of the hazards to young people in connection with their work.

The assessment must be made before young people begin work and when there is any major change in working conditions and must pay particular attention to the following points:
(a)   the fitting-out and layout of the workplace and the workstation;
(b)   the nature, degree and duration of exposure to physical, biological and chemical agents;
(c)   the form, range and use of work equipment, in particular agents, machines, apparatus and devices, and the way in which they are handled;
(d)   the arrangement of work processes and operations and the way in which these are combined (organization of work);
(e)   the level of training and instruction given to young people.

Where this assessment shows that there is a risk to the safety, the physical or mental health or development of young people, an appropriate free assessment and monitoring of their health shall be provided at regular intervals without prejudice to Directive 89/391/EEC.

The free health assessment and monitoring may form part of a national health system.

3. The employer shall inform young people of possible risks and of all measures adopted concerning their safety and health.

Furthermore, he shall inform the legal representatives of children of possible risks and of all measures adopted concerning children's safety and health.

4. The employer shall involve the protective and preventive services referred to in Article 7 of Directive 89/391/EEC in the planning, implementation and monitoring of the safety and health conditions applicable to young people.

Article 7

Vulnerability of young people—Prohibition of work

1. Member States shall ensure that young people are protected from any specific risks to their safety, health and development which are a consequence of their lack of experience, of absence of awareness of existing or potential risks or of the fact that young people have not yet fully matured.

2. Without prejudice to Article 4 (1), Member States shall to this end prohibit the employment of young people for:
(a) work which is objectively beyond their physical or psychological capacity;
(b) work involving harmful exposure to agents which are toxic, carcinogenic, cause heritable genetic damage, or harm to the unborn child or which in any other way chronically affect human health;
(c) work involving harmful exposure to radiation
(d) work involving the risk of accidents which it may be assumed cannot be recognized or avoided by young persons owing to their insufficient attention to safety or lack of experience or training; or
(e) work in which there is a risk to health from extreme cold or heat, or from noise or vibration.

Work which is likely to entail specific risks for young people within the meaning of paragraph 1 includes:
— work involving harmful exposure, to the physical, biological and chemical agents referred to in point I of the Annex, and
— processes and work referred to in point II of the Annex.

3. Member States may, by legislative or regulatory provision, authorize derogations from paragraph 2 in the case of adolescents where such derogations are indispensable for their vocational training, provided that protection of their safety and health is ensured by the fact that the work is performed under the supervision of a competent person within the meaning of Article 7 of Directive 89/391/EEC and provided that the protection afforded by that Directive is guaranteed.

SECTION III

Article 8

Working time

1. Member States which make use of the option in Article 4 (2) (b) or (c) shall adopt the measures necessary to limit the working time of children to:
(a) eight hours a day and 40 hours a week for work performed under a combined work/training scheme or an in-plant work-experience scheme;
(b) two hours on a school day and 12 hours a week for work performed in term-time outside the hours fixed for school attendance, provided that this is not prohibited by national legislation and/or practice;

in no circumstances may the daily working time exceed seven years; this limit may be raised to eight hours in the case of children who have reached the age of 15;

(c) seven hours a day and 35 hours a week for work performed during a period of at least a week when school is not operating; these limits may be raised to eight hours a day and 40 hours a week in the case of children who have reached the age of 15;

(d) seven hours a day and 35 hours a week for light work performed by children no longer subject to compulsory full-time schooling under national law.

2.   Member States shall adopt the measures necessary to limit the working time of adolescents to eight hours a day and 40 hours a week.

3.   The time spent on training by a young person working under a theoretical and/or practical combined work/training scheme or an in-plant work-experience scheme shall be counted as working time.

4.   Where a young person is employed by more than one employer, working days and working time shall be cumulative.

5.   Member States may, by legislative or regulatory provision, authorize derogations from paragraph 1 (a) and paragraph 2 either by way of exception or where there are objective grounds for so doing.

Member States shall, by legislative or regulatory provision, determine the conditions, limits and procedure for implementing such derogations.

Article 9

Night work

1.   (a) Member States which make use of the option in Article 4 (2) (b) or (c) shall adopt the measures necessary to prohibit work by children between 8 p.m. and 6 a.m.

   (b) Member States shall adopt the measures necessary to prohibit work by adolescents either between 10 p.m. and 6 a.m. or between 11 p.m. and 7 a.m.

2.   (a) Member States may, by legislative or regulatory provision, authorize work by adolescents in specific areas of activity during the period in which night work is prohibited as referred to in paragraph 1(b).
       In that event, Member States shall take appropriate measures to ensure that the adolescent is supervised by an adult where such supervision is necessary for the adolescent's protection.

   (b) If point (a) is applied, work shall continue to be prohibited between midnight and 4 a.m.

However, Member States may, by legislative or regulatory provision, authorize work by adolescents during the period in which night work is prohibited in the following cases, where there are objective grounds for so doing and provided that adolescents are allowed suitable compensatory rest time and that the objectives set out in Article 1 are not called into question:

—   work performed in the shipping or fisheries sectors;
—   work performed in the context of the armed forces or the police;
—   work performed in hospitals or similar establishments;
—   cultural, artistic, sports or advertising activities.

3.   Prior to any assignment to night work and at regular intervals thereafter, adolescents shall be entitled to a free assessment of their health and capacities, unless the work they do during the period during which work is prohibited is of an exceptional nature.

Article 10

Rest period

1.   (a)   Member States which make use of the option in Article 4 (2) (b) or (c) shall adopt the measures necessary to ensure that, for each 24-hour period, children are entitled to a minimum rest period of 14 consecutive hours.
     (b)   Member States shall adopt the measures necessary to ensure that, for each 24-hour period, adolescents are entitled to a minimum rest period of 12 consecutive hours.

2.   Member States shall adopt the measures necessary to ensure that, for each seven-day period:
—   children in respect of whom they have made use of the option in Article 4 (2) (b) or (c), and
—   adolescents

are entitled to a minimum rest period of two days, which shall be consecutive if possible.

Where justified by technical or organization reasons, the minimum rest period may be reduced, but may in no circumstances be less than 36 consecutive hours.

The minimum rest period referred to in the first and second subparagraphs shall in principle include Sunday.

3.   Member States may, by legislative or regulatory provision, provide for the minimum rest periods referred to in paragraphs 1 and 2 to be interrupted in the case of activities involving periods of work that are split up over the day or are of short duration.

4.   Member States may make legislative or regulatory provision for derogations from paragraph 1 (b) and paragraph 2 in respect of adolescents in the following cases, where there are objective grounds for so doing and provided that they are granted appropriate compensatory rest time and that the objectives set out in Article 1 are not called into question:
(a)   work performed in the shipping or fisheries sectors;
(b)   work performed in the context of the armed forces or the police;
(c)   work performed in hospitals or similar establishments;
(d)   work performed in agriculture;
(e)   work performed in the tourism industry or in the hotel, restaurant and cafe sector;
(f)   activities involving periods of work split up over the day.

Article 11

Annual rest

Member States which make use of the option referred to in Article 4 (2) (b) or (c) shall see to it that a period free of any work is included, as far as possible, in the school holidays of children subject to compulsory full-time schooling under national law.

Article 12

Breaks

Member States shall adopt the measures necessary to ensure that, where daily working time is more than four and a half hours, young people are entitled to a break of at least 30 minutes, which shall be consecutive if possible.

Article 13

Work by adolescents in the event of *force majeure*

Member States may, by legislative or regulatory provision, authorize derogations from Article 8 (2), Article 9 (1) (b), Article 10 (1) (b) and, in the case of adolescents, Article 12, for work in the circumstances referred to in Article 5 (4) of Directive 89/391/EEC, provided that such work is of a temporary nature and must be performed immediately, that adult workers are not available and that the adolescents are allowed equivalent compensatory rest time within the following three weeks.

SECTION IV

Article 14

Measures

Each Member State shall lay down any necessary measures to be applied in the event of failure to comply with the provisions adopted in order to implement this Directive; such measures must be effective and proportionate.

Article 15

Adaptation of the Annex

Adaptations of a strictly technical nature to the Annex in the light of technical progress, changes in international rules or specifications and advances in knowledge in the field covered by this Directive shall be adopted in accordance with the procedure provided for in Article 17 of Directive 89/391/EEC.

Article 16

Non-reducing clause

Without prejudice to the right of Member States to develop, in the light of changing circumstances, different provisions on the protection of young people, as long as the minimum requirements provided for by this Directive are complied with, the implementation of this Directive shall not constitute valid grounds for reducing the general level of protection afforded to young people.

Article 17

Final provisions

1. (a) Member States shall bring into force the laws, regulations and administrative provisions necessary to comply with this Directive not later than 22 June 1996 or ensure, by that date at the latest, that the two sides of industry introduce the requisite provisions by means of collective agreements, with Member States being required to make all the necessary provisions to enable them at all times to guarantee the results laid down by this Directive.

(b) The United Kingdom may refrain from implementing the first subparagraph of Article 8 (1) (b) with regard to the provision relating to the maximum weekly working time, and also Article 8 (2) and Article 9 (1) (b) and (2) for a period of four years from the date specified in subparagraph (a).

The Commission shall submit a report on the effects of this provision.

The Council, acting in accordance with the conditions laid down by the Treaty, shall decide whether this period should be extended.

(c) Member States shall forthwith inform the Commission thereof.

2. When Member States adopt the measures referred to in paragraph 1, such measures shall contain a reference to this Directive or shall be accompanied by such reference on the occasion of their official publication. The methods of making such reference shall be laid down by Member States.

3. Member States shall communicate to the Commission the texts of the main provisions of national law which they have already adopted or adopt in the field governed by this Directive.

4. Member States shall report to the Commission every five years on the practical implementation of the provisions of this Directive, indicating the viewpoints of the two sides of industry.

The Commission shall inform the European Parliament, the Council and the Economic and Social Committee thereof.

5. The Commission shall periodically submit to the European Parliament, the Council and the Economic and Social Committee a report on the application of this Directive taking into account paragraphs 1, 2, 3 and 4.

Article 18

This Directive is addressed to the Member States.

Done at Luxembourg, 22 June 1994.

For the Council

The President

E. YIANNOPOULOS

ANNEX

NON-EXHAUSTIVE LIST OF AGENTS, PROCESSES AND WORK

(Article 7 (2), second subparagraph)

I. Agents

1. *Physical agents*
    (a) Ionizing radiation;
    (b) Work in a high-pressure atmosphere, e.g. in pressurized containers, diving.

2. *Biological agents*
    (a) Biological agents belonging to groups 3 and 4 within the meaning of Article 2 (d) of Council Directive 90/679/EEC of 26 November 1990 on the protection of workers from risks related to exposure to biological agents at work (Seventh individual Directive within the meaning of Article 16 (1) of Directive 89/391/EEC).

3. *Chemical agents*
   (a) Substances and preparations classified according to Council Directive 67/548/EEC of 27 June 1967 on the approximation of laws, regulations and administrative provisions relating to the classification, packaging and labelling of dangerous substances (^{2}) with amendments and Council Directive 88/379/EEC of 7 June 1988 on the approximation of the laws, regulations and administrative provisions of the Member States relating to the classification, packaging and labelling of dangerous preparations as toxic (T), very toxic (Tx), corrosive (C) or explosive (E);
   (b) Substances and preparations classified according to Directives 67/548/EEC and 88/379/EEC as harmful (Xn) and with one or more of the following risk phrases:
   — danger of very serious irreversible effects (R39),
   — possible risk of irreversible effects (R40),
   — may cause sensitization by inhalation (R42),
   — may cause sensitization by skin contact (R43),
   — may cause cancer (R45),
   — may cause heritable genetic damage (R46),
   — danger of serious damage to health by prolonged exposure (R48),
   — may impair fertility (R60),
   — may cause harm to the unborn child (R61);
   (c) Substances and preparations classified according to Directives 67/548/EEC and 88/379/EEC as irritant (Xi) and with one or more of the following risk phrases:
   — highly flammable (R12);
   — may cause sensitization by inhalation (R42),
   — may cause sensitization by skin contact (R43),
   (d) Substances and preparations referred to Article 2 (c) of Council Directive 90/394/EEC of 28 June 1990 on the protection of workers from the risks related to exposure to carcinogens at work (Sixth individual Directive within the meaning of Article 16 (1) of Directive 89/391/EEC;
   (e) Lead and compounds thereof, inasmuch as the agents in question are absorbable by the human organism;
   (f) Asbestos.

II. Processes and work

1. Processes at work referred to in Annex I to Directive 90/394/EEC.

2. Manufacture and handling of devices, fireworks or other objects containing explosives.

3. Work with fierce of poisonous animals.

4. Animal slaughtering on an industrial scale.

5. Work involving the handling of equipment for the production, storage or application of compressed, liquified or dissolved gases.

6. Work with vats, tanks, reservoirs or carboys containing chemical agents referred to in 1.3.

7. Work involving a risk of structural collapse.

8. Work involving high-voltage electrical hazards.

9. Work the pace of which is determined by machinery and involving payment by results.

THE TEMPORARY OR MOBILE CONSTRUCTION SITES DIRECTIVE

General note. This Directive was implemented (except in certain particulars) in the UK by the Construction (Design and Management) Regulations 1994 (S.I. 1994 No. 3140) at p. 263, post.

COUNCIL DIRECTIVE

of 24 June 1992

on the implementation of minimum safety and health requirements at temporary or mobile constructions sites (eighth individual Directive within the meaning of Article 16(1) of Directive 89/391/EEC)

(92/57/EEC)

THE COUNCIL OF THE EUROPEAN COMMUNITIES,

Having regard to the Treaty establishing the European Economic Community, and in particular Article 118a thereof,

Having regard to the proposal from the Commission, submitted after consulting the Advisory Committee on Safety, Hygiene and Health Protection at Work,

In cooperation with the European Parliament,

Having regard to the opinion of the Economic and Social Committee,

Whereas Article 118a of the Treaty provides that the Council shall adopt, by means of directives, minimum requirements for encouraging improvements, especially in the working environment, to ensure a better level of protection of the safety and health of workers;

Whereas, under the terms of that Article, those directives are to avoid imposing administrative, financial and legal constraints in a way which would hold back the creation and development of small and medium-sized undertakings;

Whereas the communication from the Commission on its programme concerning safety, hygiene and health at work provides for the adoption of a Directive designed to guarantee the safety and health of workers at temporary or mobile construction sites;

Whereas, in its resolution of 21 December 1987 on safety, hygiene and health at work, the Council took note of the Commission's intention of submitting to the Council in the near future minimum requirements concerning temporary or mobile construction sites;

Whereas temporary or mobile construction sites constitute an area of activity that exposes workers to particularly high levels of risk;

Whereas unsatisfactory architectural and/or organizational options or poor planning of the works at the project preparation stage have played a role in more than half of the occupational accidents occurring on construction sites in the Community;

Whereas in each Member State the authorities responsible for safety and health at work must be informed, before the beginning of the works, of the execution of works the scale of which exceeds a certain threshold;

Whereas, when a project is being carried out, a large number of occupational accidents may be caused by inadequate coordination, particularly where various undertakings work simultaneously or in succession at the same temporary or mobile construction site;

Whereas it is therefore necessary to improve coordination between the various parties concerned at the project preparation stage and also when the work is being carried out;

Whereas compliance with the minimum requirements designed to guarantee a better standard of safety and health at temporary or mobile construction sites is essential to ensure the safety and health of workers;

Whereas, moreover, self-employed persons and employers, where they are personally engaged in work activity, may, through their activities on a temporary or mobile construction site, jeopardize the safety and health of workers;

Whereas it is therefore necessary to extend to self-employed persons and to employers where they are personally engaged in work activity on the site certain relevant provisions of Council Directive 89/655/EEC of 30 November 1989 concerning the minimum safety and health requirements for the use of work equipment by workers at work (second individual Directive), and of Council Directive 89/656/EEC of 30 November 1989 on the minimum health and safety requirements for the use by workers of personal protective equipment at the workplace (third individual Directive);

Whereas this Directive is an individual Directive within the meaning of Article 16(1) of Council Directive 89/391/EEC of 12 June 1989 on the introduction of measures to encourage improvements in the safety and health of workers at work; whereas, therefore, the provisions of the said Directive are fully applicable to temporary or mobile construction sites, without prejudice to more stringent and/or specific provisions contained in this Directive;

Whereas this Directive constitutes a practical step towards the achievement of the social dimension of the internal market with special reference to the subject matter of Council Directive 89/106/EEC of 21 December 1988 on the approximation of laws, regulations and administrative provisions of the Member States relating to construction products and the subject matter covered by Council Directive 89/440/EEC of 18 July 1989 amending Directive 71/305/EEC concerning coordination of procedures for the award of public work contracts;

Whereas, pursuant to Council Decision 74/325/EEC, the Advisory Committee on Safety, Hygiene and Health Protection at Work is consulted by the Commission with a view to drawing up proposals in this field,

HAS ADOPTED THIS DIRECTIVE:

Article 1

Subject

1.   This Directive, which is the eighth individual Directive within the meaning of Article 16(1) of Directive 89/391/EEC, lays down minimum safety and health requirements for temporary or mobile construction sites, as defined in Article 2 (a).

2.   This Directive shall not apply to drilling and extraction in the extractive industries within the meaning of Article 1 (2) of Council Decision 74/326/EEC of 27 June 1974 on the extension of the responsibilities of the Mines Safety and Health Commission to all mineral-extracting industries.

3.   The provisions of Directive 89/391/EEC are fully applicable to the whole scope referred to in paragraph 1, without prejudice to more stringent and/or specific provisions contained in this Directive.

Article 2

Definitions

For the purposes of this Directive:
(a)   'temporary or mobile construction sites' (hereinafter referred to as construction sites') means any construction site at which building or civil engineering works are carried out; a non-exhaustive list of such works is given in Annex I;
(b)   'client' means any natural or legal person for whom a project is carried out;
(c)   project supervisor' means any natural or legal person responsible for the design and/or execution and/or supervision of the execution of a project, acting on behalf of the client;
(d)   'self-employed person' means any person other than those referred to in Article 3 (a) and (b) of Directive 89/391/EEC whose professional activity contributes to the completion of a project;
(e)   'coordinator for safety and health matters at the project preparations stage' means any natural or legal person entrusted by the client and/or project supervisor, during preparation of the project design, with performing the duties referred to in Article 5;
(f)   'coordinator for safety and health matters at the project execution stage' means any natural or legal person entrusted by the client and/or project supervisor, during execution of the project, with performing the duties referred to in Article 6.

Article 3

Appointment of coordinators—Safety and health plan—Prior notice

1.   The client or the project supervisor shall appoint one or more coordinators for safety and health matters, as defined in Article 2 (e) and (f), for any construction site on which more than one contractor is present.

2.   The client or the project supervisor shall ensure that prior to the setting up of a construction site a safety and health plan is drawn up in accordance with Article 5 (b).

The Member States may, after consulting both management and the workforce, allow derogations from the provisions of the first paragraph, except where the work concerned involves particular risks as listed in Annex II.

3.   In the case of constructions sites:
—   on which work is scheduled to last longer than 30 working days and on which more than 20 workers are occupied simultaneously, or
—   on which the volume of work is scheduled to exceed 500 person-days,

the client or the project supervisor shall communicate a prior notice drawn up in accordance with Annex III to the competent authorities before work starts.

The prior notice must be clearly displayed on the construction site and, if necessary, periodically updated.

Article 4

Project preparation stage: general principles

The project supervisor, or where appropriate the client, shall take account of the general principles of prevention concerning safety and health referred to in Directive 89/391/EEC during the various stages of designing and preparing the project, in particular:

— when architectural, technical and/or organizational aspects are being decided, in order to plan the various items or stages of work which are to take place simultaneously or in succession,

— when estimating the period required for completing such work or work stages.

Account shall also be taken, each time this appears necessary, of all safety and health plans and of files drawn up in accordance with Article 5 (b) or (c) or adjusted in accordance with Article 6 (c).

Article 5

Project preparation stage: duties of coordinators

The coordinator(s) for safety and health matters during the project preparation stage appointed in accordance with Article 3(1) shall:

(a)   coordinate implementation of the provisions of Article 4;

(b)   draw up, or cause to be draw up, a safety and health plan setting out the rules applicable to the construction site concerned, taking into account where necessary the industrial activities taking place on the site; this plan must also include specific measures concerning work which falls within one or more of the categories of Annex II;

(c)   prepare a file appropriate to the characteristics of the project containing relevant safety and health information to be taken into account during any subsequent works.

Article 6

Project execution stage: duties of coordinators

The coordinator(s) for safety and health matters during the project execution stage appointed in accordance with Article 3(1) shall:

(a)   coordinate implementation of the general principles of prevention and safety:
   — when technical and/or organizational aspects are being decided, in order to plan the various items or stages of work which are to take place simultaneously or in succession,
   — when estimating the period required for completing such work or work stages;

(b)   coordinate implementation of the relevant provisions in order to ensure that employers and, if necessary for the protection of workers, self-employed persons:
   — apply the principles referred to in Article 8 in a consistent manner,
   — where required, follow the safety and health plan referred to in Article 5 (b);

(c)   make, or cause to be made, any adjustments required to the safety and health plan referred to in Article 5 (b) and the file referred to in Article 5 (c) to take account of the progress of the work and any changes which have occurred;

(d) organize cooperation between employers, including successive employers on the same site, coordination of their activities with a view to protecting workers and preventing accidents and occupational health hazards and reciprocal information as provided for in Article 6 (4) of Directive 89/391/EEC, ensuring that self-employed persons are brought into this process where necessary;

(e) coordinate arrangements to check that the working procedures are being implemented correctly;

(f) take the steps necessary to ensure that only authorized person are allowed onto the construction site.

Article 7

Responsibilities of clients, project supervisors and employers

1. Where a client or project supervisor has appointed a coordinator or coordinators to perform the duties referred to in Articles 5 and 6, this does not relieve the client or project supervisor of his responsibilities in that respect.

2. The implementation of Articles 5 and 6, and of paragraph 1 of this Article shall not affect the principle of employers' responsibility as provided for in Directive 89/391/EEC.

Article 8

Implementation of Article 6 of Directive 89/391/EEC

When the work is being carried out, the principles set out in Article 6 of Directive 89/391/EEC shall be applied, in particular as regards:

(a) keeping the construction site in good order and in a satisfactory state of cleanliness;

(b) choosing the location of workstations bearing in mind how access to these workplaces is obtained, and determining routes or areas for the passage and movement and equipment;

(c) the conditions under which various materials are handled;

(d) technical maintenance, pre-commissioning checks and regular checks on installations and equipment with a view to correcting any faults which might affect the safety and health of workers;

(e) the demarcation and laying-out of areas for the storage of various materials, in particular where dangerous materials or substances are concerned;

(f) the conditions under which the dangerous materials used are removed;

(g) the storage and disposal or removal of waste and debris;

(h) the adaptation, based on progress made with the site, of the actual period to be allocated for the various types of work or work stages;

(i) cooperation between employers and self-employed persons;

(j) interaction with industrial activities at the place within which or in the vicinity of which the construction site is located.

Article 9

Obligations of employers

In order to preserve safety and health on the construction site, under the conditions set out in Article 6 and 7, employers shall:

(a) in particular when implementing Article 8, take measures that are in line with the minimum requirements set out in Annex IV;

(b) take into account directions from the coordinator(s) for safety and health matters.

Article 10

Obligations of other groups of persons

1.   In order to preserve safety and health on the construction site, self-employed persons shall:

(a) comply in particular with the following, *mutatis mutandis*:

   (i)   the requirements of Article 6 (4) and Article 13 of Directive 89/391/EEC and Article 8 and Annex IV of this Directive;

   (ii) Article 4 of Directive 89/655/EEC and the relevant provisions of the Annex thereto;

   (iii) Article 3, Article 4 (1) to (4) and (9) and Article 5 of Directive 89/656/EEC;

(b) take into account directions from the coordinator(s) for safety and health matters.

2.   In order to preserve safety and health on the site, where employers are personally engaged in work activity on the construction site, they shall:

(a) comply in particular with the following, *mutatis mutandis*:

   (i)   Article 13 of Directive 89/391/EEC;

   (ii) Article 4 of Directive 89/655/EEC and the relevant provisions of the Annex thereto;

   (iii) Articles 3, 4(1), (2), (3), (4), (9) and 5 of Directive 89/656/EEC;

(b) take account of the comments of the coordinator(s) for safety and health.

Article 11

Information for workers

1.   Without prejudice to Article 10 of Directive 89/391/EEC, workers and/or their representatives shall be informed of all the measures to be taken concerning their safety and health on the construction site.

2.   The information must be comprehensible to the workers concerned.

Article 12

Consultation and participation of workers

Consultation and participation of workers and/or of their representatives shall take place in accordance with Article 11 of Directive 89/391/EEC on matters covered by Articles 6, 8 and 9 of this Directive, ensuring whenever necessary proper coordination between workers and/or workers' representatives in undertakings carrying out their activities at the workplace, having regard to the degree of risk and the size of the work site.

Article 13

Amendment of the Annexes

1.   Amendments to Annexes I, II and III shall be adopted by the Council in accordance with the procedure laid down in Article 118a of the Treaty.

2.   Strictly technical adaptations of Annex IV as a result of:
— the adoption of directives on technical harmonization and standardization regarding temporary or mobile construction sites, and/or
— technical progress, changes in international regulations or specifications or knowledge in the field of temporary or mobile construction sites

shall be adopted in accordance with the procedure laid down in Article 17 of Directive 89/391/EEC.

Article 14

Final provisions

1.   Member States shall bring into force the laws, regulations and administrative provisions necessary to comply with this Directive by 31 December 1993 at the latest.

They shall forthwith inform the Commission thereof.

2.   When Member States adopt these measures, they shall contain a reference to this Directive or be accompanied by such reference on the occasion of their official publication. The methods of making such a reference shall be laid down by the Member States.

3.   Member States shall communicate to the Commission the texts of the provisions of national law which they have already adopted or adopt in the field governed by this Directive.

4.   Member States shall report to the Commission every four years on the practical implementation of the provisions of this Directive, indicating the points of view of employers and workers.

The Commission shall inform the European Parliament, the Council, the Economic and Social Committee and the Advisory Committee on Safety, Hygiene and Health Protection at Work.

5.   The Commission shall submit periodically to the European Parliament, the Council and the Economic and Social Committee a report on the implementation of this Directive, taking into account paragraphs 1, 2, 3 and 4.

Article 15

This Directive is addressed to the Member States.

Done at Luxembourg, 24 June 1992.

For the Council

The President

Jose da SILVA
PENEDA

ANNEX I

NON-EXHAUSTIVE LIST OF BUILDING AND CIVIL ENGINEERING WORKS REFERRED TO IN ARTICLE 2 (A) OF THE DIRECTIVE

1. Excavation
2. Earthworks
3. Construction
4. Assembly and disassembly of prefabricated elements
5. Conversion or fitting-out
6. Alterations
7. Renovation
8. Repairs
9. Dismantling
10. Demolition
11. Upkeep
12. Maintenance — Painting and cleaning work
13. Drainage

ANNEX II

NON-EXHAUSTIVE LIST OF WORK INVOLVING PARTICULAR RISKS TO THE SAFETY AND HEALTH OF WORKERS REFERRED TO IN ARTICLE 3 (2), SECOND PARAGRAPH OF THE DIRECTIVE

1. Work which puts workers at risk of burial under earthfalls, engulfment in swampland or falling from a height, where the risk is particularly aggravated by the nature of the work or processes used or by the environment at the place of work or site.

2. Work which puts workers at risk from chemical or biological substances constituting a particular danger to the safety and health of workers or involving a legal requirement for health monitoring.

3. Work with ionizing radiation requiring the designation of controlled or supervised areas as defined in Article 20 of Directive 80/836/Euratom.

4. Work near high voltage power lines.

5. Work exposing workers to the risk of drowning.

6. Work on wells, underground earthworks and tunnels.

7. Work carried out by drivers having a system of air supply.

8. Work carried out by workers in caisson with a compressed-air atmosphere.

9. Work involving the use of explosives.

10. Work involving the assembly or dismantling of heavy prefabricated components.

ANNEX III

CONTENT OF THE PRIOR NOTICE REFERRED TO IN ARTICLE 3 (3), FIRST PARAGRAPH OF THE DIRECTIVE I

1. Date of forwarding:

2. Exact address of the construction site:

3. Client(s) (name(s) and address(es)):

4. Type of project:

5. Project supervisor(s) (name(s) and address(es)):

6. Safety and health coordinators(s) during the project preparation stage (name(s) and address(es))

7. Coordinator(s) for safety and health matters during the project execution stage (name(s) and address(es)):

8. Date planned for start of work on the construction site:

9. Planned duration of work on the construction site:

10. Estimated maximum number of workers on the construction site:

11. Planned number of contractors and self-employed persons on the construction site:

12. Details of contractors already chosen:

ANNEX IV

MINIMUM SAFETY AND HEALTH REQUIREMENTS FOR CONSTRUCTION SITES

Referred to in Article 9 (a) and Article 10(1) (a) (i) of the Directive

Preliminary remarks

The obligations laid down in this Annex apply wherever required by the features of the construction site, the activity, the circumstances or a hazard.

For the purposes of this Annex, 'rooms' covers, inter alia, hutted accommodation.

PART A

GENERAL MINIMUM REQUIREMENTS FOR ON-SITE WORKPLACES

1.   **Stability and solidity**

1.1.   Materials, equipment and, more generally, any component which, when moving in any way, may affect the safety and health of workers must be stabilized in an appropriate and safe manner.

1.2.   Access to any surface involving insufficiently resistant materials is not authorized unless appropriate equipment or means are provided to enable the work to be carried out safely.

2.   **Energy distribution installations**

2.1.   The installations must be designed, constructed and used so as not to present a fire or explosion hazard; persons must be adequately protected against the risk of electrocution caused by direct or indirect contact.

2.2.   The design, construction and choice of equipment and protection devices must take account of the type and power of the energy distributed, external conditions and the competence of persons with access to parts of the installation.

3.   **Emergency routes and exits**

3.1.   Emergency routes and exits must remain clear and lead as directly as possible to a safe area.

3.2.   In the event of danger, it must be possible for workers to evacuate all workstations quickly and as safely as possible.

3.3.   The number, distribution and dimensions of emergency routes and exits depend on the use, equipment and dimensions of the site and of the rooms and the maximum number of persons that may be present.

3.4.   Specific emergency routes and exits must be indicated by signs in accordance with the national regulations implementing Directive 77/576/EEC.

Such signs must be sufficiently resistant and be placed at appropriate points.

3.5.   Emergency routes and exits, and the traffic routes and doors giving access to them, must be free from obstruction so that they can be used at any time without hindrance.

3.6.   Emergency routes and exits requiring illumination must be provided with emergency lighting of adequate intensity in case the lighting fails.

4.   **Fire detection and fire fighting**

4.1.   Depending of the characteristics of the site, the dimensions and use of the rooms, the on-site equipment, the physical and chemical properties of the substances present and the maximum potential number of people present, an adequate number of appropriate fire-fighting devices and, where required, fire detectors and alarm systems must be provided.

4.2.   These fire-fighting devices, fire detectors and alarm systems must be regularly checked and maintained.

Appropriate tests and drills must take place at regular intervals.

4.3.   Non-automatic fire-fighting equipment be easily accessible and simple to use.

The equipment must be indicated by signs in accordance with the national regulations implementing Directive 77/576/EEC.

Such signs must be sufficiently resistant and placed at appropriate points.

5. **Ventilation**

Steps shall be taken to ensure that there is sufficient fresh air, having regard to the working methods used and the physical demands placed on the workers.

If a forced ventilation system is used, it must be maintained in working order and must not expose workers to draughts which are harmful to health.

Any breakdown must be indicated by a control system where this is necessary for workers' health.

6. **Exposure to particular risks**

6.1.   Workers must not be exposed to harmful levels of noise or to harmful external influences (e.g. gases, vapours, dust).

6.2.   If workers have to enter an area where the atmosphere is liable to contain a toxic or harmful substance or to have an insufficient oxygen level or to be inflammable, the confined atmosphere must be monitored and appropriate steps taken to prevent any hazards.

6.3.   A worker may not in any circumstances be exposed to a high-risk confined atmosphere.

He must at least be watched at all times from outside and all appropriate precautions must be taken to ensure that he can be assisted effectively and immediately.

7. **Temperature**

During working hours, the temperature must be appropriate for human beings, having regard to the working methods used and the physical demands placed on the workers.

8. **Natural and artificial lighting of workstations, rooms and traffic routes on the site**

8.1.   Workstations, rooms and traffic routes must as far as possible have sufficient natural lighting and be provided with appropriate and sufficient artificial lighting at night and when natural daylight is inadequate; where necessary, portable light sources that are protected against impact must be used.

The colour of artificial light used must not alter or affect the perception of signals or signposts.

8.2.   Lighting installations for rooms, workstations and traffic routes must be placed in such a way that there is no risk of accident to workers as a result of the type of lighting fitted.

8.3.   Rooms, workstations and traffic routes where workers are especially exposed to risks in the event of artificial lighting must be provided with emergency lighting of adequate intensity.

9.   Doors and gates

9.1.   Sliding doors must be fitted with a safety device to prevent them from being derailed and falling over.

9.2.   Doors and gates opening upwards must be fitted with a mechanism to secure them against falling back.

9.3.   Doors and gates along escape routes must be appropriately marked.

9.4.   In the immediate vicinity of gates intended primarily for vehicle traffic, there must be doors for pedestrian traffic unless it is safe for pedestrians to cross; such doors must be clearly marked and kept free at all times.

9.5.   Mechanical doors and gates must operate without any risk of accident to workers.

They must be fitted with emergency stop devices which are easily identifiable and accessible and, unless they open automatically in the event of a power-cut, it must be possible for them to be opened manually.

10.   Traffic routes—danger areas

10.1.   Traffic routes, including stairs, fixed ladders and loading bays and ramps, must be calculated, located, laid out and made negotiable to ensure easy, safe and appropriate access in such a way as not to endanger workers employed in the vicinity of these traffic routes.

10.2.   Routes used for pedestrian traffic and/or goods traffic including those used for loading and unloading must be dimensioned in accordance with the number of potential users and the type of activity concerned.

If means of transport are used on traffic routes, a sufficient safety clearance or adequate protective devices must be provided for other site users.

Routes must be clearly marked, regularly checked and properly maintained.

10.3.   Sufficient clearance must be allowed between vehicle traffic routes and doors, gates, passages for pedestrians, corridors and staircases.

10.4.   If the site includes limited-access areas, these must be equipped with devices to prevent unauthorized workers from entering.

Appropriate measures must be taken to protect workers who are authorized to enter the danger areas.

Danger areas must be clearly signposted.

11.   Loading bays and ramps

11.1.   Loading bays and ramps must be suitable for the dimensions of the loads to be transported.

11.2.   Loading bays must have at least one exit point.

11.3.   Loading ramps must be sufficiently safe to prevent workers from falling off.

12.   Freedom of movement at the workstation

The floor area at the workstation must be such as to allow workers sufficient freedom of movement to perform their work, taking account of any necessary equipment or appliances present.

13.   First aid

13.1.   The employer must ensure that first aid can be provided, and that the staff trained to provide it can be called upon, at any time.

Measures must be taken to ensure that workers who have had an accident or have suddenly been taken ill can be removed for medical treatment.

13.2.   One or more first-aid rooms must be provided where the scale of the works or the types of activity being carried out so require.

13.3.   First-aid rooms must be fitted with essential first-aid installations and equipment and be easily accessible to stretchers.

They must be signposted in accordance with the national regulations implementing Directive 77/576/EEC.

13.4.   In addition, first-aid equipment must be available at all places where working conditions so require.

This equipment must be suitably marked and easily accessible.

The address and telephone number of the local emergency service must be clearly displayed.

14.   Sanitary equipment

14.1.   Changing rooms and lockers.

14.1.1.   Appropriate changing rooms must be provided for workers if they have to wear special work clothes and if, for reasons of health or propriety, they cannot be expected to change in another area.

Changing rooms must be easily accessible, be of sufficient capacity and be provided with seating.

14.1.2.   Changing rooms must be sufficiently large and have facilities to enable each worker, where necessary, to dry his working clothes as well as his own clothing and personal effects and to lock them away.

If circumstances so require (e.g. dangerous substances, humidity, dirt), facilities must be provided to enable working clothes to be kept in a place separate from workers' own clothes and personal effects.

14.1.3.   Provisions must be made for separate changing rooms or separate use of changing rooms for men and women.

14.1.4.   If changing rooms are not required as referred to in point 14.1.1, first paragraph, each worker must be provided with a place in which he can lock away his own clothes and personal effects.

14.2.   Showers and washbasins

14.2.1.   Suitable showers in sufficient numbers must be provided for workers if required by the nature of the work or for health reasons.

Provisions must be made for separate shower rooms or separate use of shower rooms for men and women.

14.2.2.   The shower rooms must be sufficiently large to permit each worker to wash without hindrance in conditions of an appropriate standard of hygiene.

The showers must be equipped with hot and cold running water.

14.2.3.   Where showers are not required under the first paragraph of 14.2.1, a sufficient number of suitable washbasins with running water (hot water if necessary) must be provided in the vicinity of the workstations and the changing rooms.

Provisions must be made for separate washbasins, or separate use of washbasins for men and women when so required for reasons of propriety.

14.2.4.   Where the rooms housing, the showers or washbasins are separate from the changing rooms, there must be easy communication between the two.

14.3.   Lavatories and washbasins

Special facilities with an adequate number of lavatories and washbasins must be provided for workers in the vicinity of workstations, rest rooms, changing rooms and rooms housing showers or washbasins.

Provisions must be made for separate lavatories or separate use of lavatories for mens and women.

15.   Rest rooms and/or accommodation areas

15.1.   Where the safety or health of workers, in particular because of the type of activity carried out or the presence of more than a certain number of employees as well as the remote nature of the site, so require, workers must be provided with easily accessible rest rooms and/or accommodation areas.

15.2.   Rest rooms and/or accommodation areas must be large enough and equipped with an adequate number of tables and seats with backs for the number of workers concerned.

15.3.   If there are no facilities of this kind, other facilities must be provided in which workers can stay during interruptions in work.

15.4.   Fixed accommodation areas unless used only in exceptional cases, must have sufficient sanitary equipment, a rest room and a leisure room.

They must be equipped with beds, cupboards, tables and seats with backs taking account of the number of workers, and be allocated taking account, where appropriate, of the presence of workers of both sexes.

15.5.   Appropriate measures should be taken for the protection of non-smokers against discomfort caused by tobacco smoke in rest rooms and/or accommodation areas.

16.   Pregnant women and nursing mothers

Pregnant women and nursing mothers must be able to lie down to rest in appropriate conditions.

17.   Handicapped workers

Workplaces must be organized to take account of handicapped workers, if necessary.

The provision applies in particular to the doors, passageways, staircases, showers, washbasins, lavatories and workstations used or occupied directly by handicapped persons.

18.   Miscellaneous provisions

18.1.   The surroundings and the perimeter of the site must be signposted and laid out so as to be clearly visible and identifiable.

18.2.   Workers must be provided at the site with a sufficient quantity of drinking water and possibly another suitable non-alcoholic beverage both in occupied rooms and in the vicinity of workstations.

18.3.   Workers must:
    — be provided with facilities enabling them to take their meals in satisfactory conditions,
    — where appropriate, be provided with facilities enabling them to prepare their meals in satisfactory conditions.

PART B SPECIFIC MINIMUM REQUIREMENT FOR ON-SITE WORKSTATIONS

PRELIMINARY REMARK

If special situations so dictate, the classification of these minimum requirements into two sections, as below, should not regarded as binding.

Section I

ON-SITE INDOOR WORKSTATIONS

1.   Stability and solidity

Premises must have a structure and stability appropriate to the nature of their use.

2.   Emergency doors

Emergency doors must open outwards.

Emergency doors must not be so locked or fastened that they cannot be easily and immediately opened by any person who may require to use them in an emergency.

Sliding or revolving doors are not permitted if intended as emergency exits.

3.   Ventilation

If air-conditioning or mechanical ventilation installations are used, they must operate in such a way that workers are not exposed to draughts which cause discomfort.

Any deposit or dirt likely to create an immediate danger to the health of workers by polluting the atmosphere must be removed without delay.

4.   Temperature

4.1.   The temperature in rest areas, rooms for duty staff, sanitary facilities, canteens and first-aid rooms must be appropriate to the particular purpose of such areas.

4.2.   Windows, skylights and glass partitions should allow excessive effects of sunlight to be avoided, having regard to the nature of the work and the use of the room.

5.   Natural and artificial lighting

Workplaces must as far as possible have sufficient natural light and be equipped with the means of providing artificial lighting which is adequate for the purposes of protecting workers' safety and health.

6.   Floors, walls, ceilings and roofs of rooms

6.1.   The floors of workplaces must have no dangerous bumps, holes or slopes and must be fixed, stable and not slippery.

6.2.   The surfaces of floors, walls and ceilings in rooms must be such that they can be cleaned or refurbished to an appropriate standard of hygiene.

6.3.   Transparent or translucent walls, in particular all-glass partitions, in rooms or in the vicinity of workplaces and traffic routes must be clearly indicated and made of safety material or be shielded from such places or traffic routes to prevent workers from coming into contact with walls or being injured should the walls shatter.

7.   Windows and skylights

7.1.   It must be possible for workers to open, close, adjust or secure windows, skylights and ventilators in a safe manner.

When open, they must not be positioned so as to constitute a hazard to workers.

7.2.   Windows and skylights must be designed in conjunction with equipment or otherwise fitted with devices allowing them to be cleaned without risk to the workers carrying out this work or to workers present.

8.   Doors and Gates

8.1.   The position, number and dimensions of doors and gates, and the materials used in their construction, are determined by the nature and use of the rooms or areas.

8.2.   Transparent doors must be appropriately marked at a conspicuous level.

8.3.   Swing doors and gates must be transparent or have see-through panels.

8.4.   If transparent or translucent surfaces in doors and gates are not made of safety material and if there is a danger that workers may be injured if a door or gate should shatter, the surfaces must be protected against breakage.

9.   Traffic routes

Where the use and equipment of rooms so requires for the protection of workers, traffic routes must be clearly identified.

10.   Specific measures for escalators and travelators

Escalators and travelators must function safely.

They must be equipped with any necessary safety devices.

They must be fitted with easily identifiable and accessible emergency shut-down devices.

11.   Room dimensions and air space in rooms

Workrooms must have sufficient surface area and height to allow workers to perform their work without risk to their safety, health or well-being.

Section II

ON-SITE OUTDOOR WORKSTATIONS

1.   Stability and solidity

1.1.   High-level or low-level movable or fixed workstations must be solid and stable, taking account of:
— the number of workers occupying them,
— the maximum loads they may have to bear and the weight distribution,
— the outside influences to which they may be subject.
If the support and the other components of these workstations are not intrinsically stable, their stability will have to be ensured by appropriate and safe methods of fixing to avoid any untimely or spontaneous movement of the whole or of parts of the workstations.

1.2.   Checking

Stability and solidity must be checked appropriately and especially after any change in the height or depth of the workstation.

2. Energy distribution installations

2.1. On-site energy distribution installations, especially those subject to outside influences, must be regularly checked and maintained.

2.2. Installations existing before the site began must be identified, checked and clearly signposted.

2.3. Whenever possible, where overhead electric power lines exist, either they must be redirected away from the area of the site or else the current must be cut off.

If this is not possible, there will be barriers or notices to ensure that vehicles and installations are kept away.

Suitable warnings and suspended protections must be provided where vehicles have to pass beneath the lines.

3. Atmospheric influences

Workers must be protected against atmospheric influences which could affect their health and safety.

4. Falling objects

Wherever technically feasible, workers must be protected by collective methods against falling objects.

Materials and equipment must be laid out or stracked in such a way as to prevent their collapsing or overturning.

Where necessary, there must be covered passageways on the side or access to danger areas must be made impossible.

5. Falls from a height

5.1. Falls from a height must be physically prevented in particular by means of solid cradles which are sufficiently high and have at least an end-board, a main handrail and an intermediate handrail or an equivalent alternative.

5.2. In principle, work at a height must be carried out only with appropriate equipment or using collective protection devices such as cradles, platforms or safety nets.

If the use of such equipment is not possible because of the nature of the work, suitable means of access must be provided and safety harnesses or other anchoring safety methods must be used.

6. Scaffolding and leaders

6.1. All scaffolding must be properly designed, constructed and maintained to ensure that it does not collapse or move accidentally.

6.2. Work platforms, gangways and scaffolding stairways must be constructed, dimensioned, protected and used in such a way as to prevent people from falling or being exposed to falling objects.

6.3.   Scaffolding must be inspected by a competent person:
(a)   before being put into service;
(b)   subsequently, at periodic intervals;
(c)   after any modification period without use, exposure to bad weather or seismic tremors, or any other circumstance which may have affected its strength or stability.

6.4.   Ladders must be sufficiently strong and correctly maintained.

They must be correctly used, in appropriate places and in accordance with their intended purpose.

6.5.   Mobile scaffolding must be secured against spontaneous movements.

7.   Lifting equipment

7.1.   All lifting devices and accessories, including their component parts, attachments, anchorings and supports, must be:
(a)   properly designed and constructed and sufficiently strong for the use to which they are put;
(b)   correctly installed and used;
(c)   maintained in good working order;
(d)   checked and subjected to periodic tests and inspections in accordance with current legislation;
(e)   operated by qualified workers who have received appropriate training.

7.2.   All lifting devices and accessories must clearly display their maximum load values.

7.3.   Lifting equipment and accessories may not be used for other than their intended purposes.

8.   Excavating and materials-handling vehicles and machinery

8.1.   All excavating and materials-handling vehicles and machinery must be:
(a)   properly designed and constructed taking account, as far as possible, of the principles of ergonomics;
(b)   kept in good working order;
(c)   used correctly.

8.2.   Drivers and operators of excavating and materials-handling vehicles and machinery must be specially trained.

8.3.   Preventive measures must be taken to ensure that excavating and materials-handling vehicles and machinery do not fall into the excavations or into water.

8.4.   Where appropriate, excavating machinery and materials-handling machinery must be fitted with structures to protect the driver against being crushed if the machine overturns, and against falling objects.

9.   Installations, machinery, equipment

9.1.   Installations, machinery and equipment, including hand tools whether power-driven or not, must be:
(a)   properly designed and constructed taking accounts, as far as possible, of the principle of ergonomics;

(b) kept in good working order;

(c) used solely for the work for which they were designed;

(d) operated by workers who have received appropriate training.

9.2. Installations and equipment under pressure must be checked and subjected to regular tests and inspections in accordance with existing legislation.

10. Excavations, wells, underground works, tunnels and earthworks

10.1. Suitable precautions must be taken in an excavation, well, underground, working or tunnel:

(a) using an appropriate support or embankment;

(b) to prevent hazards entailed in the fall of a person, materials or objects, or flooding;

(c) to provide sufficient ventilation at all workstations so as to ensure a breathable atmosphere which is not dangerous or harmful to health;

(d) to enable workers to reach safety in the event of fire or inrush of water or materials.

10.2. Before excavation starts, measures must be taken to identify and reduce to a minimum any hazard due to underground cables and other distribution systems.

10.3. Safe routes into and out of the excavation must be provided.

10.4. Piles of earth, materials and moving vehicles must be kept away from the excavation; appropriate barriers must be built if necessary.

11. Demolition work

Where the demolition of a building or construction may present a danger:

(a) appropriate precautions, methods and procedures must be adopted;

(b) the work must be planned and undertaken only under the supervision of a competent person.

12. Metal or concrete frameworks, shutterings and heavy prefabricated components

12.1. Metal or concrete frameworks and their components, shutterings, prefabricated components or temporary support, and buttresses must be erected and dismantled only under the supervision of a competent person.

12.2. Adequate precautions must be taken to protect workers against risks arising from the temporary fragility or instability of a structure.

12.3. Shutterings, temporary supports and buttresses must de devises and designed, installed and maintained so as to safely withstand any strains and stresses which may be placed on them.

13. Cofferdams and caissons

13.1. All cofferdams and caissons must be:

(a) well constructed, of appropriate, solid materials of adequate strength;

(b) appropriately equipped so that workers can gain shelter in the event of an irruption of water and materials.

13.2.   The construction, installation, transformation or dismantling of a cofferdam or caisson must take place only under the supervision of a competent person.

13.3.   All cofferdams and caissons must be inspected by a competent person at regular intervals.

14.   Work on roofs

14.1.   Where necessary to avert a risk or where the height or the slope exceed values set by the Member States, collective preventive measures must be taken to prevent workers, and tools or other objects or materials, from falling.

14.2.   Where workers have to work on or near a roof or any other surface made of fragile materials through which it is possible to fall, preventive measures must be taken to ensure that they do not inadvertently walk on the surface made of fragile materials, or fall to the ground.

———————

THE PREGNANT WORKERS DIRECTIVE

General note. Articles 4 to 7 of this Directive have been implemented by the Management of Health and Safety at Work (Amendment) Regulations 1994 (S.I. 1994 No. 2865), at p. 260, post.

COUNCIL DIRECTIVE 92/85/EEC

of 19 October 1992

on the introduction of measures to encourage improvements in the safety and health at work of pregnant workers and workers who have recently given birth or are breastfeeding (tenth individual Directive within the meaning of Article 16 (1) of Directive 89/391/EEC)

THE COUNCIL OF THE EUROPEAN COMMUNITITES,

Having regard to the Treaty establishing the European, Economic Community, and in particular Article 118a thereof,

Having regard to the proposal from the Commission, drawn up after consultation with the Advisory Committee on Safety, Hygiene and Health Protection at work,

In cooperation with the European Parliament,

Having regard to the opinion of the Economic and Social Committee,

Whereas Article 118a of the Treaty provides that the Council shall adopt, by means of directives, minimum requirements for encouraging improvements, especially in the working environment, to protect the safety and health of workers;

Whereas this Directive does not justify any reduction in levels of protection already achieved in individual Member States, the Member States being committed, under the Treaty, to encouraging improvements in conditions in this area and to harmonising conditions while maintaining the improvements made;

Whereas, under the terms of Article 118a of the Treaty, the said directives are to avoid imposing administrative, financial and legal constraints in a way which would hold back the creation and development of small and medium-sized undertakings;

Whereas, pursuant to Decision 74/325/EEC, as last amended by the 1985 Act of Accession, the Advisory Committee on Safety, Hygiene and Health protection at Work is consulted by the Commission on the drafting of proposals in this field;

Whereas the Community Charter of the fundamental social rights of workers; adopted at the Strasbourg European Council on 9 December 1989 by the Heads of State or Government of 11 Member States, lays down, in paragraph 19 in particular, that:

Every worker must enjoy satisfactory health and safety conditions in his working environment. Appropriate measures must be taken in order to achieve further harmonisation of conditions in this area while maintaining the improvements made;

Whereas the Commission, in its action programme for the implementation of the Community Charter of the fundamental social rights of workers, has included among its aims the adoption by the Council of a Directive on the protection of pregnant women at work;

Whereas Article 15 of Council Directive 89/391/EEC of 12 June 1989 on the introduction of measures to encourage improvements in the safety and health of workers at work provides that particularly sensitive risk groups must be protected against the dangers which specifically affect them;

Whereas pregnant workers, workers who have recently birth or who are breastfeeding must be considered a specific risk group in many respects, and measures must be taken with regard to their safety and health;

Whereas the protection of the safety and health of pregnant workers, workers who have recently given birth or workers who are breastfeeding should not treat women on the labour market unfavourably nor work to the detriment of directives concerning equal treatment for men and women;

Whereas some types of activities may pose a specific risk, for pregnant workers, workers who have recently given birth or workers who are breastfeeding, of exposure to dangerous agents', processes or working conditions; whereas such risks must therefore be assessed and the result of such assessment communicated to female workers and/or their representatives;

Whereas, further, should the result of this assessment reveal the existence of a risk to the safety or health of the female worker, provision must be made for such worker to be protected;

Whereas pregnant workers and workers who are breastfeeding must not engage in activities, which have been assessed as revealing a risk of exposure, jeopardising safety and health, to certain particularly dangerous agents or working conditions;

Whereas provision should be made for pregnant workers, workers who have recently given birth or workers who are breastfeeding not to be required to work at night where such provision is necessary from the point of view of their safety and health;

Whereas the vulnerability of pregnant workers, workers who have recently given birth or who are breastfeeding makes it necessary for them to be granted the right to maternity leave of at least 14 continuous weeks, allocated before and/or after confinement, and renders necessary the compulsory nature of maternity leave of at least two weeks, allocated before and/or after confinement;

Whereas the risk of dismissal for reasons associated with their condition may have harmful effects on the physical and mental state of pregnant workers, workers who have recently given birth or who are breastfeeding; whereas provision should be made for such dismissal to be prohibited;

Whereas measures for the organisation of work concerning the protection of the health of pregnant workers, workers who, have recently given birth or workers who are breastfeeding would serve no purpose unless accompanied by the maintenance of rights linked to the employment contract, including maintenance of payment and/or entitlement to an adequate allowance;

Whereas, moreover, provision concerning maternity leave would also serve no purpose unless accompanied by the maintenance of rights linked to the employment contract and or entitlement to an adequate allowance;

Whereas the concept of an adequate allowance in the case of maternity leave must be regarded as a technical point of reference with a view to fixing the minimum level of protection and should in no circumstances be interpreted as suggesting an analogy between pregnancy and illness,

HAS ADOPTED THIS DIRECTIVE

SECTION I

PURPOSE AND DEFINITONS

Article 1

Purpose

1.   The purpose of this Directive, which is the tenth individual Directive within the meaning of Article 16 (1) of Directive 89/391/EEC, is to implement measures to encourage improvements in the safety and health at work of pregnant workers and workers who have recently given birth or who are breastfeeding.

2.   The provisions of Directive 89/391/EEC, except for Article 2 (2) thereof, shall apply in full to the whole area covered by paragraph 1, without prejudice to any more stringent and/or specific provisions contained in this Directive.

3.   This Directive may not have the effect of reducing the level of protection afforded to pregnant workers, workers who have recently given birth or who are breastfeeding as compared with the situation which exists in each Member State on the date on which this Directive is adopted.

Article 2

Definitions

For the purposes of this Directive:
(a)   *pregnant worker* shall mean a pregnant worker who informs her employer of her condition, in accordance with national legislation and/or national practice;
(b)   *worker who has recently given birth* shall mean a worker who has recently given birth within the meaning of national legislation and/or national practice and who informs her employer of her condition, in accordance with that legislation and/or practice;
(c)   *worker who is breastfeeding* shall mean a worker who is breastfeeding within the meaning of national legislation and/or national practice and who informs her employer of her condition, in accordance with that legislation and/or practice.

SECTION II

GENERAL PROVISIONS

Article 3

Guidelines

1.   In consultation with the Member States and assisted by the Advisory Committee on Safety, Hygiene and Health Protection at Work, the Commission shall draw up guidelines on the assessment of the chemical, physical and biological agents

and industrial processes considered hazardous for the safety or health of workers within the meaning of Article 2

The guidelines referred to in the first subparagraph shall also cover movements and postures, mental and physical fatigue and other types of physical and mental stress connected with the work done by workers within the meaning of Article 2.

2.   The purpose of the guidelines referred to in paragraph 1 is to serve as a basis for the assessment referred to in Article 4(1).

To this end, Member States shall bring these guidelines to the attention of all employers and all female workers and/or their representatives in the respective Member State.

Article 4

Assessment and information

1.   For all activities liable to involve a specific risk of exposure to the agents, processes or working conditions of which a non-exhaustive list is given in Annex I, the employer shall assess the nature, degree and duration of exposure, in the undertaking and/or establishment concerned, of workers within the meaning of Article 2, either directly or by way of the protective and preventive services referred to in Article 7 of Directive 89/391/EEC, in order to:
— assess any risks to the safety or health and any possible effect on the pregnancys or breastfeeding of workers within the meaning of Article 2,
— decide what measures should be taken.

2.   Without prejudice to Article 10 of Directive 89/391/EEC, workers within the meaning of Article 2 and workers likely to be in one of the situations referred to in Article 2 in the undertaking and/or establishment concerned and/or their representatives shall be informed of the results of the assessment referred to in paragraph 1 and of all measures to be taken concerning health and safety at work.

Article 5

Action further to the results of the assessment

1.   Without prejudice to Article 6 of Directive 89/391/EEC, if the results of the assessment referred to in Article 4(1) reveal a risk to the safety or health or an effect on. the pregnancy or breastfeeding of a worker within the meaning of Article 2, the employer shall take the necessary measures to ensure that, by temporarily adjusting the working conditions and/or the working hours of the worker concerned, the exposure of that worker to such risks is avoided.

2.   If the adjustment of her working conditions and/or working hours is not technically and/or objectively feasible, or cannot reasonably be required on duly substantiated grounds, the employer shall take the necessary measures to move the worker concerned to another job.

3.   If moving her to another job is not technically and/or objectively feasible or cannot reasonably be required on duly substantiated grounds, the worker concerned shall be granted leave in accordance with national legislation and/or national practice for the whole of the period necessary to protect her safety or health.

4.   The provisions of this Article shall apply *mutatis mutandis* to the case where a worker pursuing an activity which is forbidden pursuant to Article 6 becomes pregnant or starts breastfeeding and informs her employer thereof.

Article 6

Cases in which exposure is prohibited

In addition to the general provisions concerning the protection of workers, in particular those relating to the limit values for occupational exposure:

1. pregnant workers within the meaning of Article 2 (a) may under no circumstances be obliged to perform duties for which the assessment has revealed a risk of exposure, which would jeopardise safety or health, to the agents and working conditions listed in Annex II, Section A;

2. workers who are breastfeeding, within the meaning of Article 2 (c), may under no circumstances be obliged to perform duties for which the assessment has revealed a risk of exposure which would jeopardise safety or health, to the agents and working conditions listed in Annex II, Section B.

Article 7

Night work

1.   Member States shall take the necessary measures to ensure that workers referred to in Article 2 are not obliged to perform night work during their pregnancy and for a period following childbirth which shall be determined by the national authority competent for safety and health, subject to submission, in accordance with the procedures laid down by the Member States, of a medical certificate stating that this is necessary for the safety or health of the worker concerned.

2.   The measures referred to in paragraph 1 must entail the possibility, in accordance with national legislation and/or national practice, of:

(a)   transfer to daytime work; or

(b)   leave from work or extension of maternity leave where such a transfer is not technically and/or objectively feasible or cannot reasonably by required on duly substantiated grounds.

Article 8

Maternity leave

1.   Member States shall take the necessary measures to ensure that workers within the meaning of Article 2 are entitled to a continuous period of maternity leave of a least 14 weeks allocated before and/or after confinement in accordance with national legislation and/or practice.

2.   The maternity leave stipulated in paragraph 1 must include compulsory maternity leave of at least two weeks allocated before and/or after confinement in accordance with national legislation and/or practice.

Article 9

Time off for ante-natal examinations

Member States shall take the necessary measures to ensure that pregnant workers within the meaning of Article 2 (a) are entitled to, in accordance with national legislation and/or practice, time off, without loss of pay, in order to attend ante-natal examinations, if such examinations have to take place during working hours.

Article 10

Prohibition of dismissal

In order to guarantee workers, within the meaning of Article 2, the exercise of their health and safety protection rights as recognised under this Article, it shall be provided that:
1.   Member States shall take the necessary measures to prohibit the dismissal of workers, within the meaning of Article 2, during the period from the beginning of their pregnancy to the end of the maternity leave referred to in Article 8 (1), save in exceptional cases not connected with their condition which are permitted under national legislation and/or practice and, where applicable, provided that the competent authority has given its consent;
2.   if a worker, within the meaning of Article 2, is dismissed during the period referred to in point 1, the employer must cite duly substantiated grounds for her dismissal in writing;
3.   Member States shall take the necessary measures to protect workers, within the meaning of Article 2, from consequences of dismissal which is unlawful by virtue of point 1.

Article 11

Employment rights

In order to guarantee workers within the meaning of Article 2 the exercise of their health and safety protection rights as recognised in this Article, it shall be provided that:
1.   in the cases referred to in Articles 5, 6 and 7, the employment rights relating to the employment contract, including the maintenance of a payment to, and/or entitlement to an adequate allowance for, workers within the meaning of Article 2, must be ensured in accordance with national legislation and/or national practice;
2.   in the case referred to in Article 8, the following must be ensured:
     (a)   the rights connected with the employment contract of workers within the meaning of Article 2, other than those referred to in point (b) below;
     (b)   maintenance of a payment to, and/or entitlement to an adequate allowance for, workers within the meaning of Article 2;
3.   the allowance referred to in point 2 (b) shall be deemed adequate if it guarantees income at least equivalent to that which the worker concerned would receive in the event, of a break in her activities on, grounds connected with her state of health, subject to any ceiling laid down under national legislation;
4.   Member States may make entitlement to pay or the allowance referred to in points 1 and 2 (b) conditional upon the worker concerned fulfilling the conditions of eligibility for such benefits laid down under national legislation.

These conditions may under no circumstances provide for periods of previous employment in excess of 12 months immediately prior to the presumed date of confinement.

Article 12

Defence of rights

Member States shall introduce into their national legal systems such measures as are necessary to enable all workers who should themselves wronged by failure to comply with the obligations arising from this Directive to pursue their claims by judicial process (and/or, in accordance with national laws and/or practices) by recourse to other competent authorities.

Article 13

Amendments to the Annexes

1. Strictly technical adjustments to Annex I as a result of technical progress, changes in international regulations or specifications and new findings in the area covered by this Directive shall be adopted in accordance with the procedure laid down in Article 17 of Directive 89/391/EEC.

2. Annex II may be amended only in accordance with the procedure laid down in Article 118a of the Treaty.

Article 14

Final provisions

1. Member States shall bring into force the laws, regulations and administrative provisions necessary to comply with this Directive not later than two years after the adoption thereof or ensure, at the latest two years after adoption of this Directive, that the two sides of industry introduce the requisite provisions by means of collective agreements, with Member States being required to make all the necessary provisions to enable them at all times to guarantee the results laid down by this Directive. They shall forthwith inform the Commission thereof.

2. When Member States adopt the measures referred to in paragraph 1, they shall contain a reference of this Directive or shall be accompanied by such reference on the occasion of their official publication. The methods of making such a reference shall be laid down by the Member States.

3. Member States shall communicate to the Commission the texts of the essential provisions of national law which they have already adopted or adopt in the field governed by this Directive.

4. Member States shall report to the Commission every five years on the practical implementation of the provisions of this Directive, indicating the points of view of the two sides of industry.

However; Member States shall report for the first time to the Commission on the practical implementation of the provisions of this Directive, indicating the points of view of the two sides of industry, four years after its adoption.

The Commission shall inform the European Parliament, the Council, the Economic and Social Committee and the Advisory Committee on Safety, Hygiene and Health Protection at Work.

5. The Commission shall periodically submit to the European, Parliament, the Council and the Economic and Social Committee a report on the implementation of this Directive, taking into account paragraphs 1, 2, and 3.

6. The Council will re-examine this Directive, on the basis of an assessment carried out on the basis of the reports referred to in the second subparagraph of paragraph 4 and, should the need arise, of a proposal, to be submitted by the Commission at the latest five years after adoption of the Directive.

Article 15

This Directive is addressed to the Member States.

Done at Luxembourg, 19 October 1992.

For the Council

The President

D CURRY

ANNEX I

NON-EXHAUSTIVE LIST OF AGENTS, PROCESSES AND WORKING CONDITIONS

(referred to in Article 4 (1))

A. Agents

1. *Physical agents* where these are regarded as agents causing foetal lesions and/or likely to disrupt placental attachment, and in particular:
(a) shocks, vibration or movement;
(b) handling of loads entailing risks, particularly of a dorsolumbar nature;
(c) noise;
(d) ionising radiation;
(e) non-ionising radiation;
(f) extremes of cold or heat;
(g) movements   and   postures,   travelling—either   inside   or   outside   the establishment—mental   and   physical   fatigue   and   other   physical   burdens connected with the activity of the worker within the meaning of Article 2 of the Directive.

2. *Biological agents*

Biological agents of risk groups 2, 3 and 3 within the meaning of Article 2(d) numbers 2, 3, and 4 of Directive 90/679/EEC, in, so far as it is known that these agents or the therapeutic measures necessitated by such agents endanger the health of pregnant women and the unborn child and in so far as they do not yet appear in Annex II.

3. *Chemical agents*

The following chemical agents in so far as it is known that they endanger the health of pregnant women and the unborn child and in so far as they do not yet appear in Annex II:
(a) substances labelled R 40, R 45, R 46, and R 47 under Directive 67/548/EEC in so far as they do not yet appear in Annex II;
(b) chemical agents in Annex I to Directive 90/394/EEC;
(c) mercury and mercury derivatives;
(d) antimitotic drugs;
(e) carbon monoxide;

(f)   chemical agents of known and dangerous percutaneous absorption.

B.   Processes
Industrial processes listed in Annex I to Directive 90/394/EEC.

C.   Working conditions
Underground mining work.

ANNEX II

NON-EXHAUSTIVE LIST OF AGENTS AND WORKING CONDITIONS REFERRED TO IN ARTICLE 6

A.   Pregnant workers within the meaning of Article 2 (a)

1.   *Agents*

(a) Physical agents
Work in hyperbaric atmosphere, e.g. pressurised enclosures and underwater diving.

(b) Biological agents
The following biological agents:
—   toxoplasma,
—   rubella virus,

unless the pregnant workers are proved to be adequately protected against such agents by immunisation.

(c) Chemical agents
Lead and lead derivatives in so far as these agents are capable of being absorbed by the human organism.

2.   *Working conditions*

Underground mining work.

B.   Workers who are breastfeeding within the meaning of Article 2(c)

1.   *Agents*

(a) Chemical agents
Lead and lead derivatives in so far as these agents are capable of being absorbed by the human organism.

2.   *Working conditions*
Underground mining work.

THE DEREGULATION AND CONTRACTING OUT ACT 1994

(1994 c. 40)

General note. This Act, under ss 1, 37, enables the repeal of Health and Safety Regulations. It is reproduced in part only. Those sections came into force on 3 January 1995.

An Act to amend, and make provision for the amendment of statutory provisions and rules of law in order to remove or reduce certain burdens affecting persons in the carrying on of trades, businesses or professions or otherwise, and for other deregulatory purposes; to make further provision in connection with the licensing of operators of goods vehicles; to make provision for and in connection with the contracting out of certain functions vested in Ministers of the Crown, local authorities, certain governmental bodies and the holders of certain offices; and for purposes connected therewith

[3 November 1994]

PART I
DEREGULATION

CHAPTER I
GENERAL

Removal or reduction of burdens

1. Power to remove or reduce certain statutory burdens on businesses, individuals etc.—(1) If, with respect to any provision made by an enactment, a Minister of the Crown is of the opinion—

(a) that the effect of the provision is such as to impose, or authorise or require the imposition of, a burden affecting any person in the carrying on of any trade, business or profession or otherwise, and

(b) that, by amending or repealing the enactment concerned and, where appropriate, by making such other provision as is referred to in subsection (4)(a) below, it would be possible, without removing any necessary protection, to remove or reduce the burden or, as the case may be, the authorisation or requirement by virtue of which the burden may be imposed,

he may, subject to the following provisions of this section and sections 2 to 4 below, by order amend or repeal that enactment.

(2) The reference in subsection (1)(b) above to reducing the authorisation or requirement by virtue of which a burden may be imposed includes a reference to shortening any period of time within which the burden may be so imposed.

(3) In this section and sections 2 to 4 below, in relation to an order under this section,—

(a) "the existing provision" means the provision by which the burden concerned is imposed or, as the case may be, is authorised or required to be imposed; and

(b) "the relevant enactment" means the enactment containing the existing provision.

(4) An order under this section shall be made by statutory instrument and may do all or any of the following—

(a) make provision (whether by amending any enactment or otherwise) creating a burden which relates to the subject matter of, but is less onerous than that imposed by, the existing provision;

(b) make such modifications of enactments as, in the opinion of the Minister concerned, are consequential upon, or incidental to, the amendment or repeal of the relevant enactment;

(c) contain such transitional provisions and savings as appear to the Minister to be appropriate;

(d) make different provision for different cases or different areas;

but no order shall be made under this section unless a draft of the order has been laid before and approved by a resolution of each House of Parliament.

(5) In this section and sections 2 to 4 below—

(a) "Minister of the Crown" has the same meaning as in the Ministers of the Crown Act 1975 and "Minister" shall be construed accordingly;

(b) "burden" includes a restriction, requirement or condition (including one requiring the payment of fees), together with—

(i) any sanction (whether criminal or otherwise) for failure to observe the restriction or to comply with the requirement or condition; and

(ii) any procedural provisions (including provisions for appeal) relevant to that sanction; and

(c) "enactment", subject to subsection (6) below, means an enactment contained in this Act or in any other Act passed before or in the same Session as this Act, or any provision of an order under this section.

(6) In paragraph (c) of subsection (5) above—

(a) "Act" does not include anything contained in Northern Ireland legislation, within the meaning of section 24 of the Interpretation Act 1978; and

(b) the reference to an enactment is a reference to an enactment as for the time being amended, extended or applied by or under any Act mentioned in that paragraph.

(7) Where a restriction, requirement or condition is subject to a criminal sanction (as mentioned in subsection (5)(b)(i) above), nothing in this section shall authorise the making of an amendment which would have the effect of leaving the restriction, requirement or condition in place but producing a different criminal sanction or altering any procedural provisions relevant to the criminal sanction.

2. Limitations on the power under section 1.—(1) If an order under section 1 above creates a new criminal offence, then, subject to subsections (2) and (3) below, that offence shall not be punishable—

(a) on indictment with imprisonment for a term of more than two years; or

(b) on summary conviction with imprisonment for a term exceeding six months or a fine exceeding level 5 on the standard scale or both.

(2) In the case of an offence which, if committed by an adult, is triable either on indictment or summarily and is not an offence triable on indictment only by virtue of—

(a) Part V of the Criminal Justice Act 1988, or

    (b)   section 457A(4) of the Criminal Procedure (Scotland) Act 1975,

the reference in subsection (1)(b) above to level 5 on the standard scale shall be construed as a reference to the statutory maximum.

(3) If an order under section 1 above abolishes an offence contained in the relevant enactment and the maximum penalties for that offence are greater than those specified in subsection (1) above, the order may create a new criminal offence having maximum penalties not exceeding those applicable to the offence which is abolished.

(4) An order under section 1 above shall not contain any provision—
    (a)   providing for any forcible entry, search or seizure, or
    (b)   compelling the giving of evidence,

unless, and then only to the extent that, a provision to that effect is contained in the relevant enactment and is abolished by the order.

3. Preliminary consultation.—(1) Before a Minister makes an order under section 1 above, he shall—
    (a)   consult such organisations as appear to him to be representative of interests substantially affected by his proposals; and
    (b)   consult such other persons as he considers appropriate.

(2) If it appears to the Minister, as a result of the consultation required by subsection (1) above, that it is appropriate to vary the whole or any part of his proposals, he shall undertake such further consultation with respect to the variations as appears to him to be appropriate.

(3) If, after the conclusion of—
    (a)   the consultation required by subsection (1) above, and
    (b)   any further consultation undertaken as mentioned in subsection (2) above,

the Minister considers it appropriate to proceed with the making of an order under section 1 above, he shall lay before Parliament a document containing his proposals in the form of a draft of the order, together with details of the matters specified in subsection (4) below.

(4) The matters referred to in subsection (3) above are—
    (a)   the burden, authorisation or requirement which it is proposed to remove or reduce;
    (b)   whether the existing provision affords any necessary protection and, if so, how that protection is to be continued if the burden, authorisation or requirement is removed or reduced;
    (c)   whether any savings in cost are estimated to result from the proposals and, if so, either the estimated amount or the reasons why savings should be expected;
    (d)   any other benefits which are expected to flow from the removal or reduction of the burden, authorisation or requirement;
    (e)   any consultation undertaken as required by subsection (1) or subsection (2) above;
    (f)   any representations received as a result of that consultation; and
    (g)   the changes (if any) which the Minister has made to his original proposals in the light of those representations.

(5) In giving details of the representations referred to in subsection (4)(f) above, the Minister shall not disclose any information relating to a particular person or business except—

(a) with the consent of that person or of the person carrying on that business; or

(b) in such a manner as not to identify that person or business.

(6) If, before the day on which this section comes into force, any consultation was undertaken which, had it been undertaken after that day, would to any extent have satisfied the requirements of subsection (1) above, those requirements shall to that extent be taken to have been satisfied.

4. Parliamentary consideration of proposals.—(1) Where a document has been laid before Parliament under section 3(3) above, no draft of an order under section 1 above to give effect (with or without variations) to proposals in that document shall be laid before Parliament until after the expiry of the period for Parliamentary consideration, as defined in subsection (2) below.

(2) In this section "the period for Parliamentary consideration", in relation to a document, means the period of sixty days beginning on the day on which it was laid before Parliament.

(3) In reckoning the period of sixty days referred to in subsection (2) above, no account shall be taken of any time during which Parliament is dissolved or prorogued or during which either House is adjourned for more than four days.

(4) In preparing a draft of an order under section 1 above to give effect, with or without variations, to proposals in a document laid before Parliament under section 3(3) above, the Minister concerned shall have regard to any representations made during the period for Parliamentary consideration and, in particular, to any resolution or report of, or of any committee of, either House of Parliament with regard to the document.

(5) Together with a draft of an order laid before Parliament under section 1(4) above, the Minister concerned shall lay a statement giving details of—
(a) any representations, resolution or report falling within subsection (4) above; and
(b) the changes (if any) which, in the light of any such representations, resolution or report, the Minister has made to his proposals as contained in the document previously laid before Parliament under section 3(3) above.

(6) Subsection (5) of section 3 above shall apply in relation to the representations referred to in subsection (5)(a) above as it applies in relation to the representations referred to in subsection (4)(f) of that section.

CHAPTER II
MISCELLANEOUS DEREGULATORY PROVISIONS

37. Power to repeal certain health and safety provisions.—(1) The appropriate authority may by regulations repeal or, as the case may be, revoke—
(a) any provision which is an existing statutory provision for the purposes of Part I of the Health and Safety at Work etc. Act 1974 ("the 1974 Act"),
(b) any provision of regulations under section 15 of the 1974 Act (health and safety regulations) which has effect in place of a provision which was an existing statutory provision for the purposes of that Part,
(c) any provision which is an existing statutory provision for the purposes of the Health and Safety at Work (Northern Ireland) Order 1978 ("the 1978 Order"), or

(d) any provision of regulations under Article 17 of the 1978 Order (health and safety regulations) which has effect in place of a provision which was an existing statutory provision for the purposes of that Order.

(2) Before making regulations under subsection (1) above, the appropriate authority shall consult—
   (a) in the case of regulations under paragraph (a) or (b) of that subsection, the Health and Safety Commission,
   (b) in the case of regulations under paragraph (c) or (d) of that subsection, the Health and Safety Agency for Northern Ireland,

and, in either case, such other persons as the appropriate authority considers appropriate.

(3) Instead of consulting such other persons as the appropriate authority considers it appropriate to consult under subsection (2) above, the authority may require the Health and Safety Commission or, as the case may be, the Health and Safety Agency for Northern Ireland to consult such persons as it considers appropriate for the purpose of deciding how it should respond to consultation under that subsection.

(4) Instead of consulting a person whom the appropriate authority considers it appropriate to consult under subsection (2) above, the authority may require the Health and Safety Commission or, as the case may be, the Health and Safety Agency for Northern Ireland to consult the person for the purpose of deciding how it should respond to consultation under that subsection.

(5) The appropriate may require consultation under subsection (3) or (4) above to be carried out in accordance with the authority's directions.

(6) Regulations under subsection (1) above may contain such transitional provisions and savings as the appropriate authority considers appropriate.

(7) Regulations under paragraph (a) or (b) of subsection (1) above shall be made by statutory instrument, and no instrument shall be made under that paragraph unless a draft of it has been laid before, and approved by a resolution of each House of Parliament.

(8) Regulations under subsection (1)(c) or (d) above—
   (a) shall be statutory rules for the purposes of the Statutory Rules (Northern Ireland) Order 1979, and
   (b) shall be subject to affirmative resolution, as defined in section 41(4) of the Interpretation Act (Northern Ireland) 1954, as if they were statutory instruments within the meaning of that Act.

(9) In this section, "appropriate authority"—
   (a) in relation to regulations under subsection (1)(a) or (b) above, means the Secretary of State, and
   (b) in relation to regulations under subsection (1)(c) or (d) above, means the Department concerned (within the meaning of the 1978 Order, but as if any reference to that Order included a reference to this section).

PART III
SUPPLEMENTARY

82.   Short title, commencement and extent.—(1) This Act may be cited as the Deregulation and Contracting Out Act 1994.

(2)   [*not printed in this work.*]

(3) The provisions of this Act set out below shall come into force on the day on which this Act is passed, that is to say—
- (a) Chapter I of Part I,
- (b) sections 14, 18, 25 to 30, 32 to 34 and 37,
- (c)–(g) [*not printed in this work.*]
- (h) this section.

(4)   The remaining provisions of this Act, other than section 36(2), shall come into force on such day as the Secretary of State may by order made by statutory instrument appoint; and different days may be so appointed for different provisions or for different purposes.

(5)   An order under subsection (4) above may include such transitional provisions and savings as appear to the Secretary of State to be necessary or expedient in connection with the coming into force of section 36(1) or Chapters III and IV of Part I of this Act.

(6), (7)   [*not printed in this work.*]

(8)   Except in so far as any provision of this Act otherwise provides, this Act, other than Chapter I of Part I and this section, does not extend to Northern Ireland.

THE IONISING RADIATIONS (OUTSIDE WORKERS) REGULATIONS 1993

(S.I. 1993 No. 2379)

General note. These Regulations, which came into force on 1 January 1994, implement, as respects Great Britain, Council Directive 90/641/Euratom on the operational protection of outside workers exposed to the risk of ionising radiation during their activities in controlled areas (see p. 155). As to a breach of a duty under these Regulations giving rise to civil liability, see reg. 9.

ARRANGEMENT OF REGULATIONS

The Secretary of State, being the designated Minister for the purpose of section 2(2) of the European Communities Act 1972 in relation to measures relating to the basic safety standards for the health protection of the general public and workers against the dangers from ionising radiation, in the exercise of the powers conferred on him by the said section 2(2) and sections 15(1), (2), (5)(b), (6)(b) and (9) and 82(3)(a) of, and paragraphs 11, 13(3), 14, 15(1) and 16 of Schedule 3 to, the Health and Safety at Work etc Act 1974 ("the 1974 Act") and of all other powers enabling him in that behalf, for the purpose of giving effect without modifications to proposals submitted to him by the Health and Safety Commission under section 11(2)(d) of the 1974 Act after the carrying out by the said Commission of consultations in accordance with section 50(3) of that Act, hereby makes the following Regulations:—

1.   Citation and commencement. These Regulations may be cited as The Ionising Radiations (Outside Workers) Regulations 1993 and shall come into force on 1st January 1994.

2.   Interpretation.—(1) In these Regulations, unless the context otherwise requires—

"the 1985 Regulations" means the Ionising Radiations Regulations 1985;

"activities" means any service provided by an outside worker in a controlled area for which the operator is responsible;

"the Basic Safety Standards Directive" means Council Directive 80/836/Euratom laying down the basic safety standards for the health protection of the general public and workers against the dangers from ionising radiation as amended by Council Directive 84/467/Euratom;

"classified person" means—

(a) in the case of a person employed by an outside undertaking in Great Britain, a person who has been designated as a classified person under regulation 9 of the 1985 Regulations; or

(b) in the case of a person employed by an outside undertaking in Northern Ireland or in another member State, a person who has been designated as a Category A exposed worker within the meaning of Article 23 of the Basic Safety Standards Directive;

"competent authority" in relation to the competent authority of Northern Ireland or of a member State means the authority empowered to enforce the basic safety standards for the health protection of workers against dangers from ionising radiation in Northern Ireland or that member State;

"controlled area" means—

(a) in the case of an area situated in Great Britain, an area which has been designated as a controlled area under regulation 8 of the 1985 Regulations; or

(b) in the case of an area situated in Northern Ireland or in another member State, an area subject to special rules for the purposes of protection against ionising radiation and to which access is controlled as specified in Article 20 of the Basic Safety Standards Directive;

"dose assessment" means the dose assessment made and recorded by an approved dosimetry service in accordance with regulation 13 of the 1985 Regulations;

"dose estimate" means the estimate of the dose received by the outside worker made by the operator in accordance with regulation 6(2)(b);

"member State" means a member State of the Communities;

"operator" means a person in a member State who is responsible for an area which is or is required to be designated as a controlled area and is—

(a) in the case of an area situated in Great Britain, an area in which there is carried out work with ionising radiation which is required to be notified under regulation 5 of the 1985 Regulations or would be so notifiable if it were not excepted from notification by regulation 5(1)(b) of those Regulations; or

(b) in the case of an area situated in Northern Ireland or in another member State, an area in which there is carried out an activity that is required to be reported under Article 3 of the Basic Safety Standards Directive;

"outside undertaking" means the employer established in a member State of a classified person who undertakes activities of any sort in the controlled area of an operator (other than itself);

"outside worker" means a classified person employed by an outside undertaking who undertakes activities of any sort in the controlled area of any operator (other than the controlled area of the outside undertaking which employs him);

"radiation passbook" means—

(a) in the case of an outside worker employed by an outside undertaking in Great Britain, a passbook approved for the purpose of these Regulations by the Executive; or

(b) in the case of an outside worker employed by an outside undertaking in Northern Ireland or in another member State, a passbook authorised by the competent authority for Northern Ireland or that member State, as the case may be.

(2) Except where otherwise expressly provided for in these Regulations, expressions used in these Regulations shall have the same meanings as in regulation 2(1) of the 1985 Regulations.

(3) In these Regulations unless the context otherwise requires, any reference to—

(a) an employer includes a reference to a self-employed person and any duty imposed by these Regulations on an employer shall extend to a self-employed person; and

(b) an employee includes reference to a self-employed person.

(4) Duties under these Regulations imposed upon the operator shall also be imposed upon the manager of a mine or quarry (within, in either case, the meaning of section 180 of the Mines and Quarries Act 1954) in so far as those duties relate to the mine or quarry or part of the mine or quarry of which he is the manager and to matters under his control.

(5) Duties under these Regulations imposed upon the operator shall also be imposed on the holder of a nuclear site licence under the Nuclear Installations Act 1965 in so far as the duties relate to the licensed site.

(6) In these Regulations, unless the context otherwise requires—

(a) a reference to a numbered regulation is a reference to the regulation in these Regulations so numbered; and

(b) a reference to a numbered paragraph is a reference to the paragraph so numbered in the regulation in which that reference occurs.

3. Application.—(1) Without prejudice to the requirements of regulation 4 of the 1985 Regulations (co-operation between employers), regulation 6(1)(b) of these Regulations (duties of the operator) shall not apply in relation to an outside worker who enters a controlled area of the operator in the exercise of powers conferred on him by law.

(2) In the case of an outside worker (working in a controlled area situated in Great Britain) employed by an outside undertaking established in Northern Ireland or in another member State, it shall be a sufficient compliance with regulation 13 (dose assessment) and regulation 16 (medical surveillance) of the 1985 Regulations, if the outside undertaking complies with—

(a) where the outside undertaking is established in Northern Ireland, regulations 13 and 16 of the Ionising Radiations Regulations (Northern Ireland) 1985; or

(b) where the outside undertaking is established in another member State, the legislation in that State implementing Chapters II and III of the Basic Safety Standards Directive where such legislation exists.

(3) The duties imposed by regulations 4 and 5 on the outside undertaking shall only apply to outside undertakings established in Great Britain.

(4)   The duties imposed by regulation 6 on the operator shall only apply to the operator of a controlled area situated in Great Britain.

(5)   The duties imposed by regulation 7 on the outside worker shall only apply to an outside worker working in a controlled area situated in Great Britain.

(6)   Subject to paragraph (2), nothing in these Regulations shall prejudice the requirements of the 1985 Regulations.

(7)   These Regulations shall not extend to Northern Ireland.

4.   Duties of the outside undertaking.—(1) It shall be the duty of the outside undertaking which employs an outside worker to undertake activities in the controlled area of an operator—

  (a)   before commencing the activities, to make suitable arrangements to obtain from the operator information about the radiological risks relevant to the intended activities and to the controlled areas in which they are to be undertaken and about any special training that may be required;

  (b)   to ensure that the outside worker concerned has received the necessary information and training with a view to ensuring his safety in the course of those activities; and

  (c)   to make suitable arrangements with the operator to ensure that an estimate is made of the dose received by the worker in the course of those activities.

(2)   Where an outside undertaking employs an outside worker to work in Northern Ireland or another member State, the outside undertaking shall make suitable arrangements to ensure that a continuing record of the assessment of the dose received by the outside worker is maintained by the approved dosimetry service throughout the period of his employment by the outside undertaking.

5.   Radiation passbooks.—(1) The outside undertaking shall ensure that each outside worker employed by it is provided with an individual radiation passbook which shall be non-transferable and in which shall be entered the particulars set out in the Schedule to these Regulations.

(2)   The outside undertaking shall make suitable arrangements to ensure that the particulars entered in the radiation passbook are kept up to date.

(3)   The outside undertaking shall ensure that a suitable record is kept of the issue of any radiation passbook to each outside worker to whom one has been issued and of the loss of any passbook which has been reported to it in accordance with regulation 7(1)(a) and such records shall be kept for at least 5 years after the passbook ceased to be used by the outside worker.

(4)   Where the outside undertaking has had the loss of a passbook reported to it in accordance with regulation 7(1)(a), it shall ensure that an investigation is made of the circumstances of that loss, and an assessment or, if that is not reasonably practicable an estimate, is made of the dose received by the outside worker and shall ensure that the result of that investigation is entered in the record referred to in paragraph (3).

(5)   When an outside worker has returned a radiation passbook to the outside undertaking in accordance with regulation 7(1)(c), the outside undertaking shall ensure that the passbook is kept for at least 5 years from that date.

(6) Where the passbook has been returned to the outside undertaking as it is full and requires renewal or its loss has been reported to the outside undertaking, the outside undertaking shall ensure that a new passbook is issued forthwith to the outside worker and in a case where the passbook has been lost, the new passbook shall be clearly marked with the word "replacement".

6. Duties of the operator.—(1) It shall be the duty of an operator who has an outside worker undertaking activities in any controlled area under his control, before the commencement of those activities—

(a) to make suitable arrangements to provide the outside undertaking with the information referred to in regulation 4(1)(a);

(b) to take all reasonable steps to ensure by reference to the radiation passbook or by other means that the outside worker—

(i) has received any specific training required for the activities,

(ii) is medically fit to undertake the activities, and

(iii) has been provided with and has been trained to use any personal protective equipment that may be necessary for the safe performance of the activities.

(2) It shall be the duty of the operator to ensure that—

(a) the outside worker receives individual exposure monitoring, appropriate to the nature of the activities;

(b) an estimate of the dose received by the outside worker is made; and

(c) the radiation passbook is made available to the outside worker at his request.

(3) Subject to paragraph (4), as soon as is reasonably practicable after the activities referred to in paragraph (1) have been completed, it shall be the duty of the operator to ensure that an estimate of the dose received by the outside worker is entered into the radiation passbook of the outside worker.

(4) In a case where the operator no longer has access to the passbook of the outside worker when the information required by paragraph (3) becomes available to him, he shall forthwith give that information to the outside undertaking.

(5) The duty imposed on the operator under paragraph (3) to ensure that an estimate of the dose received by the outside worker is entered into the passbook of the outside worker when the activities have been completed, shall not apply in any case where having regard to—

(a) the nature and duration of the activities undertaken in the controlled areas under the control of the operator; and

(b) the pattern of past and present activities undertaken by the outside worker and the estimates of the dose previously received entered in the passbook,

and after consulting the outside undertaking, the operator, with the agreement of the outside undertaking, is satisfied that the outside worker will be most unlikely to receive in the month in which the activities are undertaken a radiation dose which exceeds one thirty-sixth part of any annual dose limit for that worker and in such a case the operator shall enter a cumulative estimate of the dose received each month.

7. Duties of the outside worker.—(1) It shall be the duty of every outside worker—

(a)   to take reasonable care of the radiation passbook issued to him, and if it is lost report the loss forthwith to the outside undertaking and in such a case co-operate with the outside undertaking in any investigation made in accordance with regulation 5(4);

(b)   not to misuse the radiation passbook issued to him or falsify or attempt to falsify any of the information contained in it;

(c)   if he leaves the employment of the outside undertaking or the radiation passbook is full and requires renewal, forthwith to give the passbook to the outside undertaking; and

(d)   to make the radiation passbook available to the operator of any controlled area in which he undertakes activities and to take the passbook with him when his activities in that controlled area have been completed.

(2)   It shall also be the duty of the outside worker to take such steps as are reasonable for a person in his position to take to ensure that an estimate of the dose that he receives in the course of those activities is either entered in his passbook or notified to the outside undertaking.

(3)   Where an outside worker who has lost a passbook subsequently finds it, he shall forthwith report its finding to the outside undertaking and return that passbook to the undertaking.

8.   Defences under these Regulations.—(1) It shall be a defence in any proceedings against an outside undertaking for a breach of a duty under these Regulations for that outside undertaking to show that—

(a)   it had entered into a contract in writing with the operator for him to perform that duty on its behalf; and

(b)   the breach of duty was a result of the operator's failure to fulfil that contract.

(2)   It shall be a defence in any proceedings against an operator for a breach of a duty under these Regulations for the operator to show that—

(a)   he had entered into a contract in writing with the outside undertaking for it to perform that duty on his behalf; and

(b)   the breach of duty was a result of the outside undertaking's failure to fulfil that contract.

(3)   The person charged shall not, without leave of the court, be entitled to rely on the defence referred to in paragraph (1) or (2) unless, within a period ending 7 clear days before the hearing, he has served on the prosecutor a notice in writing that he intends to rely on the defence and this notice shall be accompanied by a copy of the contract on which he intends to rely and, if that contract is not in English, an accurate translation of that contract into English.

(4)   For the purpose of enabling the other party to the contract to be charged with and convicted of an offence by virtue of section 36 of the Health and Safety at Work etc Act 1974, a person who establishes a defence under this regulation shall nevertheless be treated for the purposes of that section as having committed the offence.

9.   Enforcement and civil liability. Insofar as any provision of regulation 4, 5, 6 or 7 is made under section 2 of the European Communities Act 1972—

(a) the provisions of the Health and Safety at Work etc Act 1974 which relate to the approval of codes of practice and their use in criminal proceedings, enforcement and offences shall apply to that provision as if that provision had been made under section 15 of that Act; and

(b) that provision shall, in the event of a breach of any duty imposed by it, confer a right of action in civil proceedings insofar as that breach of duty causes damage.

10. Exemption certificates.—(1) Subject to paragraph (2), the Executive may, by a certificate in writing, exempt—

(a) any person or class of persons; or

(b) any premises or class of premises,

from all or any of the requirements or prohibitions imposed by these Regulations and any such exemption may be granted subject to conditions and to a limit of time and may be revoked by a certificate in writing at any time.

(2) The Executive shall not grant any such exemption unless, having regard to the circumstances of the case and in particular to—

(a) the conditions, if any, that it proposes to attach to the exemption; and

(b) any other requirements imposed by or under any enactments which apply to the case,

it is satisfied that—

(c) the health and safety of persons who are likely to be affected by the exemption will not be prejudiced in consequence of it; and

(d) compliance with the fundamental radiation protection provisions underlying regulations 6(1) and (2), 7, 8(1) and (2), 9(1), 13(2), 16(3), 24(1), 27(1) and 33(1) of the 1985 Regulations will be achieved.

11. Extension outside Great Britain. These Regulations shall apply to any work outside Great Britain to which sections 1 to 59 and 80 to 82 of the Health and Safety at Work etc Act 1974 apply by virtue of the Health and Safety at Work etc Act 1974 (Application outside Great Britain) Order 1989 as they apply to work within Great Britain.

12. Modifications relating to the Ministry of Defence etc.—(1) In this regulation any reference to—

(a) "visiting forces" is a reference to visiting forces within the meaning of any provision of Part 1 of the Visiting Forces Act 1952; and

(b) "headquarters or organisation" is a reference to a headquarters or organisation designated for the purposes of the International Headquarters and Defence Organisations Act 1964.

(2) The Secretary of State for Defence may, in the interests of national security, by a certificate in writing exempt—

(a) Her Majesty's Forces;

(b) visiting forces;

(c) any member of a visiting force working in or attached to any headquarters or organisation; or

(d) any person engaged in working with ionising radiation for, or on behalf of, the Secretary of State for Defence, from all or any of the requirements or prohibitions imposed by these Regulations and any such exemption may be granted subject to conditions and to a limit of time and may be revoked at any time by a certificate in writing, except that, where any such exemption is granted, suitable arrangements shall be made for the assessment and recording of doses of ionising radiation received by persons to whom the exemption relates.

THE SCHEDULE

Regulation 5(1)

PARTICULARS TO BE ENTERED IN THE RADIATION PASSBOOK

1. Individual serial number of the passbook.
2. A statement that the passbook has been approved by the Executive for the purpose of these Regulations.
3. Date of issue of the passbook by the approved dosimetry service.
4. The name, telephone number and mark of endorsement of the issuing approved dosimetry service.
5. The name, address, telephone and telex/fax number of the outside undertaking.
6. Full name (surname, forenames), date of birth, gender and national insurance number of the outside worker to whom the passbook has been issued.
7. Date of the last medical review of the outside worker and the relevant classification in the health record maintained under regulation 16 of the 1985 Regulations as fit, fit subject to conditions (which shall be specified and, for the purposes of these Regulations, shall include any special dose limit applicable to the outside worker) or unfit, name and signature of an authorised person and date of entry.
8. The cumulative dose assessment in mSv for the year to date for the outside worker, external (whole body, organ or tissue) and/or internal as appropriate and the date of the end of the last assessment period.
9. In respect of activities performed by the outside worker, (except where regulation 6(5) applies)—
   (a) the name and address of the relevant operator;
   (b) the period covered by the performance of the activities;
   (c) estimated dose information, which shall be, as appropriate—
       (i) an estimate of any whole body effective dose equivalent in mSv received by the outside worker;
       (ii) in the event of non-uniform exposure, an estimate of the dose equivalent in mSv to organs and tissues as appropriate;
       (iii) in the event of internal exposure, an estimate of the committed dose in mSv;
   (d) the name and signature of the person making the entry, who shall be a person authorised by the operator to make such entries.

THE MISCELLANEOUS FACTORIES (TRANSITIONAL PROVISIONS) REGULATIONS 1993

(S.I. 1993 No. 2482)

General note. These Regulations, which came into force on 17 November 1993, make provision for safety in the factories specified in the Schedules. The Regulations will cease to have effect on 1 January 1997 when the corresponding provisions in the Provision and Use of Work Equipment Regulations 1992 (S.I. 1992 No. 2932) will come into force in respect of such factories.

The Secretary of State, in exercise of the powers conferred upon him by sections 15(1) and (2) and 82(3)(a) of, and paragraph 1(1) and (2) of Schedule 3 to, the Health and Safety at Work etc Act 1974, and of all other powers enabling him in that behalf and for the purpose of giving effect without modifications to proposals submitted to him by the Health and Safety Commission under section 11(2)(d) of the said Act after the carrying out by the said Commission of consultations in accordance with section 50(3) of that Act, hereby makes the following Regulations:

1. Citation, commencement and interpretation.—(1) These Regulations may be cited as the Miscellaneous Factories (Transitional Provisions) Regulations 1993 and shall come into force on 17th November 1993.

(2) In these Regulations—
"work equipment" has the meaning assigned to it by regulation 2(1) of the Provision and Use of Work Equipment Regulations 1992;
"workplace" and "new workplace" have the meanings respectively assigned to each of them by regulation 2(1) of the Workplace (Health, Safety and Welfare) Regulations 1992.

(3) Words and phrases used in the Schedules to these Regulations and in the Factories Act 1961 shall have the same meanings in the said Schedules as in that Act.

2. Transitional provisions in factories specified in the Schedules.— (1) The provisions of Schedule 1 to these Regulations shall have effect with respect to work equipment first provided for use in any premises or undertaking before 1st January 1993.

(2) Subject to paragraph (3) of this regulation, the provisions of Schedule 2 to these Regulations shall have effect with respect to work equipment first provided for use in any premises or undertaking before 1st January 1993.

(3) Until 1st January 1996, the provisions of Schedule 2 to these Regulations shall not apply with respect to work equipment provided for use in a workplace or part of a workplace which is not—
(a) a new workplace; or
(b) a modification, an extension or a conversion.

(4)   These Regulations shall cease to have effect on 1st January 1997.

SCHEDULE 1

Regulation 2(1)

AERATED WATER

1.   Every employer of employees who work in any factory or part thereof in which is carried on the manufacture of aerated water and processes incidental thereto shall ensure that—

    (a)   all machines for filling bottles or syphons shall be so constructed, placed or fenced, as to prevent as far as possible a fragment of a bursting bottle or syphon from striking any person employed in the works; and

    (b)   the fittings of a filled syphon shall not be polished unless the syphon is held in a box or case so constructed as to prevent as far as possible the escape of fragments of a bursting syphon. Provided that this sub-paragraph shall not apply in the case of syphons filled at a pressure of less than 9 bars.

SCHEDULE 2

Regulation 2(2)

PART I
HORIZONTAL MILLING MACHINES

1.   The occupier of any factory or part thereof where a horizontal milling machine is used shall ensure that the requirements of paragraphs 2 to 7 of this Schedule are observed.

2.   Effective measures shall be taken for securing and maintaining sufficient and suitable lighting at the machines, and where artificial lighting is provided the lighting points shall be so placed or shaded as to prevent direct rays of light from impinging on the eyes of the operator while he is operating the machine.

3.—(1) The cutter or cutters of every horizontal milling machine shall be fenced, by a strong guard properly adjusted to the work, which shall enclose the whole cutting surface except such part as is necessarily exposed for the milling operations.

(2) The guard shall either:—

    (a)   be provided with adequate side flanges; or

    (b)   extend on each side of the cutter or cutters to the end of the arbor, or to the arbor support, or to a distance of not less than half the diameter of the cutter,

provided that sub-paragraph (2) of this paragraph shall not apply to cutters used for face milling.

4.   Every horizontal milling machine shall be provided with an efficient starting and stopping appliance, and the control of this appliance shall be in such a position as to be readily and conveniently operated by the person operating the machine.

5.   When suds or other cutting lubricants are used on a horizontal milling machine suitable arrangements shall be made to enable the operator to apply the suds or lubricant or to adjust the supply pipe, and suitable means shall be provided for removing the swarf.

6.   The guards or other appliances required by this Part of this Schedule shall be maintained in an efficient state and shall be constantly kept in position while the milling cutter is in motion except when the tool setter is setting up the machine.

7.   Nothing in paragraph 3 shall apply to any milling cutter—

    (a)   used on a spindle which exceeds 65 millimetres in diameter or arbor which exceeds 50 millimetres in diameter at the place where the cutter is mounted; or

    (b)   when used for—

    (i) making tools, jigs or gauges for use in the factory or similarly accurate operations where during the actual cutting process all those parts of the machine which control the relative positions of the work and the cutter can be manipulated by the operator at his unrestricted discretion,

   (ii) internal milling,

  (iii) end milling other than face milling,

  (iv) automatic gear cutting,

   (v) automatic hobbing,

  (vi) automatic profiling,

 (vii) thread milling.

PART II
JUTE

8.   The occupier of any factory or part thereof in which is carried on the spinning or weaving of jute or any process incidental thereto or the calendering or cropping of jute cloth shall ensure that in any workroom every steam pipe and steam exhaust pipe and the ends of every steam heated cylinder used in connection with a dressing machine shall be kept effectively covered with insulating material in good repair in such manner as to prevent, so far as is reasonably practicable, the escape of heat therefrom.

PART III
IRON AND STEEL FOUNDRIES

9.   The occupier of any iron foundry or steel foundry shall ensure that no person carries out any work within a distance of 4 metres from a vertical line passing through the delivery end of any spout of a cupola or furnace, being a spout used for delivering molten metal, or within a distance of 2.4 metres from a vertical line passing through the nearest part of any ladle which is in position at the end of such a spout, except, in either case, where it is necessary for the proper use or maintenance of a cupola or furnace that that work should be carried out within that distance or that work is being carried out at such a time and under such conditions that there is no danger to the person carrying it out from molten metal which is being obtained from the cupola or furnace or is in a ladle in position at the end of the spout.

10. In paragraph 9 of this Schedule, "iron foundry" and "steel foundry" means those parts of a factory in which the production of iron castings or, as the case may be, steel castings (not being the production of pig iron or the production of steel in the form of ingots and not including die-casting) is carried on by casting in moulds made of sand, loam, moulding composition or other mixture of materials, or by shell moulding or by centrifugal casting in metal moulds lined with sand, together with any part of the factory in which any of the following processes are carried on as incidental processes in connection with, and in the course of, such production, namely, the preparation and mixing of materials used in the foundry process, the preparation of moulds and cores, knockout operations and dressing or fettling operations.

THE INDUSTRIAL TRIBUNALS (CONSTITUTION AND RULES OF PROCEDURE) REGULATIONS 1993

(S.I. 1993 No. 2687 as amended by S.I. 1994 No. 536)

General note. These Regulations, which came into force on 16 December 1993, apply generally to industrial tribunal procedure on unfair dismissal etc. In this work, we reproduce only the Schedule dealing with improvement and prohibition notices under the Health and Safety at Work etc. Act 1974, s. 23.

ARRANGEMENT OF REGULATIONS

The Secretary of State, in exercise of the powers conferred on him by section 24(2) of the Health and Safety at Work etc Act 1974, section 128(1) and (5), section 154(3) and paragraphs 1, 1A and 1B of Schedule 9 to the Employment Protection (Consolidation) Act 1978, and of all other powers enabling him in that behalf, and after consultation with the Council on Tribunals, hereby makes the following Regulations:—

1. Citation, commencement and revocation.—(1) These Regulations may be cited as the Industrial Tribunals (Constitution and Procedure) Regulations 1993 and the Rules of Procedure contained in Schedules 1, 2, 3, 4 and 5 to these Regulations may be referred to, respectively, as—

    (a)   the Industrial Tribunals Rules of Procedure 1993;

    (b)   the Industrial Tribunals Complementary Rules of Procedure 1993;

    (c)   the Industrial Tribunals (Levy Appeals) Rules of Procedure 1993;

    (d)   the Industrial Tribunals (Improvement and Prohibition Notices Appeals) Rules of Procedure 1993; and

    (e)   the Industrial Tribunals (Non-Discrimination Notices Appeals) Rules of Procedure 1993.

(2)   These Regulations shall come into force on 16th December 1993.

(3)   The following Regulations are hereby revoked—
The Industrial Tribunals (England and Wales) Regulations 1965;
The Industrial Tribunals (England and Wales) (Amendment) Regulations 1967;
The Industrial Tribunals (England and Wales) (Amendment) Regulations 1970;
The Industrial Tribunals (Improvement and Prohibition Notices Appeals) Regulations 1974;
The Industrial Tribunals (Amendment) Regulations 1977;
The Industrial Tribunals (Non-Discrimination Notices Appeals) Regulations 1977;
The Industrial Tribunals (Rules of Procedure) Regulations 1985.

2.   Interpretation.—(1) In these Regulations and in Schedules 1, 2, 3, 4 and 5, unless the context otherwise requires—
"the 1978 Act" means the Employment Protection (Consolidation) Act 1978;
"the 1992 Act" means the Trade Union and Labour Relations (Consolidation) Act 1992;
"chairman" means the President or a member of the panel of chairmen selected in accordance with regulation 7(1), or the President where a Minister of the Crown so directs in accordance with section 128(6) of the 1978 Act;
"the clerk" means the person appointed as clerk to the tribunal by the Secretary of the Tribunals or a Regional Secretary to act in that capacity at one or more hearings;
"hearing" means a sitting of a tribunal duly constituted for the purpose of receiving evidence, hearing addresses and witnesses or doing anything lawfully requisite to enable the tribunal to reach a decision on any question;
"the Office of the Tribunals" means the Central Office of the Industrial Tribunals (England and Wales);
"panel of chairmen" means the panel appointed under regulation 5(1)(a);
"the President" means the President of the Industrial Tribunals (England and Wales) or the person nominated by the Lord Chancellor to discharge for the time being the functions of the President;
"Regional Chairman" means a member of the panel of chairmen who has been appointed to the position of Regional Chairman in accordance with regulation 6 (1) or who has been nominated to discharge the functions of a Regional Chairman in accordance with regulation 6(2);
"Regional Office of the Industrial Tribunals" means a regional office which has been established under the Office of the Tribunals for an area specified by the President;
"Regional Secretary" means the person for the time being acting as the secretary of a Regional Office of the Industrial Tribunals;
"Register" means the Register of applications, appeals and decisions kept in pursuance of regulation 9;
"the Secretary" means the person for the time being appointed to act as the Secretary of the Office of the Tribunals;
"tribunal" means an industrial tribunal (England and Wales) established in pursuance of regulation 4 and in relation to any proceedings means the tribunal to which the proceedings have been referred by the President or a Regional Chairman.

(2)   In these Regulations, in so far as they relate to the rules in Schedules 1 and 2, and in those Schedules, unless the context otherwise requires—
"the 1970 Act" means the Equal Pay Act 1970;

"the 1975 Act" means the Sex Discrimination Act 1975;

"the 1976 Act" means the Race Relations Act 1976;

"the 1986 Act" means the Sex Discrimination Act 1986;

"decision" in relation to a tribunal includes—

> a declaration,
>
> an order, including an order striking out any originating application or notice of appearance made under rule 4(7) or 13(2),
>
> a recommendation or an award of the tribunal, and
>
> a determination under rule 6,
>
> but does not include any other interlocutory order or any other decision on an interlocutory matter;

"equal value claim" means a claim by an applicant which rests upon entitlement to the benefit of an equality clause by virtue of the operation of section 1(2)(c) of the Equal Pay Act;

"expert" means a member of the panel of independent experts within the meaning of section 2A(4) of the Equal Pay Act;

"report" means a report required by a tribunal to be prepared by an expert, pursuant to section 2A(1)(b) of the Equal Pay Act;

"respondent" means a party to the proceedings before a tribunal other than the applicant.

(3)   [*not printed in this work*]

(4)   In these Regulations, in so far as they relate to the rules in Schedule 4, and in that Schedule, unless the context otherwise requires—

"the 1974 Act" means the Health and Safety at Work etc Act 1974;

"decision" in relation to a tribunal includes a direction under rule 4 and any order which is not an interlocutory order;

"improvement notice" means a notice under section 21 of the 1974 Act;

"inspector" means a person appointed under section 19(1) of the 1974 Act;

"prohibition notice" means a notice under section 22 of the 1974 Act;

"respondent" means the inspector who issued the improvement notice or prohibition notice which is the subject of the appeal.

(5)   [*not printed in this work*]

3.   President of Industrial Tribunals.—(1) There shall be a President of the Industrial Tribunals (England and Wales) who shall be appointed by the Lord Chancellor and shall be a person having a seven year general qualification within the meaning of section 71 of the Courts and Legal Services Act 1990.

(2)   The President may resign his office by notice in writing to the Lord Chancellor.

(3)   The President shall vacate his office at the end of the completed year of service in the course of which he attains the age of 72 years.

(4)   If the Lord Chancellor is satisfied that the President is incapacitated by infirmity of mind or body from discharging the duties of his office, or the President is adjudged to be bankrupt or makes a composition or arrangement with his creditors, the Lord Chancellor may revoke his appointment.

(5)   The functions of President under these Regulations may, if he is for any reason unable to act or during any vacancy in his office, be discharged by a person nominated for that purpose by the Lord Chancellor.

4. Establishment of industrial tribunals.—(1) The President shall from time to time determine the number of tribunals to be established in England and Wales for the purposes of determining proceedings.

(2) The President or, in relation to the area specified in relation to him, a Regional Chairman shall determine at what times and in what places in England and Wales tribunals shall sit.

5. Panels of members of tribunals.—(1) There shall be three panels of members of the Industrial Tribunals (England and Wales), namely—

(a) a panel of persons, having a seven year general qualification within the meaning of the Courts and Legal Services Act 1990, appointed by the Lord Chancellor;

(b) a panel of persons appointed by the Secretary of State after consultation with such organisations or associations of organisations representative of employees as he sees fit; and

(c) a panel of persons appointed by the Secretary of State after consultation with such organisations or associations of organisations representative of employers as he sees fit.

(2) Members of the panels constituted under these Regulations shall hold and vacate office under the terms of the instrument under which they are appointed but may resign their office by notice in writing, in the case of a member of the panel of chairmen, to the Lord Chancellor and, in any other case, to the Secretary of State; and any such member who ceases to hold office shall be eligible for reappointment.

6. Regional Chairmen.—(1) The President may from time to time appoint Regional Chairmen from the panel of chairmen and each Regional Chairman shall be responsible for the administration of justice by tribunals in the area specified by the President in relation to him.

(2) The President or the Regional Chairman for an area may from time to time nominate a member of the panel of chairmen to discharge for the time being the functions of the Regional Chairman for that area.

7. Composition of tribunals.—(1) For each hearing of any matter before a tribunal the President or the Regional Chairman shall, subject to paragraph 5, select a chairman, who shall be the President or a member of the panel of chairmen, and the President or the Regional Chairman may select himself.

(2) In any proceedings which are to be determined by a tribunal comprising a chairman (selected in accordance with paragraph (1) above) and two other members, those other members shall be selected by the President or by the Regional Chairman, as to one member from the panel of persons appointed by the Secretary of State under regulation 5(1)(b) and as to the other from the panel of persons appointed under regulation 5(1)(c).

(3) In any proceedings which are to be determined by a tribunal whose composition is described in paragraph (2), those proceedings may, with the consent of the parties, be heard and determined in the absence of any one member other than the chairman, and in that event the tribunal shall be properly constituted.

(4) The President or the Regional Chairman may at any time select from the appropriate panel another person in substitution for the chairman or other member of the tribunal previously selected to hear any proceedings before a tribunal.

(5)   Paragraph (1) does not apply where a Minister of the Crown has issued a direction in accordance with section 128(6) of the 1978 Act (direction on grounds of national security that proceedings be heard and determined by the President).

8.   Proceedings of tribunals.—(1) Subject to paragraphs (2), (3) and (4), the rules in Schedule 1 shall apply in relation to all proceedings before a tribunal except where separate rules of procedure made under the provisions of any enactment are applicable.

(2)   In proceedings to which the rules in Schedule 1 apply and which involve an equal value claim, the rules in Schedule 2 (including rule 8A) shall apply in place of rules 4, 9, 10, 12, 13 and 20 in Schedule 1.

(3)   The rules contained in Schedules 1 and 2 shall apply in proceedings to which they relate where—
- (a)   the respondent or one of the respondents resides or carries on business in England and Wales; or
- (b)   had the remedy been by way of action in the county court, the cause of action would have arisen wholly or in part in England and Wales; or
- (c)   the proceedings are to determine a question which has been referred to the tribunal by a court in England or Wales.

(4)   The rules in Schedules 3, 4 and 5 shall apply in relation to proceedings before a tribunal which relate to matters arising in England and Wales and consist, respectively, in—
- (a)   an appeal by a person assessed to levy imposed under a levy order made under section 12 of the 1982 Act;
- (b)   an appeal against an improvement or prohibition notice under section 23 of the 1974 Act; and
- (c)   an appeal against a non-discrimination notice under section 68 of the 1975 Act or section 59 of the 1976 Act.

9.   Register. The Secretary shall maintain a Register of applications, appeals and decisions which shall be open to the inspection of any person without charge at all reasonable hours.

10.   Proof of decisions of tribunals. The production in any proceedings in any court of a document purporting to be certified by the Secretary to be a true copy of an entry of a decision in the Register shall, unless the contrary is proved, be sufficient evidence of the document and of the facts stated therein.

11.   Transitional provisions relating to rules of procedure.—(1) The rules in Schedules 1, 2, 3, 4 and 5 (in this regulation referred to as "the new rules") shall apply in all proceedings to which they relate, irrespective of when those proceedings were commenced, as from 16th December 1993, and the rules of procedure in—
- (a)   Schedule 2 to the Industrial Tribunals (England and Wales) Regulations 1965;
- (b)   the Schedule to the Industrial Tribunals (Improvement and Prohibition Notices Appeal) Regulations 1974;
- (c)   the Schedule to the Industrial Tribunals (Non-Discrimination Notices Appeals) Regulations 1977;
- (d)   the Industrial Tribunals Rules of Procedure 1985 ("the 1985 rules"); and
- (e)   the Industrial Tribunals Complementary Rules of Procedure 1985,

(in this regulation together referred to as "the old rules") shall cease to have effect in relation to proceedings on that date.

(2) Anything done validly under or pursuant to the old rules before 16th December 1993 shall be treated as having been done validly for the purposes of these Regulations and the new rules, whether or not what was done could have been done under or pursuant to these Regulations and the new rules.

(3) Notwithstanding paragraph (1), in any proceedings in which a pre-hearing assessment (under Rule 6 of the 1985 rules) has taken place or commenced before 16th December 1993, Rule 6 of those rules shall continue to have effect in relation to those proceedings and no pre-hearing review (under rule 7 in Schedule 1) may take place.

(4) Where the first fixing of the date of a pre-hearing assessment occurs before 16th December 1993 but paragraph (3) does not apply, the hearing shall be refixed as a pre-hearing review (under rule 7 in Schedule 1).

12. Transitional provisions relating to composition of tribunals.—
(1) Except as mentioned in paragraph (2), a tribunal hearing an originating application on or after 16th December 1993 shall be composed of a chairman and two other members (or, with the consent of the parties, a chairman and one other member) where the first fixing of a date for the hearing of the originating application occurred before 30th November 1993.

(2) A tribunal hearing such an originating application on or after 16th December 1993 may be composed of a chairman alone for either of the following purposes—
  (a) making an order dismissing the proceedings where the appellant or applicant has given written notice of the abandonment of the proceedings; and
  (b) deciding an application in accordance with the written agreement of the parties.

SCHEDULES 1–3

[*not printed in this work*]

SCHEDULE 4

Regulation 8(4)

RULES OF PROCEDURE APPLICABLE TO APPEALS AGAINST IMPROVEMENT AND PROHIBITION NOTICES

Notice of appeal

1. An appeal shall be commenced by the appellant sending to the Secretary a notice of appeal which shall be in writing and shall set out—
  (a) the name and address of the appellant and, if different, an address within the United Kingdom to which he requires notices and documents relating to the appeal to be sent;
  (b) the date of the improvement notice or prohibition notice appealed against and the address of the premises or place concerned;
  (c) the name and address of the respondent;
  (d) particulars of the requirements or directions appealed against; and
  (e) the grounds of the appeal.

Time limit for bringing appeal

2.—(1) Subject to paragraph (2), the notice of appeal shall be sent to the Secretary within 21 days from the date of the service on the appellant of the notice appealed against.

(2) A tribunal may extend the time mentioned above where it is satisfied, on an application made in writing to the Secretary either before or after the expiration of that time, that it is not or was not reasonably practicable for an appeal to be brought within that time.

Action upon receipt of notice of appeal

3. Upon receiving a notice of appeal the Secretary shall enter particulars of it in the Register and shall send a copy of it to the respondent and inform the parties in writing of the case number of the appeal entered in the Register (which shall thereafter constitute the title of the proceedings) and of the address to which notices and other communications to the Secretary shall be sent.

Application for direction suspending the operation of a prohibition notice

4.—(1) Where an appeal has been brought against a prohibition notice and an application is made to the tribunal by the appellant in pursuance of section 24(3)(b) of the 1974 Act for a direction suspending the operation of the notice until the appeal is finally disposed of or withdrawn, the application shall be sent in writing to the Secretary and shall set out—

    (a) the case number of the appeal if known to the appellant or particulars sufficient to identify the appeal; and

    (b) the grounds on which the application is made.

(2) Upon receiving the application, the Secretary shall enter particulars of it against the entry in the Register relating to the appeal and shall send a copy of it to the respondent.

Power to require attendance of witnesses and production of documents, etc

5.—(1) A tribunal may on the application of a party made either by notice to the Secretary or at the hearing—

    (a) require a party to furnish in writing to another party further particulars of the grounds on which he relies and of any facts and contentions relevant thereto;

    (b) grant to a party such discovery or inspection of documents as might be granted by a county court; and

    (c) require the attendance of any person as a witness or require the production of any document relating to the matter to be determined,

and may appoint the time at or within which or the place at which any act required in pursuance of this rule is to be done.

(2) The tribunal shall not under paragraph (1) require the production of any document certified by the Secretary of State as being a document of which the production would be against the interests of national security.

(3) A person on whom a requirement has been made under paragraph (1) may apply to the tribunal either by notice to the Secretary or at the hearing to vary or set aside the requirement.

(4) No such application to vary or set aside shall be entertained in a case where a time has been appointed under paragraph (1) in relation to the requirement unless it is made before the time or, as the case may be, expiration on the time so appointed.

(5) Every document containing a requirement under paragraph (1)(b) or (c) shall contain a reference to the fact that under paragraph 1(7) of Schedule 9 to the 1978 Act any person who without reasonable excuse fails to comply with any such requirement shall be liable on summary conviction to a fine, and the document shall state the amount of the current maximum fine.

Time and place of hearing and appointment of assessor

6.—(1) The President or a Regional Chairman shall fix the date, time and place of the hearing of the appeal and the Secretary shall not less than 14 days (or such shorter time as may be agreed by him with the parties) before the date so fixed send to each party a notice of hearing together with information and guidance as to attendance at the hearing, witnesses and the bringing of documents (if any), representation by another person and written representations.

(2)   Where the President or a Regional Chairman so directs, the Secretary shall also send notice of the hearing to such persons as may be directed, but the requirement as to the period of notice contained in paragraph (1) shall not apply to any such notice.

(3)   The President or a Regional Chairman may, if he thinks fit, appoint in pursuance of section 24(4) of the 1974 Act a person or persons having special knowledge or experience in relation to the subject matter of the appeal to sit with the tribunal as assessor or assessors.

The hearing

7.—(1) Any hearing of an appeal shall be heard by a tribunal composed in accordance with section 128(2A), (2B) and (2C), or section 128(6), of the 1978 Act.

(2)   Any hearing of or in connection with an appeal shall take place in public except where a Minister of the Crown has directed a tribunal to sit in private on grounds of national security in accordance with paragraph 1(4A) of Schedule 9 to the 1978 Act.

(3)   Notwithstanding paragraph (2), a tribunal may sit in private, if on the application of a party the tribunal considers it appropriate to do so, for the purpose of hearing evidence—
- (a)   which relates to matters of such a nature that it would be against the interests of national security to allow the evidence to be given in public, or
- (b)   hearing evidence from any person which in the opinion of the tribunal is likely to consist of information the disclosure of which would cause substantial injury to the undertaking of the appellant or of any undertaking in which he works for reasons other than its effect on negotiations with respect to any of the matters mentioned in section 244(1) of the 1992 Act.

(4)   A member of the Council on Tribunals shall be entitled to attend any hearing in his capacity as a member.

Written representations

8.   If a party wishes to submit representations in writing for consideration by a tribunal at the hearing of the appeal, that party shall present his representations to the Secretary not less than 7 days before the hearing and shall at the same time send a copy of it to the other party.

Procedure at hearing

9.—(1) At any hearing of or in connection with an appeal a party shall be entitled to make an opening statement, to give evidence on his own behalf, to call witnesses, to cross-examine any witnesses called by the other party and to address the tribunal.

(2)   If a party shall fail to appear or to be represented at the time and place fixed for the hearing of an appeal, the tribunal may dispose of the appeal in the absence of that party or may adjourn the hearing to a later date: provided that before disposing of an appeal in the absence of a party the tribunal shall consider any written representations submitted by that party in pursuance of rule 8.

(3)   A tribunal may require any witness to give evidence on oath or affirmation and for that purpose there may be administered an oath or affirmation in due form.

Decision of tribunal

10.—(1) Where a tribunal is composed of three members its decision may be taken by a majority; and if a tribunal is composed of two members only, the chairman shall have a second or casting vote.

(2)   The decision of a tribunal shall be recorded in a document signed by the chairman which shall contain the reasons for the decision.

(3)   The clerk shall transmit the document signed by the chairman to the Secretary who shall enter it in the Register and shall send a copy of the entry to each of the parties.

(4)   The specification of the reasons for the decision shall be omitted from the Register in any case in which—
- (a)   a Minister of the Crown has directed the tribunal, in accordance with paragraph 1(4A) of Schedule 9 to the 1978 Act, to sit in private on grounds of national security, or
- (b)   evidence has been heard in private and the tribunal so directs,

and in that event a specification of the reasons shall be sent to the parties and to any superior court in any proceedings relating to such decision together with the copy of the entry.

(5)   The chairman of a tribunal shall have power by certificate under his hand to correct in documents recording the tribunal's decisions clerical mistakes or errors arising therein from any accidental slip or omission.

(6)   The clerk shall send a copy of any document so corrected and the certificate of the chairman to the Secretary who shall as soon as practicable make such correction as may be necessary in the Register and shall send a copy of the corrected entry or of the corrected specification of the reasons, as the case may be, to each of the parties.

(7)   If any decision is—

(a)   corrected under paragraph (5),

(b)   reviewed, revoked or varied under rule 11, or

(c)   altered in any way by order of a superior court,

the Secretary shall alter the entry in the Register to conform with any such certificate or order and shall send a copy of the new entry to each of the parties.

Review of tribunal's decision

11.—(1)   A tribunal shall have power on the application of a party to review and revoke or vary by certificate under the chairman's hand any of its decisions on the grounds that—

(a)   the decision was wrongly made as a result of an error on the part of the tribunal staff;

(b)   a party did not receive notice of the proceedings leading to the decision;

(c)   the decision was made in the absence of a party;

(d)   new evidence has become available since the making of the decision provided that its existence could not have been reasonably known of or foreseen; or

(e)   the interests of justice require such a review.

(2)   An application for the purposes of paragraph (1) may be made at the hearing. If the application is not made at the hearing, such application shall be made to the Secretary within 14 days from the date of the entry of a decision in the Register and must be in writing stating the grounds in full.

(3)   An application for the purposes of paragraph (1) may be refused by the chairman of the tribunal which decided the case, by the President or by a Regional Chairman if in his opinion it has no reasonable prospect of success and he shall state the reasons for his opinion.

(4)   If such an application is not refused under paragraph (3), it shall be heard by the tribunal and if it is granted the tribunal shall either vary its decision or revoke its decision and order a re-hearing.

(5)   The clerk shall send to the Secretary the certificate of the chairman as to any revocation or variation of the tribunal's decision under this rule. The Secretary shall as soon as practicable make such correction as may be necessary in the Register and shall send a copy of the entry to each of the parties.

Costs

12.—(1)   A tribunal may make an order that a party shall pay to another party either a specified sum in respect of the costs of or in connection with an appeal incurred by that other party or, in default of agreement, the taxed amount of those costs.

(2)   Any costs required by an order under this rule to be taxed may be taxed in the county court according to such of the scales prescribed by the county court rules for proceedings in the county court as shall be directed by the order.

Miscellaneous powers

13.—(1)   Subject to the provisions of these rules, a tribunal may regulate its own procedure.

(2)   A tribunal may, if it thinks fit—

(a)   postpone the day or time fixed for, or adjourn, any hearing;

(b)   before granting an application under rule 5 or 11 require the party making the application to give notice thereof to the other party;

(c)   either on the application of any person or of its own motion, direct any other person to be joined as a party to the appeal (giving such consequential directions as it considers necessary), but may do so only after having given to the person proposed to be joined a reasonable opportunity of making written or oral objection;

    (d)   make any necessary amendments to the description of a party in the Register and in other documents relating to the appeal;

    (e)   if the appellant shall at any time give notice of the abandonment of his appeal, dismiss the appeal;

    (f)   if the parties agree in writing upon the terms of a decision to be made by the tribunal, decide accordingly.

(3)   Any act required or authorised by these rules to be done by a tribunal may be done by a chairman except—

    (a)   the hearing of an appeal under rule 8;

    (b)   an act required or authorised to be so done by rule 9 or 10 which the rule implies is to be done by the tribunal which is hearing or heard the appeal;

    (c)   the hearing of an application under rule 11(1), and the variation or revocation of a decision, and ordering of a re-hearing, under rule 11(4);

    (d)   the granting of an extension of time under rule 2(2).

(4)   Any function of the Secretary may be performed by a Regional Secretary.

Notices, etc

14.—(1) Any notice given under these rules shall be in writing and all notices and documents required or authorised by these rules to be sent or given to any person hereinafter mentioned may be sent by post (subject to paragraphs (3) and (4)) or delivered to or at—

    (a)   in the case of a document directed to the Secretary, the Office of the Tribunals or such other office as may be notified by the Secretary to the parties;

    (b)   in the case of a document directed to a party, his address for service specified in the notice of appeal or in a notice under paragraph (2) or (if no address for service is so specified or if a notice sent to such an address has been returned), his last known address or place of business in the United Kingdom or, if the party is a corporation, the corporation's registered or principal office;

    (c)   in the case of a document directed to any person (other than a person specified in the foregoing provisions of this paragraph), his address or place of business in the United Kingdom, or if such a person is a corporation, the corporation's registered or principal office;

and if sent or given to the authorised representative of a party shall be deemed to have been sent or given to that party.

(2)   A party may at any time by notice to the Secretary and to the other party change his address for service under these rules.

(3)   Where a notice of appeal is not delivered, it shall be sent by the recorded delivery service.

(4)   Where for any sufficient reason service of any document or notice cannot be effected in the manner prescribed under this rule, the President or a Regional Chairman may make an order for substituted service in such manner as he may deem fit and such service shall have the same effect as service in the manner prescribed under this rule.

(5)   In the case of an appeal to which the respondent is an inspector appointed otherwise than by the Health and Safety Executive, the Secretary shall send to that executive copies of the notice of appeal and the document recording the decision of the tribunal on the appeal.

SCHEDULE 5

[not printed in this work]

THE CONTROL OF INDUSTRIAL MAJOR ACCIDENT HAZARDS (AMENDMENT) REGULATIONS 1994

(S.I.1994 No. 118)

General note. These Regulations, which came into force on 28 February 1994, amend the Control of Industrial Major Accident Hazards Regulations 1984 (S.I. 1984 No.1902) by applying those regulations to certain industrial activities for the purpose of implementing in full, in respect of Great Britain, Council Directive No. 82/501/EEC on the major accident hazards of certain industrial activities.

The Secretary of State, being the designated Minister for the purposes of Section 2(2) of the European Communities Act 1972 in relation to measures relating to the prevention and limitation of the effects of accidents arising from industrial activities involving dangerous substances, in exercise of the powers conferred on him by the said section 2 and by sections 15(1) and (2) and 82(3)(a) of, and paragraphs 1(1)(b) and (c) and (2), 15(1) and 20 of Schedule 3 to, the Health and Safety at Work etc Act 1974 ("the 1974 Act") and of all other powers enabling him in that behalf and for the purpose of giving effect without modifications to proposals submitted to him by the Health and Safety Commission under section 11(2)(d) of the 1974 Act after the carrying out by the said Commission of consultations in accordance with section 50(3) of that Act, hereby makes the following Regulations:—

1. Citation and commencement. These Regulations may be cited as the Control of Industrial Major Accident Hazards (Amendment) Regulations 1994, and shall come into force on 28th February 1994.

2. Interpretation. In these Regulations "the principal Regulations" means the Control of Industrial Major Accident Hazards Regulations 1984.

3. Amendment to the principal Regulations. Sub-paragraph (e) of paragraph (1) of regulation 3 of the principal Regulations is revoked.

4. Application of the principal Regulations. Where an industrial activity becomes subject to regulations 7 to 12 of the principal Regulations in consequence of the amendment made by regulation 3 above, then, in relation to that activity, the principal Regulations shall have effect subject to the modifications specified in the Schedule to these Regulations.

SCHEDULE

Regulation 4

MODIFICATIONS TO THE PRINCIPAL REGULATIONS IN THEIR APPLICATION TO ADDITIONAL INDUSTRIAL ACTIVITIES

1. In regulation 6(2)(a)(i), the reference to "the coming into operation of this Regulation" shall be construed as a reference to the coming into force of these Regulations.

2. In regulations 7(2) and 10(3)(a), references to the coming into operation of the principal Regulations shall be construed as references to the coming into force of these Regulations.

3. In each regulation or Schedule specified in Column 1 below, the date specified opposite thereto in Column 3 shall apply in substitution for the date referred to in that regulation or Schedule and specified in the corresponding entry in Column 2.

Column 1 Regulation or Schedule	Column 2 Existing date	Column 3 Modified date
Regulation 7(3)	8th July 1989	1st January 1997
Regulation 7(3)	1st April 1985	31st May 1994
Regulation 10(3)(b)	1st April 1985	31st May 1994
Regulation 11(3)	1st October 1985	31st August 1994
Regulation 12(5)	31st December 1991	30th November 1994
Schedule 7 paragraph 4	7th January 1985	27th February 1994

THE RAILWAYS (SAFETY CASE) REGULATIONS 1994

(S.I. 1994 No. 237)

General note. These Regulations, which came into force on 28 February 1994, provide for railway operators to prepare safety cases to submit to the relevant controller or the Health and Safety Executive. Breach of a duty under these Regulations gives rise to civil liability.

ARRRANGEMENT OF REGULATIONS

The Secretary of State, in exercise of the powers conferred on him by sections 15(1), (2), (4)(a), (5)(b), (6)(b) and 82(3)(a) of, and paragraphs 1(1)(c), 8(1), 9, 15(1) and 16 of Schedule 3 to, the Health and Safety at Work etc Act 1974 ("the 1974 Act") and for the purpose of giving effect without modifications to proposals submitted to him by the Health and Safety Commission under section 11(2)(d) of the 1974 Act after the carrying out by the said Commission of consultations in accordance with section 50(3) of that Act; and being a Minister designated for the purpose of section 2(2) of the European Communities Act 1972 in relation to measures relating to arrangements for access to rail infrastructure, in exercise of the powers conferred by the said section 2(2) and of all other powers enabling him in that behalf, hereby makes the following Regulations:

1. Citation and commencement. These Regulations may be cited as the Railways (Safety Case) Regulations 1994 and shall come into force on 28th February 1994.

2. Interpretation.—(1) In these Regulations, unless the context otherwise requires—

"audit report" means a report made pursuant to the arrangements referred to in paragraph 16 of Schedule 1;

"building operation" has the meaning assigned to it by section 176(1) of the Factories Act 1961;

"the Executive" means the Health and Safety Executive;

"factory" means a factory within the meaning of section 175 of the Factories Act 1961 and premises to which section 123(1) or (2) or 125(1) of that Act applies;

"harbour" and "harbour area" have the meanings assigned to them by regulation 2(1) of the Dangerous Substances in Harbour Areas Regulations 1987;

"infrastructure controller" means a person who controls railway infrastructure;

"mine" and "quarry" have the meanings assigned to them by section 180 of the Mines and Quarries Act 1954;

"notified" means notified in writing, and related expressions shall be construed accordingly;

"owner" in relation to a station means the person with the freehold interest in the premises comprising the station where those premises are situated in England or Wales and the proprietor of the *dominium utile* where those premises are situated in Scotland;

"railway" has the meaning assigned to it by section 67(1) of the Transport and Works Act 1992 except that it does not include any part of a railway—

    (a) within a harbour or harbour area, or which is part of a factory, mine or quarry unless, in each case, it is being used or is intended to be used for the carriage of fare paying passengers;

    (b) used solely for the purpose of carrying out a building operation or work of engineering construction;

    (c) within a maintenance or goods depot;

"railway infrastructure" means fixed assets used for the operation of a railway including its permanent way and plant used for signalling or exclusively for supplying electricity for operational purposes to the railway, but it does not include a station;

"railway operator" means a person who is an infrastructure controller or operates trains or stations;

"revision" means proposed revision where by virtue of regulation 6(2) the revision has not been made;

"safety case" shall be construed in accordance with paragraph (2);

"safety representative" has the meaning assigned to it by regulation 2(1) of the Safety Representatives and Safety Committees Regulations 1977;

"station" means a railway passenger station or terminal, but does not include any permanent way or plant used for signalling or exclusively for supplying electricity for operational purposes to the railway;

"train" includes any rolling stock (within the meaning of the Railways Act 1993);

"work of engineering construction" has the meaning assigned to it by section 176(1) of the Factories Act 1961;

"workplace" has the meaning assigned to it by regulation 2(1) of the Safety Representatives and Safety Committees Regulations 1977.

(2)   Any reference in these Regulations to a safety case is a reference to a document

containing the particulars required by the provision of these Regulations pursuant to which the safety case is prepared, and in so far as the document contains other particulars it shall not be treated as part of the safety case for the purposes of these Regulations; and a safety case may—

(a) contain the particulars so required by reference to the same particulars contained in another safety case prepared by the same person if the first mentioned safety case is to be submitted for acceptance to the same person who has accepted the other safety case;

(b) be prepared by a person in respect of more than one operation intended to be undertaken by him if in the event of separate safety cases being prepared in respect of those operations they would have to be accepted by the same person pursuant to these Regulations.

(3) Any provision of these Regulations requiring particulars to be included in a safety case—

(a) which are also required to be included by virtue of a more general provision of the Regulations is without prejudice to the generality of the more general provision;

(b) (except in relation to the particulars specified in paragraph 14 of Schedule 1) shall require no more detail to be included than is necessary to enable the person to whom it is submitted for acceptance to satisfy himself on the matters referred to in paragraph (4) or (5) or regulation 10(8)(a).

(4) Any reference in these Regulations to an infrastructure controller accepting a safety case or revision (otherwise than by virtue of regulation 10(8)), is a reference to that controller notifying the person who prepared it that he is satisfied that the procedures and arrangements described in it which affect or are likely to affect the performance of his own health and safety duties will, when properly implemented with those described in any other safety case or revision thereof which that controller has prepared or accepted pursuant to these Regulations, be capable of ensuring compliance by that controller with those duties in relation to the operation to which the first mentioned safety case or revision relates.

(5) Any reference in these Regulations to the Executive accepting a safety case or revision is a reference to the Executive notifying the person who prepared it that it is satisfied with the case for health and safety made out in it.

(6) Any reference in these Regulations to the health and safety duties of an infrastructure controller is a reference to the duties imposed on him by the relevant statutory provisions (other than these Regulations).

(7) Where a railway operator is succeeded by a new railway operator, anything done in pursuance of these Regulations by the former railway operator shall, for the purposes of these Regulations, be treated as having been done by his successor; and for this purpose a person shall be treated as a successor in so far as control of the relevant railway infrastructure or the operation of the trains or stations concerned, as appropriate, has been transferred to him.

(8) Any reference in these Regulations to a person in control of any railway infrastructure is a reference to a person who, in the course of a business or other undertaking carried on by him (whether for profit or not), is in operational control of that infrastructure, except that where such control is for the time being exercised by a person undertaking maintenance, repair or alteration work on the infrastructure, it is a reference to a person who would be in operational control of the infrastructure if such work were not being undertaken.

(9) Any reference in these Regulations to a person operating a train or station is a reference to the person operating the train or station for the time being in the course of a business or other undertaking carried on by him (whether for profit or not), but it does not include a self-employed person by reason only that he himself drives or otherwise controls the movement of a train.

(10) Unless the context otherwise requires, any reference in these Regulations to—

    (a) a numbered regulation or Schedule is a reference to the regulation or Schedule in these Regulations so numbered;

    (b) a numbered paragraph is a reference to the paragraph so numbered in the regulation or Schedule in which the reference appears.

3. Use of railway infrastructure.—(1) A person in control of any railway infrastructure shall not use or permit it to be used for the operation of trains or stations unless—

    (a) he has prepared a safety case containing the particulars specified in Schedules 1 and 2;

    (b) the Executive has accepted that safety case;

    (c) where he is not the person operating those trains or stations, the person undertaking that operation has agreed in writing to comply with any reasonable request he may make as respects any aspect of the operation which affects or is likely to affect the performance of the health and safety duties of the person in control of the railway infrastructure; and

    (d) the person operating those trains or stations has complied with regulation 4 or 5, as appropriate.

(2) A person in control of any railway infrastructure shall not accept a safety case pursuant to these Regulations unless his own safety case has been accepted pursuant to paragraph (1)(b).

4. Safety case for train operations.—(1) A person shall not operate a train in relation to any railway infrastructure unless—

    (a) he has prepared a safety case containing the particulars specified in Schedule 1, and

    (b) the safety case has been accepted—

        (i) by the relevant infrastructure controller at least 28 days before the operation commences; or

        (ii) where he is the relevant infrastructure controller, by the Executive.

(2) In this regulation "the relevant infrastructure controller" means the person in control of the railway infrastructure in relation to which the train is to be operated, and where there are different such persons for different parts of that infrastructure paragraph (1) shall apply separately in relation to each such part.

5. Safety case for station operations.—(1) A person shall not operate a station unless—

    (a) he has prepared a safety case containing the particulars specified in Schedule 1, and

    (b) the safety case has been accepted—

        (i) where another person is the owner of the station and is the only relevant infrastructure controller, by that controller at least 28 days before the operation commences,

        (ii) in any other case, by the Executive after taking account of any views given to it by the relevant infrastructure controller as respects matters which affect or are likely to affect the performance of his health and safety duties.

(2)   In this regulation "the only relevant infrastructure controller" means the person in control of all the railway infrastructure serving the station and "the relevant infrastructure controller" means the only relevant infrastructure controller or where there are different persons in control of different parts of the railway infrastructure serving the station, it means each of them.

6.   Revision of safety cases.—(1) A person who has prepared a safety case pursuant to these Regulations shall revise its contents whenever it is appropriate; but nothing in this paragraph shall require the revision to be sent to another person.

(2)   Where a revision proposed to be made under paragraph (1) will render the safety case materially different from the last version sent to the person who accepted it pursuant to these Regulations, the revision shall not be made—

(a)   unless the revision has been sent to that person;

(b)   unless that person has accepted the revision or (where he is an infrastructure controller) has notified the person who prepared the safety case that the revision does not affect and is not likely to affect the performance of the health and safety duties of the infrastructure controller; and

(c)   where the person who accepted the safety case is an infrastructure controller, until 28 days after the revision has been accepted or until 28 days after a notification has been made under sub-paragraph (b),

and where the revision is to a safety case accepted pursuant to paragraph (ii) of regulation 5(1)(b) the Executive shall, before accepting the revision, take account of any views given to it by the relevant infrastructure controller referred to in that paragraph as respects the matters referred to in that paragraph.

(3)   A person who has prepared a safety case which has been accepted pursuant to these Regulations shall make a thorough review of its contents at least every three years.

7.   Duty to conform with safety case.—(1) Where a person has prepared and has had accepted a safety case pursuant to these Regulations he shall ensure that the procedures and arrangements described in the safety case and any revision thereof are followed.

(2)   In criminal proceedings for a contravention of paragraph (1) it shall be a defence for the accused to prove that—

(a)   in the particular circumstances of the case it was not in the best interests of the health and safety of persons to follow the procedures or arrangements concerned and there was insufficient time to revise the safety case pursuant to regulation 6, or

(b)   the commission of the offence was due to a contravention by another person of regulation 8 and the accused had taken all reasonable precautions and exercised all due diligence to ensure that the procedures or arrangements were followed.

8.   Co-operation.—(1) Every person to whom this regulation applies shall co-operate so far as is necessary with a railway operator (in this regulation referred to as "the duty holder") to enable him to comply with the provisions of these Regulations.

(2) This regulation applies to—
    (a) any other railway operator whose operations affect or are affected by operations carried out by the duty holder;
    (b) an employer of persons or a self-employed person carrying out work on or in relation to premises or plant owned or controlled by the duty holder.

9. Notifications, consultations and documents.—(1) Where a safety case has been received by an infrastructure controller for acceptance pursuant to these Regulations or a revision thereof has been received by him pursuant to regulation 6(2), the controller shall notify the Executive of that fact forthwith, and, except in the case of a revision, of the address notified to him pursuant to paragraph (4)(a).

(2) Where an infrastructure controller accepts a safety case or revision pursuant to these Regulations (other than by virtue of regulation 10(8)) or sends a notification pursuant to regulation 6(2)(b) in relation to a revision (other than by virtue of regulation 10(9)), he shall send a copy of the safety case or revision and a copy of the notification referred to in regulation 2(4) or the notification referred to in regulation 6(2)(b), as appropriate, to the Executive forthwith.

(3) Where an infrastructure controller accepts a safety case or revision pursuant to these Regulations (other than by virtue of regulation 10(8)) he shall identify in the notification referred to in regulation 2(4) the procedures and arrangements described in the safety case or revision which affect or are likely to affect the performance of his health and safety duties and the extent to which they do so.

(4) A person who prepares a safety case pursuant to these Regulations shall—
    (a) when submitting that safety case to a person for acceptance, notify that person of an address in Great Britain for the purposes of sub-paragraphs (b) to (f) below, and, where the person submitting that safety case is an infrastructure controller, paragraph (7);
    (b) keep the accepted safety case and any revision thereof or a copy thereof at that address;
    (c) keep each audit report made by him or a copy thereof at that address;
    (d) ensure that a record is made of any action taken in consequence of such an audit report and keep that record or a copy thereof at that address;
    (e) ensure that a report is made of every review carried out pursuant to regulation 6(3) and ensure that a copy of it is sent to the person who has accepted the safety case; and
    (f) keep such report or a copy thereof at that address.

(5) A person who submits to the Executive a safety case for acceptance pursuant to regulation 5 or who submits to the Executive a revision to a safety case accepted under that regulation, shall send a copy of the safety case or revision to the relevant infrastructure controller referred to in that regulation.

(6) Where an infrastructure controller scrutinises a safety case submitted to him for acceptance pursuant to these Regulations or a revision submitted to him pursuant to regulation 6(2), he shall make a record of the steps he has taken in that scrutiny and of the results thereof.

(7) Where an infrastructure controller accepts a safety case or revision he shall keep a copy of that safety case or revision, every report sent to him pursuant to paragraph (4)(e) and the record referred to in paragraph (6) at the address he has notified pursuant to paragraph (4)(a).

(8) Each report and record required to be kept by this regulation shall be kept for a period of 3 years after it has been made, and the safety case and revision shall be kept for so long as it is current.

(9) It shall be sufficient compliance with paragraphs (4) and (7) for the information in the documents to be kept at the address notified on film or by electronic means provided that the information is capable of being reproduced as a written copy at that address and it is secure from loss or unauthorised interference.

(10) Where a person has notified an address pursuant to sub-paragraph (a) of paragraph (4), he may notify to the person who has accepted the safety case a different address in Great Britain for the purposes of the provisions referred to in that sub-paragraph, and where he does so references in those provisions and in paragraph (9) where applicable to the address notified shall be construed as the address in the last notification made under this paragraph.

(11) An employer who prepares in respect of a workplace a safety case or revision thereto pursuant to these Regulations shall consult safety representatives on its preparation.

(12) Regulation 7(1) of the Safety Representatives and Safety Committees Regulations 1977 shall have effect as if the reference to safety representatives being entitled to inspect and take copies of documents were, in a case where by virtue of paragraph (9) information is kept on film or in electronic form, a reference to them being entitled to be given appropriate facilities to enable them to read it and to take a copy of it.

10.   Acceptance of safety cases by the Secretary of State.—(1) Where an infrastructure controller refuses to accept a safety case or revision thereof submitted to him by a person pursuant to these Regulations he shall notify that person of the reasons for that decision.

(2) A failure by an infrastructure controller to accept within a reasonable time a safety case submitted to him for acceptance pursuant to these Regulations or a revision submitted to him pursuant to regulation 6(2), shall, subject to paragraph (3), be treated as a refusal to accept it for the purposes of the following provisions of this regulation.

(3) Where an infrastructure controller has notified a person under regulation 6(2)(b) that a revision does not affect and is not likely to affect the performance of his health and safety duties, the refusal or failure to accept that revision shall not be treated as a refusal or failure for the purposes of this regulation.

(4) The person the acceptance of whose safety case or revision has been refused by an infrastructure controller may submit it for acceptance to the Secretary of State within 28 days of receiving the notification referred to in paragraph (1) or after the expiry of the time referred in paragraph (2), as appropriate, and where he does so submit it he shall—

(a)   send a copy of any such notification to the Secretary of State and to the Executive;
(b)   notify the infrastructure controller and the Executive that he has submitted the safety case or revision to the Secretary of State, and
(c)   send a copy of the safety case or revision to the Executive.

(5) On receiving the notification referred to in paragraph (4)(b) the infrastructure controller shall provide the Secretary of State with a copy of every safety case or

revision thereof he has prepared or accepted pursuant to these Regulations and which it is necessary for the Secretary of State to see to come to a view on the matters referred to in paragraph (8)(a).

(6) Where a safety case or revision is submitted for acceptance pursuant to paragraphs (2) and (4), the Secretary of State may decline to deal with it if he considers that the infrastructure controller has not had reasonable time to scrutinise the safety case or revision, as appropriate.

(7) In performing his functions under this regulation the Secretary of State shall take account of any advice given to him with respect thereto by or on behalf of the Health and Safety Commission.

(8) The Secretary of State shall notify his decision in writing to the person who submitted the safety case or revision to him, the infrastructure controller and the Executive; if he decides to accept it—

    (a) the notification shall state that he is satisfied that the procedures and arrangements described in the safety case or revision which affect or are likely to affect the performance of the health and safety duties of the infrastructure controller will, when properly implemented with those described in any other safety case or revision thereof the infrastructure controller has prepared or accepted pursuant to these Regulations, be capable of ensuring compliance by that controller with his health and safety duties in relation to the operation to which the first mentioned safety case or revision relates;

    (b) these regulations shall have effect as if—

        (i) the safety case or revision had been accepted by the infrastructure controller, and

        (ii) the references in regulations 4 and 5 to "at least 28 days" did not apply and regulation 6(2)(c) did not apply.

(9) Where the Secretary of State decides not to accept a revision to a safety case because he is satisfied that the revision does not affect and is not likely to affect the health and safety duties of the infrastructure controller, the notification referred to in paragraph (8) shall state that fact and these Regulations shall have effect as if—

    (a) the infrastructure controller had sent to the person who prepared the safety case a notification pursuant to regulation 6(2)(b), and

    (b) regulation 6(2)(c) did not apply.

11. Exemptions.—(1) Subject to paragraph (2) and to any Community obligation of the United Kingdom the Executive may, by a certificate in writing, exempt any person or class of persons from any requirement or prohibition imposed by these Regulations and any such exemption may be granted subject to conditions and with or without limit of time and may be revoked by a certificate in writing at any time.

(2) The Executive shall not grant any such exemption unless, having regard to the circumstances of the case, and in particular to—

    (a) the conditions, if any, which it proposes to attach to the exemption; and

    (b) any other requirements imposed by or under any enactment which apply to the case,

it is satisfied that the health and safety of persons who are likely to be affected by the exemption will not be prejudiced in consequence of it.

(3) Subject to any Community obligation of the United Kingdom, the Secretary of State for Defence may, in the interests of national security, by a certificate in writing

exempt any person or class of persons from the requirements of these Regulations and any such exemption may be granted subject to conditions and to a limit of time and may be revoked by the said Secretary of State by a further certificate in writing at any time.

12.   Transitional provisions. The provisions of Schedule 3 shall have effect.

13.   Revocations. The provisions of the Railways Regulations 1992 specified in column 1 of Schedule 4 shall be revoked to the extent specified in the corresponding entry in column 2 of that Schedule.

SCHEDULE 1

Regulations 3, 4, 5

PARTICULARS TO BE INCLUDED IN A SAFETY CASE

1.   The name and address of the person who has prepared the safety case (in this Schedule referred to as "the duty holder").

2.   A description of the operation intended to be undertaken by the duty holder.

3.   A general description of the premises or plant intended to be used by the duty holder for the operation intended to be undertaken by him.

4.   Particulars of any—
 (a)   technical specifications; and
 (b)   procedures or arrangements relating to operations or maintenance,
which the duty holder intends to follow in connection with the operation intended to be undertaken by him, in so far as they affect the health and safety of persons.

5.   A statement of the duty holder's general policy with respect to the health and safety of persons affected by the operation he intends to undertake, including the health and safety objectives he intends to achieve in relation to it.

6.   A statement of the significant findings of the risk assessment the duty holder has made pursuant to regulation 3 of the Management of Health and Safety at Work Regulations 1992 and particulars of the arrangements he has made pursuant to regulation 4(1) thereof.

7.   Particulars to demonstrate that the management system of the duty holder is adequate to ensure that the relevant statutory provisions will (in respect of matters within his control) be complied with in relation to the operation he intends to undertake.

8.   Particulars to demonstrate that the duty holder has an adequate organisation for carrying out the policy referred to in paragraph 5 and adequate arrangements for ensuring the competence of his employees as respects health and safety.

9.   Particulars to demonstrate that the duty holder has established adequate arrangements for the passing of information relevant to health and safety to persons within his undertaking and to other railway operators whose operations affect or are affected by the operation intended to be carried out by the duty holder.

10.   Particulars of the arrangements the duty holder has established for consulting his employees on matters of health and safety.

11.   Particulars to demonstrate that the duty holder has established adequate arrangements for investigating accidents and other incidents which could endanger persons, for co-ordinating such investigations with the investigations carried out by other railway operators and for participating in investigations carried out by other railway operators.

12.   Particulars of the arrangements the duty holder has established with a view to securing the health and safety of persons, for managing work carried out by persons who are not his employees on or in relation to premises or plant which he owns or controls.

13.   Particulars of the procedures the duty holder has established for dealing with accidents and with emergencies or other incidents which could endanger persons.

14.   Where the safety case is prepared pursuant to regulation 5, particulars of the procedures and arrangements the duty holder has established—

(a)   to prevent risks to the health and safety of persons arising from the movement or overcrowding of persons in the station; and

(b)   for the evacuation of persons from the station in an emergency.

15.   Particulars of the safety procedures the duty holder has established for the design and procurement of premises and plant to be used by him or under his control.

16.   Particulars to demonstrate that the duty holder has established adequate arrangements for audit and the making of reports thereof.

17.   Particulars of the arrangements the duty holder has established to enable him to comply with regulation 8, including—

(a)   in a case where the duty holder is to submit the safety case to an infrastructure controller for acceptance pursuant to these Regulations, particulars to demonstrate that the duty holder has established adequate arrangements for enabling the controller to follow with respect to that safety case the arrangements described in his own safety case pursuant to paragraph 3 of Schedule 2;

(b)   in a case where the duty holder is to submit a safety case to the Executive for acceptance pursuant to regulation 5, particulars to demonstrate that the duty holder has established adequate arrangements for enabling the relevant infrastructure controller referred to in that regulation to follow with respect to that safety case the arrangements described in his own safety case pursuant to paragraph 4 of Schedule 2.

18.   In this Schedule—

(a)   "audit" means systematic assessment of the adequacy of the management system to achieve the purpose referred to in paragraph 7 carried out by persons who are sufficiently independent of the system (but who may be employed by the duty holder) to ensure that such assessment is objective;

(b)   "management system" means the organisation and arrangements established by the duty holder for managing his undertaking;

(c)   any reference to an operation intended to be undertaken by a duty holder is—

(i)   where the safety case is prepared pursuant to regulation 3, a reference to the operations he intends to carry out in relation to the railway infrastructure concerned;

(ii)   where the safety case is prepared pursuant to regulation 4 or 5, a reference to the train or station operations concerned.

SCHEDULE 2

Regulation 3

ADDITIONAL PARTICULARS TO BE INCLUDED IN A SAFETY CASE OF AN INFRASTRUCTURE CONTROLLER

1.   Particulars of the arrangements established by the infrastructure controller who has prepared the safety case for scrutinising—

(a)   any safety cases or revisions thereof sent to him for acceptance pursuant to regulation 4, 5 or 6 and the criteria he will use for accepting them;

(b)   copies of any safety cases or revisions thereof sent to him pursuant to regulation 9(5).

2.   Particulars to demonstrate that the arrangements and criteria referred to in paragraph 1(a) will enable him before accepting a safety case or revision thereof to be satisfied on the matters referred to in regulation 2(4).

3.   Particulars of the arrangements he has established for ensuring that railway operators who have had their safety cases accepted by him follow the procedures and arrangements described in them in so far as those procedures and arrangements affect or are likely to affect the performance of his health and safety duties.

4.   Particulars of the arrangements he has established for ensuring that persons operating stations served by any railway infrastructure he controls who have had their safety cases accepted by the Executive pursuant to regulation 5, follow the procedures and arrangements described in them in so far as those procedures and arrangements affect or are likely to affect the performance of his health and safety duties.

SCHEDULE 3

Regulation 12

Transitional Provisions

1.   Where a person is undertaking a relevant operation on 28th February 1994 it shall, to the extent that the operation is undertaken in the same place as it was on that date, be sufficient compliance by him with regulation 3(1)(a) and (b), 4 or 5 if the safety case referred to in that provision is prepared and accepted within 2 years after that date.

2.   Where pursuant to regulation 4 or 5 a person submits in respect of a train or station operation to be carried out by him a safety case for acceptance to an infrastructure controller who by virtue of paragraph 1 has not had his own safety case accepted by the Executive, paragraph 1 shall, to the extent that it relates to regulation 3, cease to apply to that controller in respect of that operation.

3.   Where a relevant operation is not being undertaken on 28th February 1994 in consequence of normal operating schedules, maintenance, repair or an emergency, the operation shall nevertheless be treated for the purposes of paragraph 1 as being undertaken on that date.

4.   Where a safety case is prepared after the relevant operation has commenced references in regulation 2(2)(b) and Schedule 1 to the operation intended to be undertaken by the person or duty holder respectively, shall include references to the operation already commenced by him.

5.   In this Schedule "relevant operation" in relation to regulation 3(1)(a) and (b), 4 or 5 means the activity which would, apart from this Schedule, be prohibited by that regulation.

SCHEDULE 4

Regulation 13

Revocations of the Railways Regulations 1992

Column 1 *Regulation*	Column 2 *Extent of revocation*
Regulation 8	Paragraphs (6) to (11).
Regulation 9	In paragraph (4) the words "other than a dispute falling within paragraph (7)".
	Paragraphs (7) and (8).
Regulation 14	In paragraph (1) the references to paragraphs (6), (7), (8), (9) and (10) of regulation 8 and paragraph (8) of regulation 9.
Regulation 15	The whole regulation.

THE RAILWAYS (SAFETY CRITICAL WORK) REGULATIONS 1994

(S.I. 1994 No. 299)

General note. These Regulations, which came into force on 1 April 1994, regulate the undertaking of safety critical work on a transport system. Breach of a duty under these Regulations gives rise to civil liability.

The Secretary of State, in exercise of powers conferred on him by sections 15(1), (2), (4)(a), (5)(b), (6)(b) and 82(3)(a) of, and paragraphs 1(1)(c), 6(2), 7, 8(1) and 14 of Schedule 3 to, the Health and Safety at Work etc Act 1974 and of all other powers enabling him in that behalf for the purpose of giving effect without modifications to proposals submitted to him by the Health and Safety Commission under section 11(2)(d) of the said Act after the carrying out by the said Commission of consultations in accordance with section 50(3) of that Act, hereby makes the following Regulations:

1. Citation and commencement. These Regulations may be cited as the Railways (Safety Critical Work) Regulations 1994, and shall come into force on 1st April 1994.

2. Interpretation.—(1) In these Regulations, unless the context otherwise requires—

"approve" means approve for the time being in writing, and "approved" shall be construed accordingly;

"building operation" has the meaning assigned to it by section 176(1) of the Factories Act 1961;

"the Executive" means the Health and Safety Executive;

"factory" has the meaning assigned to it by section 175 of the Factories Act 1961 and premises to which section 123(1) or (2) or 125(1) of that Act applies;

"harbour" and "harbour area" have the meanings assigned to them by regulation 2(1) of the Dangerous Substances in Harbour Area Regulations 1987;

"means of identification" means a card or other document containing the name of the employee to whom it is issued, his photograph, the name of his employer and such other particulars as the employer wishes to include;

"mine" and "quarry" have the meanings assigned to them by section 180 of the Mines and Quarries Act 1954;

"railway operator" has the meaning assigned to it by the Railways (Safety Case) Regulations 1994 as if, in those Regulations, "railway" included any transport system and "train" included any vehicle;

"relevant assessments" means assessments (including medical assessments) which are relevant for the purpose of ascertaining the competence and fitness of the employee to undertake the safety critical work concerned (whether or not they have been approved under regulation 3(3));

"safety critical work" means work by a person—

(a) as a driver, guard, conductor or signalman or in any other capacity in which he can control or affect the movement of a vehicle;

(b)   in a maintenance capacity or as a supervisor of, or look-out for, persons
working in a maintenance capacity; and for this purpose, a person
works in a maintenance capacity if his work involves—

    (i)   maintenance, repair or alteration of—

        (aa) the permanent way or other means of guiding or supporting
vehicles,

        (bb) signals or any other means of controlling the movement of
vehicles, or

        (cc) any means of supplying electricity to vehicles or to the
means of guiding or supporting vehicles, or

    (ii) coupling or uncoupling vehicles; or

    (iii) checking that vehicles are working properly before they are used on
any occasion,

which could affect the health or safety of persons on a transport system;

"transport system" means a transport system to which Chapter I of Part II of the
Transport and Works Act 1992 applies or would apply were it not for the
exclusion in section 26(2) of that Act, except that it does not include any
part of a transport system—

(a)   within a harbour or harbour area, or which is part of a factory, mine or
quarry unless, in each case, it is being used or is intended to be used for
the carriage of fare paying passengers;

(b)   used solely for the purpose of carrying out a building operation or
work of engineering construction;

(c)   within a maintenance or goods depot;

"vehicle" means a vehicle used on a transport system and includes a mobile
traction unit used on such a system;

"work of engineering construction" has the meaning assigned to it by section
176(1) of the Factories Act 1961.

(2)   These Regulations shall apply to a self-employed person as they apply to an
employer and an employee and as if that self-employed person were both an
employer and employee.

(3)   Any reference in these Regulations to a numbered paragraph is a reference to
the paragraph so numbered in the regulation in which the reference appears.

3.   Competence and fitness.—(1) No employer shall permit any of his employees
to undertake any safety critical work unless—

(a)   the employee is competent and fit to undertake that work;

(b)   there is in existence an adequate record of any relevant assessments
undergone by the employee;

(c)   the employer has issued the employee with a means of identification;

(d)   the employer has established suitable arrangements to enable a railway
operator who is affected by the work to examine the record referred to in
sub-paragraph (b) above, or be informed of its contents.

(2)   An employee shall carry with him the means of identification referred to in
paragraph (1)(c) when he is undertaking any safety critical work.

(3)   The Executive may for the purposes of this regulation approve for the time
being assessments to be undergone by employees undertaking safety critical work
and in the case each such assessment the procedures to be followed and the
standard to be achieved in relation thereto and the intervals within which the
assessment is to be undergone again.

(4) Where the Executive has approved assessments under paragraph (3) then, without prejudice to the generality of sub-paragraph (a) of paragraph (1), an employee shall not be treated for the purposes of that sub-paragraph as competent and fit to undertake the work to which the assessments relate unless he has undergone each such assessment in accordance with any procedures so approved and within any intervals so approved, and in the case of each such assessment has achieved a standard not less than that so approved.

(5) Without prejudice to the generality of paragraph (3)—

  (a) assessments approved under that paragraph may include medical assessments made by registered medical practitioners approved by the Executive;

  (b) intervals approved under that paragraph may include intervals approved by reference to the time of resuming work following an event specified for the purpose in the approval.

(6) Where an approval is given under paragraph (3) notice of it shall be published in such manner as the Executive considers appropriate for bringing it to the attention of employers likely to be affected by the approval.

(7) An approval under this regulation may be given in respect of a class of safety critical work.

(8) In any proceedings against a person for an offence of contravening this regulation, it shall be a defence for that person to prove that he took all reasonable precautions and exercised all due diligence to avoid the commission of that offence.

4. Hours of work.—(1) Every employer shall ensure, so far as is reasonably practicable, that no employee of his undertakes any safety critical work for such number of hours as would be liable to cause him fatigue which could endanger safety; and in determining whether he would be so liable regard shall be had to the length of time between periods on duty.

(2) For the purposes of paragraph (1) a person shall be regarded as undertaking work throughout the period he is on duty.

5. Exemptions.—(1) Subject to paragraph (2), the Executive may, by a certificate in writing, exempt any person or class of persons from any requirement or prohibition imposed by these Regulations and any such exemption may be granted subject to conditions and with or without limit of time and may be revoked by a certificate in writing at any time.

(2) The Executive shall not grant any such exemption unless, having regard to the circumstances of the case, and in particular to—

  (a) the conditions, if any, which it proposes to attach to the exemption; and

  (b) any other requirements imposed by or under any enactment which apply to the case,

it is satisfied that the health and safety of persons who are likely to be affected by the exemption will not be prejudiced in consequence of it.

THE PERSONAL PROTECTIVE EQUIPMENT (EC DIRECTIVE) (AMENDMENT) REGULATIONS 1994

(S.I. 1994 No. 2326)

General note. These Regulations, which came into force fully on 1 January 1995, give effect to Council Directive 93/95/EEC of 29th October 1993 amending Directive 89/686/EEC on the approximation of the laws of the Member States relating to personal protective equipment (the "PPE Directive"). They also give effect to the amendments made by Council Directive 93/68/EEC of 22nd July 1993 (the "CE Marking Directive") to the PPE Directive. Breach of a duty under these Regulations gives rise to civil liability.

The Secretary of State, being designated for the purposes of section 2(2) of the European Communities Act 1972 in relation to measures relating to safety as regards personal protective equipment, in exercise of the powers conferred on him by section 2(2) of the said Act hereby makes the following Regulations:

1.—(1) These Regulations may be cited as the Personal Protective Equipment (EC Directive) (Amendment) Regulations 1994.

(2) This paragraph, regulation 2 below and (so far as it relates to them) paragraph (1) above shall come into force on 1st October 1994.

(3) The other provisions of these Regulations shall come into force on 1st January 1995; and regulation 2 below shall thereupon cease to have effect.

(4) Regulation 2 of the Personal Protective Equipment (EC Directive) (Amendment) Regulations 1993 is hereby revoked.

2. Paragraph 31 of Schedule 1 to the Provision and Use of Work Equipment Regulations 1992 and Schedule 1 to the Personal Protective Equipment at Work Regulations (Northern Ireland) 1993 shall have effect as if references therein to Council Directive 89/686/EEC of 21st December 1989 on the approximation of the laws of the Member States relating to personal protective equipment were references to that Directive as amended by Council Directive 93/95/EEC of 29th October 1993.

3.—(1) The Personal Protective Equipment (EC Directive) Regulations 1992 ("the principal Regulations"), paragraph 31 of Schedule 1 to the aforementioned Provision and Use of Work Equipment Regulations 1992, Schedule 1 to the Personal Protective Equipment at Work Regulations 1992 and Schedule 1 to the aforementioned Personal Protective Equipment at Work Regulations (Northern Ireland) 1993 shall have effect as if references therein to the aforementioned Council Directive 89/686/EEC (in the principal Regulations and in this regulation referred to as "the Directive") were references to the Directive as amended by both the aforementioned Council Directive 93/95/EEC and Article 7 of Council Directive 93/68/EEC of 22nd July 1993; and references to "the Directive" in regulation 4 below shall be construed accordingly.

(2) The copy of the Directive printed in the Schedule to the principal Regulations shall be read as if it were amended as provided in the Schedule to the aforementioned Personal Protective Equipment (EC Directive) (Amendment) Regulations 1993 and the Schedule to these Regulations.

4.—(1) In a case in which Article 13(4) of the Directive (CE marking affixed unduly) applies and Article 7 thereof (safety) does not, an enforcement authority, in performance of the duty imposed by regulation 3(2)(c) of the principal Regulations, may give to the appropriate person a notice—

  (a) stating that the enforcement authority suspects that the CE marking has been affixed to PPE unduly within the meaning of Article 13(4) of the Directive,

  (b) specifying the respect in which it is so suspected and giving particulars thereof,

  (c) requiring the appropriate person—

    (i) to secure that the PPE conforms as regards the provisions of the Directive concerning the CE marking within such period as may be specified in the notice, or

    (ii) to provide evidence within that period, to the satisfaction of the enforcement authority, that the CE marking has been properly affixed, and

  (d) warning the appropriate person that if the non-conformity continues or satisfactory evidence is not provided within that period, action may be taken in accordance with section 14,16 or 17 of the Consumer Protection Act 1987;

and in such a case sections 14,16 and 17 of the Consumer Protection Act 1987 (applied by regulation 3(2)(b) of the principal Regulations) shall not be applied until such a notice has so been served and the appropriate person upon whom it has been served has failed to comply with its requirements.

(2) In paragraph (1) above—

"appropriate person" means the manufacturer of the PPE in question or any authorised representative of his established within the European Economic Area;

"enforcement authority" means a weights and measures authority in Great Britain or a district council in Northern Ireland;

"PPE" means a product to which the Directive applies.

5. Until the end of 1996, sections 13, 14, 16 and 17 of the Consumer Protection Act 1987, regulation 10(1) of the Provision and Use of Work Equipment Regulations 1992, regulation 4(3)(e) of each of the Personal Protective Equipment at Work Regulations 1992 and the Personal Protective Equipment at Work Regulations (Northern Ireland) 1993 and regulation 4 above shall not be applied in respect of a failure of a product to comply with the current version of the Directive in any particular if it would have complied with the previous version of the Directive in that particular; and in this regulation—

  (a) "the current version of the Directive" means Council Directive 89/686/EEC of 21st December 1989 as amended as set out in regulation 3(1) above, and

  (b) "the previous version of the Directive" means that Directive before its amendment by Council Directive 93/68/EEC of 22nd July 1993.

SCHEDULE

AMENDMENTS TO THE DIRECTIVE

In paragraphs 5 and 6, the words "Contracting Parties" are substituted for the word "Community" by virtue of paragraph 8 of Protocol 1 annexed to the Agreement on the European Economic Area signed at Oporto on 2nd May 1992 as adjusted by the Protocol signed at Brussels on 17th March 1993.

1. Throughout the text, the term "EC mark" is replaced by "CE marking".

2. In Article 4 the first paragraph is replaced by the following text:

> "1. Member States may not prohibit, restrict or hinder the placing on the market of PPE or PPE components which comply with the provisions of this Directive and which bear the CE marking attesting their conformity to all the provisions of this Directive, including the certification procedures in Chapter II.".

3. The following paragraph is added to Article 5:

> "6. (a) Where the PPE is subject to other Directives concerning other aspects and which also provide for the affixing of the CE marking, the latter shall indicate that the PPE is also presumed to conform to the provisions of the other Directives.
>
> (b) However, where one or more of these Directives allow the manufacturer, during a transitional period, to choose which arrangements to apply, the CE marking shall indicate conformity to the provisions only of those Directives applied by the manufacturer. In this case, particulars of the Directives applied, as published in the Official Journal of the European Communities, must be given in the documents, notices or instructions required by the Directives and accompanying such PPE.".

4. In Article 9 the first paragraph is replaced by the following:

> "1. Member States shall notify the Commission and the other Member States of the bodies which they have appointed to carry out the procedures referred to in Article 8 together with the specific tasks which these bodies have been appointed to carry out and the identification numbers assigned to them beforehand by the Commission.
>
> The Commission shall publish in the Official Journal of the European Communities a list of the notified bodies and their identification numbers and the tasks for which they have been notified. The Commission shall ensure that this list is kept up to date.".

5. The introductory sentence of Article 12 is replaced by the following text:

> "The EC declaration of conformity is the procedure whereby the manufacturer or his authorised representative established within the Contracting Parties:".

6. Article 13 is replaced by the following text:

Article 13

1. The CE conformity marking shall consist of the initials "CE" in the form shown in the specimen in Annex IV. in the event of the involvement of a notified body in the production control phase as indicated in Article 11, its identification number shall be added.

2. The CE marking must be affixed to each piece of manufactured PPE so as to be visible, legible and indelible throughout the expected life of the PPE; however, if this is not possible in view of the characteristics of the product, the CE marking may be affixed to the packaging.

3. The affixing of markings on the PPE which are likely to deceive third parties as to the meaning and form of the CE marking shall be prohibited. Any other marking may be affixed to the PPE or its packaging provided that the visibility and legibility of the CE marking is not thereby reduced.

4. Without prejudice to Article 7:
   (a) where a Member State establishes that the CE marking has been affixed unduly, the manufacturer or his authorised representative established within the Contracting Parties shall be obliged to make the product conform as regards the provisions concerning the CE marking and to end the infringement under the conditions imposed by the Member State;
   (b) where non-conformity continues, the Member State must take all appropriate measures to restrict or prohibit the placing on the market of the product in question or to ensure that it is withdrawn from the market in accordance with the procedures laid down in Article 7.".

7. The following text is added to section 1.4 of Annex II:

   "(h) where appropriate, the references of the Directives applied in accordance with Article 5(6)(b);
   (i) the name, address and identification number of the notified body involved in the design stage of the PPE.".

8. Annex IV is replaced by the following text:

"*ANNEX IV*
CE CONFORMITY MARKING AND INFORMATION

— The CE conformity marking shall consist of the initials "CE" taking the following form:

— If the CE marking is reduced or enlarged the proportions given in the above graduated drawing must be respected.
— The various components of the CE marking must have substantially the same vertical dimension, which may not be less than 5mm. This minimum dimension may be waived for small-scale PPE.

Additional information
— The last two digits of the year in which the CE marking was affixed; this information is not required in the case of the PPE referred to in Article 8(3)."

THE MANAGEMENT OF HEALTH AND SAFETY AT WORK (AMENDMENT) REGULATIONS 1994

(S.I. 1994 No. 2865)

General note. These Regulations, which came into force on 1 December 1994, amend the Management of Health and Safety at Work Regulations 1992 (S.I. 1992 No.2051) to give effect in Great Britain to Arts. 4 to 7 of Council Directive 92/85/EEC on the introduction of measures to encourage improvements in the safety and health at work of pregnant workers and workers who have recently given birth or who are breastfeeding. The Regulations add a new reg. 13A and amend reg. 15 of the principal Regulations. Breach of a duty imposed on an employer does give rise to civil liability to the extent that it relates to risk referred to in reg. 13A(1) to an employee.

The Secretary of State, in exercise of the powers conferred on him by sections 15(1) and 47(2) of, and paragraphs 7 and 8(1) of Schedule 3 to, the Health and Safety at Work etc Act 1974 and of all other powers enabling him in that behalf, and for the purpose of giving effect without modifications to the proposals submitted to him by the Health and Safety Commission under section 11(2)(d) of the said Act of 1974 after the carrying out by the Commission of consultations in accordance with section 50(3) of that Act, hereby makes the following Regulations:

1. Citation and commencement. These Regulations may be cited as the Management of Health and Safety at Work (Amendment) Regulations 1994 and shall come into force on 1st December 1994.

2. Amendment of the Management of Health and Safety at Work Regulations 1992.—(1)   The Management of Health and Safety at Work Regulations 1992 (in these Regulations referred to as "the 1992 Regulations") shall be amended in accordance with the following provisions of this regulation.

(2)   In regulation 1(2) of the 1992 Regulations there shall be added the following definitions—

    (a)   before the definition of "the assessment":

        "'the 1978 Act' means the Employment Protection (Consolidation) Act 1978;" and

    (b)   after the definition of "fixed-term contract of employment":

        "'given birth' means delivered a living child or, after twenty-four weeks of pregnancy, a stillborn child;

        'maternity leave period' in relation to an employee is the period referred to in section 33(1) of the 1978 Act;

        'new or expectant mother' means an employee who is pregnant; who has given birth within the previous six months; or who is breastfeeding;"

(3)   After regulation 13 of the 1992 Regulations the following provisions shall be added:—

    "13A.—(1)   Where—

        (a)   the persons working in an undertaking include women of child-bearing age; and

(b)   the work is of a kind which could involve risk, by reason of her condition, to the health and safety of a new or expectant mother, or to that of her baby, from any processes or working conditions, or physical, biological or chemical agents, including those specified in Annexes I and II of Council Directive 92/85/EEC in the introduction of measures to encourage improvements in the safety and health at work of pregnant workers and workers who have recently given birth or are breastfeeding,

the assessment required by regulation 3(1) shall also include an assessment of such risk.

(2)   Where, in the case of an individual employee, the taking of any other action the employer is required to take under the relevant statutory provisions would not avoid the risk referred to in paragraph (1) the employer shall, if it is reasonable to do so, and would avoid such risks, alter her working conditions or hours of work.

(3)   If it is not reasonable to alter the working conditions or hours of work, or if it would not avoid such risk, the employer shall, subject to section 46 of the 1978 Act, suspend the employee from work for so long as is necessary to avoid such risk.

(4)   In paragraphs (1) to (3) references to risk, in relation to risk from any infectious or contagious disease, are references to a level of risk at work which is in addition to the level to which a new or expectant mother may be expected to be exposed outside the workplace.

13B.   Where—
   (a)   a new or expectant mother works at night; and
   (b)   a certificate from a registered medical practitioner or a registered midwife shows that it is necessary for her health or safety that she should not be at work for any period of such work identified in the certificate

the employer shall, subject to section 46 of the 1978 Act, suspend her from work for so long as is necessary for her health or safety.

13C.—(1)   Nothing in paragraph (2) or (3) of regulation 13A shall require the employer to take any action in relation to an employee until she has notified the employer in writing that she is pregnant, has given birth within the previous six months, or is breastfeeding.

(2)   Nothing in paragraph (2) or (3) of regulation 13A or in regulation 13B shall require the employer to maintain action taken in relation to an employee—
   (a)   in a case—
      (i)   to which regulation 13A(2) or (3) relates; and
      (ii)   where the employee has notified her employer that she is pregnant,
   where she has failed, within a reasonable time of being requested to do so in writing by her employer, to produce for the employer's inspection a certificate from a registered medical practitioner or a registered midwife showing that she is pregnant;

(b)   once the employer knows that she is no longer a new or expectant mother; or

(c)   if the employer cannot establish whether she remains a new or expectant mother."

(4)   Regulation 14 of the 1992 Regulations shall be amended by inserting in paragraph (1)(a), after "obligations"—

"other than those in regulations 13A to 13C,".

(5)   Regulation 15 shall be amended by substituting therefor the following regulation:

"15.—(1)   Breach of a duty imposed by these Regulations shall not confer a right of action in any civil proceedings.

(2)   Paragraph (1) shall not apply to any duty imposed by these Regulations on an employer to the extent that it relates to risk referred to in regulation 13A(1) to an employee.".

THE CONSTRUCTION (DESIGN AND MANAGEMENT) REGULATIONS 1994

(S.I. 1994 No. 3140)

General note. These Regulations, which came into force on 31 March 1995, give effect as respects Great Britain (except in certain particulars) to Council Directive 92/57/EEC on the implementation of minimum safety and health requirements at temporary or mobile construction sites (see pp. 182–202). Breach of a duty imposed by the Regulations (other than a duty imposed by regs. 10 and 16(1)(c)) does not result in civil liability (reg. 21).

ARRANGEMENT OF REGULATIONS

Whereas the Health and Safety Commission has submitted to the Secretary of State, under section 11(2)(d) of the Health and Safety at Work etc Act 1974 ("the 1974 Act"), proposals for the purpose of making regulations after the carrying out by the said Commission of consultations in accordance with section 50(3) of the 1974 Act;

And whereas the Secretary of State has made modifications to the said proposals under section 50(1) of the 1974 Act and has consulted the said Commission thereon in accordance with section 50(2) of that Act;

Now therefore, the Secretary of State, in exercise of the powers conferred on him by sections 15(1), (2), (3)(a) and (c), (4)(a), (6)(b) and (9), and 82(3)(a) of, and paragraphs 1(1)(c), 6(1), 14, 15(1), 20 and 21 of Schedule 3 to, the 1974 Act, and of all other powers enabling him in that behalf and for the purpose of giving effect to the said proposals of the said Commission with modifications as aforesaid, hereby makes the following Regulations:

1. Citation and commencement. These Regulations may be cited as the Construction (Design and Management) Regulations 1994 and shall come into force on 31st March 1995.

2. Interpretation.—(1) In these Regulations, unless the context otherwise requires—

"agent" in relation to any client means any person who acts as agent for a client in connection with the carrying on by the person of a trade, business or other undertaking (whether for profit or not);

"cleaning work" means the cleaning of any window or any transparent or translucent wall, ceiling or roof in or on a structure where such cleaning involves a risk of a person falling more than 2 metres;

"client" means any person for whom a project is carried out, whether it is carried out by another person or is carried out in-house;

"construction phase" means the period of time starting when construction work in any project starts and ending when construction work in that project is completed;

"construction work" means the carrying out of any building, civil engineering or engineering construction work and includes any of the following—

(a) the construction, alteration, conversion, fitting out, commissioning, renovation, repair, upkeep, redecoration or other maintenance (including cleaning which involves the use of water or an abrasive at high pressure or the use of substances classified as corrosive or toxic for the purposes of regulation 7 of the Chemicals (Hazard Information and Packaging) Regulations 1993), de-commissioning, demolition or dismantling of a structure,

(b) the preparation for an intended structure, including site clearance, exploration, investigation (but not site survey) and excavation, and laying or installing the foundations of the structure,

(c) the assembly of prefabricated elements to form a structure or the disassembly of prefabricated elements which, immediately before such disassembly, formed a structure,

(d) the removal of a structure or part of a structure or of any product or waste resulting from demolition or dismantling of a structure or from disassembly of prefabricated elements which, immediately before such disassembly, formed a structure, and

(e) the installation, commissioning, maintenance, repair or removal of mechanical, electrical, gas, compressed air, hydraulic, telecommunications, computer or similar services which are normally fixed within or to a structure,

but does not include the exploration for or extraction of mineral resources or activities preparatory thereto carried out at a place where such exploration or extraction is carried out;

"contractor" means any person who carries on a trade, business or other undertaking (whether for profit or not) in connection with which he—

(a)   undertakes to or does carry out or manage construction work,

(b)   arranges for any person at work under his control (including, where he is an employer, any employee of his) to carry out or manage construction work;

"design" in relation to any structure includes drawing, design details, specification and bill of quantities (including specification of articles or substances) in relation to the structure;

"designer" means any person who carries on a trade, business or other undertaking in connection with which he—

(a)   prepares a design, or

(b)   arranges for any person under his control (including, where he is an employer, any employee of his) to prepare a design,

relating to a structure or part of a structure;

"developer" shall be construed in accordance with regulation 5(1);

"domestic client" means a client for whom a project is carried out not being a project carried out in connection with the carrying on by the client of a trade, business or other undertaking (whether for profit or not);

"health and safety file" means a file, or other record in permanent form, containing the information required by virtue of regulation 14(d);

"health and safety plan" means the plan prepared by virtue of regulation 15;

"planning supervisor" means any person for the time being appointed under regulation 6(1)(a);

"principal contractor" means any person for the time being appointed under regulation 6(1)(b);

"project" means a project which includes or is intended to include construction work;

"structure" means—

(a)   any building, steel or reinforced concrete structure (not being a building), railway line or siding, tramway line, dock, harbour, inland navigation, tunnel, shaft, bridge, viaduct, waterworks, reservoir, pipe or pipe-line (whatever, in either case, it contains or is intended to contain), cable, aqueduct, sewer, sewage works, gasholder, road, airfield, sea defence works, river works, drainage works, earthworks, lagoon, dam, wall, caisson, mast, tower, pylon, underground tank, earth retaining structure, or structure designed to preserve or alter any natural feature, and any other structure similar to the foregoing, or

(b)   any formwork, falsework, scaffold or other structure designed or used to provide support or means of access during construction work, or

(c)   any fixed plant in respect of work which is installation, commissioning, de-commissioning or dismantling and where any such work involves a risk of a person falling more than 2 metres.

(2)   In determining whether any person arranges for a person (in this paragraph called "the relevant person") to prepare a design or to carry out or manage construction work regard shall be had to the following, namely—

(a)   a person does arrange for the relevant person to do a thing where—

(i)   he specifies in or in connection with any arrangement with a third person that the relevant person shall do that thing (whether by nominating the relevant person as a subcontractor to the third person or otherwise), or

(ii)   being an employer, it is done by any of his employees in-house;

(b)   a person does not arrange for the relevant person to do a thing where—
  (i)   being a self-employed person, he does it himself or, being in partnership it is done by any of his partners; or
  (ii) being an employer, it is done by any of his employees otherwise than in-house, or
  (iii) being a firm carrying on its business anywhere in Great Britain whose principal place of business is in Scotland, it is done by any partner in the firm; or
  (iv) having arranged for a third person to do the thing, he does not object to the third person arranging for it to be done by the relevant person,

and the expressions "arrange" and "arranges" shall be construed accordingly.

(3)   For the purposes of these Regulations—
  (a)   a project is carried out in-house where an employer arranges for the project to be carried out by an employee of his who acts, or by a group of employees who act, in either case, in relation to such a project as a separate part of the undertaking of the employer distinct from the part for which the project is carried out; and
  (b)   construction work is carried out or managed in-house where an employer arranges for the construction work to be carried out or managed by an employee of his who acts or by a group of employees who act, in either case, in relation to such construction work as a separate part of the undertaking of the employer distinct from the part for which the construction work is carried out or managed; and
  (c)   a design is prepared in-house where an employer arranges for the design to be prepared by an employee of his who acts, or by a group of employees who act, in either case, in relation to such design as a separate part of the undertaking of the employer distinct from the part for which the design is prepared.

(4)   For the purposes of these Regulations, a project is notifiable if the construction phase—
  (a)   will be longer than 30 days; or
  (b)   will involve more than 500 person days of construction work,

and the expression "notifiable" shall be construed accordingly.

(5)   Any reference in these Regulations to a person being reasonably satisfied—
  (a)   as to another person's competence is a reference to that person being satisfied after the taking of such steps as it is reasonable for that person to take (including making reasonable enquiries or seeking advice where necessary) to satisfy himself as to such competence; and
  (b)   as to whether another person has allocated or will allocate adequate resources is a reference to that person being satisfied that after the taking of such steps as it is reasonable for that person to take (including making reasonable enquiries or seeking advice where necessary)—
    (i)   to ascertain what resources have been or are intended to be so allocated; and
    (ii) to establish whether the resources so allocated or intended to be allocated are adequate.

(6)   Any reference in these Regulations to—
  (a)   a numbered regulation or Schedule is a reference to the regulation in or Schedule to these Regulations so numbered; and
  (b)   a numbered paragraph is a reference to the paragraph so numbered in the regulation in which the reference appears.

3.   Application of regulations.—(1) Subject to the following paragraphs of this regulation, these Regulations shall apply to and in relation to construction work.

(2) Subject to paragraph (3), regulations 4 to 12 and 14 to 19 shall not apply to or in relation to construction work included in a project where the client has reasonable grounds for believing that—

(a) the project is not notifiable; and

(b) the largest number of persons at work at any one time carrying out construction work included in the project will be or, as the case may be, is less than 5.

(3) These Regulations shall apply to and in relation to construction work which is the demolition or dismantling of a structure notwithstanding paragraph (2).

(4) These Regulations shall not apply to or in relation to construction work in respect of which the local authority within the meaning of regulation 2(1) of the Health and Safety (Enforcing Authority) Regulations 1989 is the enforcing authority.

(5) Regulation 14(b) shall not apply to projects in which no more than one designer is involved.

(6) Regulation 16(1)(a) shall not apply to projects in which no more than one contractor is involved.

(7) Where construction work is carried out or managed in-house or a design is prepared in-house, then, for the purposes of paragraphs (5) and (6), each part of the undertaking of the employer shall be treated as a person and shall be counted as a designer or, as the case may be, contractor, accordingly.

(8) Except where regulation 5 applies, regulations 4, 6, 8 to 12 and 14 to 19 shall not apply to or in relation to construction work included or intended to be included in a project carried out for a domestic client.

4.   Clients and agents of clients.—(1) A client may appoint an agent or another client to act as the only client in respect of a project and where such an appointment is made the provisions of paragraphs (2) to (5) shall apply.

(2) No client shall appoint any person as his agent under paragraph (1) unless the client is reasonably satisfied that the person he intends to appoint as his agent has the competence to perform the duties imposed on a client by these Regulations.

(3) Where the person appointed under paragraph (1) makes a declaration in accordance with paragraph (4), then, from the date of receipt of the declaration by the Executive, such requirements and prohibitions as are imposed by these Regulations upon a client shall apply to the person so appointed (so long as he remains as such) as if he were the only client in respect of that project.

(4) A declaration in accordance with this paragraph—

(a) is a declaration in writing, signed by or on behalf of the person referred to in paragraph (3), to the effect that the client or agent who makes it will act as client for the purposes of these Regulations; and

(b) shall include the name of the person by or on behalf of whom it is made, the address where documents may be served on that person and the address of the construction site; and

(c) shall be sent to the Executive.

(5)   Where the Executive receives a declaration in accordance with paragraph (4), it shall give notice to the person by or on behalf of whom the declaration is made and the notice shall include the date the declaration was received by the Executive.

(6)   Where the person referred to in paragraph (3) does not make a declaration in accordance with paragraph (4), any requirement or prohibition imposed by these Regulations on a client shall also be imposed on him but only to the extent it relates to any matter within his authority.

5.   Requirements on developer.—(1) This regulation applies where the project is carried out for a domestic client and the client enters into an arrangement with a person (in this regulation called "the developer") who carries on a trade, business or other undertaking (whether for profit or not) in connection with which—

(a)   land or an interest in land is granted or transferred to the client; and

(b)   the developer undertakes that construction work will be carried out on the land; and

(c)   following the construction work, the land will include premises which, as intended by the client, will be occupied as a residence.

(2)   Where this regulation applies, with effect from the time the client enters into the arrangement referred to in paragraph (1), the requirements of regulations 6 and 8 to 12 shall apply to the developer as if he were the client.

6.   Appointments of planning supervisor and principal contractor.—
(1) Subject to paragraph (6)(b), every client shall appoint—

(a)   a planning supervisor; and

(b)   a principal contractor,

in respect of each project.

(2)   The client shall not appoint as principal contractor any person who is not a contractor.

(3)   The planning supervisor shall be appointed as soon as is practicable after the client has such information about the project and the construction work involved in it as will enable him to comply with the requirements imposed on him by regulations 8(1) and 9(1).

(4)   The principal contractor shall be appointed as soon as is practicable after the client has such information about the project and the construction work involved in it as will enable the client to comply with the requirements imposed on him by regulations 8(3) and 9(3) when making an arrangement with a contractor to manage construction work where such arrangement consists of the appointment of the principal contractor.

(5)   The appointments mentioned in paragraph (1) shall be terminated, changed or renewed as necessary to ensure that those appointments remain filled at all times until the end of the construction phase.

(6)   Paragraph (1) does not prevent—

(a)   the appointment of the same person as planning supervisor and as principal contractor provided that person is competent to carry out the functions under these Regulations of both appointments; or

(b)   the appointment of the client as planning supervisor or as principal contractor or as both, provided the client is competent to perform the relevant functions under these Regulations.

7. Notification of project.—(1) The planning supervisor shall ensure that notice of the project in respect of which he is appointed is given to the Executive in accordance with paragraphs (2) to (4) unless the planning supervisor has reasonable grounds for believing that the project is not notifiable.

(2) Any notice required by paragraph (1) shall be given in writing or in such other manner as the Executive may from time to time approve in writing and shall contain the particulars specified in paragraph (3) or, where applicable, paragraph (4) and shall be given at the times specified in those paragraphs.

(3) Notice containing such of the particulars specified in Schedule 1 as are known or can reasonably be ascertained shall be given as soon as is practicable after the appointment of the planning supervisor.

(4) Where any particulars specified in Schedule 1 have not been notified under paragraph (3), notice of such particulars shall be given as soon as is practicable after the appointment of the principal contractor and, in any event, before the start of construction work.

(5) Where a project is carried out for a domestic client then, except where regulation 5 applies, every contractor shall ensure that notice of the project is given to the Executive in accordance with paragraph (6) unless the contractor has reasonable grounds for believing that the project is not notifiable.

(6) Any notice required by paragraph (5) shall—
  (a) be in writing or such other manner as the Executive may from time to time approve in writing;
  (b) contain such of the particulars specified in Schedule 1 as are relevant to the project; and
  (c) be given before the contractor or any person at work under his control starts to carry out construction work.

8. Competence of planning supervisor, designers and contractors.—
(1) No client shall appoint any person as planning supervisor in respect of a project unless the client is reasonably satisfied that the person he intends to appoint has the competence to perform the functions of planning supervisor under these Regulations in respect of that project.

(2) No person shall arrange for a designer to prepare a design unless he is reasonably satisfied that the designer has the competence to prepare that design.

(3) No person shall arrange for a contractor to carry out or manage construction work unless he is reasonably satisfied that the contractor has the competence to carry out or, as the case may be, manage, that construction work.

(4) Any reference in this regulation to a person having competence shall extend only to his competence—
  (a) to perform any requirement; and
  (b) to conduct his undertaking without contravening any prohibition,

imposed on him by or under any of the relevant statutory provisions.

9. Provision for health and safety.—(1) No client shall appoint any person as planning supervisor in respect of a project unless the client is reasonably satisfied that the person he intends to appoint has allocated or, as appropriate, will allocate adequate resources to enable him to perform the functions of planning supervisor under these Regulations in respect of that project.

(2)   No person shall arrange for a designer to prepare a design unless he is reasonably satisfied that the designer has allocated or, as appropriate, will allocate adequate resources to enable the designer to comply with regulation 13.

(3)   No person shall arrange for a contractor to carry out or manage construction work unless he is reasonably satisfied that the contractor has allocated or, as appropriate, will allocate adequate resources to enable the contractor to comply with the requirements and prohibitions imposed on him by or under the relevant statutory provisions.

10.   Start of construction phase. Every client shall ensure, so far as is reasonably practicable, that the construction phase of any project does not start unless a health and safety plan complying with regulation 15(4) has been prepared in respect of that project.

11.   Client to ensure information is available.—(1) Every client shall ensure that the planning supervisor for any project carried out for the client is provided (as soon as is reasonably practicable but in any event before the commencement of the work to which the information relates) with all information mentioned in paragraph (2) about the state or condition of any premises at or on which construction work included or intended to be included in the project is or is intended to be carried out.

(2)   The information required to be provided by paragraph (1) is information which is relevant to the functions of the planning supervisor under these Regulations and which the client has or could ascertain by making enquiries which it is reasonable for a person in his position to make.

12.   Client to ensure health and safety file is available for inspection.—
(1) Every client shall take such steps as it is reasonable for a person in his position to take to ensure that the information in any health and safety file which has been delivered to him is kept available for inspection by any person who may need information in the file for the purpose of complying with the requirements and prohibitions imposed on him by or under the relevant statutory provisions.

(2)   It shall be sufficient compliance with paragraph (1) by a client who disposes of his entire interest in the property of the structure if he delivers the health and safety file for the structure to the person who acquires his interest in the property of the structure and ensures such person is aware of the nature and purpose of the health and safety file.

13.   Requirements on designer.—(1) Except where a design is prepared in-house, no employer shall cause or permit any employee of his to prepare, and no self-employed person shall prepare, a design in respect of any project unless he has taken reasonable steps to ensure that the client for that project is aware of the duties to which the client is subject by virtue of these Regulations and of any practical guidance issued from time to time by the Commission with respect to the requirements of these Regulations.

(2)   Every designer shall—
    (a)   ensure that any design he prepares and which he is aware will be used for the purposes of construction work includes among the design considerations adequate regard to the need—
        (i)   to avoid foreseeable risks to the health and safety of any person at work carrying out construction work or cleaning work in or on the structure

at any time, or of any person who may be affected by the work of such a person at work,

   (ii)   to combat at source risks to the health and safety of any person at work carrying out construction work or cleaning work in or on the structure at any time, or of any person who may be affected by the work of such a person at work, and

   (iii)   to give priority to measures which will protect all persons at work who may carry out construction work or cleaning work at any time and all persons who may be affected by the work of such persons at work over measures which only protect each person carrying out such work;

(b)   ensure that the design includes adequate information about any aspect of the project or structure or materials (including articles or substances) which might affect the health or safety of any person at work carrying out construction work or cleaning work in or on the structure at any time or of any person who may be affected by the work of such a person at work; and

(c)   co-operate with the planning supervisor and with any other designer who is preparing any design in connection with the same project or structure so far as is necessary to enable each of them to comply with the requirements and prohibitions placed on him in relation to the project by or under the relevant statutory provisions.

(3) Sub-paragraphs (a) and (b) of paragraph (2) shall require the design to include only the matters referred to therein to the extent that it is reasonable to expect the designer to address them at the time the design is prepared and to the extent that it is otherwise reasonably practicable to do so.

14. Requirements on planning supervisor. The planning supervisor appointed for any project shall—

(a)   ensure, so far as is reasonably practicable, that the design of any structure comprised in the project—
   (i)   includes among the design considerations adequate regard to the needs specified in heads (i) to (iii) of regulation 13(2)(a), and
   (ii)   includes adequate information as specified in regulation 13(2)(b);

(b)   take such steps as it is reasonable for a person in his position to take to ensure co-operation between designers so far as is necessary to enable each designer to comply with the requirements placed on him by regulation 13;

(c)   be in a position to give adequate advice to—
   (i)   any client and any contractor with a view to enabling each of them to comply with regulations 8(2) and 9(2), and to
   (ii)   any client with a view to enabling him to comply with regulations 8(3), 9(3) and 10;

(d)   ensure that a health and safety file is prepared in respect of each structure comprised in the project containing—
   (i)   information included with the design by virtue of regulation 13(2)(b), and
   (ii)   any other information relating to the project which it is reasonably foreseeable will be necessary to ensure the health and safety of any person at work who is carrying out or will carry out construction work or cleaning work in or on the structure or of any person who may be affected by the work of such a person at work;

(e)   review, amend or add to the health and safety file prepared by virtue of sub-paragraph (d) of this regulation as necessary to ensure that it contains the information mentioned in that sub-paragraph when it is delivered to the client in accordance with sub-paragraph (f) of this regulation; and

(f)   ensure that, on the completion of construction work on each structure comprised in the project, the health and safety file in respect of that structure is delivered to the client.

15. Requirements relating to the health and safety plan.—(1) The planning supervisor appointed for any project shall ensure that a health and safety plan in respect of the project has been prepared no later than the time specified in paragraph (2) and contains the information specified in paragraph (3).

(2) The time when the health and safety plan is required by paragraph (1) to be prepared is such time as will enable the health and safety plan to be provided to any contractor before arrangements are made for the contractor to carry out or manage construction work.

(3) The information required by paragraph (1) to be contained in the health and safety plan is—
  (a)   a general description of the construction work comprised in the project;
  (b)   details of the time within which it is intended that the project, and any intermediate stages, will be completed;
  (c)   details of risks to the health or safety of any person carrying out the construction work so far as such risks are known to the planning supervisor or are reasonably foreseeable;
  (d)   any other information which the planning supervisor knows or could ascertain by making reasonable enquiries and which it would be necessary for any contractor to have if he wished to show—
       (i)   that he has the competence on which any person is required to be reasonably satisfied by regulation 8, or
       (ii) that he has allocated or, as appropriate, will allocate, adequate resources on which any person is required to be reasonably satisfied by regulation 9;
  (e)   such information as the planning supervisor knows or could ascertain by making reasonable enquiries and which it is reasonable for the planning supervisor to expect the principal contractor to need in order for him to comply with the requirement imposed on him by paragraph (4); and
  (f)   such information as the planning supervisor knows or could ascertain by making reasonable enquiries and which it would be reasonable for any contractor to know in order to understand how he can comply with any requirements placed upon him in respect of welfare by or under the relevant statutory provisions.

(4) The principal contractor shall take such measures as it is reasonable for a person in his position to take to ensure that the health and safety plan contains until the end of the construction phase the following features:
  (a)   arrangements for the project (including, where necessary, for management of construction work and monitoring of compliance with the relevant statutory provisions) which will ensure, so far as is reasonably practicable, the health and safety of all persons at work carrying out the construction work and all persons who may be affected by the work of such persons at work, taking account of—
       (i)   risks involved in the construction work,
       (ii) any activity specified in paragraph (5); and
  (b)   sufficient information about arrangements for the welfare of persons at work by virtue of the project to enable any contractor to understand how he can comply with any requirements placed upon him in respect of welfare by or under the relevant statutory provisions.

(5) An activity is an activity referred to in paragraph (4)(a)(ii) if—
- (a) it is an activity of persons at work; and
- (b) it is carried out in or on the premises where construction work is or will be carried out; and
- (c) either—
  - (i) the activity may affect the health or safety of persons at work carrying out the construction work or persons who may be affected by the work of such persons at work, or
  - (ii) the health or safety of the persons at work carrying out the activity may be affected by the work of persons at work carrying out the construction work.

16. Requirements on and powers of principal contractor.—(1) The principal contractor appointed for any project shall—
- (a) take reasonable steps to ensure co-operation between all contractors (whether they are sharing the construction site for the purposes of regulation 9 of the Management of Health and Safety at Work Regulations 1992 or otherwise) so far as is necessary to enable each of those contractors to comply with the requirements and prohibitions imposed on him by or under the relevant statutory provisions relating to the construction work;
- (b) ensure, so far as is reasonably practicable, that every contractor, and every employee at work in connection with the project complies with any rules contained in the health and safety plan;
- (c) take reasonable steps to ensure that only authorised persons are allowed into any premises or part of premises where construction work is being carried out;
- (d) ensure that the particulars required to be in any notice given under regulation 7 are displayed in a readable condition in a position where they can be read by any person at work on construction work in connection with the project; and
- (e) promptly provide the planning supervisor with any information which—
  - (i) is in the possession of the principal contractor or which he could ascertain by making reasonable enquiries of a contractor, and
  - (ii) it is reasonable to believe the planning supervisor would include in the health and safety file in order to comply with the requirements imposed on him in respect thereof in regulation 14, and
  - (iii) is not in the possession of the planning supervisor.

(2) The principal contractor may—
- (a) give reasonable directions to any contractor so far as is necessary to enable the principal contractor to comply with his duties under these Regulations;
- (b) include in the health and safety plan rules for the management of the construction work which are reasonably required for the purposes of health and safety.

(3) Any rules contained in the health and safety plan shall be in writing and shall be brought to the attention of persons who may be affected by them.

17. Information and training.—(1) The principal contractor appointed for any project shall ensure, so far as is reasonably practicable, that every contractor is provided with comprehensible information on the risks to the health or safety of that contractor or of any employees or other persons under the control of that contractor arising out of or in connection with the construction work.

(2) The principal contractor shall ensure, so far as is reasonably practicable, that every contractor who is an employer provides any of his employees at work carrying out the construction work with—

    (a) any information which the employer is required to provide to those employees in respect of that work by virtue of regulation 8 of the Management of Health and Safety at Work Regulations 1992; and

    (b) any health and safety training which the employer is required to provide to those employees in respect of that work by virtue of regulation 11(2)(b) of the Management of Health and Safety at Work Regulations 1992.

18. Advice from, and views of, persons at work. The principal contractor shall—

    (a) ensure that employees and self-employed persons at work on the construction work are able to discuss, and offer advice to him on, matters connected with the project which it can reasonably be foreseen will affect their health or safety; and

    (b) ensure that there are arrangements for the co-ordination of the views of employees at work on construction work, or of their representatives, where necessary for reasons of health and safety having regard to the nature of the construction work and the size of the premises where the construction work is carried out.

19. Requirements and prohibitions on contractors.—(1) Every contractor shall, in relation to the project—

    (a) co-operate with the principal contractor so far as is necessary to enable each of them to comply with his duties under the relevant statutory provisions;

    (b) so far as is reasonably practicable, promptly provide the principal contractor with any information (including any relevant part of any risk assessment in his possession or control made by virtue of the Management of Health and Safety at Work Regulations 1992) which might affect the health or safety of any person at work carrying out the construction work or of any person who may be affected by the work of such a person at work or which might justify a review of the health and safety plan;

    (c) comply with any directions of the principal contractor given to him under regulation 16(2)(a);

    (d) comply with any rules applicable to him in the health and safety plan;

    (e) promptly provide the principal contractor with the information in relation to any death, injury, condition or dangerous occurrence which the contractor is required to notify or report by virtue of the Reporting of Injuries, Diseases and Dangerous Occurrences Regulations 1985; and

    (f) promptly provide the principal contractor with any information which—

        (i) is in the possession of the contractor or which he could ascertain by making reasonable enquiries of persons under his control, and

        (ii) it is reasonable to believe the principal contractor would provide to the planning supervisor in order to comply with the requirements imposed on the principal contractor in respect thereof by regulation 16(1)(e), and

        (iii) which is not in the possession of the principal contractor.

(2)   No employer shall cause or permit any employee of his to work on construction work unless the employer has been provided with the information mentioned in paragraph (4).

(3)   No self-employed person shall work on construction work unless he has been provided with the information mentioned in paragraph (4).

(4)   The information referred to in paragraphs (2) and (3) is—
   (a)   the name of the planning supervisor for the project;
   (b)   the name of the principal contractor for the project; and
   (c)   the contents of the health and safety plan or such part of it as is relevant to the construction work which any such employee or, as the case may be, which the self-employed person, is to carry out.

(5)   It shall be a defence in any proceedings for contravention of paragraph (2) or (3) for the employer or self-employed person to show that he made all reasonable enquiries and reasonably believed—
   (a)   that he had been provided with the information mentioned in paragraph (4); or
   (b)   that, by virtue of any provision in regulation 3, this regulation did not apply to the construction work.

20.   Extension outside Great Britain. These Regulations shall apply to any activity to which sections 1 to 59 and 80 to 82 of the Health and Safety at Work etc Act 1974 apply by virtue of article 7 of the Health and Safety at Work etc Act 1974 (Application outside Great Britain) Order 1989 other than the activities specified in sub-paragraphs (b), (c) and (d) of that article as they apply to any such activity in Great Britain.

21.   Exclusion of civil liability. Breach of a duty imposed by these Regulations, other than those imposed by regulation 10 and regulation 16(1)(c), shall not confer a right of action in any civil proceedings.

22.   Enforcement. Notwithstanding regulation 3 of the Health and Safety (Enforcing Authority) Regulations 1989, the enforcing authority for these Regulations shall be the Executive.

23.   Transitional provisions. Schedule 2 shall have effect with respect to projects which have started, but the construction phase of which has not ended, when these Regulations come into force.

24.   Repeals, revocations and modifications.—(1) Subsections (6) and (7) of section 127 of the Factories Act 1961 are repealed.

(2)   Regulations 5 and 6 of the Construction (General Provisions) Regulations 1961 are revoked.

(3)   The Construction (Notice of Operations and Works) Order 1965 is revoked.

(4)   For item (i) of paragraph 4(a) of Schedule 2 to the Health and Safety (Enforcing Authority) Regulations 1989, the following item shall be substituted—
   "(i)   regulation 7(1) of the Construction (Design and Management) Regulations 1994 (SI 1994/3140) (which requires projects which include or are intended to include construction work to be notified to the Executive) applies to the project which includes the work; or".

SCHEDULE 1

Regulation 7

PARTICULARS TO BE NOTIFIED TO THE EXECUTIVE

1. Date of forwarding.
2. Exact address of the construction site.
3. Name and address of the client or clients (see note).
4. Type of project.
5. Name and address of the planning supervisor.
6. A declaration signed by or on behalf of the planning supervisor that he has been appointed as such.
7. Name and address of the principal contractor.
8. A declaration signed by or on behalf of the principal contractor that he has been appointed as such.
9. Date planned for start of the construction phase.
10. Planned duration of the construction phase.
11. Estimated maximum number of people at work on the construction site.
12. Planned number of contractors on the construction site.
13. Name and address of any contractor or contractors already chosen.

Note: Where a declaration has been made in accordance with regulation 4(4), item 3 above refers to the client or clients on the basis that that declaration has not yet taken effect.

SCHEDULE 2

Regulation 23

TRANSITIONAL PROVISIONS

1. Until 1st January 1996, regulation 6 shall not apply in respect of a project the construction phase of which started before the coming into force of these Regulations.

2. Where at the coming into force of these Regulations the time specified in regulation 6(3) for the appointment of the planning supervisor has passed, the time for appointing the planning supervisor by virtue of regulation 6(1)(a) shall be as soon as is practicable after the coming into force of these Regulations.

3. Where at the coming into force of these Regulations the time specified in regulation 6(4) for the appointment of the principal contractor has passed, the time for appointing the principal contractor by virtue of regulation 6(1)(b) shall be as soon as is practicable after the coming into force of these Regulations.

4. Regulation 7 shall not require notification of any project where notice of all construction work included in the project has been given in accordance with section 127(6) of the Factories Act 1961 before the coming into force of these Regulations.

5. Regulation 10 shall not apply to any project the construction phase of which starts before 1st August 1995.

6. Regulation 11 shall not apply to any project the construction phase of which started before the coming into force of these Regulations.

7. Until 1st August 1995, regulation 13 and regulation 14(a) shall not apply in respect of any design the preparation of which started before the coming into force of these Regulations.

THE CONTROL OF SUBSTANCES HAZARDOUS TO HEALTH REGULATIONS 1994

(S.I. 1994 No. 3246 as amended by S.I. 1994 No. 3247)

General note. These Regulations, which came into force on 16 January 1995, re-enact, with minor modifications, the Control of Substances Hazardous to Health Regulations 1988 (S.I. 1988 No. 1657). The Regulations also implement as regards Great Britain Council Directive 90/679/EEC on the protection of workers from risks related to exposure to biological agents at work. Breach of a duty imposed by these Regulations gives rise to civil liability; see the Health and Safety at Work etc. Act 1974, s. 47(2).

ARRANGEMENT OF REGULATIONS

The Secretary of State being the Minister designated for the purpose of section 2(2) of the European Communities Act 1972 in relation to the abolition of restrictions on the import or export of goods, in the exercise of the powers conferred on him by the said section 2(2) and sections 15(1), (2), (3)(a) and (b), (4), (5)(b), (6)(b) and (9), 52(2) and (3) and 82(3)(a) of, and paragraphs 1(1) and (2), 2, 3(1), 6(1), 8, 9, 11, 13(1) and (3), 14, 15(1) and 16 of Schedule 3 to, the Health and Safety at Work etc Act 1974 ("the 1974 Act") and of all other powers enabling him in that behalf and for the purpose of giving effect without modifications to proposals submitted to him by the Health and Safety Commission under section 11(2)(d) of the 1974 Act after the carrying out by the said Commission of consultations in accordance with section 50(3) of that Act, hereby makes the following Regulations:

1. Citation and commencement. These Regulations may be cited as the Control of Substances Hazardous to Health Regulations 1994 and shall come into force on 16th January 1995.

2. Interpretation.—(1) In these Regulations, unless the context otherwise requires—

"the 1974 Act" means the Health and Safety at Work etc Act 1974;

"the Agreement" means the Agreement on the European Economic Area signed at Oporto on 2nd May 1992 as adjusted by the Protocol signed at Brussels on 17th March 1993 and adopted as respects Great Britain by the European Economic Area Act 1993;

"approved" means approved for the time being in writing;

"approved supply list" has the meaning assigned to it in regulation 4 of the Chemicals (Hazard Information and Packaging for Supply) Regulations 1994 (S.I. 1994/3247);

"biological agent" means any micro-organism, cell culture, or human endoparasite, including any which have been genetically modified, which may cause any infection, allergy, toxicity or otherwise create a hazard to human health;

"carcinogen" means—

(a) any substance or preparation which if classified in accordance with the classification provided for by regulation 5 of the Chemicals (Hazard Information and Packaging for Supply) Regulations 1994 would be in the category of danger, carcinogenic (category 1) or carcinogenic (category 2) whether or not the substance or preparation would be required to be classified under those Regulations; or

(b) any substance or preparation—

(i) listed in Schedule 8; and

(ii) any substance or preparation arising from a process specified in Schedule 8 which is a substance hazardous to health;

"the Executive" means the Health and Safety Executive;

"fumigation" means an operation in which a substance is released into the atmosphere so as to form a gas to control or kill pests or other undesirable organisms and "fumigate" and "fumigant" shall be construed accordingly;

"maximum exposure limit" for a substance hazardous to health means the maximum exposure limit for that substance set out in Schedule 1 in relation to the reference period specified therein when calculated by a method approved by the Health and Safety Commission;

"member State" means a State which is a Contracting Party to the Agreement, but until the Agreement comes into force in relation to Liechtenstein does not include the State of Liechtenstein;

"micro-organism" means a microbiological entity, cellular or non-cellular, which is capable of replication or of transferring genetic material;

"occupational exposure standard" for a substance hazardous to health means the standard approved by the Health and Safety Commission for that substance in relation to the specified reference period when calculated by a method approved by the Health and Safety Commission;

"registered dentist" has the meaning assigned to it in section 53(1) of the Dentists Act 1984;

"registered medical practitioner" means a fully registered person within the meaning of the Medical Act 1983;

"substance" means any natural or artificial substance whether in solid or liquid form or in the form of a gas or vapour (including micro-organisms);

"substance hazardous to health" means any substance (including any preparation) which is—

   (a) a substance which is listed in Part 1 of the approved supply list as dangerous for supply within the meaning of the Chemicals (Hazard Information and Packaging for Supply) Regulations 1994 and for which an indication of danger specified for the substance in Part V of that list is very toxic, toxic, harmful, corrosive or irritant;

   (b) a substance specified in Schedule 1 (which lists substances assigned maximum exposure limits) or for which the Health and Safety Commission has approved an occupational exposure standard;

   (c) a biological agent;

   (d) dust of any kind, when present at a substantial concentration in air;

   (e) a substance, not being a substance mentioned in sub-paragraphs (a) to (d) above, which creates a hazard to the health of any person which is comparable with the hazards created by substances mentioned in those sub-paragraphs.

(2)   In these Regulations, any reference to an employee being exposed to a substance hazardous to health is a reference to the exposure of that employee to a substance hazardous to health arising out of or in connection with work which is under the control of his employer.

(3)   In these Regulations, unless the context otherwise requires—

   (a) a reference to a numbered regulation or Schedule is a reference to the regulation or Schedule in these Regulations so numbered; and

   (b) a reference to a numbered paragraph is a reference to the paragraph so numbered in the regulation or Schedule in which that reference appears.

General note. Para. (1) amended by S.I. 1994 No. 3247, reg. 19(12).

3.   Duties under these Regulations.—(1) Where any duty is placed by these Regulations on an employer in respect of his employees, he shall, so far as is reasonably practicable, be under a like duty in respect of any other person, whether at work or not, who may be affected by the work carried on by the employer except that the duties of the employer—

   (a) under regulation 11 (health surveillance) shall not extend to persons who are not his employees; and

   (b) under regulations 10 and 12(1) and (2) (which relate respectively to monitoring and information, training etc) shall not extend to persons who are not his employees, unless those persons are on the premises where the work is being carried on.

(2)   These Regulations shall apply to a self-employed person as they apply to an employer and an employee and as if that self-employed person were both an employer and employee, except that regulations 10 and 11 shall not apply to a self-employed person.

(3)   The duties imposed by these Regulations shall not extend to the master or crew of a seagoing ship or to the employer of such persons in relation to the normal shipboard activities of a ship's crew under the direction of the master.

4.   Prohibitions relating to certain substances.—(1) Those substances described in column 1 of Schedule 2 are prohibited to the extent set out in the corresponding entry in column 2 of that Schedule.

(2)   The importation into the United Kingdom, other than from another member State, of the following substances and articles is prohibited, namely—

   (a)   2-naphthylamine, benzidine, 4-aminodiphenyl, 4-nitrodiphenyl, their salts and any substance containing any of those compounds in a total concentration equal to or greater than 0.1 per cent by mass;

   (b)   matches made with white phosphorus,

and any contravention of this paragraph shall be punishable under the Customs and Excise Management Act 1979 and not as a contravention of a health and safety regulation.

(3)   A person shall not supply during the course of or for use at work any substance or article specified in paragraph (2).

(4)   A person shall not supply during the course of or for use at work, benzene or any substance containing benzene unless its intended use is not prohibited by item 11 of Schedule 2.

5.   Application of regulations 6 to 12.—(1) Regulations 6 to 12 shall have effect with a view to protecting persons against risks to their health, whether immediate or delayed, arising from exposure to substances hazardous to health except—

   (a)   where and to the extent that the following Regulations apply, namely—
      (i)   the Control of Lead at Work Regulations 1980,
      (ii)   the Control of Asbestos at Work Regulations 1987;

   (b)   where the substance is hazardous to health solely by virtue of its radioactive, explosive or flammable properties, or solely because it is at a high or low temperature or a high pressure;

   (c)   where the risk to health is a risk to the health of a person to whom the substance is administered in the course of his medical treatment;

   (d)   below ground in any mine within the meaning of section 180 of the Mines and Quarries Act 1954.

(2)   In paragraph 1(c) "medical treatment" means medical or dental examination or treatment which is conducted by, or under the direction of, a registered medical practitioner or registered dentist and includes any such examination, treatment or administration of any substance conducted for the purpose of research.

(3)   Nothing in these Regulations shall prejudice any requirement imposed by or under any enactment relating to public health or the protection of the environment.

6.   Assessment of health risks created by work involving substances hazardous to health.—(1) An employer shall not carry on any work which is liable to expose any employees to any substance hazardous to health unless he has made a suitable and sufficient assessment of the risks created by that work to the health of those employees and of the steps that need to be taken to meet the requirements of these Regulations.

(2) The assessment required by paragraph (1) shall be reviewed regularly and forthwith if—
(a) there is reason to suspect that the assessment is no longer valid; or
(b) there has been a significant change in the work to which the assessment relates,

and, where as a result of the review, changes in the assessment are required, those changes shall be made.

7. Prevention or control of exposure to substances hazardous to health.—(1) Every employer shall ensure that the exposure of his employees to substances hazardous to health is either prevented or, where this is not reasonably practicable, adequately controlled.

(2) So far as is reasonably practicable, the prevention or adequate control of exposure of employees to a substance hazardous to health, except to a carcinogen or a biological agent, shall be secured by measures other than the provision of personal protective equipment.

(3) Without prejudice to the generality of paragraph (1), where the assessment made under regulation 6 shows that it is not reasonably practicable to prevent exposure to a carcinogen by using an alternative substance or process, the employer shall apply all the following measures, namely—
(a) the total enclosure of the process and handling systems unless this is not reasonably practicable;
(b) the use of plant, processes and systems of work which minimise the generation of, or suppress and contain, spills, leaks, dust, fumes and vapours of carcinogens;
(c) the limitation of the quantities of a carcinogen at the place of work;
(d) the keeping of the number of persons who might be exposed to a carcinogen to a minimum;
(e) the prohibition of eating, drinking and smoking in areas that may be contaminated by carcinogens;
(f) the provision of hygiene measures including adequate washing facilities and regular cleaning of walls and surfaces;
(g) the designation of those areas and installations which may be contaminated by carcinogens, and the use of suitable and sufficient warning signs; and
(h) the safe storage, handling and disposal of carcinogens and use of closed and clearly labelled containers.

(4) Where the measures taken in accordance with paragraph (2) or (3), as the case may be, do not prevent, or provide adequate control of, exposure to substances hazardous to health to which those paragraphs apply, then, in addition to taking those measures, the employer shall provide those employees with such suitable personal protective equipment as will adequately control their exposure to those substances.

(5) Any personal protective equipment provided by an employer in pursuance of this regulation shall comply with any enactment (whether in an Act or instrument) which implements in Great Britain any provision on design or manufacture with respect to health or safety in any relevant Community directive listed in Schedule 1 to the Personal Protective Equipment at Work Regulations 1992 which is applicable to that item of personal protective equipment.

(6)   Where there is exposure to a substance for which a maximum exposure limit is specified in Schedule 1, the control of exposure shall, so far as the inhalation of that substance is concerned, only be treated as being adequate if the level of exposure is reduced so far as is reasonably practicable and in any case below the maximum exposure limit.

(7)   Without prejudice to the generality of paragraph (1), where there is exposure to a substance for which an occupational exposure standard has been approved, the control of exposure shall, so far as the inhalation of that substance is concerned, be treated as being adequate if—

(a)   that occupational exposure standard is not exceeded; or

(b)   where that occupational exposure standard is exceeded, the employer identifies the reasons for the standard being exceeded and takes appropriate action to remedy the situation as soon as is reasonably practicable.

(8)   Where respiratory protective equipment is provided in pursuance of this regulation, then it shall—

(a)   be suitable for the purpose; and

(b)   comply with paragraph (5) or, where no requirement is imposed by virtue of that paragraph, be of a type approved or shall conform to a standard approved, in either case, by the Executive.

(9)   In the event of the failure of a control measure which might result in the escape of carcinogens into the workplace, the employer shall ensure that—

(a)   only those persons who are responsible for the carrying out of repairs and other necessary work are permitted in the affected area and they are provided with suitable respiratory protective equipment and protective clothing; and

(b)   employees and other persons who may be affected are informed of the failure forthwith.

(10) Schedule 9 of these Regulations shall have effect in relation to biological agents.

(11) In this regulation, "adequate" means adequate having regard only to the nature of the substance and the nature and degree of exposure to substances hazardous to health and "adequately" shall be construed accordingly.

8.   Use of control measures etc.—(1) Every employer who provides any control measure, personal protective equipment or other thing or facility pursuant to these Regulations shall take all reasonable steps to ensure that it is properly used or applied as the case may be.

(2)   Every employee shall make full and proper use of any control measure, personal protective equipment or other thing or facility provided pursuant to these Regulations and shall take all reasonable steps to ensure it is returned after use to any accommodation provided for it and, if he discovers any defect therein, shall report it forthwith to his employer.

9.   Maintenance, examination and test of control measures etc.—(1) Every employer who provides any control measure to meet the requirements of regulation 7 shall ensure that it is maintained in an efficient state, in efficient working order and in good repair and, in the case of personal protective equipment, in a clean condition.

(2) Where engineering controls are provided to meet the requirements of regulation 7, the employer shall ensure that thorough examinations and tests of those engineering controls are carried out—

    (a) in the case of local exhaust ventilation plant, at least once every 14 months, or for local exhaust ventilation plant used in conjunction with a process specified in column 1 of Schedule 3, at not more than the interval specified in the corresponding entry in column 2 of that Schedule;

    (b) in any other case, at suitable intervals.

(3) Where respiratory protective equipment (other than disposable respiratory protective equipment) is provided to meet the requirements of regulation 7, the employer shall ensure that at suitable intervals thorough examinations and, where appropriate, tests of that equipment are carried out.

(4) Every employer shall keep a suitable record of the examinations and tests carried out in pursuance of paragraphs (2) and (3) and of any repairs carried out as a result of those examinations and tests, and that record or a suitable summary thereof shall be kept available for at least 5 years from the date on which it was made.

10. Monitoring exposure at the workplace.—(1) In any case in which—

    (a) it is requisite for ensuring the maintenance of adequate control of the exposure of employees to substances hazardous to health; or

    (b) it is otherwise requisite for protecting the health of employees,

the employer shall ensure that the exposure of employees to substances hazardous to health is monitored in accordance with a suitable procedure.

(2) Where a substance or process is specified in column 1 of Schedule 4, monitoring shall be carried out at least at the frequency specified in the corresponding entry in column 2 of that Schedule.

(3) The employer shall keep a suitable record of any monitoring carried out for the purpose of this regulation and that record or a suitable summary thereof shall be kept available—

    (a) where the record is representative of the personal exposures of identifiable employees, for at least 40 years;

    (b) in any other case, for at least 5 years.

11. Health surveillance.—(1) Where it is appropriate for the protection of the health of his employees who are, or are liable to be, exposed to a substance hazardous to health, the employer shall ensure that such employees are under suitable health surveillance.

(2) Health surveillance shall be treated as being appropriate where—

    (a) the employee is exposed to one of the substances specified in Column 1 of Schedule 5 and is engaged in a process specified in Column 2 of that Schedule, unless that exposure is not significant; or

    (b) the exposure of the employee to a substance hazardous to health is such that an identifiable disease or adverse health effect may be related to the exposure, there is a reasonable likelihood that the disease or effect may occur under the particular conditions of his work and there are valid techniques for detecting indications of the disease or the effect.

(3) The employer shall ensure that a health record, containing particulars approved by the Executive, in respect of each of his employees to whom paragraph (1) relates is

made and maintained and that that record or a copy thereof is kept in a suitable form for at least 40 years from the date of the last entry made in it.

(4) Where an employer who holds records in accordance with paragraph (3) ceases to trade, he shall forthwith notify the Executive thereof in writing and offer those records to the Executive.

(5) If an employee is exposed to a substance specified in Schedule 5 and is engaged in a process specified therein, the health surveillance required under paragraph (1) shall include medical surveillance under the supervision of an employment medical adviser or appointed doctor at intervals of not more than 12 months or at such shorter intervals as the employment medical adviser or appointed doctor may require.

(6) Where an employee is subject to medical surveillance in accordance with paragraph (5) and an employment medical adviser or appointed doctor has certified by an entry in the health record of that employee that in his professional opinion that employee should not be engaged in work which exposes him to that substance or that he should only be so engaged under conditions specified in the record, the employer shall not permit the employee to be engaged in such work except in accordance with the conditions, if any, specified in the health record, unless that entry has been cancelled by an employment medical adviser or appointed doctor.

(7) Where an employee is subject to medical surveillance in accordance with paragraph (5) and an employment medical adviser or appointed doctor has certified by an entry in his health record that medical surveillance should be continued after his exposure to that substance has ceased, the employer shall ensure that the medical surveillance of that employee is continued in accordance with that entry while he is employed by the employer, unless that entry has been cancelled by an employment medical adviser or appointed doctor.

(8) On reasonable notice being given, the employer shall allow any of his employees access to the health record which relates to him.

(9) An employee to whom this regulation applies shall, when required by his employer and at the cost of the employer, present himself during his working hours for such health surveillance procedures as may be required for the purposes of paragraph (1) and, in the case of an employee who is subject to medical surveillance in accordance with paragraph (5), shall furnish the employment medical adviser or appointed doctor with such information concerning his health as the employment medical adviser or appointed doctor may reasonably require.

(10) Where, for the purpose of carrying out his functions under these Regulations, an employment medical adviser or appointed doctor requires to inspect any workplace or any record kept for the purposes of these Regulations, the employer shall permit him to do so.

(11) Where an employee or an employer is aggrieved by a decision recorded in the health record by an employment medical adviser or appointed doctor to suspend an employee from work which exposes him to a substance hazardous to health (or to impose conditions on such work), he may, by an application in writing to the Executive within 28 days of the date on which he was notified of the decision, apply for that decision to be reviewed in accordance with a procedure approved for the purposes of this paragraph by the Health and Safety Commission, and the result of that review shall be notified to the employee and employer and entered in the health record in accordance with the approved procedure.

(12) In this regulation—

"appointed doctor" means a registered medical practitioner who is appointed for the time being in writing by the Executive for the purposes of this regulation;

"employment medical adviser" means an employment medical adviser appointed under section 56 of the 1974 Act;

"health surveillance" includes biological monitoring.

12. Information, instruction and training for persons who may he exposed to substances hazardous to health.—(1) An employer who undertakes work which may expose any of his employees to substances hazardous to health shall provide that employee with such information, instruction and training as is suitable and sufficient for him to know—

(a) the risks to health created by such exposure; and

(b) the precautions which should be taken.

(2) Without prejudice to the generality of paragraph (1), the information provided under that paragraph shall include—

(a) information on the results of any monitoring of exposure at the workplace in accordance with regulation 10 and, in particular, in the case of any substance hazardous to health specified in Schedule 1, the employee or his representatives shall be informed forthwith, if the results of such monitoring show that the maximum exposure limit has been exceeded; and

(b) information on the collective results of any health surveillance undertaken in accordance with regulation 11 in a form calculated to prevent it from being identified as relating to any particular person.

(3) Every employer shall ensure that any person (whether or not his employee) who carries out any work in connection with the employer's duties under these Regulations has the necessary information, instruction and training.

13. Provisions relating to certain fumigations.—(1) This regulation shall apply to fumigations in which the fumigant used or intended to be used is hydrogen cyanide, ethylene oxide, phosphine or methyl bromide, except that this regulation shall not apply to fumigations using the fumigant specified in column 1 of Schedule 6 when the nature of the fumigation is that specified in the corresponding entry in column 2 of that Schedule.

(2) An employer shall not undertake any fumigation to which this regulation applies unless he has—

(a) notified the persons specified in Part I of Schedule 7 of his intention to undertake the fumigation; and

(b) provided to those persons the information specified in Part II of that Schedule,

at least 24 hours in advance, or such shorter time in advance, as the persons required to be notified may agree.

(3) An employer who undertakes a fumigation to which this regulation applies shall ensure that, before the fumigant is released, suitable warning notices have been affixed at all points of reasonable access to the premises or to those parts of the premises in which the fumigation is to be carried out and that after the fumigation has been completed, and the premises are safe to enter, those warning notices are removed.

14. Exemption certificates.—(1) Subject to paragraph (2) and to any of the provisions imposed by the Communities in respect of the protection of workers from the risks related to exposure to chemical, physical and biological agents at work, the Executive may, by a certificate in writing, exempt any person or class of persons or any substance or class of substances from all or any of the requirements or prohibitions imposed by these Regulations and any such exemption may be granted subject to conditions and to a limit of time and may be revoked by a certificate in writing at any time.

(2) The Executive shall not grant any such exemption unless having regard to the circumstances of the case and, in particular, to—

(a) the conditions, if any, which it proposes to attach to the exemption; and

(b) any other requirements imposed by or under any enactments which apply to the case,

it is satisfied that the health and safety of persons who are likely to be affected by the exemption will not be prejudiced in consequence of it.

15. Extension outside Great Britain.—(1) Subject to paragraph (2), these Regulations shall apply to and in relation to any activity outside Great Britain to which sections 1 to 59 and 80 to 82 of the 1974 Act apply by virtue of article 4, 5 or 7 of the Health and Safety at Work etc Act 1974 (Application outside Great Britain) Order 1989 as those provisions apply within Great Britain.

(2) These Regulations shall not extend to Northern Ireland except insofar as they relate to imports of substances and articles referred to in regulation 4(2) into the United Kingdom.

16. Defence in proceedings for contravention of these Regulations. In any proceedings for an offence consisting of a contravention of these Regulations it shall be a defence for any person to prove that he took all reasonable precautions and exercised all due diligence to avoid the commission of that offence.

17. Exemptions relating to the Ministry of Defence etc.—(1) In this regulation, any reference to—

(a) "visiting forces" is a reference to visiting forces within the meaning of any provision of Part I of the Visiting Forces Act 1952; and

(b) "headquarters or organisation" is a reference to a headquarters or organisation designated for the purposes of the International Headquarters and Defence Organisations Act 1964.

(2) The Secretary of State for Defence may, in the interests of national security, by a certificate in writing exempt—

(a) Her Majesty's Forces;

(b) visiting forces;

(c) any member of a visiting force working in or attached to any headquarters or organisation; or

(d) any person engaged in work involving substances hazardous to health, if that person is under the direct supervision of a representative of the Secretary of State for Defence,

from all or any of the requirements or prohibitions imposed by these Regulations and any such exemption may be granted subject to conditions and to a limit of time and may be revoked at any time by a certificate in writing, except that, where any such exemption is granted, suitable arrangements shall be made for the assessment of the health risks created by the work involving substances hazardous to health and for adequately controlling the exposure to those substances of persons to whom the exemption relates.

(3) Regulation 11(11) shall not apply in relation to—
  (a) Her Majesty's Forces;
  (b) visiting forces; or
  (c) any member of a visiting force working in or attached to any headquarters or organisation.

18. Revocations and savings.—(1) Paragraphs 19, 20 and 21 in Part VIII of Schedule 2 to the Personal Protective Equipment at Work Regulations 1992 are revoked.

(2) Regulation 3 of the Health and Safety (Miscellaneous Modifications) Regulations 1993 is revoked.

(3) Paragraph (9) of regulation 21 of the Chemicals (Hazard Information and Packaging) Regulations 1993 is revoked.

(4) The following Regulations are revoked—
  (a) The Health and Safety (Dangerous Pathogens) Regulations 1981;
  (b) The Control of Substances Hazardous to Health Regulations 1988;
  (c) The Control of Substances Hazardous to Health (Amendment) Regulations 1991;
  (d) The Control of Substances Hazardous to Health (Amendment) Regulations 1992;

(5) Any record or register required to be kept under any regulations revoked by paragraph (4) shall, notwithstanding those revocations, be kept in the same manner and for the same period as specified in those regulations as if these Regulations had not been made, except that the Executive may approve the keeping of records at a place or in a form other than at the place where, or in the form in which, records were required to be kept under the regulations so revoked.

19. Extension of meaning of "work". For the purposes of Part I of the 1974 Act the meaning of "work" shall be extended to include any activity involving the consignment, storage or use of any of the biological agents listed in Part V of Schedule 9 and the meaning of "at work" shall be extended accordingly, and in that connection the references to employer in paragraphs 12 and 13 of that Schedule include references to any person carrying on such an activity.

20. Modification of section 3(2) of the 1974 Act. Section 3(2) of the 1974 Act shall be modified in relation to an activity involving the consignment, storage or use of any of the biological agents referred to in regulation 19 so as to have effect as if the reference therein to a self-employed person is a reference to any person who is not an employer or an employee and the reference therein to his undertaking includes a reference to such an activity.

SCHEDULE 1

Regulations 2(1), 7(6) and 12(2)

List of Substances Assigned Maximum Exposure Limits

The maximum exposure limits of the dusts included in the list below refer to the total inhalable dust fraction, unless otherwise stated.

| | | *Reference periods* | | | |
| | | *Long-term maximum exposure limit (8-hour TWA reference period)* | | *Short-term maximum exposure limit (15-minute reference period)* | |
Substance	*Formula*	*ppm*	*mg m^{-3}*	*ppm*	*mg m^{-3}*
Acrylamide	$CH_2=CHCONH_2$	–	0.3	–	–
Acrylonitrile	$CH_2=CHCN$	2	4	–	–
Arsenic & compounds except arsine (as As)	As	–	0.1	–	–
Benzene	C_6H_6	5	16	–	–
Beryllium and beryllium compounds (as Be)	Be	–	0.002	–	–
Bis (chloromethyl) ether	$ClCH_2OCH_2Cl$	0.001	0.005	–	–
Buta-1, 3-diene	$CH_2=CHCH=CH_2$	10	22	–	–
2–Butoxyethanol	$C_4H_9OCH_2CH_2OH$	25	120	–	–
Cadmium & cadmium compounds, except cadmium oxide fume, cadmium sulphide and cadmium sulphide pigments (as Cd)	Cd	–	0.025	–	–
Cadmium oxide fume (as Cd)	CdO	–	0.025	–	0.05
Cadmium sulphide and cadmium sulphide pigments (respirable dust as Cd)	CdS	–	0.04	–	–
Carbon disulphide	CS_2	10	30	–	–
Chromium (VI) compounds (as Cr)	Cr	–	0.05	–	–
Cobalt and cobalt compounds (as Co)	Co	–	0.1	–	–
1,2–Dibromoethane (Ethylene dibromide)	$BrCH_2CH_2Br$	0.5	4	–	–
1,2–Dichloroethane (Ethylene dichloride)	$ClCH2CH_2Cl$	5	20	–	–
Dichloromethane	CH_2Cl_2	100	350	300	1050
2,2'–Dichloro4,4'–methylene dianiline (mboca)	$CH_2(C_6H_3ClNH_2)_2$	–	0.005	–	–
1–Chloro-2,3-epoxypropane (Epichlorohydrin)	$OCH_2{-}CH{-}CH_2Cl$	0.5	2	1.5	6
2–Ethoxyethanol	$C_2H_5OCH_2CH_2OH$	10	37	–	–
2–Ethoxyethyl acetate	$C_2H_5OCH_2CH_2OOCCH_3$	10	54	–	–
Ethylene oxide	CH_2CH_2O	5	10	–	–
Formaldehyde	HCHO	2	2.5	2	2.5
Grain dust		–	10	–	–

Substance	Formula	Long-term maximum exposure limit (8-hour TWA reference period)		Short-term maximum exposure limit (15-minute reference period)	
		ppm	mg m^{-3}	ppm	mg m^{-3}
Hydrogen cyanide	HCN	–	–	10	10
Isocyanates, all (as-NCO)		–	0.02	–	0.07
Man-made mineral fibre°		–	5	–	–
2–Methoxyethanol	$CH_3OCH_2CH_2OH$	5	16	–	–
2–Methoxyethyl acetate	$CH_3COOCH_2CH_2OCH_3$	5	24	–	–
4,4'–Methylenedianiline	$CH_2(C_6H_4NH_2)_2$	0.01	0.08	–	–
Nickel and its inorganic compounds (except nickel carbonyl):					
water-soluble nickel compounds (as Ni)	Ni	–	0.1	–	–
nickel and water-insoluble nickel compounds (as Ni)		–	0.5	–	–
2–Nitropropane	$CH_3CH(NO_2)CH_3$	5	18	–	–
Rubber process dust		–	6	–	–
Rubber fume*		–	0.6	–	–
Silica, respirable crystalline	SiO_2	–	0.4	–	–
Styrene	$C_6H_5CH=CH_2$	100	420	250	1050
1, 1, 1–Trichloroethane	CH_3CCl_3	350	1900	450	2450
Trichloroethylene	$CCl_2=CHCl$	100	535	150	802
Vinyl chloride#	$CH_2=CHCl$	7	–	–	–
Vinylidene chloride	$CH_2=CCl_2$	10	40	–	–
Wood dust (hard wood)		–	5	–	–

° In addition to the maximum exposure limit specified above man-made mineral fibre is also subject to a maximum exposure limit of 2 fibres ml^{-1}, 8-hour TWA, when measured or calculated by a method approved by the Health and Safety Commission.

* Limit relates to cyclohexane soluble material.

\# In addition to the maximum exposure limit specified above vinyl chloride is also subject to an overriding annual exposure limit of 3 ppm.

SCHEDULE 2

Regulation 4(1)

PROHIBITION OF CERTAIN SUBSTANCES HAZARDOUS TO HEALTH FOR CERTAIN PURPOSES

Column 1 *Description of substance*	**Column 2** *Purpose for which the substance is prohibited*
1. 2-naphthylamine; benzidine; 4-aminodiphenyl; 4-nitrodiphenyl; their salts and any substance containing any of those compounds, in any other substance in a total concentration equal to or greater than 0.1 per cent by mass.	Manufacture and use for all purposes including any manufacturing process in which a substance described in column 1 of this item is formed.
2. Sand or other substance containing free silica.	Use as an abrasive for blasting articles in any blasting apparatus (see note 1).

Column 1	**Column 2**
Description of substance	*Purpose for which the substance is prohibited*

3. A substance—
   (a) containing compounds of silicon calculated as silica to the extent of more than 3 per cent by weight of dry material; or
   (b) composed of or containing dust or other matter deposited from a fettling or blasting process.

Use as a parting material in connection with the making of metal castings (see notes 2 and 3).

4. Carbon disulphide.

Use in the cold–cure process of vulcanising in the proofing of cloth with rubber

5. Oils other than white oil, or oil of entirely animal or vegetable origin or entirely of mixed animal and vegetable origin (see note 4).

Use for oiling the spindles of self-acting mules

6. Ground or powdered flint or quartz other than natural sand.

Use in relation to the manufacture or decoration of pottery for the following purposes:
   (a) the placing of ware for the biscuit fire;
   (b) the polishing of ware;
   (c) as the ingredient of a wash for saggars, trucks, bats, cranks, or other articles used in supporting ware during firing; and
   (d) as dusting or supporting powder in potters' shops.

7. Ground or powdered flint or quartz other than—
   (a) natural sand; or
   (b) ground or powdered flint or quartz which forms parts of a slop or paste.

Use in relation to the manufacture or decoration of pottery for any purpose except—
   (a) use in a separate room or building for
       (i) the manufacture of powdered flint or quartz, or
       (ii) the making of frits or glazes or the making of colours or coloured slips for the decoration of pottery;
   (b) use for the incorporation of the substance into the body of ware in an enclosure in which no person is employed and which is constructed and ventilated to prevent the escape of dust.

8. Dust or powder of a refractory material containing not less than 80 per cent of silica other than natural sand.

Use for sprinkling the moulds of silica bricks, namely bricks or other articles composed of refractory material and containing not less than 80 per cent of silica.

9. White phosphorus.

Use in the manufacture of matches.

10. Hydrogen cyanide.

Use in fumigation except when—
   (a) released from an inert material in which hydrogen cyanide is absorbed;
   (b) generated from a gassing powder (see note 5); or

Column 1 *Description of substance*	**Column 2** *Purpose for which the substance is prohibited*
	(c) applied from a cylinder through suitable piping and applicators other than for fumigation in the open air to control or kill mammal pests.
11. Benzene and any substance containing benzene in a concentration equal to or greater than 0.1 per cent by mass, other than (a) motor fuels covered by Council Directive 85/210/EEC (OJ No. L96, 3.4.1985, p. 25); (b) waste covered by Council Directives 75/442/EEC (OJ No. L194, 25.7.1975, p. 39) and 78/319/EEC (OJ No. L84, 31.3.78, p. 43).	Use for all purposes except use in industrial processes, and for the purposes of research, development and analysis.

Notes

1. "Blasting apparatus" means apparatus for cleaning, smoothing, roughening or removing of part of the surface of any article by the use as an abrasive of a jet of sand, metal shot or grit or other material propelled by a blast of compressed air or steam or by a wheel.

2. This prohibition shall not prevent the use as a parting material of the following substances: natural sand; zirconium silicate (zircon); calcined china clay; calcined aluminous fireclay; sillimanite; calcined or fused alumina; olivine.

3. "Use as a parting material" means the application of the material to the surface or parts of the surface of a pattern or of a mould so as to facilitate the separation of the pattern from the mould or the separation of parts of the mould.

4. "White oil" means a refined mineral oil conforming to a specification approved by the Executive and certified by its manufacturer as so conforming.

5. "Gassing powder" means a chemical compound in powder form which reacts with atmospheric moisture to generate hydrogen cyanide.

SCHEDULE 3

Regulation 9(2)(a)

FREQUENCY OF THOROUGH EXAMINATION AND TEST OF LOCAL EXHAUST VENTILATION PLANT USED IN CERTAIN PROCESSES

Column 1 *Process*	**Column 2** *Minimum frequency*
Processes in which blasting is carried out in or incidental to the cleaning of metal castings, in connection with their manufacture.	1 month
Processes, other than wet processes, in which metal articles (other than of gold, platinum or iridium) are ground, abraded or polished using mechanical power, in any room for more than 12 hours in any week.	6 months
Processes giving off dust or fume in which nonferrous metal castings are produced.	6 months
Jute cloth manufacture.	1 month

SCHEDULE 4

Regulation 10(2)

Specific Substances and Processes for which Monitoring is Required

Column 1
Substance or process

Column 2
Minimum frequency

Vinyl chloride monomer.	Continuous or in accordance with a procedure approved by the Health and Safety Commission.
Vapour or spray given off from vessels at which an electrolytic chromium process is carried on, except trivalent chromium.	Every 14 days.

SCHEDULE 5

Regulation 11(2)(a) and (5)

Medical Surveillance

Column 1
Substances for which medical surveillance is appropriate

Column 2
Processes

Vinyl chloride monomer (VCM).	In manufacture, production, reclamation, storage, discharge, transport, use or polymerisation.
Nitro or amino derivatives of phenol and of benzene or its homologues.	In the manufacture of nitro or amino derivatives of phenol and of benzene or its homologues and the making of explosives with the use of any of these substances.
Potassium or sodium chromate or dichromate.	In manufacture.
1-Naphthylamine and its salts. Orthotolidine and its salts. Dianisidine and its salts. Dichlorbenzidine and its salts.	In manufacture, formation or use of these substances.
Auramine. Magenta.	In manufacture.
Carbon disulphide. Disulphur dichloride. Benzene, including benzol. Carbon tetrachloride. Trichloroethylene.	Processes in which these substances are used, or given off as vapour, in the manufacture of indiarubber or of articles or goods made wholly or partially of indiarubber.
Pitch.	In manufacture of blocks of fuel consisting of coal, coal dust, coke or slurry with pitch as a binding substance.

SCHEDULE 6

FUMIGATIONS EXCEPTED FROM REGULATION 13

Column 1 *Fumigant*	**Column 2** *Nature of fumigation*
Hydrogen cyanide.	Fumigations carried out for research.
	Fumigations in fumigation chambers.
	Fumigations in the open air to control or kill mammal pests.
Methyl bromide.	Fumigations carried out for research.
	Fumigations in fumigation chambers.
	Fumigations of soil outdoors under gas-proof sheeting where not more than 1,000 kg is used in any period of 24 hours on the premises.
	Fumigations of soil under gas-proof sheeting in glasshouses where not more than 500 kg is used in any period of 24 hours on the premises.
	Fumigations of compost outdoors under gas-proof sheeting where not more than 10 kg of methyl bromide is used in any period of 24 hours on the premises.
	Fumigations under gas-proof sheeting inside structures other than glasshouses and mushroom houses where not more than 5 kg of methyl bromide is used in each structure during any period of 24 hours.
	Fumigations of soil or compost in mushroom houses where not more than 5 kg of methyl bromide is used in any one fumigation in any period of 24 hours.
	Fumigations of containers where not more than 5 kg of methyl bromide is used in any one fumigation in a period of 24 hours.
Phosphine.	Fumigations carried out for research.
	Fumigations in fumigation chambers.
	Fumigations under gas-proof sheeting inside structures where not more than 1 kg of phosphine in each structure is used in any period of 24 hours.
	Fumigations in containers where not more than 0.5 kg of phosphine is used in any one fumigation in any period of 24 hours.
	Fumigations in individual impermeable packages.
	Fumigations in the open air to control or kill mammal pests.
Ethylene oxide.	Fumigations carried out for research.
	Fumigations in fumigation chambers.

SCHEDULE 7

Regulation 13(2)

NOTIFICATION OF CERTAIN FUMIGATIONS

PART I
PERSONS TO WHOM NOTIFICATIONS MUST BE MADE

1.   In the case of a fumigation to be carried out within the area of a harbour authority, advance notification of fumigation shall, for the purposes of regulation 13(2)(a), be given to—

    (a)   that authority;

    (b)   an inspector appointed under section 19 of the 1974 Act, if that inspector so requires; and

    (c)   where the fumigation—

        (i)   is to be carried out on a sea-going ship, the chief fire officer of the area in which the ship is situated and the officer in charge of the office of Her Majesty's Customs and Excise at the harbour, or

        (ii)   is the space fumigation of a building, the chief fire officer of the area in which the building is situated.

2.   In the case of a fumigation, other than a fumigation to which paragraph (1) applies, advance notification of fumigation shall be given to—

    (a)   the police officer for the time being in charge of the police station for the police district in which the fumigation is carried out;

    (b)   an inspector appointed under section 19 of the 1974 Act if that inspector so requires; and

    (c)   where the fumigation is to be carried out on a sea-going ship or is the space fumigation of a building, the chief fire officer of the area in which the ship or building is situated.

PART II
INFORMATION TO BE GIVEN IN ADVANCE NOTICE OF FUMIGATIONS

3.   The information to be given in a notification made for the purposes of regulation 13(2) shall include the following:—

    (a)   the name, address and place of business of the fumigator and his telephone number;

    (b)   the name of person requiring the fumigation to be carried out;

    (c)   the address and description of the premises where the fumigation is to be carried out;

    (d)   the date on which the fumigation is to be carried out and the estimated time of commencement and completion;

    (e)   the name of the operator in charge of the fumigation; and

    (f)   the fumigant to be used.

SCHEDULE 8

Regulation 2(1)

OTHER SUBSTANCES AND PROCESSES TO WHICH THE DEFINITION OF "CARCINOGEN" RELATES

Aflatoxins

Arsenic

Bichromate manufacture involving the roasting of chromite ore

Electrolytic chromium processes, excluding passivation, which involve hexavalent chromium compounds

Mustard gas (B, B'Dichlorodiethyl sulphide)

Calcining, sintering or smelting of nickel copper matte or acid leaching or electrorefining of roasted matte

Coal soots, coal tar, pitch and coal tar fumes

The following mineral oils:
- (i)   unrefined and mildly refined vacuum distillates;
- (ii) catalytically cracked petroleum oils with final boiling points above 320°C;
- (iii) used engine oils;

Auramine manufacture

Leather dust in boot and shoe manufacture, arising during preparation and finishing

Hard wood dusts

Isopropyl alcohol manufacture (strong acid process)

Rubber manufacturing and processing giving rise to rubber process dust and rubber fume

Magenta manufacture

SCHEDULE 9

Regulation 7(10)

SPECIAL PROVISIONS RELATING TO BIOLOGICAL AGENTS

PART I
PROVISIONS OF GENERAL APPLICATION TO BIOLOGICAL AGENTS

Interpretation

1.   In this Schedule—

"cell culture" means the *in-vitro* growth of cells derived from multicellular organisms;

"diagnostic service" means any activity undertaken solely with the intention of—

- (a)   testing for the presence of or identifying a biological agent,
- (b)   isolating or identifying other organisms from specimens or samples containing or suspected of containing a biological agent,
- (c)   analysing specimens or samples from a human patient or animal in which a biological agent is or is suspected of being present for purposes relating to the assessment of the clinical progress, or assistance in the clinical management, of that patient or animal,

and "diagnosis" shall be construed accordingly;

"Group" means one of the four hazard Groups specified in paragraph 3 to which biological agents are assigned.

Application

2.—(1) This Schedule shall have effect with a view to protecting employees against risks to their health, whether immediate or delayed, arising from exposure to biological agents except that paragraph 11 shall not apply in relation to a particular biological agent where the results of the assessment made under regulation 6 indicate that—

- (a)   the activity does not involve a deliberate intention to work with or use that biological agent; and
- (b)   there is no significant risk to the health of employees associated with that biological agent.

(2)   Unless otherwise expressly provided, the provisions of this Schedule shall have effect in addition to and not in substitution for other provisions of these Regulations.

Classification of biological agents

3.—(1) The Health and Safety Commission shall approve and publish for the purposes of this Schedule a document, which may be revised or re-issued from time to time, entitled "Categorisation of Biological Agents according to hazard and categories of containment" containing a list of biological agents together with the classification of each agent which it has approved, and any reference in this Schedule to "approved classification" in relation to a particular biological agent shall be construed as a reference to the classification of that agent which appears in the said document.

(2)   Where a biological agent has an approved classification any reference in these Regulations to a particular Group in relation to that agent shall be taken as a reference to the Group to which that agent has been assigned in that approved classification.

(3)   Where a biological agent does not have an approved classification, the employer shall provisionally classify that agent in accordance with sub-paragraph (4) below, having regard to the nature of the agent and the properties of which he may reasonably be expected to be aware.

(4)   When provisionally classifying a biological agent the employer shall assign that agent to one of the following Groups according to its level of risk of infection and, if in doubt as to which of two alternative Groups is the most appropriate, he shall assign it to the higher of the two—

- (a)   Group 1—unlikely to cause human disease;
- (b)   Group 2—can cause human disease and may be a hazard to employees; it is unlikely to spread to the community and there is usually effective prophylaxis or treatment available;
- (c)   Group 3—can cause severe human disease and may be a serious hazard to employees; it may spread to the community, but there is usually effective prophylaxis or treatment available;
- (d)   Group 4—causes severe human disease and is a serious hazard to employees; it is likely to spread to the community and there is usually no effective prophylaxis or treatment available.

Assessment of health risks

4.   Without prejudice to the generality of regulation 6, every employer who intends to carry on any work which is liable to expose his employees to any biological agent shall take account of the Group into which that agent is classified when making an assessment of the risks created by that work.

Prevention of exposure to a biological agent

5.   Without prejudice to the generality of regulation 7(1), if the nature of the activity so permits, every employer shall ensure that the exposure of his employees to a particular biological agent is prevented by substituting a biological agent which is less hazardous.

Control of exposure to biological agents

6.—(1) Where there is a risk of exposure to a biological agent and it is not otherwise reasonably practicable to prevent that exposure then it shall be adequately controlled, in particular by the following measures which are to be applied in the light of the results of the assessment—

- (a)   keeping as low as practicable the number of employees exposed or likely to be exposed to the biological agent;
- (b)   designing work processes and engineering control measures so as to prevent or minimise the release of biological agents into the place of work;
- (c)   displaying the biohazard sign shown in Part IV of this Schedule and other relevant warning signs;
- (d)   drawing up plans to deal with accidents involving biological agents;
- (e)   specifying appropriate decontamination and disinfection procedures;
- (f)   instituting means for the safe collection, storage and disposal of contaminated waste, including the use of secure and identifiable containers, after suitable treatment where appropriate;
- (g)   making arrangements for the safe handling and transport of biological agents, or materials that may contain such agents, within the workplace;
- (h)   specifying procedures for taking, handling and processing samples that may contain biological agents;
- (i)   providing collective protection measures and, where exposure cannot be adequately controlled by other means, individual protection measures including, in particular, the supply of appropriate protective clothing or other special clothing;

    (j)   where appropriate, making available effective vaccines for those employees who are not already immune to the biological agent to which they are exposed or are liable to be exposed;

    (k)   instituting hygiene measures compatible with the aim of preventing or reducing the accidental transfer or release of a biological agent from the workplace, including, in particular—

        (i)   the provision of appropriate and adequate washing and toilet facilities, and

        (ii)   the prohibition of eating, drinking, smoking and application of cosmetics in working areas where there is a risk of contamination by biological agents.

(2) In this paragraph, "appropriate" in relation to clothing and hygiene measures means appropriate for the risks involved and the conditions at the place where exposure to the risk may occur.

Special control measures for health and veterinary care facilities

7. In health and veterinary care isolation facilities where there are human patients or animals which are, or are suspected of being, infected with a Group 3 or Group 4 biological agent, the employer shall select the most suitable containment measures from those listed in Part II of this Schedule with a view to controlling adequately the risk of infection.

Special control measures for laboratories, animal rooms and industrial processes

8.—(1) Every employer who is engaged in any of the activities specified in sub-paragraph (3) below shall ensure that measures taken to control adequately the exposure of his employees to biological agents include, in particular, the most suitable combination of containment measures from those listed in Parts II and III of this Schedule as appropriate, taking into account—

    (a)   the nature of the activity specified in sub-paragraph (3) below;

    (b)   the minimum containment level specified in sub-paragraph (4) below;

    (c)   the assessment of risk made under regulation 6; and

    (d)   the nature of the biological agent concerned.

(2)   (a)   An employer who is engaged in any of the activities specified in sub-paragraphs (a) or (b) of paragraph (3) below shall select measures from Part II of this Schedule;

    (b)   an employer who is engaged in the activity specified in sub-paragraph (c) of paragraph (3) below shall select measures from Part III of this Schedule and, subject to paragraph (4) below, when making that selection he may combine measures from different categories of containment on the basis of a risk assessment related to any particular process or part of a process.

(3) The activities referred to in sub-paragraph (1) above are—

    (a)   research, development, teaching or diagnostic work in laboratories which involves the handling of a Group 2, Group 3 or Group 4 biological agent or material containing such an agent;

    (b)   keeping or handling of laboratory animals which have been deliberately infected with a Group 2, Group 3 or Group 4 biological agent or which are, or are suspected of being, naturally infected with such an agent; and

    (c)   industrial processes which involve the use of a Group 2, Group 3 or Group 4 biological agent.

(4) The minimum containment level referred to in sub-paragraph (1) above shall be—

    (a)   level 2 for activities involving the handling of a Group 2 biological agent;

    (b)   level 3 for activities involving the handling of a Group 3 biological agent;

    (c)   level 4 for activities involving the handling of a Group 4 biological agent;

    (d)   level 2 for laboratories which do not intentionally work with biological agents but handle materials in respect of which there exist uncertainties about the presence of a Group 2, Group 3 or Group 4 biological agent;

    (e)   level 3 or 4, where appropriate, for laboratories which do not intentionally work with biological agents but where the employer knows or suspects that such a containment level is necessary; except where guidelines approved by the Health and Safety Commission indicate that, in the particular case, a lower containment level is appropriate; and

(f)   level 3 for activities where it has not been possible to carry out a conclusive assessment but concerning which it appears that the activity might involve a serious health risk for employees.

Examination and maintenance of personal protective equipment

9.—(1) Every employer who provides personal protective equipment, including protective clothing, to meet the requirements of these Regulations as they apply to biological agents shall ensure that it is—
(a)   properly stored in a well-defined place;
(b)   checked and cleaned at suitable intervals; and
(c)   when discovered to be defective, repaired or replaced before further use.
(2)   Personal protective equipment which may be contaminated by biological agents shall be—
(a)   removed on leaving the working area; and
(b)   kept apart from uncontaminated clothing and equipment.
(3)   The employer shall ensure that the equipment referred to in sub-paragraph (2) above is subsequently decontaminated and cleaned or, if necessary, destroyed.

Information for employees

10.—(1) Every employer shall provide written instructions at the workplace and, if appropriate, display notices which shall include the procedure to be followed in the case of—
(a)   an accident or incident which has or may have resulted in the release of a biological agent which could cause severe human disease;
(b)   the handling of a Group 4 biological agent or material that may contain such an agent.
(2)   Every employee shall report forthwith, to his employer or to any other employee of that employer with specific responsibility for the health and safety of his fellow employees, any accident or incident which has or may have resulted in the release of a biological agent which could cause severe human disease.
(3)   Every employer shall inform his employees or their representatives—
(a)   forthwith, of any accident or incident which has or may have resulted in the release of a biological agent which could cause severe human disease; and
(b)   as soon as practicable thereafter, of
(i)   the causes of such an accident or incident; and
(ii)   the measures taken or to be taken to rectify the situation.

List of employees exposed to certain biological agents

11.—(1) Subject to paragraph 2(1), every employer shall keep a list of employees exposed to a Group 3 or Group 4 biological agent, indicating the type of work done and, where known, the biological agent to which they have been exposed, and records of exposures, accidents and incidents, as appropriate.
(2)   Subject to sub-paragraph (3) below, the list shall be kept for at least 10 years following the last known exposure of the employee concerned.
(3)   In the case of those exposures which may result in infections—
(a)   with biological agents known to be capable of establishing persistent or latent infections;
(b)   that, in the light of present knowledge, are undiagnosable until illness develops many years later;
(c)   that have particularly long incubation periods before illness develops;
(d)   that result in illnesses which recrudesce at times over a long period despite treatment; or
(e)   that may have serious long-term sequelae,
the list shall be kept for 40 years following the last known exposure.
(4)   The employment medical adviser or appointed doctor referred to in regulation 11, and any employee of that employer with specific responsibility for the health and safety of his fellow employees, shall have access to the list.
(5)   Each employee shall have access to the information on the list which relates to him personally.

Notification of the use of biological agents

12.—(1) Subject to sub-paragraphs (5) and (6) below, an employer shall not store or use for the first time one or more biological agents in Group 2, 3 or 4 at particular premises unless he has notified the Executive in writing of his intention to do so at least 30 days in advance or before such shorter time as the Executive may approve and with that notification has furnished the particulars specified in sub-paragraph (3) below.

(2) Subject to sub-paragraphs (5) and (7) below, notification in accordance with sub-paragraph (1) above shall also be made of the storage or use for the first time of—

(a) each subsequent biological agent where that agent is specified in Part V of this Schedule;

(b) each subsequent Group 3 biological agent where that agent does not have an approved classification.

(3) The particulars to be included in the notification referred to in sub-paragraphs (1) and (2) above shall be—

(a) the name and address of the employer and the address of the premises where the biological agent will be stored or used;

(b) the name, qualifications and relevant experience of any employee of that employer with specific responsibility for the health and safety of his fellow employees;

(c) the results of the assessment made under regulation 6;

(d) the Group to which the biological agent has been assigned and, if the agent is specified in Part V of this Schedule or is a Group 3 agent which does not have an approved classification, the identity of the agent; and

(e) the preventive and protective measures that are to be taken.

(4) Where there are substantial changes to processes or procedures of importance to health or safety at work which render the original notification invalid the employer shall notify the Executive forthwith in writing of those changes.

(5) Sub-paragraphs (1) and (2) above shall not apply in relation to a particular biological agent where an intention to store or use that biological agent has been previously notified to the Executive in accordance with the Genetically Modified Organisms (Contained Use) Regulations 1992.

(6) Sub-paragraph (1) above shall not apply to an employer who intends to provide a diagnostic service in relation to Group 2 or Group 3 biological agents, other than those Group 3 agents specified in Part V of this Schedule, unless it will involve a process likely to propagate or concentrate that agent.

(7) Sub-paragraph (2) above shall not apply to an employer who intends to provide a diagnostic service unless it will involve a process likely to propagate or concentrate a biological agent which does not have an approved classification.

Notification of the consignment of biological agents

13.—(1) An employer shall not consign any of the biological agents specified in Part V of this Schedule or anything containing, or suspected of containing, such an agent to any other premises, whether or not those premises are under his ownership or control, unless he has notified the Executive in writing of his intention to do so at least 30 days in advance or before such shorter time as the Executive may approve and with that notification has furnished the particulars specified in sub-paragraph (4) below.

(2) Sub-paragraph (1) above shall not apply where—

(a) the biological agent or material containing or suspected of containing such an agent is being consigned solely for the purpose of diagnosis;

(b) material containing or suspected of containing the biological agent is being consigned solely for the purpose of disposal; or

(c) the biological agent is or is suspected of being present in a human patient or animal which is being transported for the purpose of medical treatment.

(3) Where a biological agent specified in Part V of this Schedule is imported into Great Britain, the consignee shall give the notice required by sub-paragraph (1) above.

(4) The particulars to be included in the notification referred to in sub-paragraph (1) above shall be—

(a)   the identity of the biological agent and the volume of the consignment;
(b)   the name of the consignor;
(c)   the address of the premises from which it will be transported;
(d)   the name of the consignee;
(e)   the address of the premises to which it shall be transported;
(f)   the name of the transport operator responsible for the transportation;
(g)   the name of any individual who will accompany the consignment;
(h)   the method of transportation;
(i)   the packaging and any containment precautions which will be taken;
(j)   the route which will be taken; and
(k)   the proposed date of transportation.

Notification to the Health Ministers

14.—(1) Upon receipt of any notification submitted in accordance with paragraphs 12 or 13 concerning a biological agent specified in Part V of this Schedule, the Executive shall notify the appropriate Health Minister forthwith in writing that that agent is to be or is no longer to be stored, used or consigned.

(2)   In sub-paragraph (1) above "Health Minister" means, in respect of England, Scotland or Wales, the Secretary of State concerned with health in that country.

PART II

CONTAINMENT MEASURES FOR HEALTH AND VETERINARY CARE FACILITIES,
LABORATORIES AND ANIMAL ROOMS

	Containment measures		*Containment levels*	
		2	3	4
1.	The workplace is to be separated from any other activities in the same building.	No	Yes	Yes
2.	Input air and extract air to the workplace are to be filtered using HEPA or equivalent.	No	Yes, on extract air	Yes, on input and double on extract air
3.	Access is to be restricted to authorised persons only.	Yes	Yes	Yes, via air-lock key procedure
4.	The workplace is to be sealable to permit disinfection.	No	Yes	Yes
5.	Specified disinfection procedures.	Yes	Yes	Yes
6.	The workplace is to be maintained at an air pressure negative to atmosphere.	No, unless mechanically ventilated	Yes	Yes
7.	Efficient vector control eg rodents and insects.	Yes, for animal containment	Yes, for animal containment	Yes
8.	Surfaces impervious to water and easy to clean.	Yes, for bench	Yes, for bench and floor (and walls for animal containment)	Yes, for bench, floor, walls and ceiling
9.	Surfaces resistant to acids, alkalis, solvents, disinfectants.	Yes, for bench	Yes, for bench and floor (and walls for animal containment)	Yes, for bench, floor, walls and ceiling

Containment measures	Containment levels		
	2	3	4
10. Safe storage of biological agents.	Yes	Yes	Yes, secure storage
11. An observation window, or alternative, is to be present, so that occupants can be seen.	No	Yes	Yes
12. A laboratory is to contain its own equipment.	No	Yes, so far as is reasonably practicable	Yes
13. Infected material, including any animal, is to be handled in a safety cabinet or isolator or other suitable containment.	Yes, where aerosol produced	Yes, where aerosol produced	yes (Class III cabinet)
14. Incinerator for disposal of animal carcases.	Accessible	Accessible	Yes, on site

Note:

"Class III cabinet" means a safety cabinet defined as such in British Standard 5726: Part I: 1992, or unit offering an equivalent level of operator protection as defined in British Standard 5726: Part I: 1992.

Part III
Containment Measures for Industrial Processes

Containment measures	Containment levels		
	2	3	4
1 Viable micro-organisms should be contained in a system which physically separates the process from the environment (closed system).	Yes	Yes	Yes
2 Exhaust gases from the closed system should be treated so as to—	Minimise release	Prevent release	Prevent release
3 Sample collection, addition of materials to a closed system and transfer of viable microorganisms to another closed system, should be performed so as to—	Minimise release	Prevent release	Prevent release
4 Bulk culture fluids should not be removed from the closed system unless the viable microorganisms have been—	Inactivated by validated means	Inactivated by validated chemical or physical means	Inactivated by validated chemical or physical means
5 Seals should be designed so as to—	Minimise release	Prevent release	Prevent release

	Containment measures	*Containment levels*		
		2	3	4
6	Closed systems should be located within a controlled area—	Optional	Optional	Yes, and purpose-built
	(a) biohazard signs should be posted;	Optional	Yes	Yes
	(b) access should be restricted to nominated personnel only;	Optional	Yes	Yes, via air-lock
	(c) personnel should wear protective clothing;	Yes, work clothing	Yes	Yes, a complete change
	(d) decontamination and washing facilities should be provided for personnel;	Yes	Yes	Yes
	(e) personnel should shower before leaving the controlled area;	No	Optional	Yes
	(f) effluent from sinks and showers should be collected and inactivated before release;	No	Optional	Yes
	(g) the controlled area should be adequately ventilated to minimise air contamination;	Optional	Optional	Yes
	(h) the controlled area should be maintained at an air pressure negative to atmosphere;	No	Optional	Yes
	(i) input and extract air to the controlled area should be HEPA filtered;	No	Optional	Yes
	(j) the controlled area should be designed to contain spillage of the entire contents of closed system;	Optional	Yes	Yes
	(k) the controlled area should be sealable to permit fumigation.	No	Optional	Yes
7.	Effluent treatment before final discharge.	Inactivated by validated means	Inactivated by validated chemical or physical means	Inactivated by validated physical means

PART IV
BIOHAZARD SIGN

The biohazard sign required by paragraph 6 of Part I of this Schedule shall be in the form shown below—

PART V
LIST OF BIOLOGICAL AGENTS REFERRED TO IN PARAGRAPHS 12(2)(A), 13(1) AND (3) AND 14(1) OF PART I OF THIS SCHEDULE

(1)   All Group 4 biological agents.
(2)   Rabies virus.
(3)   Simian herpes B virus.
(4)   Venezuelan equine encephalitis virus.
(5)   Tick-borne encephalitis group viruses in Group 3.
(6)   Monkeypox virus.
(7)   Mopeia virus.

THE CHEMICALS (HAZARD INFORMATION AND PACKAGING FOR SUPPLY) REGULATIONS 1994

(S.I. 1994 No 3247)

General note. These Regulations, which came into force on 31 January 1995, revoke and replace with amendments the Chemicals (Hazard Information and Packaging) Regulations 1993 (S.I. 1993 No. 1743). Like the 1993 Regulations, these Regulations, as respects Great Britain, implement Council Directive 92/32/EEC (amending for the 7th time Council Directive 67/548/EEC), in so far as its provisions relate to the classification, packaging and labelling of dangerous substances ("the substances Directive"); and Council Directive 88/379/EEC on the classification, packaging and labelling of dangerous preparations ("the preparations Directive"). These Regulations also implement certain Directives which adapt to technical progress and modify the substances Directive and the preparations Directive. As to breach of a duty imposed by these Regulations giving rise to civil liability, see reg.16.

ARRANGEMENT OF REGULATIONS

Schedule 6.   Particulars to be shown on labels for substances and preparations dangerous for supply and certain other preparations.

Schedule 7.   British and International Standards relating to child resistant fastenings and tactile warning devices.

Schedule 8.   Modifications to certain enactments relating to the flash point of flammable liquids.

The Secretary of State, being the designated Minister for the purpose of section 2(2) of the European Communities Act 1972 in relation to the regulation and control of classification, packaging and labelling of dangerous substances and preparations, and for measures relating to consumer protection, in the exercise of the powers conferred on him by the said section 2(2) and sections 15(1), (2), (3), (4)(a), (5)(b), (6)(b) and (9), 80(1) and (4) and 82(3)(a) of, and paragraphs 1(1)(b) and (c), (4) and (5), 15 and 16 of Schedule 3 to, the Health and Safety at Work etc Act 1974 ("the 1974 Act") and of all other powers enabling him in that behalf—

(a)   for the purpose of giving effect without modifications to proposals submitted to him by the Health and Safety Commission under section 11(2)(d) of the 1974 Act after the carrying out by the said Commission of consultations in accordance with section 50(3) of that Act; and

(b)   it appearing to him that the modifications to the enactments referred to in regulation 19(3) below are expedient in consequence of the Regulations referred to below after the carrying out by him of consultations in accordance with section 80(4) of the 1974 Act,

hereby makes the following Regulations:—

1.   Citation and commencement. These Regulations may be cited as the Chemicals (Hazard Information and Packaging for Supply) Regulations 1994 and shall come into force on 31st January 1995.

2.   Interpretation.—(1) In these Regulations, unless the context otherwise requires—

"aerosol dispenser" means an article which consists of a non-reusable receptacle containing a gas compressed, liquefied or dissolved under pressure, with or without liquid, paste or powder and fitted with a release device allowing the contents to be ejected as solid or liquid particles in suspension in a gas, as a foam, paste or powder or in a liquid state;

"the Agreement" means the Agreement on the European Economic Area signed at Oporto on 2nd May 1992 as adjusted by the Protocol signed at Brussels on 17th March 1993 and adopted as respects the United Kingdom by the European Economic Area Act 1993;

"approved classification and labelling guide" means the guide entitled "Approved Guide to the Classification and Labelling of Substances and Preparations Dangerous for Supply (2nd Edition)" approved by the Health and Safety Commission on 18th October 1994 for the purposes of these Regulations;

"approved supply list" means the list described in regulation 4;

"category of danger" means, in relation to a substance or preparation dangerous for supply, one of the categories of danger specified in column 1 of Part I of Schedule 1;

"classification" means, in relation to a substance or preparation dangerous for supply, classification in accordance with regulation 5;

"commercial sample" means, in relation to a substance or preparation dangerous for supply, a sample of that substance or preparation provided to the recipient with a view to subsequent purchase;

"the Community" means the European Economic Community and other States in the European Economic Area;

"concentration limits" means, in relation to a substance dangerous for supply, the concentration limits for the substance (if any) specified in column 4 of Part V of the approved supply list or, where that substance is not listed in the approved supply list or appears in it without specified concentration limits, it means the concentration limits for that substance ascertained from Part II of Schedule 3;

"EEC number" means, in relation to a substance dangerous for supply—

(a) in the case of a substance that is included in the approved supply list, the number (if any) specified in column 3 of Part V of that list;

(b) in the case of a substance that is not included in the approved supply list or for which an EEC number is not given in Part V of that list, the number for that substance (if any) specified in the European Inventory of Existing Commercial Chemical Substances (EINECS); or

(c) in the case of a substance that is a new substance within the meaning of regulation 2(1) of the Notification of New Substances Regulations 1993, the number for that substance (if any) listed in the European List of Notified Chemical Substances (ELINCS);

"the European Economic Area" means the Area referred to in the Agreement;

"the Executive" means the Health and Safety Executive;

"flash point" means the flash point determined in accordance with Part III of Schedule 1;

"freight container" means a container as defined in regulation 2(1) of the Freight Containers (Safety Convention) Regulations 1984;

"index number" means, in relation to a substance dangerous for supply which appears in Part I of the approved supply list, the number for that substance specified in column 2 of that Part;

"indication of danger" means, in relation to a substance or preparation dangerous for supply, one or more of the indications of danger referred to in column 1 of Schedule 2 and—

(a) in the case of a substance dangerous for supply listed in Part I of the approved supply list, it is one or more indications of danger for that substance specified by a symbol-letter in column 3 of Part V of that list; or

(b) in the case of a substance dangerous for supply not so listed or a preparation dangerous for supply, it is one or more indications of danger determined in accordance with the classification of that substance or preparation under regulation 5 and the approved classification and labelling guide;

"member State" means a State which is a Contracting Party to the Agreement, but until the Agreement comes into force in relation to Liechtenstein does not include the State of Liechtenstein;

"package" means, in relation to a substance or preparation dangerous for supply, the package in which the substance or preparation is supplied and which is liable to be individually handled during the course of the supply and includes the receptacle containing the substance or preparation and any other packaging associated with it and any pallet or other device which enables more than one receptacle containing a substance or preparation dangerous for supply to be handled as a unit, but does not include—

(a) a freight container (other than a tank container), a skip, a vehicle or other article of transport equipment; or

(b) in the case of supply by way of retail sale, any wrapping such as a paper or plastic bag into which the package is placed when it is presented to the purchaser;

"packaging" means, in relation to a substance or preparation dangerous for supply, as the context may require, the receptacle, or any components, materials or wrappings associated with the receptacle for the purpose of enabling it to perform its containment function or both;

"pesticide" shall be construed in accordance with paragraph 1 of Schedule 4;

"poisons advisory centre" means a body approved for the time being for the purposes of regulation 14 by the Secretary of State for Health in consultation with the Secretaries of State for Scotland and Wales, the Health and Safety Commission and such other persons or bodies as appear to her to be appropriate;

"preparations" means mixtures or solutions of two or more substances;

"preparation dangerous for supply" means a preparation which is in one or more of the categories of danger specified in column 1 of Schedule 1;

"property" means, in relation to a substance or preparation dangerous for supply, a property described in column 2 of Part I of Schedule 1 and further described in the approved classification and labelling guide;

"receptacle" means, in relation to a substance or preparation dangerous for supply, a vessel, or the innermost layer of packaging, which is in contact with the substance and which is liable to be individually handled when the substance is used and includes any closure or fastener;

"risk phrase" means, in relation to a substance or preparation dangerous for supply, a phrase listed in Part III of the approved supply list and in these Regulations specific risk phrases may be designated by the letter "R" followed by a distinguishing number or combination of numbers but the risk phrase shall be quoted in full on any label or safety data sheet on which the risk phrase is required to be shown;

"safety phrase" means, in relation to a substance or preparation dangerous for supply, a phrase listed in Part IV of the approved supply list and in these Regulations specific safety phrases may be designated by the letter "S" followed by a distinguishing number or combination of numbers, but the safety phrase shall be quoted in full on any label or safety data sheet in which the safety phrase is required to be shown;

"substances" means chemical elements and their compounds in the natural state or obtained by any production process, including any additive necessary to preserve the stability of the product and any impurity deriving from the process used, but excluding any solvent which may be separated without affecting the stability of the substance or changing its composition;

"substance dangerous for supply" means—

(a) a substance listed in Part I of the approved supply list; or

(b) any other substance which is in one or more of the categories of danger specified in column 1 of Schedule 1;

"supplier" means a person who supplies a substance or preparation dangerous for supply, and in the case of a substance which is imported (whether or not from a member State) includes the importer established in Great Britain of that substance or preparation;

"supply" in relation to a substance or preparation—

(a) means, subject to sub-paragraph (b) and (c) below, supply of that substance or preparation, whether as principal or agent for another, in the course of or for use at work, by way of—

    (i)   sale or offer for sale,

    (ii) commercial sample, or

    (iii) transfer from a factory, warehouse or. other place of work and its curtilage to another place of work, whether or not in the same ownership;

(b) for the purposes of sub-paragraphs (a) and (b) of regulation 16(2), except in relation to regulations 7 and 12, in any case for which by virtue of those sub-paragraphs the enforcing authority for these Regulations is the Royal Pharmaceutical Society or the local weights and measures authority, has the meaning assigned to it by section 46 of the Consumer Protection Act 1987 and also includes offer to supply and expose for supply; or

(c) in relation to regulations 7 and 12 shall have the meaning assigned to it by regulations 7(2) and 12(12) respectively;

"symbol" means the symbol shown in column 3 of Schedule 2 for the indication of danger shown in column 1 of that Schedule, and "symbol-letter" means the letter shown in the corresponding entry in column 2 of that Schedule.

(2) Unless the context otherwise requires, where in these Regulations reference is made to a quantity of a substance or preparation dangerous for supply expressed in litres, that reference shall mean—

(a) in the case of a liquid, the volume in litres of that liquid;

(b) in the case of a gas, the volume in litres of the receptacle containing that gas; and

(c) in the case of a solid, the same number of kilograms of that solid,

and for the purposes of aggregation, one kilogram of a solid shall be deemed to be equivalent to one litre of a liquid or gas.

(3) Subject to regulation 19, nothing in these Regulations shall prejudice any other requirement imposed by or under any enactment which relates to a substance or preparation dangerous for supply.

(4) Unless the context otherwise requires, any reference in these Regulations to—

(a) a numbered regulation or Schedule is a reference to the regulation or Schedule in these Regulations so numbered; and

(b) a numbered paragraph is a reference to the paragraph so numbered in the regulation or Schedule in which the reference appears.

3. Application of these Regulations.—(1) These Regulations shall apply to any substance or preparation which is dangerous for supply except—

(a) a substance or preparation which is dangerous by reason that it is a radioactive substance within the meaning of the Ionising Radiations Regulations 1985 but is not otherwise dangerous for supply;

(b) a substance or preparation which is—

    (i)   intended for use as an animal feeding stuff within the meaning of section 66(1) of the Agriculture Act 1970, and

    (ii) in a finished state intended for the final user;

(c) a cosmetic product within the meaning of regulation 2(1) of the Cosmetic Products (Safety) Regulations 1989 (including any aerosol dispenser containing a cosmetic product);

    (d) a substance or preparation which is—
        (i) intended for use as a medicinal product within the meaning of section 130 of the Medicines Act 1968, or
       (ii) a substance or preparation specified in an order made under section 104 or 105 of the Medicines Act 1968 which is for the time being in force and which directs that specified provisions of that Act shall have effect in relation to that substance or preparation as such provisions have effect in relation to medicinal products within the meaning of that Act;
    (e) a substance or preparation which is a controlled drug within the meaning of the Misuse of Drugs Act 1971 except that these Regulations shall apply to drugs which are excepted from section 4(1)(b) of that Act (which makes it unlawful to supply a controlled drug) by regulations made under section 7(1)(a) of that Act;
    (f) a substance or preparation which is dangerous by reason that it contains disease producing micro-organisms but is not otherwise dangerous for supply;
    (g) a substance or preparation which is a sample taken by an authority responsible for the enforcement of any requirement imposed by or under any enactment;
    (h) munitions, and preparations which are supplied with a view to producing a practical effect by explosion or a pyrotechnic effect;
    (i) a substance or preparation which is—
        (i) intended for use as food within the meaning of section 1 of the Food Safety Act 1990, and
       (ii) in a finished state intended for the final user;
    (j) a substance or preparation which is under customs control;
    (k) subject to Council Regulation EC 2455/92 on the export notification and information exchange of dangerous substances, a substance or preparation which is intended for export to a country which is not a member State;
    (l) a pesticide which has been approved under the Food and Environment Protection Act 1985;
    (m) a substance or preparation which is transferred from a factory, warehouse or other place of work and its curtilage to another place of work in the same ownership and in the immediate vicinity;
    (n) a substance to which paragraph (7) of regulation 6 of the Notification of New Substances Regulations 1993 applies (including new substances not yet fully tested) which is labelled in accordance with the provisions of that paragraph; or
    (o) substances, preparations and mixtures thereof in the form of wastes which are covered by Council Directives 91/156/EEC and 91/689/EEC.

(2) Regulations 8 to 12 shall only apply to substances or preparations dangerous for supply which are supplied in packages.

(3) Regulations 8 to 12 shall not apply to—
    (a) substances which are supplied with a view to producing a practical effect by explosion or a pyrotechnic effect; or
    (b) propane, butane or liquefied petroleum gas.

(4) Paragraph (3) of regulation 9, paragraph (1) of regulation 10 and paragraph (3) of regulation 12 shall notwithstanding paragraph (1) apply to the preparations referred to in those paragraphs (unless expressly otherwise provided for) whether or not those preparations would otherwise be dangerous for supply within the meaning of regulation 2(1).

(5)   Where a substance or preparation dangerous for supply has been imported for delivery to its importer at his place of work, the provisions of these Regulations which relate to the labelling of that substance or preparation shall not apply until ten days after it has been delivered to the importer, if during that period it is not—

(a)   supplied to any other person; or

(b)   subjected to any form of manipulation, treatment or processing which results in the substance or preparation being exposed, or for any purpose (other than labelling in accordance with these Regulations) which results in any receptacle containing the substance or preparation being removed from its outer packaging.

(6)   These Regulations shall not extend to Northern Ireland.

4.   Meaning of the approved supply list. The "approved supply list" means the list entitled "Information Approved for the Classification and Labelling of Substances and Preparations Dangerous for Supply (2nd Edition)" approved by the Health and Safety Commission on 18 October 1994 for the purposes of these Regulations and comprises—

(a)   in Part I—

(i)   in column 1, a list of the names of the substances for which the Commission has approved information, and

(ii)   in the corresponding entries in columns 2 and 3 respectively the index number and (if any) the CAS Number (for reference only) for the substance;

(b)   in Part II—

(i)   in column 1, a list of the index numbers of the substances for which the Commission has approved information, and

(ii)   in the corresponding entries in column 2 the names of those substances;

(c)   in Part III, a numbered list of the risk phrases and combinations of risk phrases which the Commission has approved;

(d)   in Part IV, a numbered list of the safety phrases and combinations of safety phrases which the Commission has approved;

(e)   in Part V, the information which the Commission has approved for each substance referred to in Part I, namely—

(i)   in column 1, the index number and abbreviated name (for reference only), and

(ii)   in the corresponding entries in columns 2 to 4, respectively the classification, the labelling data (including the EEC Number) and any concentration limits which the Commission has approved for the substance for the classification of preparations containing that substance;

(f)   in Part VI, a list of the conventional oral toxicity (LD_{50}) values which the Commission has approved in relation to pesticides for the purpose of classifying those pesticides in accordance with Schedule 4,

together with such notes and explanatory material as are requisite for the use of the list.

5.   Classification of substances and preparations dangerous for supply.—(1) A supplier shall not supply a substance or preparation dangerous for supply, unless it has been classified in accordance with the following paragraphs of this regulation.

(2) In the case of a substance which is listed in the approved supply list, the classification shall be that specified in the entry for that substance in column 2 of Part V of that list.

(3) In the case of a substance which is a new substance within the meaning of regulation 2(1) of the Notification of New Substances Regulations 1993 and which has been notified in accordance with regulation 4 or 6(1) or (2) of those Regulations, the substance shall be classified in conformity with that notification.

(4) In the case of any other substance dangerous for supply, after an investigation to become aware of relevant and accessible data which may exist, the substance shall be classified by placing it into one or more of the categories of danger specified in column 1 of Part I of Schedule 1 corresponding to the properties of the substance specified in the entry opposite thereto in column 2 and by assigning appropriate risk phrases by the use of the criteria set out in the approved classification and labelling guide.

(5) Subject to paragraph (6), a preparation to which these Regulations apply shall be classified as dangerous for supply in accordance with Schedule 3 by the use of the criteria set out in the approved classification and labelling guide.

(6) A preparation which is intended for use as a pesticide (other than a pesticide which has been approved under the Food and Environment Protection Act 1985) shall be classified as dangerous for supply in accordance with Schedule 4.

6. Safety data sheets for substances and preparations dangerous for supply.—(1) Subject to paragraphs (2) and (5), the supplier of a substance or preparation dangerous for supply shall provide the recipient of that substance or preparation with a safety data sheet containing information under the headings specified in Schedule 5 to enable the recipient of that substance or preparation to take the necessary measures relating to the protection of health and safety at work and relating to the protection of the environment and the safety data sheet shall clearly show its date of first publication or latest revision, as the case may be.

(2) In this regulation "supply" shall not include supply by way of—
   (a) offer for sale;
   (b) transfer from a factory, warehouse or another place of work and its curtilage to another place of work in the same ownership; or
   (c) returning substances or preparations to the person who supplied them, providing that the properties of that substance or preparation remain unchanged.

(3) The supplier shall keep the safety data sheet up to date and revise it forthwith if any significant new information becomes available regarding safety or risks to human health or the protection of the environment in relation to the substance or preparation concerned and the revised safety data sheet shall be clearly marked with the word "revision".

(4) Except in circumstances to which paragraph (5) relates, the safety data sheet shall be provided free of charge no later than the date on which the substance or preparation is first supplied to the recipient and where the safety data sheet has been revised in accordance with paragraph (3), a copy of the revised safety data sheet shall be provided free of charge to all recipients who have received the substance or preparation in the last 12 months and the changes in it shall be brought to their notice.

(5) Safety data sheets need not be provided with substances or preparations dangerous for supply sold to the general public in circumstances to which

regulation 16(2)(a) or (b) applies (relating to supply from a shop etc) if sufficient information is furnished to enable users to take the necessary measures as regards the protection of health and safety, except that safety data sheets shall be provided free of charge at the request of persons who intend the substance or preparation to be used at work, but in those circumstances paragraph (4) (in so far as it relates to the subsequent provision of revised data sheets) shall not apply to such requests.

(6)   The particulars required to be given in the safety data sheets shall be in English, except that where a substance or preparation is intended to be supplied to a recipient in another member State, the safety data sheet may be in an official language of that State.

7.   Advertisements for substances dangerous for supply.—(1) A person who supplies or offers to supply a substance dangerous for supply shall ensure that the substance is not advertised unless mention is made in the advertisement of the hazard or hazards presented by the substance.

(2)   In this regulation the word "supply" has the same meaning as in section 46 of the Consumer Protection Act 1987.

8.   Packaging of substances and preparations dangerous for supply. The supplier of a substance or preparation which is dangerous for supply shall not supply any such substance or preparation unless it is in a package which is suitable for that purpose, and in particular, unless—

    (a)   the receptacle containing the substance or preparation and any associated packaging are designed, constructed, maintained and closed so as to prevent any of the contents of the receptacle from escaping when subjected to the stresses and strains of normal handling, except that this sub-paragraph shall not prevent the fitting of a suitable safety device;

    (b)   the receptacle and any associated packaging, in so far as they are likely to come into contact with the substance or preparation, are made of materials which are neither liable to be adversely affected by that substance nor liable in conjunction with that substance to form any other substance which is itself a risk to the health or safety of any person; and

    (c)   where the receptacle is fitted with a replaceable closure, that closure is designed so that the receptacle can be repeatedly re-closed without its contents escaping.

9.   Labelling of substances and preparations dangerous for supply.—
(1) Subject to regulations 9 and 10 of the Carriage of Dangerous Goods by Road and Rail (Classification, Packaging and Labelling) Regulations 1994 (which allow combined carriage and supply labelling in certain circumstances) and paragraphs (5) to (9), a supplier shall not supply a substance or preparation which is dangerous for supply unless the particulars specified in paragraph (2) relating to a substance or in paragraph (3) relating to a preparation, as the case may be, are clearly shown in accordance with the requirements of regulation 11—

    (a)   on the receptacle containing the substance or preparation; and

    (b)   if that receptacle is inside one or more layers of packaging, on any such layer which is likely to be the outermost layer of packaging during the supply or the use of the substance or preparation, unless such packaging permits the particulars shown on the receptacle or other packaging to be clearly seen.

(2)   The particulars required under paragraph (1) in relation to a substance dangerous for supply shall be—
  (a)   the name and full address and telephone number of a person in a member State who is responsible for supplying the substance, whether he be its manufacturer, importer or distributor;
  (b)   the name of the substance, being the name or one of the names for the substance listed in Part I of the approved supply list, or if it is not so listed an internationally recognised name; and
  (c)   the following particulars ascertained in accordance with Part I of Schedule 6, namely—
      (i)   the indication or indications of danger and the corresponding symbol or symbols (if any),
      (ii)   the risk phrases (set out in full),
      (iii)   the safety phrases (set out in full), and
      (iv)   the EEC number (if any), and, in the case of a substance dangerous for supply which is listed in Part I of the approved supply list, the words "EEC label".

(3)   The particulars required under paragraph (1) in relation to a preparation which is, or (where sub-paragraph (d) below applies) may be, dangerous for supply shall be—
  (a)   the name and full address and telephone number of a person in a member State who is responsible for supplying the preparation, whether he be its manufacturer, importer or distributor;
  (b)   the trade name or other designation of the preparation;
  (c)   the following particulars ascertained in accordance with Part I of Schedule 6, namely—
      (i)   identification of the constituents of the preparation which result in the preparation being classified as dangerous for supply,
      (ii)   the indication or indications of danger and the corresponding symbol or symbols (if any),
      (iii)   the risk phrases (set out in full),
      (iv)   the safety phrases (set out in full),
      (v)   in the case of a pesticide, the modified information specified in paragraph 5 of Part I of Schedule 6, and
      (vi)   in the case of a preparation intended for sale to the general public, the nominal quantity (nominal mass or nominal volume); and
  (d)   where required by paragraph 5(5), of Part I of Schedule 3, the words specified in that paragraph.

(4)   Where the Executive receives a notification of a derogation provided for by paragraph 3(1) of Part I of Schedule 6, it shall forthwith inform the European Commission thereof.

(5)   Indications such as "non-toxic" or "non-harmful" or any other statement indicating that the substance or preparation is not dangerous for supply shall not appear on the package.

(6)   Except for the outermost packaging of a package in which a substance or preparation is transferred, labelling in accordance with this regulation shall not be required where a substance or preparation dangerous for supply is supplied by way of transfer from a factory, warehouse or other place of work and its curtilage to another place of work, if, at that other place of work it is not subject to any form of manipulation, treatment or processing which results in the substance or preparation

dangerous for supply being exposed or, for any purpose other than labelling in accordance with these Regulations, results in any receptacle containing the substance or preparation being removed from its outer packaging.

(7) Except in the case of a substance or preparation dangerous for supply for which the indication of danger is required to be explosive, very toxic or toxic or which is classified as sensitizing, labelling under this regulation shall not be required for such small quantities of that substance or preparation that there is no reason to fear danger to persons handling that substance or preparation or to other persons.

(8) Where, in the case of a substance or preparation dangerous for supply, other than a pesticide, the package in which the substance or preparation is supplied does not contain more than 125 millilitres of the substance or preparation, the risk phrases required by paragraph (2)(c)(ii) or (3)(c)(iii), and the safety phrases required by paragraph (2)(c)(iii) or (3)(c)(iv), as the case may be, need not be shown if the substance or preparation is classified only in one or more of the categories of danger, highly flammable, flammable, oxidising or irritant or in the case of substances not intended to be supplied to the public, harmful.

(9) Where, because of the size of the label, it is not reasonably practicable to provide the safety phrases required under paragraph (2)(c)(iii) or (3)(c)(iv), as the case may be, on the label, that information may be given on a separate label or on a sheet accompanying the package.

10. Particular labelling requirements for certain preparations.—(1) In the case of preparations to which Part II of Schedule 6 applies the appropriate provisions of that Part of the Schedule shall have effect to regulate the labelling of such preparations even if the preparations referred to in Part IIB of that Schedule would not otherwise be dangerous for supply.

(2) In the case of preparations packaged in aerosol dispensers, the flammability criteria set out in Part II of Schedule 1 shall have effect for the classification and labelling of those preparations for supply in place of the categories of danger "extremely flammable", "highly flammable" or "flammable" set out in Part I of that Schedule, and where a dispenser contains a substance so classified, that dispenser shall be labelled in accordance with the provisions of paragraph 2 of the said Part II.

11. Methods of marking or labelling packages.—(1) Any package which is required to be labelled in accordance with regulations 9 and 10 may carry the particulars required to be on the label clearly and indelibly marked on a part of that package reserved for that purpose and, unless the context otherwise requires, any reference in these Regulations to a label includes a reference to that part of the package so reserved.

(2) Subject to paragraph (7), any label required to be carried on a package shall be securely fixed to the package with its entire surface in contact with it and the label shall be clearly and indelibly printed.

(3) The colour and nature of the marking shall be such that the symbol (if any) and wording stand out from the background so as to be readily noticeable and the wording shall be of such size and spacing as to be easily read.

(4) The package shall be so labelled that the particulars can be read horizontally when the package is set down normally.

(5) Subject to paragraph (7), the dimensions of the label required under regulation 9 shall be as follows—

Capacity of Package	Dimensions of label
(a) not exceeding 3 litres	if possible at least 52 x 74 millimetres
(b) exceeding 3 litres but not exceeding 50 litres	at least 74 x 105 millimetres
(c) exceeding 50 litres but not exceeding 500 litres	at least 105 x 148 millimetres
(d) exceeding 500 litres	at least 148 x 210 millimetres

(6) Any symbol required to be shown in accordance with regulation 9(2)(c)(i) or 9(3)(c)(ii) and specified in column 3 of Schedule 2 shall be printed in black on an orange-yellow background and its size (including the orange-yellow background) shall be at least equal to an area of one-tenth of that of a label which complies with paragraph (5) and shall not in any case be less than 100 square millimetres.

(7) If the package is an awkward shape or so small that it is unsuitable to attach a label complying with paragraphs (2) and (5), the label shall be attached in some other appropriate manner.

(8) The particulars required to be shown on the label shall be in English, except that where a substance or preparation is intended to be supplied to a recipient in another member State, the label may be in an official language of that State.

12. Child resistant fastenings and tactile warning devices.—(1) The British and International Standards referred to in this regulation are further described in Schedule 7.

(2) This regulation shall not apply in relation to a pesticide.

(3) Subject to paragraph (5), a person shall not supply a substance or preparation referred to in paragraph (4) in a receptacle of any size fitted with a replaceable closure unless the packaging complies with the requirements of BS EN 28317 or ISO 8317.

(4) Paragraph (3) shall apply to—
   (a) substances and preparations dangerous for supply which are required to be labelled with the indication of danger "very toxic", "toxic", or "corrosive";
   (b) preparations containing methanol in a concentration equal to or more than 3% by weight;
   (c) preparations containing dichloromethane in a concentration equal to or more than 1% by weight;
   (d) liquid preparations having a kinematic viscosity measured by rotative viscometry in accordance with BS 2782 method 730 B or ISO 3291 of less than $7 \times 10^{-6} m^2 s^{-1}$ at 40°C and containing aliphatic or aromatic hydrocarbons or both in a total concentration equal to or more than 10% by weight, except where such a preparation is supplied in an aerosol dispenser.

(5) Paragraph (3) shall not apply if the person supplying it can show that it is obvious that the packaging in which the substance or preparation is supplied is sufficiently safe for children because they cannot obtain access to the contents without the help of a tool.

(6) If the packaging in which the substance or preparation is supplied was approved on or before 31 May 1993 by the British Standards Institution as complying with the requirements of the British Standards Specification BS 6652: 1989 it shall be treated in all respects as complying with the requirements of BS EN 28317.

(7) A person shall not supply a preparation dangerous for supply if the packaging in which the preparation is supplied has—

    (a) a shape or designation or both likely to attract or arouse the active curiosity of children or to mislead consumers; or

    (b) a presentation or a designation or both used for human or animal foodstuffs, medicinal or cosmetic products.

(8) A person shall not supply a substance or preparation referred to in paragraph (9) in a receptacle of any size, unless the packaging carries a tactile warning of danger in accordance with BS 7280 or EN Standard 272.

(9) Paragraph (8) shall apply to substances and preparations dangerous for supply which are required to be labelled with the indication of danger "very toxic", "toxic", "corrosive", "harmful", "extremely flammable" or "highly flammable".

(10) A duly authorised officer of the enforcing authority, for the purpose of ascertaining whether there has been a contravention of paragraph (3) may require the person supplying a substance or preparation to which that paragraph applies to provide him with a certificate from a qualified test house stating that—

    (a) the closure is such that it is not necessary to test to BS EN 28317 or ISO 8317; or

    (b) the closure has been tested and found to conform to that standard.

(11) For the purpose of paragraph (10) a "qualified test house" means a laboratory that conforms to BS 7501 or EN 45 000.

(12) In this regulation, "supply" means offer for sale, sell or otherwise make available to the general public.

13. Retention of classification data for substances and preparations dangerous for supply. A person who classifies a substance in accordance with regulation 5(4) or a preparation dangerous for supply shall keep a record of the information used for the purposes of classifying it for at least 3 years after the date on which the substance or preparation was supplied by him for the last time and shall make the record or a copy of it available to the appropriate enforcing authority referred to in regulation 16(2) at its request.

14. Notification of the constituents of certain preparations dangerous for supply to the poisons advisory centre.—(1) This regulation shall apply to any preparation which is classified on the basis of one or more of its health effects referred to in column 1 of Schedule 1.

(2) Subject to regulation 17 (transitional provisions), the supplier of a preparation to which this regulation applies shall, if it was first supplied before these Regulations came into force (or, if it was first supplied after that date, before first supplying it), notify the poisons advisory centre of the information required to be in the safety data sheet prepared for the purposes of regulation 6 relating to the preparation.

(3) The supplier shall ensure that the information supplied to the poisons advisory centre in pursuance of paragraph (2) is kept up to date.

(4) The poisons advisory centre shall only disclose any information sent to it in pursuance of paragraph (2) or (3) on a request by, or by a person working under the direction of, a registered medical practitioner in connection with the medical treatment of a person who may have been affected by the preparation.

15. Exemption certificates.—(1) Subject to paragraph (2) and to any of the provisions imposed by the Community in respect of the free movement of dangerous substances and preparations, the Executive may by a certificate in writing exempt any person or class of persons, substance or preparation to which these Regulations apply, or class of such substances or preparations, from all or any of the requirements or prohibitions imposed by or under these Regulations and any such exemption may be granted subject to conditions and to a limit of time and may be revoked at any time by a certificate in writing.

(2) The Executive shall not grant any such exemption unless, having regard to the circumstances of the case, and in particular to—

(a) the conditions, if any, which it proposes to attach to the exemption; and

(b) any requirements imposed by or under any enactments which apply to the case,

it is satisfied that the health or safety of persons who are likely to be affected by the exemption will not be prejudiced in consequence of it.

16. Enforcement, civil liability and defence.—(1) Insofar as any provision of regulations 5 to 14 is made under section 2 of the European Communities Act 1972—

(a) subject to paragraph (2), the provisions of the Health and Safety at Work etc Act 1974 which relate to the approval of codes of practice and their use in criminal proceedings, to enforcement and to offences shall apply to that provision as if that provision had been made under section 15 of that Act; and

(b) a breach of a duty imposed by that provision shall confer a right of action in civil proceedings, insofar as that breach of duty causes damage.

(2) Notwithstanding regulation 3 of the Health and Safety (Enforcing Authority) Regulations 1989, the enforcing authority for these Regulations shall be the Executive, except that—

(a) where a substance or preparation dangerous for supply is supplied in or from premises which are registered under section 75 of the Medicines Act 1968, the enforcing authority shall be the Royal Pharmaceutical Society;

(b) where a substance or preparation dangerous for supply is supplied otherwise than as in sub-paragraph (a) above—

(i) in or from any shop, mobile vehicle, market stall or other retail outlet, or

(ii) otherwise to members of the public, including by way of free sample, prize or mail order,

the enforcing authority shall be the local weights and measures authority; and

(c) for regulations 7 and 12, the enforcing authority shall be the local weights and measures authority.

(3) In every case where by virtue of paragraph (2) these Regulations are enforced by the Royal Pharmaceutical Society or the local weights and measures authority, they shall be enforced as if they were safety regulations made under section 11 of the Consumer Protection Act 1987 and the provisions of section 12 of that Act shall apply to these Regulations as if they were safety regulations and as if the maximum period of imprisonment on summary conviction specified in subsection (5) thereof were 3 months instead of 6 months.

(4) In any proceedings for an offence under these Regulations, it shall be a defence for any person to prove that he took all reasonable precautions and exercised all due diligence to avoid the commission of that offence.

17.   Transitional provisions.—(1) Until 31st July 1995 it shall be a sufficient compliance with the requirements of these Regulations (except regulation 12(3)) if a substance or preparation is classified, packaged and labelled and a safety data sheet provided for it in accordance with the Chemicals (Hazard Information and Packaging) Regulations 1993 as in force immediately before these Regulations came into force.

(2)   Until 31st July 1995 it shall be a sufficient compliance with regulation 12(3) (relating to child resistant fastenings) if the packaging complies with the requirements of the Child Resistant Packaging (Safety) Regulations 1986 as in force immediately before these Regulations came into force.

(3)   Until 1st March 1995 in any case in which—
- (a)   the package or receptacle in which one or more substances or preparations dangerous for supply is supplied contains a total quantity of 25 litres or less;
- (b)   the substances or preparations were packaged and labelled before 1st September 1994 and were not removed from their package or receptacle since that date; and
- (c)   it was not reasonably practicable either—
  - (i)   to repackage and relabel the substances or preparations before they were supplied, or
  - (ii)   to supply them on a date earlier than the date on which they were in fact supplied,

it shall be a sufficient compliance with the requirements of these Regulations (not being the requirement to provide the safety data sheds described in regulation 6(1)) if the substances or preparations are classified, packaged and labelled in accordance with the Classification, Packaging and Labelling of Dangerous Substances Regulations 1984 as in force immediately before 1st September 1993 (on which date the Chemicals (Hazard Information and Packaging) Regulations 1993 came into force).

(4)   Regulation 14 (notification to the poisons advisory centre) shall not apply until the date on which the Secretary of State has approved the poisons advisory centre and it shall be a sufficient compliance with that regulation if the information required to be provided in relation to any preparation is received by the poisons advisory centre—
- (a)   in the case of a preparation which is required to have the indication of danger, very toxic, toxic or corrosive, before 6 months after that date;
- (b)   in the case of a preparation which is required to have the indication of danger, harmful or irritant, before 1 year after that date; or
- (c)   in either case, before such later date as the Executive may approve.

18.   Extension outside Great Britain. These Regulations shall apply to any activity outside Great Britain to which sections 1 to 59 and 80 to 82 of the Health and Safety at Work etc Act 1974 apply by virtue of the Health and Safety at Work etc Act 1974 (Application Outside Great Britain) Order 1989 as they apply to activities within Great Britain.

19.   Revocations and modifications.—(1) The following Regulations are revoked:—
- (a)   the Child Resistant Packaging (Safety) Regulations 1986;
- (b)   the Child Resistant Packaging (Safety) (Amendment) Regulations 1990;
- (c)   the Child Resistant Packaging (Safety) (Amendment) Regulations 1993;
- (d)   the Chemicals (Hazard Information and Packaging) Regulations 1993.

(2)   Where a substance or preparation dangerous for supply is required to be labelled in accordance with these Regulations and is so labelled, that labelling shall be deemed to satisfy the requirements of—

(a)   section 5 of the Petroleum (Consolidation) Act 1928 including that section as applied to any dangerous substance by an Order in Council made under section 19 of that Act;

(b)   regulation 6 of the Highly Flammable Liquids and Liquefied Petroleum Gases Regulations 1972; and

(c)   regulations 3 and 4 of the Farm and Garden Chemicals Regulations 1971.

(3)   The following Local Acts shall be modified in accordance with sub-paragraphs (a) and (b) below—

(a)   in section 4 of Part II of the London County Council (General Powers) Act 1912, for the definition of "flash point" there shall be substituted the following definition—

"'flash point' means the flash point determined in accordance with Part III of Schedule 1 to the Chemicals (Hazard Information and Packaging for Supply) Regulations 1994 (S.I. 1994/3247)";

(b)   in section 38 of the London Building Acts (Amendment) Act 1939 for subsection (2A), there shall be substituted the following subsection—

"(2A)   In this section, "flash point" means the flash point determined in accordance with Part III of Schedule 1 to the Chemicals (Hazard Information and Packaging for Supply) Regulations 1994 (S.I. 1994/3247).".

(4)   In the first Note following the table in Part II of Schedule 2 to the Control of Industrial Major Accident Hazards Regulations 1984 for the words "the Chemicals (Hazard Information and Packaging) Regulations 1993 (S.I. No 1746)" there shall be substituted the words "the Chemicals (Hazard Information and Packaging for Supply) Regulations 1994 (S.I. 1994/3247)".

(5)   In note 2 to Schedule 1 of the Dangerous Substances in Harbour Areas Regulations 1987 for the words "the Chemicals (Hazard Information and Packaging) Regulations 1993" there shall be substituted the words "the Chemicals (Hazard Information and Packaging for Supply) Regulations 1994 (S.I. 1994/3247)".

(6)   In paragraph 1(1)(a) of Schedule 2 to the Control of Asbestos at Work Regulations 1987 for the words "the Chemicals (Hazard Information and Packaging) Regulations 1993 (S.I. 1993/1746)" there shall be substituted the words "the Chemicals (Hazard Information and Packaging for Supply) Regulations 1994 (S.I. 1994/3247)".

(7)   In   regulation 2(1)   of   the   Health   and   Safety   (Enforcing   Authority) Regulations 1989—

(a)   in the definition of "preparation dangerous for supply" for the words "the Chemicals (Hazard Information and Packaging) Regulations 1993 (S.I. 1993 No 1746)" there shall be substituted the words "the Chemicals (Hazard Information and Packaging for Supply) Regulations 1994 (S.I. 1994/3247)"; and

(b)   in the definition of "substance dangerous for supply" for the words "the Chemicals (Hazard Information and Packaging) Regulations 1993" there shall be substituted the words "the Chemicals (Hazard Information and Packaging for Supply) Regulations 1994".

(8) The Notification of New Substances Regulations 1993 shall be amended as follows—

    (a) in regulation 2(1) in the definition of "the approved supply list" for the words "the Chemicals (Hazard Information and Packaging) Regulations 1993" there shall be substituted the words "the Chemicals (Hazard Information and Packaging for Supply) Regulations 1994 (S.I. 1994/3247)"; and

    (b) in regulations 4(d), 6(7) and 18(3)(h) in each place where the words occur, for the words "the Chemicals (Hazard Information and Packaging) Regulations 1993" there shall be substituted the words "the Chemicals (Hazard Information and Packaging for Supply) Regulations 1994".

(9) The provisions of the Petroleum (Consolidation) Act 1928 referred to in column 1 of Part I of Schedule 8 and the provisions of the instruments referred to in column 1 of Part II of that Schedule (all of which relate to the flash points of flammable liquids) shall be modified to the extent specified in the corresponding entries in column 2 of that Schedule.

(10) In the Carriage of Dangerous Goods by Road and Rail (Classification, Packaging and Labelling) Regulations 1994—

    (a) in regulation 2(1), for the definition of "the supply Regulations" there shall be substituted the following definition—

        "'the supply Regulations' means the Chemicals (Hazard Information and Packaging for Supply) Regulations 1994 (S.I. 1994/3247), except that for the purposes of regulation 14 (transitional defences) it means the Chemicals (Hazard Information and Packaging) Regulations 1993 (S.I. 1993/1746 as amended by S.I. 1993/3050) excluding those amendments made by paragraphs 2 to 19, 21 to 29 and 31 to 33 of Schedule 9;";

    (b) in regulation 11(5) for the words "regulation 14" there shall be substituted the words "regulation 11"; and

    (c) in paragraphs (1), (2)(a) and (3)(a) of regulation 14, the words "as in force immediately before these Regulations came into force" shall be deleted in each place where those words occur.

(11) In regulation 3(2) of the Dangerous Substances and Preparations (Safety) (Consolidation) Regulations 1994 for the words "the Chemicals (Hazard Information and Packaging) Regulations 1993" there shall be substituted the words "the Chemicals (Hazard Information and Packaging for Supply) Regulations 1994 (S.I. 1994/3247)".

(12) In regulation 2(1) of the Control of Substances Hazardous to Health Regulations 1994—

    (a) in the definition of "approved supply list" for the words "regulation 4(1) of the Chemicals (Hazard Information and Packaging) Regulations 1993" there shall be substituted the words "regulation 4 of the Chemicals (Hazard Information and Packaging for Supply) Regulations 1994 (S.I. 1994/3247)";

    (b) in sub-paragraph (a) of the definition of "carcinogen" for the words "the Chemicals (Hazard Information and Packaging) Regulations 1993" there shall be substituted the words "the Chemicals (Hazard Information and Packaging for Supply) Regulations 1994"; and

    (c) in sub-paragraph (a) of the definition of "substance hazardous to health" for the words "the Chemicals (Hazard Information and Packaging) Regulations 1993" there shall be substituted the words "the Chemicals (Hazard Information and Packaging for Supply) Regulations 1994".

SCHEDULE 1

Regulations 2(1), 5(4) and 10(3)

CLASSIFICATION OF SUBSTANCES AND PREPARATIONS DANGEROUS FOR SUPPLY

PART I
CATEGORIES OF DANGER

Column 1 *Category of danger*	Column 2 *Property* (See Note 1)	Column 3 *Symbol-letter*
PHYSICO-CHEMICAL PROPERTIES		
Explosive	Solid, liquid, pasty or gelatinous substances and preparations which may also react exothermically without atmospheric oxygen thereby quickly evolving gases, and which under defined test conditions detonate, quickly deflagrate or upon heating explode when partially confined.	E
Oxidizing	Substances and preparations which give rise to a highly exothermic reaction in contact with other substances, particularly flammable substances.	O
Extremely flammable	Liquid substances and preparations having an extremely low flash point and a low boiling point and gaseous substances and preparations which are flammable in contact with air at ambient temperature and pressure. (See Note 2).	F+
Highly flammable	The following substances and preparations, namely— (a) substances and preparations which may become hot and finally catch fire in contact with air at ambient temperature without any application of energy, (b) solid substances and preparations which may readily catch fire after brief contact with a source of ignition and which continue to burn or to be consumed after removal of the source of ignition, (c) liquid substances and preparations having a very low flash point, or (d) substances and preparations which, in contact with water or damp air, evolve highly flammable gases in dangerous quantities. (See Note 2).	F
Flammable	Liquid substances and preparations having a low flash point. (See Note 2).	none

Column 1 *Category of danger*	Column 2 *Property* (See Note 1)	Column 3 *Symbol-letter*
HEALTH EFFECTS		
Very toxic	Substances and preparations which in very low quantities cause death or acute or chronic damage to health when inhaled, swallowed or absorbed via the skin.	T+
Toxic	Substances and preparations which in low quantities cause death or acute or chronic damage to health when inhaled, swallowed or absorbed via the skin.	T
Harmful	Substances and preparations which may cause death or acute or chronic damage to health when inhaled, swallowed or absorbed via the skin.	Xn
Corrosive	Substances and preparations which may, on contact with living tissues, destroy them.	C
Irritant	Non-corrosive substances and preparations which, through immediate, prolonged or repeated contact with the skin or mucous membrane, may cause inflammation.	Xi
Sensitizing	Substances and preparations which, if they are inhaled or if they penetrate the skin, are capable of eliciting a reaction by hypersensitization such that on further exposure to the substance or preparation, characteristic adverse effects are produced.	
Sensitizing by inhalation		Xn
Sensitizing by skin contact		Xi
Carcinogenic (See Note 3)	Substances and preparations which, if they are inhaled or ingested or if they penetrate the skin, may induce cancer or increase its incidence.	
Category 1		T
Category 2		T
Category 3		Xn
Mutagenic (See Note 3)	Substances and preparations which, if they are inhaled or ingested or if they penetrate the skin, may induce heritable genetic defects or increase their incidence.	
Category 1		T
Category 2		T
Category 3		Xn
Toxic for reproduction (See Note 3)	Substances and preparations which, if they are inhaled or ingested or if they penetrate the skin, may produce or increase the incidence of non-heritable adverse effects in the progeny and/or an impairment of male or female reproductive functions or capacity.	

Column 1 *Category of danger*	Column 2 *Property* (See Note 1)	Column 3 *Symbol-letter*
Category 1		T
Category 2		T
Category 3		Xn
Dangerous for the environment (See Note 4)	Substances which, were they to enter into the environment, would present or might present an immediate or delayed danger for one or more components of the environment.	N

Notes

1. As further described in the approved classification and labelling guide.
2. Preparations packed in aerosol dispensers shall be classified as flammable in accordance with the additional criteria set out in Part II of this Schedule.
3. The categories are specified in the approved classification and labelling guide.
4. (a) In certain cases specified in the approved supply list and in the approved classification and labelling guide substances classified as dangerous for the environment do not require to be labelled with the symbol for this category of danger.

    (b) This category of danger does not apply to preparations.

PART II
CLASSIFICATION OF SUBSTANCES AND PREPARATIONS DANGEROUS FOR SUPPLY IN AEROSOL DISPENSERS AS FLAMMABLE

1. A substance or preparation which is packed in an aerosol dispenser shall be classified as dangerous for supply at least as "flammable" if that dispenser contains either—
    (a) more than 45 per cent by weight of flammable substances; or
    (b) more than 250 grams of flammable substances.

For the purposes of this paragraph, "flammable substances" means highly flammable gases or flammable liquids having flash points equal to or less than 100°C.

2. Where an aerosol dispenser contains a substance or preparation which is classified in accordance with paragraph 1 as flammable it shall show in accordance with the requirements of regulation 10 either—
    (a) the word "flammable"; or
    (b) the symbol having the symbol-letter F in column 2 of Schedule 2,
or both the word "flammable" and that symbol.

PART III
METHODS FOR THE DETERMINATION OF FLASH POINT

1. For the purpose of classifying a substance or preparation dangerous for supply in accordance with Part I of this Schedule, the flash point shall be determined—
    (a) by one of the equilibrium methods referred to in paragraph 3; or
    (b) by one of the non-equilibrium methods referred to in paragraph 4, except that when the flash point so determined falls within one of the following ranges, namely:—

(i)   −2° C to +2°C,

(ii)   19°C to 23°C, or

(iii)   53° C to 57° C,

that flash point shall be confirmed by one of the equilibrium methods referred to in paragraph 3 using like apparatus.

2.   The use of any method or apparatus referred to in paragraphs 3, 4 and 5 is subject to the conditions specified in the appropriate standard particularly having regard to the nature of the substance (eg viscosity) and to the flash point range and also to the advice provided in paragraphs 21 to 25 of the approved classification and labelling guide.

3.   The equilibrium methods referred to in paragraph 1(a) are those defined in the following standards, namely International Standards ISO 1516, ISO 3680, ISO 1523 and ISO 3679.

4.   The non-equilibrium methods referred to in paragraph 1(b) use the apparatus referred to below in accordance with the following standards namely:—

    (a)   Abel Apparatus—

        (i)   British Standard BS 2000 Part 170,

        (ii)   French Standard NF M07–011,

        (iii)   French Standard NF T66–009;

    (b)   Abel-Pensky Apparatus—

        (i)   German Standard DIN 51755, Part 1 (for temperatures from 5 to 65 degrees C),

        (ii)   German Standard DIN 51755, Part 2 (for temperatures below 5 degrees C),

        (iii)   French Standard NF M07–036,

        (iv)   European Standard EN 57;

    (c)   Tag Apparatus—

        (i)   American Standard ASTM D-56;

    (d)   Pensky-Martens Apparatus—

        (i)   British Standard BS 6664 Part 5,

        (ii)   International Standard ISO 2719,

        (iii)   American Standard ASTM D–93,

        (iv)   French Standard NF M07–019,

        (v)   German Standard DIN 51758,

        (vi)   European Standard EN 11.

5. To determine the flash point of viscous liquids (paints, gums and similar) containing solvents, only apparatus and test methods suitable for determining the flash point of viscous liquids may be used namely:—

    —   International Standards ISO 3679, ISO 3680, ISO 1523 and German Standard DIN 53213, Part 1.

SCHEDULE 2

Regulation 2(1)

INDICATIONS OF DANGER AND SYMBOLS FOR SUBSTANCES AND PREPARATIONS DANGEROUS FOR SUPPLY

Column 1 *Indication of danger*	Column 2 *Symbol-letter*	Column 3 *Symbol*
Explosive	E	

Column 1 *Indication of danger*	Column 2 *Symbol-letter*	Column 3 *Symbol*
Oxidizing	O	
Extremely flammable	F +	
Highly flammable	F	
Very toxic	T+	
Toxic	T	
Harmful	Xn	
Corrosive	C	

| Column 1 | Column 2 | Column 3 |
Indication of danger	*Symbol-letter*	*Symbol*
Irritant	Xi	
Dangerous for the environment	N	

SCHEDULE 3

Regulations 5(5) and 9(3)(d)

CLASSIFICATION PROVISIONS FOR PREPARATIONS DANGEROUS FOR SUPPLY

PART I
GENERAL PROVISIONS

Application

1. The provisions of this Schedule shall apply for the classification of preparations (other than pesticides).

Interpretation

2. In this Schedule, for the purposes of classification—

"physico-chemical properties" means the properties to be applied for the classifications "explosive", "oxidizing", "extremely flammable", "highly flammable" or "flammable";

"health effects" means the effects to be assessed for the classifications "very toxic", "toxic", "harmful", "corrosive", "irritant", "carcinogenic", "mutagenic or "toxic for reproduction".

Classification of preparations by physico-chemical properties

3.—(1) The requisite physico-chemical properties for the classification of preparations shall be determined in accordance with the criteria set out in the approved classification and labelling guide.

(2) Preparations shall be classified as explosive, oxidizing, extremely flammable, highly flammable or flammable when they satisfy the criteria referred to in sub-paragraph (1) above for the category of danger.

(3) By way of derogation from sub-paragraph (2), the determination of explosive, oxidizing, extremely flammable, highly flammable or flammable properties is not necessary provided that none of the constituents possess such properties and that, on the basis of information available to the manufacturer, the preparation is unlikely to present dangers of this kind.

Classification of preparations by health effects

4.—(1) The health effects of a preparation shall be assessed by one or more of the following methods—

(a) by the conventional method described in the following paragraphs using concentration limits; or

(b) by the criteria set out in the approved classification and labelling guide in relation to the preparation for an appropriate classification and label.

(2) Any one or more of the health effects of the preparation which are not assessed by the method set out in sub-paragraph (1)(b) above shall be assessed in accordance with the conventional method.

(3) Where the health effects have been established by both methods, the results of the method set out in sub-paragraph (1)(b) above shall be used for classifying the preparation except in the case of carcinogenic and mutagenic effects and toxic effects for reproduction, when the conventional method set out in sub-paragraph (1)(a) shall always be used.

(4) Where it can be demonstrated that—

(a) the health effects on man differ from those suggested by a toxicological determination or a conventional assessment, then the preparation shall be classified according to its effects on man;

(b) owing to effects such as potentiation a conventional assessment would underestimate the health effects, these effects shall be taken into account in classifying the preparation; or

(c) owing to effects such as antagonism a conventional assessment would overestimate the health effects, these effects shall be taken into account in classifying the preparation.

(5) For preparations of a known composition classified in accordance with the method set out in sub-paragraph (1)(b) above, a new health effect assessment either by the method set out in sub-paragraph (1)(a) or (1)(b) above shall be performed whenever—

(a) changes of composition of the initial concentration of a weight/weight percentage of one or more of the constituents are introduced by the manufacturer which exceed the permitted variations set out in the following table—

Initial concentration range of the constituent	Permitted variation in actual concentration of the constituent
≤ 2.5%	± 15%
> 2.5 ≤ 10%	± 10%
> 10 ≤ 25%	± 6%
> 25 ≤ 50%	± 5%
> 50 ≤ 100%	± 2.5%

(b) changes of composition involving the substitution or addition of one or more constituents, which may or may not be dangerous within the definitions in Schedule 1, are introduced by the manufacturer.

Classification by the conventional method

5.—(1) In accordance with paragraph 4(1)(a), the health effects shall be assessed by the conventional method described below using concentration limits.

(2) Where the substances concerned are dangerous for supply and are listed as dangerous for supply in the approved supply list and are assigned concentration limits necessary for the application of the method of assessment described below, these concentration limits shall be used.

(3) Where the substances concerned are dangerous for supply and do not appear in the approved supply list as dangerous for supply or appear there without the concentration limits necessary for the application of the method of evaluation described below, the concentration limits shall be assigned in accordance with Part II of this Schedule.

(4) In its application to preparations that are gases, this Part shall be modified so that references to concentrations expressed as percentage by weight are to concentrations expressed as the same percentage by volume.

(5) Where a preparation contains at least one substance which, in accordance with regulation 6(7) of the Notification of New Substances Regulations 1993 bears the warning "Caution—Substance not yet fully tested", the label of the preparation must bear the words "Caution—This preparation contains a substance not yet fully tested" if the substance is present in a concentration equal to or in excess of 1% by weight.

(6) A substance referred to in sub-paragraph (5) above must, whatever its concentration level, be treated on the same basis as the other substances present in the preparation when applying the method of evaluation by calculation, if its labelling gives at least an indication of the health effect.

Classification by the conventional method as very toxic

6. The following preparations shall be regarded as very toxic—

(a) owing to their acute lethal effects, preparations containing one or more substances classified or regarded as very toxic in concentrations exceeding—
   (i) either the concentration specified in the approved supply list for the substance or substances under consideration, or
   (ii) the concentration specified in paragraph 1 of Part II of this Schedule (Table I or Table IA in the case of gases) where the substance or substances do not appear in the approved supply list or appear in it without concentration limits;

(b) owing to their acute lethal effects, preparations containing more than one substance classified or regarded as very toxic in individual concentrations not exceeding the limits specified in the approved list or in paragraph 1 of Part II of this Schedule (Table I or Table IA), if the sum of the quotients obtained by dividing the percentage weight of each very toxic substance in the preparation by the very toxic limit specified for that substance is 1 or more, ie—

$$\sum\left(\frac{P_{T+}}{L_{T+}}\right) \geq 1$$

where—

P_{T+} the percentage by weight of each very toxic substance in the preparation,

L_{T+} the very toxic limit specified for each very toxic substance expressed as a percentage.

(c) owing to their non-lethal irreversible effects after a single exposure, preparations containing one or more substances dangerous for supply which produce such effects in individual concentrations exceeding—
   (i) either the concentration specified in the approved supply list for the substance or substances under consideration, or
   (ii) the concentration specified in paragraph 2 of Part II of this Schedule (Table II or Table IIA in the case of gases) where the substance or substances do not appear in the approved supply list or appear in it without concentration limits.

Classification by the conventional method as toxic

7. The following preparations shall be regarded as toxic—

(a) owing to their acute lethal effects, preparations containing one or more substances classified or regarded as very toxic or toxic in concentrations exceeding—
   (i) either the concentration specified in the approved supply list for the substance or substances under consideration, or
   (ii) the concentration specified in paragraph 1 of Part II of this Schedule (Table I or Table IA) where the substance or substances do not appear in the approved supply list or appear in it without concentration limits;

(b) owing to their acute lethal effects, preparations containing more than one substance classified or regarded as very toxic or toxic in individual concentrations not exceeding the limits specified in the approved supply list or in paragraph 1 of

Part II of this Schedule (Table I or Table IA) if the sum of the quotients obtained by dividing the percentage weight of each very toxic or toxic substance in the preparation by the toxic limit specified for that substance is 1 or more, ie—

$$\sum \left(\frac{P_{T+}}{L_T} + \frac{P_T}{L_T} \right) \geq 1$$

where—

P_{T+} the percentage by weight of each very toxic substance in the preparation,

P_T the percentage by weight of each toxic substance in the preparation,

L_T the toxic limit specified for each very toxic or toxic substance expressed as a percentage;

(c) owing to their non-lethal irreversible effects after a single exposure, preparations containing one or more substances dangerous for supply which produce such effects in individual concentrations exceeding—

   (i) either the concentration specified in the approved supply list for the substance or substances under consideration, or

   (ii) the concentration specified in paragraph 2 of Part II of this Schedule (Table II or Table IIA) where the substance or substances do not appear in the approved supply list or appear in it without concentration limits;

(d) owing to their long term effects after repeated or prolonged exposure, preparations containing one or more substances dangerous for supply which produce such effects in individual concentrations exceeding—

   (i) either the concentration specified in the approved supply list for the substance or substances under consideration, or

   (ii) the concentration specified in paragraph 3 of Part II of this Schedule (Table III or Table IIIA in the case of gases) where the substance or substances do not appear in the approved supply list or appear in it without concentration limits.

Classification by the conventional method as harmful

8. The following preparations shall be regarded as harmful—

(a) owing to their acute lethal effects, preparations containing one or more substances classified or regarded as very toxic, toxic or harmful in concentrations exceeding—

   (i) either the concentration specified in the approved supply list for the substance or substances under consideration, or

   (ii) the concentration specified in paragraph 1 of Part II of this Schedule (Table I or Table IA) where the substance or substances do not appear in the approved supply list or appear in it without concentration limits;

(b) owing to their acute lethal effects, preparations containing more than one substance classified or regarded as very toxic, toxic or harmful in individual concentrations not exceeding the limits specified in the approved supply list or in paragraph 1 of Part II of this Schedule (Table I or Table IA) if the sum of the quotients obtained by dividing the percentage weight of each very toxic, toxic or harmful substance in the preparation by the harmful limit specified for that substance is 1 or more, ie—

$$\sum \left(\frac{P_{T+}}{L_{Xn}} + \frac{P_T}{L_{Xn}} + \frac{P_{Xn}}{L_{Xn}} \right) \geq 1$$

where—

P_{T+} the percentage by weight of each very toxic substance in the preparation,

P_T the percentage by weight of each toxic substance in the preparation,

P_{Xn} the percentage by weight of each harmful substance in the preparation,

L_{Xn} the harmful limit specified for each very toxic, toxic or harmful substance expressed as a percentage;

(c)   owing to their non-lethal irreversible effects after a single exposure, preparations containing one or more substances dangerous for supply which produce such effects in individual concentrations exceeding—

   (i)   either the concentration specified in the approved supply list for the substance or substances under consideration, or

   (ii) the concentration specified in paragraph 2 of Part II of this Schedule (Table II or Table IIA) where the substance or substances do not appear in the approved supply list or appear in it without concentration limits;

(d)   owing to their long-term effects after repeated or prolonged exposure, preparations containing one or more substances dangerous for supply that produce such effects in individual concentrations exceeding—

   (i)   either the concentration specified in the approved supply list for the substance or substances under consideration, or

   (ii) the concentration specified in paragraph 3 of Part II of this Schedule (Table III or Table IIIA in the case of gases) where the substance or substances do not appear in the approved supply list or appear in it without concentration limits;

(e)   owing to their sensitizing effects by inhalation, preparations containing at least one substance dangerous for supply to which is assigned the risk phrase R42 (may cause sensitization by inhalation) that produces such effects in individual concentrations exceeding—

   (i)   either the concentration specified in the approved supply list for the substance or substances under consideration, or

   (ii) the concentration specified in paragraph 5 of Part II of this Schedule (Table V or Table VA in the case of gases) where the substance or substances do not appear in the approved supply list or appear in it without concentration limits.

Classification by the conventional method as corrosive

9.—(1) In this Schedule a preparation shall be regarded as "very corrosive" if it has been classified as corrosive with the risk phrase R35 (causes severe burns).

(2)   The following preparations shall be regarded as very corrosive—

(a)   preparations containing one or more substances classified or regarded as very corrosive in concentrations exceeding—

   (i)   either the concentration specified in the approved supply list for the substance or substances under consideration, or

   (ii) the concentration specified in paragraph 4 of Part II of this Schedule (Table IV or Table IVA in the case of gases) where the substance or substances do not appear in the approved supply list or appear in it without concentration limits;

(b)   preparations containing more than one substance classified or regarded as very corrosive in individual concentrations not exceeding the limits specified either in the approved supply list or in paragraph 4 of Part II of this Schedule (Table IV or Table IVA) if the sum of the quotients obtained by dividing the percentage weight of each very corrosive substance in the preparation by the corrosive (R35) limit specified for that substance is 1 or more, ie—

$$\sum \left(\frac{P_{C.R35}}{L_{C.R35}} \right) \geq 1$$

where—

$P_{C.R35}$ the percentage by weight of each very corrosive substance in the preparation,

$L_{C.R35}$ the corrosive (R35) limit specified for each very corrosive substance expressed as a percentage by weight.

10. The following preparations shall also be regarded as corrosive—
(a) preparations containing one or more substances classified or regarded as corrosive to which is assigned the risk phrase R35 or R34 (causes burns) in individual concentrations exceeding—
   (i) either the concentration specified in the approved supply list for the substance or substances under consideration, or
   (ii) the concentration specified in paragraph 4 of Part II of this Schedule (Table IV or Table IVA) where the substance or substances do not appear in the approved supply list or appear in it without concentration limits;
(b) preparations containing more than one substance classified or regarded as corrosive to which is assigned the risk phrase R35 or R34 in individual concentrations not exceeding the limits specified either in the approved supply list or in paragraph 4 of Part II of this Schedule (Table IV or Table IVA) if the sum of the quotients obtained by dividing the percentage weight of each corrosive substance in the preparation by the corrosive (R34) limit specified for that substance is 1 or more, ie—

$$\sum \left(\frac{P_{C.R35}}{L_{C.R34}} + \frac{P_{C.R34}}{L_{C.R34}} \right) \geq 1$$

where—
$P_{C.R35}$ the percentage by weight of each corrosive substance to which is assigned the risk phrase R35 in the preparation,
$P_{C.R34}$ the percentage by weight of each corrosive substance to which is assigned the risk phrase R34 in the preparation,
$L_{C.R34}$ the corrosive (R34) limit specified for each corrosive substance to which is assigned the risk phrase R35 or R34 expressed as a percentage by weight.

Classification by the conventional method as irritant
11. The following preparations shall be regarded as liable to cause serious eye damage—
(a) preparations containing one or more substances classified or regarded as irritant to which is assigned the risk phrase R41 (risk of serious damage to eyes) in individual concentrations exceeding—
   (i) either the concentration specified in the approved supply list for the substance or substances under consideration, or
   (ii) the concentration specified in paragraph 4 of Part II of this Schedule (Table IV or Table IVA) where the substance or substances do not appear in the approved supply list or appear in it without concentration limits;
(b) preparations containing more than one substance classified or regarded as corrosive to which is assigned the risk phrase R35 or R34, or irritant to which is assigned the risk phrase R41, in individual concentrations not exceeding the limits specified either in the approved supply list or in paragraph 4 of Part II of this Schedule (Table IV or IVA) if the sum of the quotients obtained by dividing the percentage weight of each irritant substance in the preparation by the irritant (R41) limit specified for that substance is 1 or more, ie—

$$\sum \left(\frac{P_{C.R35}}{L_{Xi.R41}} + \frac{P_{C.R34}}{L_{Xi.R41}} + \frac{P_{Xi.R41}}{L_{Xi.R41}} \right) \geq 1$$

where—
$P_{C.R35}$ the percentage by weight of each corrosive substance to which is assigned the risk phrase R35 in the preparation,
$P_{C.R34}$ the percentage by weight of each corrosive substance to which is assigned the risk phrase R34 in the preparation,

$P_{Xi.R41}$ the percentage by weight of each irritant substance to which is assigned the risk phrase R41 in the preparation,

$L_{Xi.R41}$ the irritant (R41) limit specified for each irritant substance expressed as a percentage by weight to which is assigned the risk phrase R41 in the preparation.

12. The following preparations shall be regarded as skin irritants—

(a) preparations containing one or more substances classified or regarded as corrosive, to which is assigned the risk phrase R35 or R34, or irritant, to which is assigned the risk phrase R38 (irritating to skin) in individual concentrations exceeding—
   (i) either the concentration specified in the approved supply list for the substance or substances under consideration, or
   (ii) the concentration specified in paragraph 4 of Part II of this Schedule (Table IV or Table IVA) where the substance or substances do not appear in the approved supply list or appear in it without concentration limits;

(b) preparations containing more than one substance classified or regarded as corrosive, to which is assigned the risk phrase R35 or R34, or irritant, to which is assigned the risk phrase R38, in individual concentrations not exceeding the limits specified either in the approved supply list or in paragraph 4 of Part II of this Schedule (Table IV or Table IVA) if the sum of the quotients obtained by dividing the percentage weight of each substance in the preparation by the irritant (R38) limit specified for that substance is 1 or more, ie—

$$\sum \left(\frac{P_{C.R34}}{L_{Xi.R38}} + \frac{P_{C.R35}}{L_{Xi.R38}} + \frac{P_{Xi.R38}}{L_{Xi.R38}} \right) \geq 1$$

where—

$P_{C.R35}$ the percentage by weight of each corrosive substance to which is assigned the risk phrase R35 in the preparation,

$P_{C.R34}$ the percentage by weight of each corrosive substance to which is assigned the risk phrase R34 in the preparation,

$P_{Xi.R38}$ the percentage by weight of each irritant substance to which is assigned the risk phrase R38 in the preparation,

$L_{Xi.R38}$ the irritant (R38) limit specified for each corrosive or irritant substance expressed as a percentage by weight to which is assigned the risk phrase R35, R34 or R38 in the preparation;

(c) owing to their sensitizing effects by skin contact preparations containing at least one substance dangerous for supply to which is assigned phrase R43 (may cause sensitization by skin contact) that produces such effects in individual concentrations exceeding—
  — either the concentration specified in the approved supply list for the substance under consideration, or
  — the concentration specified in paragraph 5 of Part II of this Schedule (Table V or Table VA) where the substance or substances do not appear in the approved supply list or appear in it without concentration limits.

13. The following preparations shall be regarded as eye irritants—

(a) preparations containing one or more substances classified or regarded as irritant to which is assigned the risk phrase R41 (risk of serious damage to eyes) or R36 (irritating to eyes) in individual concentrations exceeding—
   (i) either the concentration specified in the approved supply list for the substance or substances under consideration, or
   (ii) the concentration specified in paragraph 4 of Part II of this Schedule (Table IV or Table IVA) where the substance or substances do not appear in the approved supply list or appear in it without concentration limits;

(b) preparations containing more than one substance classified or regarded as irritant to which is assigned the risk phrase R41 or R36 in individual concentrations not exceeding the limits specified either in the approved supply list or in paragraph 4 of Part II of this Schedule (Table IV or Table IVA) if the sum of the quotients obtained by dividing the percentage weight of each irritant substance in the preparation by the irritant (R36) limit specified for that substance is 1 or more, ie—

$$\sum\left(\frac{P_{Xi.R41}}{L_{Xi.R36}}+\frac{P_{Xi.R36}}{L_{Xi.R36}}\right)\geq 1$$

where—

$P_{Xi.R41}$ the percentage by weight of each irritant substance to which is assigned the risk phrase R41 in the preparation,

$P_{Xi.R36}$ the percentage by weight of each irritant substance to which is assigned the risk phrase R36 in the preparation,

$L_{Xi.R36}$ the irritant (R36) limit specified for each irritant substance expressed as a percentage by weight to which is assigned the risk phrase R41 or R36 in the preparation.

14.   The following preparations shall be regarded as irritants for the respiratory system—
   (a) preparations containing one or more substances classified or regarded as irritant to which is assigned the risk phrase R37 (irritating to the respiratory system) in individual concentrations exceeding—
      (i) either the concentration specified in the approved supply list for the substance or substances under consideration, or
      (ii) the concentration specified in paragraph 4 of Part II of this Schedule (Table IV or Table IVA) where the substance or substances do not appear in the approved supply list or appear in it without concentration limits;
   (b) preparations containing more than one substance classified or regarded as irritant to which is assigned the risk phrase R37 in individual concentrations not exceeding the limits specified either in the approved supply list or in paragraph 4 of Part II of this Schedule (Table IV or Table IVA) if the sum of the quotients obtained by dividing the percentage weight of each irritant substance in the preparation by the irritant (R37) limit specified for that substance is 1 or more, ie—

$$\sum\left(\frac{P_{Xi.R37}}{L_{Xi.R37}}\right)\geq 1$$

where—

$P_{Xi.R37}$ the percentage by weight of each irritant substance to which is assigned the risk phrase R37 in the preparation,

$L_{Xi.R37}$ the irritant (R37) limit specified for each irritant substance expressed as a percentage by weight to which is assigned the risk phrase R37 in the preparation.

Classification by the conventional method as carcinogenic

15.—(1) Preparations shall be regarded as carcinogenic and assigned at least the symbol and indication of danger "toxic" if they contain a substance producing such effects to which is assigned either the risk phrase R45 (may cause cancer) or R49 (may cause cancer by inhalation) which denotes carcinogenic substances in category 1 or category 2 in a concentration equal to or exceeding—
   (a) either the concentration specified in the approved supply list for the substance or substances under consideration, or

(b) the concentration specified in paragraph 6 of Part II of this Schedule (Table VI or Table VIA in the case of gases) where the substance or substances do not appear in the approved supply list or appear in it without concentration limits.

(2) Preparations shall be regarded as suspect for humans owing to their possible carcinogenic effects and assigned at least the symbol and indication of danger "harmful" if they contain a substance producing such effects to which is assigned the risk phrase R40 (possible risk of irreversible effects) which denotes carcinogenic substances in category 3 in a concentration equal to or exceeding—

(a) either the concentration specified in the approved supply list for the substance or substances under consideration, or

(b) the concentration specified in paragraph 6 of Part II of this Schedule (Table VI or Table VIA) where the substance or substances do not appear in the approved supply list or appear in it without concentration limits.

Classification by the conventional method as mutagenic

16.—(1) Preparations shall be regarded as mutagenic and assigned at least the symbol and indication of danger "toxic" if they contain a substance producing such effects to which is assigned the risk phrase R46 (may cause heritable genetic damage) which denotes mutagenic substances in category 1 in a concentration equal to or exceeding—

(a) either the concentration specified in the approved supply list for the substance or substances under consideration, or

(b) the concentration specified in paragraph 6 of Part II of this Schedule (Table VI or Table VIA) where the substance or substances do not appear in the approved supply list or appear in it without concentration limits.

(2) Preparations shall be regarded as mutagenic and assigned at least the symbol and indication of danger "toxic" if they contain a substance producing such effects to which is assigned the risk phrase R46 (may cause heritable genetic damage) which denotes mutagenic substances in category 2 in a concentration equal to or exceeding—

(a) either the concentration specified in the approved supply list for the substance or substances under consideration, or

(b) the concentration specified in paragraph 6 of Part II of this Schedule (Table VI or Table VIA) where the substance or substances do not appear in the approved supply list or appear in it without concentration limits.

(3) Preparations shall be regarded as suspect for humans because of their possible mutagenic effects and assigned at least the symbol and indication of danger "harmful" if they contain a substance producing such effects to which is assigned the risk phrase R40 (possible risk of irreversible effects) which denotes mutagenic substances in category 3 in a concentration equal to or exceeding—

(a) either the concentration specified in the approved supply list for the substance or substances under consideration, or

(b) the concentration specified in paragraph 6 of Part II of this Schedule (Table VI or Table VIA) where the substance or substances do not appear in the approved supply list or appear in it without concentration limits.

Classification by the conventional method as toxic for reproduction

17.—(1) Preparations shall be regarded as toxic for reproduction and assigned at least the symbol and indication of danger "toxic" if they contain a substance producing such effects to which is assigned the appropriate risk phrase as ascertained from the approved classification and labelling guide which denotes substances toxic for reproduction in category 1 in a concentration equal to or exceeding—

(a) either the concentration specified in the approved supply list for the substance or substances under consideration, or

(b) the concentration specified in paragraph 6 of Part II of this Schedule (Table VI or Table VIA) where the substance or substances do not appear in the approved supply list or appear in it without concentration limits;

(2)   Preparations shall be regarded as having to be treated as toxic for reproduction and assigned at least the symbol and indication of danger "toxic" if they contain a substance producing such effects to which is assigned the appropriate risk phrase in category 2 in a concentration equal to or exceeding—

(a)   either the concentration specified in the approved supply list for the substance or substances under consideration, or

(b)   the concentration specified in paragraph 6 of Part II of this Schedule (Table VI or Table VIA) where the substance or substances do not appear in the approved supply list or appear in it without concentration limits.

(3)   Preparations shall be regarded as having to be treated as toxic for reproduction and assigned at least the symbol and indication of danger "harmful" if they contain a substance producing such effects to which is assigned the appropriate risk phrase as ascertained from the approved classification and labelling guide which denotes substances toxic for reproduction in category 3 in a concentration equal to or exceeding–

(a)   either the concentration specified in the approved supply list for the substance or substances under consideration, or

(b)   the concentration specified in paragraph 6 of Part II of this Schedule (Table VI or Table VIA) where the substance or substances do not appear in the approved supply list or appear in it without concentration limits.

Lower limits of concentration

18.—(1)   For preparations to which this Schedule applies, no account shall be taken of substances, whether or not listed in the approved supply list, whether existing as impurities or as additives, if their concentration by weight is less than–

(a)   0.1% for substances classified as very toxic, toxic, carcinogenic (category 1 or 2) or mutagenic (category 1 or 2);

(b)   0.5% for substances classified as toxic for reproduction (category 1 or 2);

(c)   1% for substances classified as harmful, corrosive, irritant, sensitizing, carcinogenic (category 3) or mutagenic (category 3); or

(d)   5% for substances classified as toxic to reproduction (category 3),

unless lower limits are referred to in Part V of the approved supply list, or in the case of gases in Part II of this Schedule.

(2)   Some substances may have more than one health effect and each of these properties shall be characterised by its specific concentration limit.

PART II

CONCENTRATION LIMITS TO BE USED IN APPLYING THE CONVENTIONAL METHOD OF ASSESSING HEALTH EFFECTS IN ACCORDANCE WITH PART I OF THIS SCHEDULE WHERE NO SUCH LIMITS ARE GIVEN IN THE APPROVED SUPPLY LIST

An assessment must be made of the health effects that the use of a substance or a preparation might entail. For that purpose the dangerous health effects have been subdivided into:

1.   acute lethal effects;

2.   non-lethal irreversible effects after a single exposure;

3.   severe effects after repeated or prolonged exposure;

4.   corrosive effects, irritant effects;

5.   sensitizing effects;

6.   carcinogenic effects, mutagenic effects, toxic effects for reproduction.

The systematic assessment of the dangerous health effects is expressed by means of concentration limits, expressed as weight/weight percentage except for gaseous preparations (Tables A) where they are expressed as a volume/volume percentage and in conjunction with the classification of a substance.

The classification of the substance is expressed either by a symbol and one or more risk phrases or by categories (category 1, category 2 or category 3) also expressed by risk phrases when substances are shown to be carcinogenic, mutagenic or toxic for reproduction. Therefore it is important to consider, in addition to the symbol, all the phrases denoting specific risks which are assigned to each substance under consideration.

1. Acute lethal effects

1.1   *Other than gaseous preparations*

The concentration limits fixed in Table 1 determine the classification of the preparation in relation to the individual concentration of the substance(s) present whose classification is also shown.

TABLE I

Classification of the substance	Classification of the preparation		
	T+	T	X_n
T+ with R26, R27, R28	concentration≥7%	1%≤concentration<7%	0.1%≤concentration<1%
T with R23, R24, R25		concentration≥25%	3%≤concentration<25%
X_n with R20, R21, R22			concentration≥25%

The R phrases denoting risk shall be assigned to the preparation in accordance with the following criteria:
— the label shall include one or more of the above mentioned R phrases according to the classification used,
— in general, the R phrases selected should be those applicable to the substance(s) present in the concentration which gives rise to the most severe classification.

1.2   *Gaseous preparations*

The concentration limits expressed as a volume/volume percentage in Table IA below determine the classification of the gaseous preparations in relation to the individual concentration of the gas(es) present whose classification is also shown.

TABLE IA

Classification of the substance (gas)	Classification of the preparation		
	T+	T	X_n
T+ with R26, R27, R28	concentration≥1%	0.2%≤concentration<1%	0.02%≤concentration<0.2%
T with R23, R24, R25		concentration≥5%	0.5%≤concentration<5%
X_n with R20, R21, R22			concentration≥5%

The R phrases denoting risk shall be assigned to the preparation in accordance with the following criteria:
— the label shall include one or more of the above mentioned R phrases according to the classification used,
— in general, the R phrases selected should be those applicable to the substance(s) present in the concentration which gives rise to the most severe classification.

2.   Non-lethal irreversible effects after a single exposure

2.1   *Other than gaseous preparations*

For substances that produce non-lethal irreversible effects after a single exposure (R39/route of exposure, R40/route of exposure), the individual concentration limits specified in Table II determine, when appropriate, the classification of the preparation.

TABLE II

Classification of the substance	Classification of the preparation		
	T+	T	X_n
T+ with R39/ route of exposure	concentration≥10% R39(*) obligatory	1%≤concentration<10% R39(*) obligatory	0.1%≤concentration<1% R40(*)(†) obligatory
T with R39/ route of exposure		concentration≥10% R39(*) obligatory	1%≤concentration<10% R40(*)(†) obligatory
X_n with R40/ route of exposure			concentration≥10% R40(*)(†) obligatory

(*) In order to indicate the route of administration/exposure the combined R phrases listed in paragraphs 44, 45 and 46 of the approved classification and labelling guide shall be used.

(†) R40 here refers to substances classified as harmful. Concentration limits for substances required to be labelled R40 but classified as carcinogenic or mutagenic are given in Table VI.

2.2   *Gaseous preparations*

For gases that produce non-lethal irreversible effects after a single exposure (R39/route of exposure, R40/route of exposure), the individual concentration limits specified in Table IIA, expressed as a volume/volume percentage, determine, when appropriate, the classification of the preparation.

TABLE IIA

Classification of the substance (gas)	Classification of the preparation		
	T+	T	X_n
T+ with R39/ route of exposure	concentration≥1% R39(*) obligatory	0.2%≤concentration<1% R39(*) obligatory	0.02%≤concentration<0.2% R40(*)(†) obligatory
T with R39/ route of exposure		concentration≥5% R39(*) obligatory	0.5%≤concentration<5% R40(*)(†) obligatory
X_n with R40/ route of exposure			concentration≥5% R40(*)(†) obligatory

(*) In order to indicate the route of administration/exposure the combined R phrases listed in paragraphs 44, 45 and 46 of the approved classification and labelling guide shall be used.

(†) R40 here refers to substances classified as harmful. Concentration limits for substances required to be labelled R40 but classified as carcinogenic or mutagenic are given in Table VI.

3.   Severe effects after repeated or prolonged exposure

3.1   *Other than gaseous preparations*

For substances that produce severe effects after repeated exposure (R48/route of exposure), the individual concentration limits specified in Table III determine, when appropriate, the classification of the preparation.

TABLE III

Classification of the substance	Classification of the preparation	
	T	X_n
T with R48/ route of exposure	concentration ≥ 10% R48(*) obligatory	1% ≤ concentration < 10% R48(*) obligatory
X_n with R48/ route of exposure		concentration ≥ 10% R48(*) obligatory

(*) In order to indicate the route of administration/exposure the combined R phrases listed in paragraphs 44, 45 and 46 of the approved classification and labelling guide shall be used.

3.2   *Gaseous preparations*
For gases that produce severe effects after repeated or prolonged exposure (R48/route of exposure), the individual concentration limits specified in Table IIIA below, expressed as a volume/volume percentage, determine, when appropriate, the classification of the preparation.

TABLE IIIA

Classification of the substance (gas)	Classification of the preparation	
	T	X_n
T with R48/ route of exposure	concentration ≥ 5% R48(*) obligatory	0.5%≤concentration<5% R48(*) obligatory
X_n with R48/ route of exposure		concentration≥5% R48(*) obligatory

(*) In order to indicate the route of administration/exposure the combined R phrases listed in paragraphs 44, 45 and 46 of the approved classification and labelling guide shall be used.

4.   Corrosive and irritant effects including serious damage to eye

4.1   *Other than gaseous preparations*
For substances that produce corrosive effects (R34, R35) or irritant effects (R36, R37, R38, R41), the individual concentration limits specified in Table IV determine, when appropriate, the classification of the preparation.

4.2   *Gaseous preparations*
For gases that produce such effects (R34, R35– or R36, R37, R38, R41), the individual concentration limits specified in Table IVA below, expressed as a volume/volume percentage determine, when appropriate, the classification of the preparation.

TABLE IV

Classification of the substance	*Classification of the preparation*			
	C with R35	*C with R34*	*X_i with R41*	*X_i with R36, R37, R38*
C with R35	concentration ≥10% R35 obligatory	5%≤concentration <10% R34 obligatory	(*)	1%≤concentration <5% R36/R38 obligatory
C with R34		concentration≥10% R34 obligatory	(*)	5%≤concentration <10% R36/R38 obligatory
X_i with R41			concentration≥10% R41 obligatory	5%≤concentration <10% R36 obligatory
X_i with R36, R37, R38				concentration ≥20% R36, R37 and R38 are obligatory in the light of the concentration present if they apply to the substances under consideration

(*) According to the approved classification and labelling guide (paragraph 57) when a substance or preparation is classified as corrosive and assigned the risk phrase R34 or R35, the risk phrase R41 does not need to be included. Consequently, if the preparation contains corrosive substances with R35 or R34 below the concentration limits for a classification of the preparation as corrosive, such substances can contribute to a classification of the preparation as irritant (R41) or irritant (R36).

Therefore when the formulae of paragraphs 11(b) and 13(b) of Part I of this Schedule are applied the following concentration limits must be used, unless different values are fixed in the approved supply list.

(a) when formula 11(b) is applied the limit values for $L_{Xi\ R41}$ are:
— 10% for the substances X_i R41,
— 10% for the substances C R34,
— 5% for the substances C R35;

(b) when the formula 13(b) is applied the limit values for $L_{Xi\ R36}$ are:
— 20% for the substances X_i R36,
— 5% for the substances X_i R41,
— 5% for the substances C R34,
— 1% for the substances C R35.

TABLE IVA

Classification of the substance (gas)	Classification of the preparation			
	C with R35	C with R34	X_i with R41	X_i with R36, R37, R38
C with R35	concentration ≥1% R35 obligatory	0.2%≤concentration <1% R34 obligatory	(*)	0.02%≤concentration <0.2% R37 obligatory
C with R34		concentration≥5% R34 obligatory	(*)	0.5%≤concentration <5% R37 obligatory
X_i with R41			concentration≥5% R41 obligatory	0.5%≤concentration <5% R36 obligatory
X_i with R36, R37, R38			concentration≥5% R41 obligatory	concentration ≥5% R36, R37, R38 obligatory as appropriate

(*) According to the approved classification and labelling guide (paragraph 57) when a substance or preparation is classified as corrosive and assigned the risk phrase R34 or R35, the risk phrase R41 does not need to be included. Consequently, if the preparation contains corrosive substances with R35 or R34 below the concentration limits for a classification of the preparation as corrosive, such substances can contribute to a classification of the preparation as irritant (R41) or irritant (R36).

Therefore when the formulae of paragraphs 11(b) and 13(b) of Part I of this Schedule are applied the following concentration limits must be used, unless different values are fixed in the approved supply list.

    (a)   when formula 11(b) is applied the limit values for $L_{Xi\ R41}$ are:
- 10% for the substances X_i R41,
- 10% for the substances C R34,
- 5% for the substances C R35;

    (b)   when the formula 13(b) is applied the limit values for $L_{Xi\ R36}$ are:
- 20% for the substances X_i R36,
- 5% for the substances X_i R41,
- 5% for the substances C R34,
- 1% for the substances C R35.

5.   Sensitizing effects

5.1   *Other than gaseous preparations*

Substances that produce such effects are classified as sensitizing and assigned:
- the symbol Xn and phrase R42 if this effect can be produced by inhalation,
- the symbol Xi and phrase R43 if this effect can be produced through contact with the skin,
- the symbol Xn and phrase R42/43 if this effect can be produced by inhalation and through contact with the skin.

The individual concentration limits specified in Table V determine, when appropriate, the classification of the preparation.

TABLE V

Classification of the substance	Classification of the preparation	
	Sensitizing with R42	*Sensitizing with R43*
Sensitizing with R42	concentration ≥ 1% R42 obligatory	
Sensitizing with R43		concentration ≥ 1% R43 obligatory
Sensitizing with R42/43	concentration ≥ 1% R42/43 obligatory	

5.2   *Gaseous preparations*

Gases that produce such effects are classified as sensitizing and assigned:
— the symbol Xn and phrase R42 if this effect can be produced by inhalation,
— the symbol Xn and phrase R42/43 if this effect can be produced by inhalation and through contact with the skin.

The individual concentration limits specified in Table VA below, expressed as a volume/volume percentage, determine, when appropriate, the classification of the preparation.

TABLE VA

Classification of the substance (gas)	Classification of the preparation	
	Sensitizing with R42	*Sensitizing with R43*
Sensitizing with R42	concentration ≥ 0.2% R42 obligatory	
Sensitizing with R42/43	concentration ≥ 0.2% R42/43 obligatory	

6.   Carcinogenic/mutagenic/toxic effects for reproduction

6.1   *Other than gaseous preparations*

For substances which produce such effects and for which specific concentration limits do not yet appear in the approved supply list, concentration limits laid down in Table VI shall determine, where appropriate, the classification of the preparation.

TABLE VI

Classification of the substance	Classification of the preparation	
	Categories 1 and 2	*Category 3*
Carcinogenic substances of category 1 or 2 with R45 or R49	≥ 0.1% carcinogenic R45, R49 obligatory as appropriate	
Carcinogenic substances of category 3 with R40(*)		≥ 1% carcinogenic R40(*) obligatory
Mutagenic substances of category 1 or 2 with R46	≥ 0.1% mutagenic R46 obligatory	

Classification of the substance	Classification of the preparation	
	Categories 1 and 2	*Category 3*
Mutagenic substances of category 3 with R40(*)		≥ 1% mutagenic R40(*) obligatory
Substances "toxic for reproduction" of category 1 or 2 with R60 (fertility)	≥ 0.5% toxic for reproduction (fertility) R60 obligatory	
Substances "toxic for reproduction" of category 3 with R62 (fertility)		≥ 5% toxic for reproduction (fertility) R62 obligatory
Substances "toxic for reproduction" of category 1 or 2 with R61 (development)	≥ 0.5% toxic for reproduction (development) R61 obligatory	
Substances "toxic for reproduction" of category 3 with R63 (development)		≥ 5% toxic for reproduction (fertility) R63 obligatory

(*) R40 here refers to substances classified as carcinogenic or mutagenic. Concentration limits for substances required to be labelled R40 but classified as harmful are given in Table II.

6.2   *Gaseous preparations*

For gases which produce such effects and for which specific concentration limits do not yet appear in the approved supply list, concentration limits laid down in Table VIA, expressed as a volume/volume percentage, shall determine, where appropriate, the classification of the preparation.

TABLE VIA

Classification of the substance (gas)	Classification of the preparation	
	Categories 1 and 2	*Category 3*
Carcinogenic substances of category 1 or 2 with R45 or R49	≥ 0.1% carcinogenic R45, R49 obligatory as appropriate	
Carcinogenic substances of category 3 with R40(*)		≥ 1% carcinogenic R40(*) obligatory
Mutagenic substances of category 1 or 2 with R46	≥ 0.1% mutagenic R46 obligatory	
Mutagenic substances of category 3 with R40 (*)		≥ 1% mutagenic R40(*) obligatory

Classification of the substance (gas)	Classification of the preparation	
	Categories 1 and 2	Category 3
Substances "toxic for reproduction" of category 1 or 2 with R60 (fertility)	≥ 0.2% toxic for reproduction (fertility) R60 obligatory	
Substances "toxic for reproduction" of category 3 with R62 (fertility)		≥ 1% toxic for reproduction (fertility) R62 obligatory
Substances "toxic for reproduction" of category 1 or 2 with R61 (development)	≥ 0.2% toxic for reproduction (development) R61 obligatory	
Substances "toxic for reproduction" of category 3 with R63 (development)		≥ 1% toxic for reproduction (development) R63 obligatory

(*) R40 here refers to substances classified as carcinogenic or mutagenic. Concentration limits for substances required to be labelled R40 but classified as harmful are given in Table IIA.

SCHEDULE 4

Regulations 2(1) and 5(6)

CLASSIFICATION PROVISIONS FOR PREPARATIONS INTENDED TO BE USED AS PESTICIDES

Interpretation

1. A pesticide means a preparation designed—
   (a) to destroy organisms harmful to plants or to plant products or to protect plants and plant products from such organisms;
   (b) to improve or regulate plant production, with the exception of a fertiliser and a soil conditioner;
   (c) to preserve plant products except—
      (i) a wood preservative which does not contain preservatives which penetrate into the wood, or
      (ii) a food preservative to which the Preservatives in Food Regulations 1979 apply;
   (d) to destroy undesired plants;
   (e) to destroy parts of plants or to prevent undesired growth; or
   (f) to render harmless or to destroy, or to give protection against, any nuisance or harmful animals or insect pests and to control organisms with harmful or unwanted effects on water systems, buildings or other structures, or manufactured products.

Classification as very toxic, toxic or harmful

2.—(1) A preparation intended for use as a pesticide shall be classified as very toxic, toxic or harmful if its toxicity as determined by an internationally recognised test method in accordance with sub-paragraph (2) below is within the range for that classification in the table set out at the end of this sub-paragraph.

Classification	LD_{50} absorbed orally in rat, mg/kg		LD_{50} absorbed percutaneously in rat or rabbit, mg/kg		LC_{50} absorbed by inhalation in rat, mg/litre (4 hours)
	Solids other than baits and tablets	Liquids and bait preparations and pesticides in tablet form	Solids other than baits and tablets	Liquids and bait preparations and pesticides in tablet form	Gases, liquefied gases, fumigants and aerosols, in powders having particle size ≤ 50 microns
Very toxic	≤ 5	≤ 25	≤ 10	≤ 50	≤ 0.5
Toxic	> 5 to 50	> 25 to 200	> 10 to 100	> 50 to 400	> 0.5 to 2
Harmful	> 50 to 500	> 200 to 2,000	>100 to 1,000	> 400 to 4,000	> 2 to 20

(2) Subject to sub-paragraphs (3) and (4) below, pesticides shall be classified as very toxic, toxic or harmful by carrying out toxicity tests on the pesticide in the form in which it is intended to be used and these tests shall be suitable having regard to the nature and intended method of use of the pesticide and in particular—

    (a)   in the case of pesticides which can be absorbed through the skin, the percutaneous LD_{50} value shall be used where it is such that it would place a pesticide in a more restrictive class than the oral LD_{50} value or the inhalation LC_{50} value; and

    (b)   in the case of gases, liquefied gases, fumigants and aerosols and powders in which the diameter of the particles does not exceed 50 microns, the inhalation LC_{50} value shall be used.

(3) In a case where a preparation to which this Schedule applies—

    (a)   contains only one active ingredient;

    (b)   the toxicity of that active ingredient is known; and

    (c)   there are valid grounds for believing that the toxicity determined on the basis of a calculation carried out in accordance with this sub-paragraph would not differ substantially from the toxicity determined by biological testing carried out in accordance with sub-paragraphs (1) and (2) above, the toxicity of the preparation may be calculated in accordance with the formula—

$$\frac{L \times 100}{C}$$

where L is the oral toxicity (LD_{50}) of the active ingredient and C its concentration as a percentage by weight and in this sub-paragraph where the active ingredient is listed in column 1 of Part VI of the approved supply list, its toxicity shall be taken as the conventional LD_{50} value given in the corresponding entry in column 2 of that Part.

(4) Account shall also be taken of any fact which suggests that—

    (a)   the preparation in normal use involves a risk to human health;

    (b)   the preparation is less toxic or harmful than its ingredients seem to indicate; or

    (c)   in relation to a particular preparation, the rat is not the most suitable animal for testing.

(5) Classification for properties other than very toxic, toxic or harmful shall be carried out in accordance with the provisions of regulation 5(5).

SCHEDULE 5

Regulation 6(1)

HEADINGS UNDER WHICH PARTICULARS ARE TO BE PROVIDED IN SAFETY DATA SHEETS

The safety data sheet referred to in regulation 6 shall contain the following obligatory headings:

1. Identification of the substance/preparation and company/undertaking.
2. Composition/information on ingredients.
3. Hazards identification.
4. First-aid measures.
5. Fire-fighting measures.
6. Accidental release measures.
7. Handling and storage.
8. Exposure controls/Personal protection.
9. Physical and chemical properties.
10. Stability and reactivity.
11. Toxicological information.
12. Ecological information.
13. Disposal considerations.
14. Transport information.
15. Regulatory information.
16. Other information.

SCHEDULE 6

Regulations 9 and 10(1)

PARTICULARS TO BE SHOWN ON LABELS FOR SUBSTANCES AND PREPARATIONS DANGEROUS FOR SUPPLY AND CERTAIN OTHER PREPARATIONS

PART I
GENERAL PROVISIONS RELATING TO LABELS

Labelling particulars for substances dangerous for supply

1.—(1) In the case of a substance dangerous for supply which is listed in Part I of the approved supply list, the particulars to be shown on the label in accordance with regulation 9(2)(c) shall be the particulars specified for the substance in the relevant entry in column 3 of Part V of that list.

(2) Subject to paragraph 4, in the case of a substance dangerous for supply which is not listed in Part I of the approved supply list the particulars required to be shown on the label in accordance with regulation 9(2)(c) shall be determined from the classification of the substance in accordance with regulation 5 in conjunction with the approved classification and labelling guide.

Labelling particulars for preparations dangerous for supply

2.—(1) Subject to paragraphs 3, 4 and 5, the provisions of this paragraph shall have effect in relation to the labelling of preparations dangerous for supply.

(2) Subject to sub-paragraph (4) below, the chemical names of the substances dangerous for supply present in the preparation shall be shown in accordance with the following rules—

(a) in the case of a preparation classified as requiring the indication of danger T+, T or Xn, only substances requiring those indications of danger present in the preparation in concentrations exceeding the lowest limit (Xn limit) for the substance laid down in column 4 of Part V of the approved supply list, or if no such limit is laid down the relevant limit laid down in Part II of Schedule 3 need be referred to;

(b)   in the case of a preparation classified as requiring the indication of danger C, only substances requiring that indication of danger present in the preparation in concentrations exceeding the lowest limit (Xi limit) for the substance laid down in column 4 of Part V of the approved supply list, or if no such limit is laid down the relevant limit laid down in Part II of Schedule 3 need be referred to; and

(c)   if the preparation is assigned one or more of the standard risk phrases R39, R40, R42, R43, R42/43, R45, R46, R48, R49, R60, R61 or R62, the name of any substance causing the preparation to be so assigned shall be referred to.

(3)   The chemical name referred to in sub-paragraph (2) above shall be—

(a)   in the case of a substance listed in Part I of the approved supply list, the name or one of the names under which it is listed; or

(b)   in the case of a substance not so listed, an internationally recognised name.

(4)   For the purposes of labelling, no account shall be taken of any substance in the preparation if its concentration is less than the concentration referred to in paragraph 18(1) of Part I of Schedule 3.

(5)   Subject to sub-paragraph (4) above, the particulars to be shown on the label in accordance with regulation 9(3)(c)(ii), (iii) and (iv) shall be determined from the classification of the preparation made in accordance with regulation 5 in conjunction with the approved classification and labelling guide.

Derogation for naming the ingredients of certain preparations containing harmful substances

3.—(1)   Where a person can demonstrate to. the Executive that the disclosure of the chemical identity of a substance required to show the indication of danger Xn (not being a substance which would cause the preparation to be assigned one of the risk phrases referred to in paragraph 2(2)(c)) on the label will put at risk the confidential nature of his property, he shall be permitted to refer to that substance either by means of a name that identifies the most important functional chemical groups of the substance or by means of an alternative name giving equivalent information.

(2)   In such a case the manufacturer shall notify the Executive of his intention so to label the preparation.

(3)   Regulation 18 of the Notification of New Substances Regulations 1993 (which relates to confidentiality of information notified) shall apply to information notified under sub-paragraph (2) above as it applies to information notified under those Regulations.

Indications of danger and symbols for substances and preparations dangerous for supply

4.—(1)   Except in the case of a substance dangerous for supply which is listed in Part I of the approved supply list, where a substance or preparation is required to have more than one indication of danger in either of the following groups listed in decreasing order of severity, namely—

(a)   explosive, oxidizing, extremely flammable and highly flammable; or

(b)   very toxic, toxic, corrosive, harmful and irritant,

only one of the indications of danger with its symbol from each group corresponding to the most severe indication of danger in that group needs be shown.

(2)   The risk phrases R 12 (extremely flammable) and R 11 (highly flammable) need not be used if they repeat the indication of danger shown on the label.

Designation of pesticides to which Schedule 4 applies

5.—(1)   A preparation which is a pesticide shall be designated by—

(a)   the trade name or trade designation of the preparation;

(b)   the name and concentration of each active ingredient in the preparation and the concentration thereof shall be expressed—

    (i) in the case of pesticides which are supplied as solids, in aerosol dispensers, or
        as volatile or viscous liquids, as percentage by weight,
    (ii) for other liquids as percentage by weight or as grams per litre, or
    (iii) for gases, as percentage by volume;
 (c) the name of each other ingredient which is—
    (i) required to have the indication of danger T+ or T, if the concentration
        thereof exceeds 0.2 per cent by weight,
    (ii) required to have the indication of danger C or Xn, if the concentration
        thereof exceeds 5 per cent by weight.
(2) The label shall also show—
 (a) the net quantity of the preparation;
 (b) the batch number; and
 (c) in the case of preparations which are required to have the indication of danger
     T+, T or Xn, an indication that the container must not be re-used except in the
     case of containers that are specifically designed for re-use, recharging or refilling
     by the supplier of the pesticide.

PART II
PARTICULAR PROVISIONS CONCERNING CERTAIN PREPARATIONS

A
Special provisions for preparations dangerous for supply

Preparations to be supplied to the general public

1.—(1) The labels on packages of preparations dangerous for supply intended to be
supplied to the general public must bear relevant safety phrase S1, S2, S45 or S46 in
accordance with the approved classification and labelling guide.

(2) When such preparations are classified as very toxic, toxic, or corrosive and where it is
physically impossible to give the information on the package itself, packages containing such
preparations must be accompanied by precise and easily understandable instructions for use
including, where appropriate, instructions for the destruction of the empty package.

Preparations intended for use by spraying

2. The labels on packages containing preparations dangerous for supply intended to be
used for spraying shall bear the safety phrase S23 and safety phrase S38 or S51 assigned in
accordance with the approved classification and labelling guide.

**Preparations containing a substance affected by the risk phrase R33 (danger of
cumulative effects)**

3. When a preparation dangerous for supply contains at least one substance required to
show the risk phrase R33, that phrase must be shown on the label of the preparation when the
concentration of that substance is equal to or higher than 1% unless a different value for that
substance is shown in Part V of the approved supply list.

**Preparations containing a substance affected by the risk phrase R64 (may
cause harm to breast-fed babies)**

4. When a preparation dangerous for supply contains at least one substance required to
show the risk phrase R64, that phrase must be shown on the label of the preparation when the
concentration of that substance is equal to or higher than 1% unless a different value for that
substance is shown in Part V of the approved supply list.

B
Special provisions for preparations whether or not dangerous for supply

Paints and varnishes containing lead

1.—(1) Labels of packages of paints and varnishes containing lead in quantities exceeding 0.15% expressed as weight of metal of the total weight of the preparation, as determined in accordance with ISO Standard 6503/1984, shall show the following particulars—

> "Contains lead. Should not be used on surfaces that are liable to be chewed or sucked by children.".

(2) In the case of packages containing less than 125 millilitres of such preparations the particulars may be—

> "Warning. Contains lead.".

Cyanoacrylate based adhesives

2.—(1) The immediate packages of glues based on cyanoacrylates shall bear the following inscription—

> "Cyanoacrylate.
> Danger.
> Bonds skin and eyes in seconds.
> Keep out of the reach of children.".

(2) Appropriate safety advice shall accompany the package.

Preparations containing isocyanates

3. The package labels of preparations containing isocyanates (whether as monomers, oligomers, prepolymers etc or as mixtures thereof) shall bear the following inscriptions—

> "Contains isocyanates.
> See information supplied by the manufacturer.".

Certain preparations containing epoxy constituents

4. The package labels of preparations containing epoxy constituents with an average molecular weight ≤ 700 shall bear the following inscriptions—

> "Contains epoxy constituents.
> See information supplied by the manufacturer.".

Preparations intended to be sold to the general public that contain active chlorine

5. The package labels of preparations containing more than 1% of active chlorine which are intended to be sold to the general public shall bear the following inscription—

> "Warning! Do not use with other products. May release dangerous gases (chlorine)."

Preparations containing cadmium (alloys) intended to be used for brazing or soldering

6. The package labels of preparations containing cadmium (alloys) intended to be used for brazing or soldering shall bear the following inscription—

> "Warning! Contains cadmium.
> Dangerous fumes are formed during use.
> See information supplied by the manufacturer.
> Comply with the safety instructions.".

SCHEDULE 7

Regulation 12(1)

PROVISIONS RELATING TO CHILD RESISTANT CLOSURES AND TACTILE WARNING DEVICES

The British and International Standards referred in regulation 12 are as follows:—

"BS 2782" means the British Standard Specification for the determination of the viscosity of polymers in the liquid, emulsified or dispersed state using a rotational viscometer working at a defined shear rate, BS 2782: Part 7: Method 730B: 1978 (1991) which was published by the British Standards Institution and came into effect on 31 October 1978;

"ISO 3219" means the International Standard ISO 3219 (December 15 1977 edition) adopted by the International Standards Organisation (ISO);

"BS EN 28317" means the British Standard Specification for packagings resistant to opening by children, BS EN 28317:1993 which was published by the British Standards Institution and came into effect on 15 February 1993;

"ISO 8317" means the International Standard ISO 8317 (1 July 1989 edition) relating to "Child-resistant packaging — Requirements for the testing of reclosable packages adopted by the International Standards Organisation (ISO)";

"BS 6652" means the British Standard Specification for packagings resistant to opening by children, BS 6652:1989 which was published by the British Standards Institution and came into effect on 30 June 1989;

"BS 7280" means the British Standard Specification for the requirements for tactile danger warnings for packaging BS 7280:1990 which was published by the British Standards Institution and came into effect on 28 February 1990;

"EN 272" means European Standard EN 272 (20 August 1989 edition) relating to tactile warning of danger;

"BS 7501" means the British Standard on the general criteria for the operation of testing laboratories BS 7501:1989 which was published by the British Standards Institution and came into effect on 31 October 1989;

"EN 45 000" means European Standards Series 45 000 which sets out the general criteria which laboratories must adhere to in order to obtain accreditation for the certification of child resistant fastenings.

SCHEDULE 8

Regulation 19(9)

MODIFICATIONS TO CERTAIN ENACTMENTS RELATING TO THE FLASH POINT OF FLAMMABLE LIQUIDS

PART I

MODIFICATION TO THE PETROLEUM (CONSOLIDATION) ACT 1928

Column 1 *Provision*	Column 2 *Extent of modification*
Petroleum (Consolidation) Act 1928	
Section 23	
Definition of petroleum-spirit	In the definition of petroleum-spirit for the words "the Chemicals (Hazard Information and Packaging) Regulations 1993 (SI 1993 No 1746)" substitute the words "the Chemicals (Hazard Information and Packaging for Supply) Regulations 1994 (SI 1994/3247)".

PART II
MODIFICATIONS TO INSTRUMENTS

Column 1	Column 2
Provision	*Extent of modification*

Petroleum (Mixtures) Order 1929

Article 1

For the words "the Chemicals (Hazard Information and Packaging) Regulations 1993 (SI 1993 No 1746)" substitute the words "the Chemicals (Hazard Information and Packaging for Supply) Regulations 1994 (SI 1994/3247)".

Part II of the Schedule

Paragraph 1 (liquid mixtures)

For the words "the Chemicals (Hazard Information and Packaging) Regulations 1993" substitute the words "the Chemicals (Hazard Information and Packaging for Supply) Regulations 1994".

Paragraph 2 (sedimentary and viscous mixtures)

In sub-paragraphs (1), (2) and (4) in each place where the words occur, for the words "the Chemicals (Hazard Information and Packaging) Regulations 1993" substitute the words "the Chemicals (Hazard Information and Packaging for Supply) Regulations 1994".

Paragraph 3 (solid mixtures)

For the words "the Chemicals (Hazard Information and Packaging) Regulations 1993" substitute the words "the Chemicals (Hazard Information and Packaging for Supply) Regulations 1994".

The Dry Cleaning Special Regulations 1949

Regulation 2(2)

In the definition of "Flash point", for the words "the Chemicals (Hazard Information and Packaging) Regulations 1993 (SI 1993 No 1746)" substitute the words "the Chemicals (Hazard Information and Packaging for Supply) Regulations 1994 (SI 1994/3247)".

The Factories (Testing of Aircraft Engines and Accessories) Special Regulations 1952

Regulation 2(2)

In the definition of "Petroleum-spirit", for the words "the Chemicals (Hazard Information and Packaging) Regulations 1993 (SI 1993 No 1746)" substitute the words "the Chemicals (Hazard Information and Packaging for Supply) Regulations 1994 (SI 1994/3247)".

Column 1 *Provision*	Column 2 *Extent of modification*
The Shipbuilding and Ship-repairing Regulations 1960	
Regulation 3(2)	In the definition of "Abel closed cup test", for the words "the Chemicals (Hazard Information and Packaging) Regulations 1993 (SI 1993 No 1746)" substitute the words "the Chemicals (Hazard Information and Packaging for Supply) Regulations 1994 (SI 1994/3247)".
The Highly Flammable Liquids and Liquefied Petroleum Gases Regulations 1972	
Regulation 2(2)	In sub-paragraph (a) of the definition of "highly flammable liquid", for the words "the Chemicals (Hazard Information and Packaging) Regulations 1993 (SI 1993 No. 1746)" substitute the words "the Chemicals (Hazard Information and Packaging for Supply) Regulations 1994 (SI 1994/3247)".

THE ELECTRICAL EQUIPMENT (SAFETY) REGULATIONS 1994

(S.I. 1994 No. 3260)

General note. These Regulations, which came into force on 9 January 1995, consolidate with amendments the Low Voltage Electrical Equipment (Safety) Regulations 1989 (S.I. 1989 No.728). They implement the requirements of Council Directive No. 73/23/EEC on the harmonisation of the laws of member States relating to electrical equipment designed for use within certain voltage limits, as amended by Council Directive No. 93/68/EEC (the "CE marking" Directive). The Regulations do not apply to any electrical equipment which is placed on the market before 1 January 1997 and which complies with the provisions of the 1989 Regulations.

Whereas the Secretary of State has, in accordance with section 11(5) of the Consumer Protection Act 1987, consulted such organisations as appear to him to be representative of interests substantially affected by these Regulations, such other persons as he considers appropriate and the Health and Safety Commission:

And whereas the Secretary of State is a Minister designated for the purposes of section 2 of the European Communities Act 1972 in relation to measures for safety and consumer protection as respects electrical equipment and any provisions concerning the composition, labelling, marketing, classification or description of electrical equipment.

Now, therefore, the Secretary of State in exercise of powers conferred on him by section 11 of the said Act of 1987 and by section 2 of the said Act of 1972 and of all other powers enabling him in that behalf hereby makes the following Regulations:—

1. Citation and commencement. These Regulations may be cited as the Electrical Equipment (Safety) Regulations 1994 and shall come into force on 9th January 1995.

2. Revocation, defence and consequential amendment.—(1) The Low Voltage Electrical Equipment (Safety) Regulations 1989 are hereby revoked provided that the said Regulations of 1989 shall continue to apply to electrical equipment to which these Regulations do not apply by virtue of paragraph (4) of regulation 4 below.

(2) In Schedule 1 to the Provision and Use of Work Equipment Regulations 1992 for paragraph 1 there shall be substituted—

"1. Council Directive 73/23/EEC on the harmonization of the laws of Member States relating to electrical equipment designed for use within certain voltage limits (OJ No. L77, 26.3.1973, p. 29) as amended by Article 13 of Council Directive 93/68/EEC (OJ No. L220, 30.8.1993, p. 1.)."

(3) In any proceedings against a person for an offence under any of the relevant statutory provisions (as defined in section 53(1) of the Health and Safety at Work etc Act 1974 or article 2(2) of the Health and Safety at Work (Northern Ireland) Order 1978 which impose requirements with respect to any matter it shall be a defence for that person to show that the requirements of these Regulations were satisfied in relation to that matter.

(4)   Where an improvement notice or a prohibition notice has been served on any person pursuant to section 21 or, as the case may be, section 22 of the Health and Safety at Work etc Act 1974 (or pursuant to article 23 or, as the case may be, article 24 of the Health and Safety at Work (Northern Ireland) Order 1978), if the person upon whom the notice was served appeals to an industrial tribunal pursuant to section 24 of the said Act (or article 26 of the said Order) and shows that the notice relates to any matter in respect of which the requirements of these Regulations are satisfied, the tribunal shall cancel the notice.

3.   Interpretation.—(1) In these Regulations—
"the 1987 Act" means the Consumer Protection Act 1987;
"authorised representative" means a representative established within the Community appointed by a manufacturer of electrical equipment to act on his behalf in relation to these Regulations;
"the CE marking Directive" means Council Directive No 93/68/EEC;
"CE marking" means the CE conformity marking referred to in regulation 9 consisting of the initials "CE" taking the form of the specimen given in Schedule 1;
"the Community" means the European Economic Community and other States in the European Economic Area;
"electrical equipment" means, unless the context otherwise requires, any electrical equipment to which these Regulations apply by virtue of regulation 4 below;
"EEA Agreement" means the Agreement on the European Economic Area signed at Oporto on 2 May 1992 as adjusted by the Protocol signed at Brussels on 17 March 1993;
"end user" means the consumer which expression shall include an industrial and commercial consumer;
"harmonised standard" means a standard harmonised in accordance with Article 5 of the low voltage Directive;
"international safety provision" means a safety provision of a standard which has been published by the International Commission on the Rules for the Approval of Electrical Equipment or the International Electrotechnical Commission and which has been published in the Official Journal of the Communities pursuant to Article 6 of the low voltage Directive;
"the low voltage Directive" means Council Directive No 73/23/EEC on the harmonisation of the laws of member States relating to electrical equipment designed for use within certain voltage limits as amended by the CE marking Directive;
"member State" means a State which is a Contracting Party to the EEA Agreement but until the EEA Agreement comes into force in relation to Liechtenstein does not include the state of Liechtenstein;
"national safety provision" means a safety provision which has the force of law in a member State of the Community or which is contained in a standard published and not withdrawn by a national standards body, not being a safety provision which is to the same effect as a safety provision of a harmonised standard or as an international safety provision;
"national standards body" means a body which has been notified under Article 11 of the low voltage Directive for the purposes of Article 5 of that Directive;
"safe" has the same meaning as in section 19(1) of the 1987 Act, except that, for the purpose of these Regulations, the references in that subsection to "risk"

shall be construed as including references to any risk of—
(a) death or injury to domestic animals; and
(b) damage to property;
and as excluding any risk arising from the improper installation or maintenance of the electrical equipment in question or from the use of the equipment in applications for which it is not made;
"safety provision" means a provision made for the purpose of ensuring that the equipment in question is safe;
"supply" (except in reference to the electricity supply) includes offering to supply, agreeing to supply, exposing for supply and possessing for supply, and cognate expressions shall be construed accordingly.

(2) For the purposes of regulation 7(2) below a national safety provision is applicable to equipment in a particular member State if—
(a) the provision has the force of law in that member State or the national standards body publishing it has its principal office there, and
(b) the equipment was not manufactured in any other member State.

(3) Any reference in these Regulations to an electric shock is a reference to an electric shock of such severity as to be liable to cause death or personal injury.

4. Application.—(1) Subject to paragraphs (2) and (3) below, these Regulations apply to any electrical equipment (including any electrical apparatus or device) designed or adapted for use with voltage (in the case of alternating current) of not less than 50 volts nor more than 1,000 volts or (in the case of direct current) of not less than 75 volts nor more than 1,500 volts.

(2) These Regulations do not apply to the electrical equipment set out in Schedule 2 to these Regulations.

(3) These Regulations do not apply to any electrical equipment supplied for export to a place which is not within any member State.

(4) These Regulations do not apply to any electrical equipment which is placed on the market before 1st January 1997 and which complies with the provisions of the Low Voltage Electrical Equipment (Safety) Regulations 1989.

5. Requirement for electrical equipment to be safe etc.—(1) Electrical equipment shall be—
(a) safe;
(b) constructed in accordance with principles generally accepted within the member States as constituting good engineering practice in relation to safety matters and in particular shall be designed and constructed to ensure that it is safe when connected to the electricity supply system by providing a level of protection against electric shock which relies on a combination of insulation and the protective earthing conductor contained within the electricity supply system or which achieves that level of protection by other means; and
(c) in conformity with the principal elements of the safety objectives for electrical equipment set out in Schedule 3 to these Regulations.

(2) In determining whether electrical equipment satisfies the requirements of paragraph (1) above, no regard shall be had to any liability of the equipment to cause radio-electrical interference.

(3) In determining whether electrical equipment which—
(a) has previously been supplied to any end user; or

(b) is supplied solely by virtue of its being hired out whether in connection with the supply of other goods and services or otherwise provided that it satisfies the requirements of sub-paragraph (a) above

satisfies the requirements of paragraph 1 above, no regard shall be had to General Condition 1(b) of Schedule 3.

6. Harmonised standards. Electrical equipment which satisfies the safety provisions of harmonised standards shall be taken to comply with the requirements of regulation 5(1) above unless there are reasonable grounds for suspecting that the electrical equipment does not so comply.

7. Conformity with other standards and requirements.—(1) Where there are no relevant harmonised standards, electrical equipment which satisfies international safety provisions shall be taken to comply with the requirements of regulation 5(1) above unless there are reasonable grounds for suspecting that the electrical equipment does not so comply.

(2) Where there are no relevant harmonised standards and no relevant international safety provisions, electrical equipment which has been manufactured in accordance with the national safety provisions applicable to that equipment in a member State and the compliance of the equipment with such provisions results in the equipment being at the time when the equipment is supplied in the United Kingdom at least as safe as it would be if it satisfied the requirements of regulation 5(1) above shall be taken to comply with the requirements of regulation 5(1) above unless there are reasonable grounds for suspecting that the electrical equipment does not so comply.

8. Reports on safety etc of electrical equipment. Where the conformity of any electrical equipment with the requirements of regulation 5(1) is called into question (whether in any proceedings or otherwise) any report prepared by a body notified in accordance with the procedure set out in Article 11 of the low voltage Directive for the purpose of Article 8.2 of that Directive may be relied upon for the purpose of establishing that the equipment does in fact satisfy those requirements and due regard shall be had to any such report by any person or court by whom the question of conformity falls to be determined.

9. CE marking.—(1) Subject to regulation 12, the manufacturer of electrical equipment or his authorised representative shall affix to all electrical equipment to which these Regulations apply (or to their packaging, instruction sheet or guarantee certificate) in a visible, easily legible and indelible form the CE marking as shown in Schedule 1 by way of confirmation that the electrical equipment conforms with all the requirements of these Regulations which relate to it.

(2) No person shall affix to electrical equipment any markings liable to deceive third parties as to the meaning and form of the CE marking affixed in accordance with these Regulations or which reduces the visibility or legibility of the CE marking so affixed.

(3) (a) Where electrical equipment is subject to other legally binding Community provisions which also provide for the affixing of the CE marking, the latter shall, subject to (b) below be taken to indicate conformity with the requirements of such provisions.
    (b) Where a Community provision referred to in (a) above allows the manufacturer, during a transitional period, a choice of arrangements the CE marking shall indicate conformity only in respect of those requirements

of the provision which are applied by the manufacturer and particulars of the provisions as published in the Official Journal of the European Communities must be given in the documents, notices or instructions which are required by the provisions and accompany the electrical equipment.

10. EC declaration of conformity. Subject to regulation 12, the manufacturer of electrical equipment or his authorised representative shall draw up in respect of all electrical equipment to which these Regulations apply a written declaration of conformity which shall comprise:—
    (a)   the name and address of the manufacturer or his authorised representative;
    (b)   a description of the electrical equipment;
    (c)   a reference to the harmonised standards;
    (d)   where appropriate, references to the specifications with which conformity is declared;
    (e)   identification of the signatory who has been empowered to enter into commitments on behalf of the manufacturer or his authorised representative; and
    (f)   the last two digits of the year in which the CE marking was affixed.

11. Internal Production Control.—(1) Subject to regulation 12 and to paragraphs (2) and (3) below, the manufacturer of electrical equipment shall compile the technical documentation listed in Schedule 4 and keep it for a period of at least ten years after manufacture of electrical equipment of that model has ceased, together with the EC declaration of conformity referred to in regulation 10 above, available for inspection by an enforcement authority (which for the purposes of this regulation shall include, where appropriate, the Health and Safety Executive and the Northern Ireland Department for Economic Development) or any of its officers.

(2) Where the manufacturer of electrical equipment is not established in the Community, the technical documentation shall be kept in the manner provided for in paragraph (1) above by the manufacturer's authorised representative.

(3) Where the manufacturer of electrical equipment is established outside the Community and has no authorised representative established in the Community, the technical documentation shall be kept in the manner provided for in paragraph (1) above by the person who supplies the electrical equipment on the first occasion that it is supplied in the Community.

(4) Every manufacturer of electrical equipment shall ensure that his manufacturing process produces electrical equipment which conforms to the technical documentation referred to in paragraph (1).

12. Secondhand and hired equipment. Regulations 9(1), 10 and 11 shall not apply in relation to electrical equipment which—
    (a)   has previously been supplied to any end user; or
    (b)   is supplied solely by virtue of its being hired out whether in connection with the supply of other goods and services or otherwise provided that it satisfies the provisions of sub-paragraph (a) above.

13. Compliance Notices.—(1) Except in the case of electrical equipment which in the opinion of the enforcement authority is likely to jeopardise the safety or health of any person, where an enforcement authority has reasonable grounds for suspecting that the affixing of the CE marking to electrical equipment to which these Regulations apply involves a contravention of these Regulations or any part of them, it may serve a notice (a "compliance notice") on the manufacturer of that electrical equipment or his authorised representative established in the Community and in such a case sections 13, 14, 16 or 17 of the 1987 Act or sections 21 or 22 of the 1974 Act shall not be applied until such a notice has been so served and the person upon whom it has been served has failed to comply with its requirements.

(2) Schedule 5 shall have effect in respect of a compliance notice.

14. Prohibition on supply.—(1) Subject to paragraph (2) below, no person shall supply any electrical equipment in respect of which the requirements of regulations 5(1) and 9(1) above are not satisfied.

(2) For the purposes of this regulation a supply shall include the provision of electrical equipment by a manufacturer for use in his own premises and where a supply consists solely of such provision paragraph (1) above shall apply to the supply as if the words "and 9(1)" were omitted.

15. Duties of enforcement authorities. Every authority and council on whom a duty is imposed by virtue of section 27 of the 1987 Act—
  (a) shall have regard, in performing that duty, in so far as it relates to any provision of these Regulations, to matters specified in any direction issued by the Secretary of State with respect to that provision; and
  (b) shall give immediate notice to the Secretary of State of any suspension notice served by it or any application made by it for an order for forfeiture of any goods to which these Regulations apply or any other thing done in respect of any such goods for the purposes of or in connection with sections 14 to 17 of that Act.

16. Commencement of Proceedings. Subject to regulation 17(3), in England, Wales and Northern Ireland a magistrates' court may try an information (in the case of England and Wales) or a complaint (in the case of Northern Ireland) in respect of an offence committed under section 12 of the 1987 Act in relation to a contravention of these Regulations if (in the case of England and Wales) the information is laid or (in the case of Northern Ireland) the complaint is made within twelve months from the time when the offence is committed, and in Scotland summary proceedings for such an offence may be begun at any time within twelve months from the time when the offence is committed.

17. Regulations to be treated as safety regulations within the meaning of the 1987 Act.—(1) Subject to paragraph (2) below, these Regulations shall be treated for all purposes as if they were safety regulations within the meaning of section 45(1) of the 1987 Act.

(2) Where a contravention of regulation 14 above arises from the supply of electrical equipment which fails to satisfy the requirements of regulation 5(1) above or of goods which would cause the relevant equipment to contravene those requirements because there is in each case a risk of death or injury to domestic animals or damage to property, or both, but no risk of the death of a person or of personal injury, the person who contravenes regulation 14 shall be guilty of an offence punishable on summary conviction with imprisonment for not more than three months or with a fine not exceeding level five on the standard scale.

(3) Without prejudice to the provisions of paragraphs (1) and (2) above and the provisions of Part IV of the 1987 Act, in so far as these Regulations apply in relation to such electrical equipment as is mentioned in paragraph (4) below—

  (a) the Health and Safety Executive ("the Executive") (or, for Northern Ireland, the Department for Economic Development ("the Department")) may make arrangements for the enforcement of these Regulations, and

  (b) the provisions of the Health and Safety at Work etc Act 1974 ("the 1974 Act") (or the Health and Safety at Work (Northern Ireland) Order 1978 ("the 1978 Order")) mentioned in paragraph (5) below shall apply as if—

  (i)   these Regulations were health and safety regulations and, accordingly, relevant statutory provisions within the meaning of the 1974 Act (or the 1978 Order),

  (ii) any reference therein to an enforcing authority were a reference to the Executive (or the Department),

  (iii) any reference therein to any provision of the 1974 Act (or the 1978 Order) were a reference to that provision as, and so far as, it is applied by this paragraph,

and section 34(3) of the 1974 Act and article 32(3) of the 1978 Order shall have effect with the substitution for the words "six months" of the words "twelve months".

(4) The electrical equipment referred to in paragraph (3) above is—

  (a) electrical equipment designed for use or operation, whether exclusively or not, by persons at work; and

  (b) electrical equipment designed for use, otherwise than at work, in non-domestic premises made available to persons at a place where they may use the equipment provided for their use there.

(5) The provisions referred to in paragraph (3) above are sections 18(6) and (7)(b), sections 19 to 26 (save for subsections (3), (4) and (6) of section 23), subsections (1)(e) to (h) and (o), (2), (2A), (3) (save for the words "Subject to any provision made by virtue of section 15(6)(d) or (e) or by virtue of paragraph 2(2) of Schedule 3") and (4)(e) of section 33, section 34(3), (4) and (5), sections 35 to 39 (save for subsection (3) of section 36) and section 42 of the 1974 Act and articles 2(3), 21 to 28, paragraphs (1)(e) to (l), (2), (4), (5)(d) and (e) and (6) of article 31, paragraphs (3) and (4) of article 32 and articles 33 to 36 of the Order.

(6) The Executive or the Department shall, where action has been taken by it to prohibit or restrict the supply of any electrical equipment which bears the CE marking, forthwith inform the Secretary of State of the action taken, and the reason for it.

18.   Requirement to give information about electrical equipment which does not bear the CE marking.   A person who supplies electrical equipment which does not bear the CE marking laid down in regulation 9(1) shall, on his being required at a reasonable time to give such information, to an enforcement authority, the Executive or the Department, or to any of its officers, all the information which he has about—

  (a) the date when the electrical equipment was first supplied in the Community; and

  (b) the basis on which the electrical equipment does not bear the CE marking and information.

SCHEDULE 1

Regulation 3(1)

SPECIMEN FORM OF CE MARKING TO BE PLACED ON OR TO ACCOMPANY ELECTRICAL EQUIPMENT

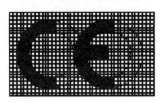

—If the CE marking is reduced or enlarged the proportions given in the above graduated drawing must be respected.

—The various components of the CE marking must have substantially the same vertical dimension, which may not be less than 5 mm.

SCHEDULE 2

Regulation 4(2)

ELECTRICAL EQUIPMENT EXCLUDED FROM THESE REGULATIONS

Equipment for use in an explosive atmosphere

Equipment for radiology and medical purposes

Parts for goods lifts and passenger lifts

Electricity supply meters

Plugs and socket outlets for domestic use

Fence controllers

Specialised electrical equipment for use on ships, aircraft or railways, which complies with the safety provisions drawn up by international bodies in which the member States participate.

SCHEDULE 3

Regulation 5(1)

PRINCIPAL ELEMENTS OF THE SAFETY OBJECTIVES FOR ELECTRICAL EQUIPMENT DESIGNED FOR USE WITHIN CERTAIN VOLTAGE LIMITS

1. **General conditions**

    (a) The essential characteristics, the recognition and observance of which will ensure that electrical equipment will be used safely and in applications for which it was made, shall be marked on the equipment, or, if this is not possible, on an accompanying notice.

    (b) The manufacturer's brand name or trade mark should be clearly printed on the electrical equipment or, where that is not possible, on the packaging.

    (c) The electrical equipment, together with its component parts should be made in such a way as to ensure that it can be safely and properly assembled and connected.

    (d) The electrical equipment should be so designed and manufactured as to ensure that protection against the hazards set out in points 2 and 3 of this Schedule is assured providing that the equipment is used in applications for which it was made and is adequately maintained.

2. Protection against hazards arising from the electrical equipment

(a) Persons and domestic animals must be adequately protected against danger of physical injury or other harm which might be caused by electrical contact direct or indirect;

(b) Temperatures, arcs or radiation which would cause a danger must not be produced;

(c) Persons, domestic animals and property must be adequately protected against non-electrical dangers caused by the electrical equipment which are revealed by experience;

(d) The insulation must be suitable for foreseeable conditions.

3. Protection against hazards which may be caused by external influences on the electrical equipment

(a) The electrical equipment must meet the expected mechanical requirements in such a way that persons, domestic animals and property are not endangered;

(b) The electrical equipment must be resistant to non-mechanical influences in expected environmental conditions, in such a way that persons, domestic animals and property are not endangered;

(c) In foreseeable conditions of overload the electrical equipment must not endanger persons, domestic animals and property.

SCHEDULE 4

Regulation 11(1)

TECHNICAL DOCUMENTATION

1.   Technical documentation must be such as to enable enforcement authorities to assess the conformity of electrical equipment to the requirements of these Regulations. It must, as far as is relevant for such assessment, cover the design, manufacture and operation of electrical equipment.

2.   The technical documentation must include:—

(a) a general description of the electrical equipment;

(b) conceptual design and manufacturing drawings and schemes of components, sub-assemblies, circuits etc;

(c) descriptions and explanations necessary for the understanding of the drawings and schemes referred to in (b) and the operation of the electrical equipment;

(d) a list of the standards applied in full or in part and descriptions of the solutions adopted to satisfy the requirements of regulation 5(1) where standards have not been applied;

(e) results of design calculations made, examinations carried out etc;

(f) test reports.

SCHEDULE 5

Regulation 13

COMPLIANCE NOTICE

1.   The notice shall—

(a) specify the description of the electrical equipment to which the notice relates;

(b) state that the enforcement authority suspects that affixing of the CE marking to the electrical equipment involves a contravention of a provision or provisions of these Regulations and the reasons for that suspicion;

(c) specify the provision or provisions referred to in paragraph (b) above;

(d) require that person—

(i) to secure that any electrical equipment to which the notice relates conforms as regards the provisions concerning the CE marking and to end the infringement within such period as may be specified by the notice; or

      (ii) to provide evidence within that period to the satisfaction of the enforcement authority that all the provisions of these Regulations have been complied with; and

  (e) warn that person that if the non-conformity continues (or if satisfactory evidence has not been produced under sub-paragraph (ii) of paragraph (d) above) within the period specified in the notice, further action may be taken under these Regulations in respect of that electrical equipment or any electrical equipment of the same type supplied by that person.

2.   The notice may include directions as to the measures to be taken by that person to secure conformity of that electrical equipment with the provisions of these Regulations including different ways of securing conformity.

THE HEALTH AND SAFETY AT WORK ETC ACT 1974 (APPLICATION OUTSIDE GREAT BRITAIN) ORDER 1995

(S.I. 1995 No. 263)

General note. This Order, which came into force on 15 March 1995, revokes and replaces with modifications the Health and Safety at Work etc Act 1974 (Application outside Great Britain) Order 1989 (S.I. 1989 No. 840). The main changes of substance are the application of the Health and Safety at Work etc Act 1974, ss. 1 to 59 and 80 to 82, to wells and to pipelines. Breach of a duty under this Order gives rise to civil liability.

Her Majesty, in exercise of the powers conferred by section 84(3) and (4) of the Health and Safety at Work etc Act 1974, is pleased, by and with the advice of Her Privy Council, to order, and it is hereby ordered, as follows:—

1. Citation, commencement and revocation.—(1) This Order may be cited as the Health and Safety at Work etc Act 1974 (Application outside Great Britain) Order 1995 and shall come into force on 15th March 1995.

(2) The Health and Safety at Work etc Act 1974 (Application outside Great Britain) Order 1989 is hereby revoked.

2. Interpretation.—(1) In this Order, unless the context otherwise requires—
"the 1974 Act" means the Health and Safety at Work etc Act 1974;
"designated area" means any area designated by order under section 1(7) of the Continental Shelf Act 1964 and "within a designated area" includes over and under it;
"offshore installation" shall be construed in accordance with article 4(2) and (3) of this Order;
"the prescribed provisions of the 1974 Act" means sections 1 to 59 and 80 to 82 of the 1974 Act;
"stand-by vessel" means a vessel which is ready to give assistance in the event of an emergency on or near an offshore installation;
"territorial waters" means United Kingdom territorial waters adjacent to Great Britain and "within territorial waters" includes on, over and under them;
"vessel" includes a hovercraft and any floating structure which is capable of being staffed.

(2) For the purposes of this Order, any structures and devices on top of a well shall be treated as forming part of the well.

(3) For the purposes of this Order, a person shall be deemed to be engaged in diving operations throughout any period from the time when he commences to prepare for diving until the time when—
(a) he is no longer subjected to raised pressure;
(b) he has normal inert gas partial pressure in his tissues; and
(c) if he entered the water, he has left it,

and diving operations include the activity of any person in connection with the health and safety of a person who is, or is deemed to be, engaged in diving operations.

3.   Application of the 1974 Act outside Great Britain.—(1) The prescribed provisions of the 1974 Act shall, to the extent specified in the following articles of this Order, apply to and in relation to the premises and activities outside Great Britain which are so specified as those provisions apply within Great Britain.

(2)   The reference in paragraph (1) of this article to premises and activities includes a reference to any person, article or substance on those premises or engaged in or, as the case may be, used or for use in connection with any such activity, but does not include a reference to an aircraft which is airborne.

4.   Offshore installations.—(1) The prescribed provisions of the 1974 Act shall apply within territorial waters or a designated area to and in relation to—
   (a)   any offshore installation and any activity on it;
   (b)   any activity, including diving operations, in connection with an offshore installation, or any activity which is immediately preparatory thereto, whether carried on from the installation itself, on or from a vessel or in any other manner, other than—
      (i)   transporting, towing or navigating the installation; and
      (ii)   any activity on or from a vessel being used as a stand-by vessel;
   (c)   diving operations involving the survey and preparation of the sea bed for an offshore installation.

(2)   In this Order "offshore installation" means—
   (a)   the fixed structures consisting of six towers referred to in the Schedule to this Order as NSR M-1 and NSR R-1, NSR R-2, NSR R-3, NSR R-4 and NSR R-5 and settled on the sea bed at the locations specified in the Schedule and the related cables between each of those towers at sea bed level and the related cables which lie or extend outside the said locations; or
   (b)   subject to paragraph (3) of this article, a structure which is, or is to be, or has been, used while standing or stationed in water, or on the foreshore or other land intermittently covered with water—
      (i)   for the exploitation, or exploration with a view to exploitation, of mineral resources by means of a well;
      (ii)   for the storage of gas in or under the shore or bed of any water or the recovery of gas so stored;
      (iii)   for the conveyance of things by means of a pipe; or
      (iv)   mainly for the provision of accommodation for persons who work on or from a structure falling within any of the provisions of this sub-paragraph,
      and which is not an excepted structure.

(3)   For the purposes of paragraph (2)(b) of this article, the excepted structures are—
   (a)   a structure which is connected with dry land by a permanent structure providing access at all times and for all purposes;
   (b)   a well;
   (c)   a structure which has ceased to be used for any of the purposes specified in paragraph (2)(b) of this article and has since been used for a purpose not so specified;
   (d)   a mobile structure which has been taken out of use and is not for the time being intended to be used for any of the purposes specified in paragraph (2)(b) of this article; and
   (e)   any part of a pipeline.

5.   Wells.—(1) Subject to paragraph (2) of this article, the prescribed provisions of the 1974 Act shall apply within territorial waters or a designated area to and in relation to—

  (a)   a well and any activity in connection with it; and
  (b)   an activity which is immediately preparatory to any activity in sub-paragraph (a) above.

(2)   Paragraph (1) of this article includes keeping a vessel on station for the purpose of working on a well but otherwise does not include navigation or an activity connected with navigation.

6.   Pipelines.—(1) The prescribed provisions of the 1974 Act shall apply within territorial waters or a designated area to and in relation to—

  (a)   any pipeline;
  (b)   any pipeline works;
  (c)   the following activities in connection with pipeline works—
      (i)   the loading, unloading, fuelling or provisioning of a vessel;
      (ii) the loading, unloading, fuelling, repair and maintenance of an aircraft on a vessel,

being in either case a vessel which is engaged in pipeline works.

(2)   In this article—

  "pipeline" means a pipe or system of pipes for the conveyance of any thing, together with—
      (a)   any apparatus for inducing or facilitating the flow of any thing through, or through a part of, the pipe or system;
      (b)   any apparatus for treating or cooling any thing which is to flow through, or through part of, the pipe or system;
      (c)   valves, valve chambers and similar works which are annexed to, or incorporated in the course of, the pipe or system;
      (d)   apparatus for supplying energy for the operation of any such apparatus or works as are mentioned in the preceding paragraphs;
      (e)   apparatus for the transmission of information for the operation of the pipe or system;
      (f)   apparatus for the cathodic protection of the pipe or system; and
      (g)   a structure used or to be used solely for the support of a part of the pipe or system;

  but not including a pipeline of which no initial or terminal point is situated in the United Kingdom or within territorial waters, United Kingdom territorial waters adjacent to Northern Ireland, or a designated area;

  "pipeline works" means—
      (a)   assembling or placing a pipeline or length of pipeline including the provision of internal or external protection for it;
      (b)   inspecting, testing, maintaining, adjusting, repairing, altering or renewing a pipeline or length of pipeline;
      (c)   changing the position of or dismantling or removing a pipeline or length of pipeline;
      (d)   opening the bed of the sea for the purposes of the works mentioned in sub-paragraphs (a) to (c) of this definition, and tunnelling or boring for those purposes;
      (e)   any activities incidental to the activities described in sub-paragraphs (a) to (d) of this definition;

(f) diving operations in connection with any of the works mentioned in sub-paragraphs (a) to (e) of this definition or for the purpose of determining whether a place is suitable as part of the site of a proposed pipeline and the carrying out of surveying operations for settling the route of a proposed pipeline.

7. Mines.—(1) The prescribed provisions of the 1974 Act shall apply to and in relation to the working of a mine, and to work for the purpose of or in connection with the working of any part of a mine, within territorial waters or extending beyond them.

(2) In this article "mine" and "working of a mine" have the same meaning as in the Mines and Quarries Act 1954.

8. Other activities within territorial waters. The prescribed provisions of the 1974 Act shall apply within territorial waters to and in relation to—
  (a) the construction, reconstruction, alteration, repair, maintenance, cleaning, demolition and dismantling of any building or other structure not being a vessel, or any preparation for any such activity;
  (b) the loading, unloading, fuelling or provisioning of a vessel;
  (c) diving operations;
  (d) the construction, reconstruction, finishing, refitting, repair, maintenance, cleaning or breaking up of a vessel except when carried out by the master or any officer or member of the crew of that vessel; and
  (e) the maintaining on a station of a vessel which would be an offshore installation were it not a structure to which paragraph (3)(d) of article 4 of this Order applies,

except that this article shall not apply to vessels which are registered outside the United Kingdom and are on passage through territorial waters.

9. Legal proceedings.—(1) Proceedings for any offence under section 33 of the 1974 Act, being an offence to which that section applies by virtue of this Order, may be taken, and the offence may for all incidental purposes be treated as having been committed, in any place in Great Britain.

(2) Section 3 of the Territorial Waters Jurisdiction Act 1878 (which requires certain consents for the institution of proceedings) shall not apply to proceedings for any offence to which paragraph (1) of this article relates.

Miscellaneous provisions

10. The prescribed provisions of the 1974 Act shall apply in accordance with this Order to individuals whether or not they are British subjects, and to bodies corporate whether or not they are incorporated under the law of any part of the United Kingdom.

11. Nothing in this Order except article 9(2) of this Order shall be taken to limit or prejudice the operation which any Act or legislative instrument may, apart from this Order, have in territorial waters or elsewhere.

SCHEDULE

Article 4(2)(a)

LOCATION OF TOWERS

Title		Degrees	Minutes	Seconds	
Master 1	Latitude	53	44	45	N
NSR M-1	Longitude	02	33	30	E
Remote 1	Latitude	53	56	00	N
NSR R-1	Longitude	02	24	00	E
Remote 2	Latitude	53	55	45	N
NSR R-2	Longitude	02	51	00	E
Remote 3	Latitude	53	38	30	N
NSR R-3	Longitude	02	56	45	E
Remote 4	Latitude	53	29	57	N
NSR R-4	Longitude	02	30	50	E
Remote 5	Latitude	53	42	00	N
NSR R-5	Longitude	02	08	30	E

THE OFFSHORE INSTALLATIONS AND PIPELINE WORKS (MANAGEMENT AND ADMINISTRATION) REGULATIONS 1995

(S.I. 1995 No. 738)

General note. These Regulations, which came into force for most purposes on 20 June 1995, contain requirements for the management and administration of offshore oil and gas installations, for health and safety purposes. The Regulations give effect, in relation to offshore installations in territorial waters adjacent to Great Britain or in the UK sector of the continental shelf, to certain provisions of Council Directive 92/91/EEC concerning the minimum requirements for improving the safety and health protection of workers in the mineral-extracting industries through drilling. The Regulations also give effect to Art. 11.2 of Council Directive 89/391/EEC on the introduction of measures to encourage improvements in the safety and health of workers at work (in part). Breach of a duty under these Regulations gives rise to civil liability; see the Health and Safety at Work etc. Act 1974, s. 47(2).

ARRANGEMENT OF REGULATIONS

The Secretary of State, in exercise of the powers conferred on him by sections 15(1), (2), (3)(a) and (5)(b), and 82(3)(a) of, and paragraphs 6, 14, 15(1) and 16 of Schedule 3 to, the Health and Safety at Work etc Act 1974 and of all other powers enabling him in that behalf and for the purpose of giving effect without modifications to proposals submitted to him by the Health and Safety Commission under section 11(2)(d) of the 1974 Act after the carrying out by the said Commission of consultations in accordance with section 50(3) of that Act, hereby makes the following Regulations:

1.   Citation and commencement. These Regulations may be cited as the Offshore Installations and Pipeline Works (Management and Administration) Regulations 1995 and shall come into force on 20th June 1995, except regulation 23(2), which shall come into force on 20th June 1997.

2.   Interpretation.—(1) In these Regulations, unless the context otherwise requires—

"the 1969 Act" means the Employers' Liability (Compulsory Insurance) Act 1969;

"the 1971 Act" means the Mineral Workings (Offshore Installations) Act 1971;

"the 1995 Order" means the Health and Safety at Work etc Act 1974 (Application outside Great Britain) Order 1995;

"apparatus or works" means—

(a)   apparatus or works described in paragraphs (a) to (f); and

(b)   a structure described in paragraph (g),

of the definition of "pipeline" in article 6(2) of the 1995 Order;

"associated structure" means, in relation to an offshore installation, a vessel, aircraft or hovercraft attendant on the installation or any floating structure used in connection with the installation;

"concession owner" in relation to an offshore installation means the person who at any time has the right to exploit or explore mineral resources in any area, or to store gas in any area and to recover gas so stored if, at that time, the installation is, or is to be, used in the exercise of that right;

"duty holder" means—

(a)   in relation to a fixed installation, the operator; and

(b)   in relation to a mobile installation, the owner;

"fixed installation" means an offshore installation other than a mobile installation;

"installation manager" means, in relation to an offshore installation, the person appointed for the purposes of regulation 6(1)(a) who is for the time being in charge of it;

"mobile installation" means an offshore installation (other than a floating production platform) which can be moved from place to place without major dismantling or modification, whether or not it has its own motive power;

"offshore installation" shall be construed in accordance with regulation 3;

"operator" in relation to a fixed installation means the person appointed by a concession owner to execute any function of organising or supervising any operation to be carried out by such installation or, where no such person has been appointed, the concession owner;

"owner" in relation to a mobile installation means the person who controls the operation of the installation;

"pipeline" means a pipeline within the meaning of article 6(2) of the 1995 Order;

"pipeline works" means pipeline works within the meaning of article 6(2) of the 1995 Order;

"relevant employee" means an employee—
- (a) who is ordinarily resident in the United Kingdom, or
- (b) who is not ordinarily resident in the United Kingdom but who has been present in the United Kingdom and relevant waters in the course of employment there for a continuous period of not less than 7 days;

"relevant waters" means—
- (a) tidal waters and parts of the sea in or adjacent to Great Britain up to the seaward limits of territorial waters; and
- (b) any area designated by order under section 1(7) of the Continental Shelf Act 1964; and

"vessel" includes a hovercraft and any floating structure which is capable of being staffed.

(2) Any reference in these Regulations to operating an offshore installation is a reference to using the installation for any of the purposes described in regulation 3(1).

(3) For the purpose of these Regulations any structures and devices on top of a well shall be treated as forming part of the well.

(4) Unless the context otherwise requires, any reference in these Regulations to—
- (a) a numbered regulation is a reference to the regulation in these Regulations so numbered;
- (b) a numbered paragraph is a reference to the paragraph so numbered in the regulation in which the reference appears; and
- (c) a numbered Schedule is a reference to the Schedule in these Regulations so numbered.

3. Meaning of "offshore installation".—(1) Subject to the provisions of this regulation, in these Regulations the expression "offshore installation" means a structure which is, or is to be, or has been used, while standing or stationed in relevant waters, or on the foreshore or other land intermittently covered with water—
- (a) for the exploitation, or exploration with a view to exploitation, of mineral resources by means of a well;
- (b) for the storage of gas in or under the shore or bed of relevant waters or the recovery of gas so stored;
- (c) for the conveyance of things by means of a pipe; or
- (d) mainly for the provision of accommodation for persons who work on or from a structure falling within any of the provisions of this paragraph,

and which is not an excepted structure.

(2) For the purposes of paragraph (1), the excepted structures are—
- (a) a structure which is connected with dry land by a permanent structure providing access at all times and for all purposes;
- (b) a well;
- (c) a structure or device which does not project above the sea at any state of the tide;
- (d) a structure which has ceased to be used for any of the purposes specified in paragraph (1), and has since been used for a purpose not so specified;
- (e) a mobile structure which has been taken out of use and is not for the time being intended to be used for any of the purposes specified in paragraph (1); and
- (f) any part of a pipeline.

(3) For the purposes of these Regulations there shall be deemed to be part of an offshore installation—

    (a) any well for the time being connected to it by pipe or cable;

    (b) such part of any pipeline connected to it as is within 500 metres of any part of its main structure;

    (c) any apparatus or works which are situated—

        (i) on or affixed to its main structure; or

        (ii) wholly or partly within 500 metres of any part of its main structure and associated with a pipe or system of pipes connected to any part of that installation.

(4) Where two or more structures are, or are to be, connected permanently above the sea at high tide they shall for the purposes of these Regulations be deemed to comprise a single offshore installation.

4. Application.—(1) These Regulations shall apply—

    (a) in Great Britain; and

    (b) to and in relation to offshore installations, wells, pipelines and activities outside Great Britain to which sections 1 to 59 and 80 to 82 of the Health and Safety at Work etc Act 1974 apply by virtue of articles 4(1) and (2)(b), 5 and 6 of the 1995 Order.

(2) Regulations 6 to 21 shall not apply in relation to an offshore installation which is in transit to or from a location; and an offshore installation is not in transit to or from a location while it is being manoeuvred at the location.

(3) Save where otherwise expressly provided, nothing in regulations 6 to 13 or 15 to 18 shall impose a duty in relation to an offshore installation while there are no persons aboard.

5. Notification concerning offshore installations.—(1) The duty holder shall, no later than the date on which an offshore installation is due to enter or leave relevant waters, notify the Executive in writing of the date of its intended entry into or departure from such waters.

(2) Where there is a change of duty holder in relation to an offshore installation, the new duty holder shall ensure that it is not operated until the Executive has been notified in writing of—

    (a) the date of such change;

    (b) the name and address of the new duty holder; and

    (c) where the address furnished pursuant to sub-paragraph (b) is outside Great Britain, an address in Great Britain to which communications to him may be sent.

6. Managers.—(1) The duty holder shall ensure that—

    (a) the offshore installation is at all times under the charge of a competent person appointed by him to manage on his behalf the installation and the persons on it; and a reference to the installation manager is a reference to such person while he is in charge;

    (b) the installation manager is provided with appropriate resources to be able to carry out effectively his function, and the duties he may have to discharge under regulation 8; and

    (c) the identity of the installation manager is known to or readily ascertainable by every person on the installation.

(2) For the purpose of paragraph (1)(a), a person is not in charge of an offshore installation when he is not on it unless he remains in communication with it and, in a case where it might be necessary to exercise his functions, is able to reach it promptly.

7. Restraint and putting ashore.—(1) If an installation manager has reasonable cause to believe that it is necessary or expedient to do so for the purpose of securing the safety of the offshore installation or the safety or health of persons on or near it, he may take such measures against a person on the installation, including—
(a) restraint of his person; and
(b) putting him ashore in the United Kingdom as soon as is practicable thereafter,

as are reasonable.

(2) If it appears likely that a person will not be put ashore within twenty-four hours of being put under restraint, the installation manager shall forthwith give notice to the duty holder of his being kept under restraint and of the reason for it.

8. Co-operation.—(1) Every person shall co-operate—
(a) with the installation manager, and any other person on whom any duty is placed by regulations 5 to 19, so far as is necessary to enable him to comply with the relevant statutory provisions, including this regulation;
(b) with the installation manager, so far as is necessary to enable him to discharge his functions described in regulations 6 and 7; and
(c) with the helicopter landing officer, so far as is necessary to enable him to perform his function referred to in regulation 13.

(2) In addition to the duty placed on him by paragraph (1), an installation manager shall co-operate with the manager of another offshore installation, where an activity carried out from, by means of or on one of the installations could affect the health and safety of persons on the other installation or of persons engaged in an activity in connection with the other installation.

(3) The duty in paragraph (1) is without prejudice to any duty owed by a master, captain or person in charge of any vessel or aircraft.

9. Records.—(1) The duty holder shall ensure that there is kept on the offshore installation or at a suitable place nearby a record of the persons who are for the time being on, or working from the installation, and containing, in relation to each such person—
(a) his full name; and
(b) the name and address of his employer, if any,

and in this regulation such a record is referred to as "the offshore record".

(2) The duty holder shall ensure that, as soon as possible after an entry is made in the offshore record, a like entry is made together with the following additional information—
(a) the nationality of the person working on or from the installation;
(b) his date of birth;
(c) his usual residence; and
(d) the name, address and relationship of any next of kin of his,

in another record, in this regulation referred to as "the onshore record".

(3)   The duty holder shall ensure that an entry in the onshore record relating to any person is thereafter kept readily available at an address in Great Britain until 28 days after he ceases to be on or to work from the installation.

10.   Permits to work. In cases where, because of—

(a)   the kind of work which may be done on the offshore installation; or

(b)   the circumstances in which work may be done on the offshore installation,

it is necessary for the health or safety of persons to do so, the duty holder shall introduce arrangements for securing that, in such a case, a person does not do such work save in accordance with the terms of a permit in writing, given by a competent person authorised by or on behalf of the duty holder.

11.   Instructions. The duty holder shall ensure that, where necessary for the health and safety of persons—

(a)   comprehensible instructions on procedures to be observed on the offshore installation are put in writing; and

(b)   the relevant part of such instructions is brought to the attention of every person who is to do anything to which that part relates.

12.   Communication. The duty holder shall ensure that arrangements, which are appropriate for health and safety purposes, are in place for effective communication—

(a)   between the offshore installation and the shore, vessels, aircraft and other installations; and

(b)   where a helicopter is to land on or take off from an offshore installation aboard which there will be no persons immediately before the landing, or after the take-off, between the helicopter and—

(i)   a suitable offshore installation with persons on board; or

(ii)   where there is no such installation, suitable premises ashore.

13.   Helicopters. The duty holder shall ensure that—

(a)   a competent person appointed to be in control of helideck operations on the offshore installation (in these Regulations referred to as "the helicopter landing officer") is present on the installation;

(b)   such person is in control throughout such operations; and

(c)   such procedures are established, and plant provided, as will secure, so far as is reasonably practicable, that helideck operations, including the landing and take-off of helicopters, are without risks to health and safety.

14.   Operational information. The duty holder shall make arrangements for the collection and keeping of—

(a)   such meteorological and oceanographic information; and

(b)   such information relating to the motions of the offshore installation,

as is necessary for securing, so far as is reasonably practicable, the safe operation of the installation and the safety of persons on or near it.

15.   Information to persons.—(1) The duty holder shall ensure that the address and telephone number of the office of the Executive for the sector in which the offshore installation is situated is known to or readily ascertainable by every person on the installation.

(2)   The employer of a person who is not on an offshore installation, and who is engaged in—
(a)   an activity in connection with an offshore installation;
(b)   an activity in connection with a well;
(c)   pipeline works; or
(d)   any of the following activities in connection with pipeline works—
(i)   the loading, unloading, fuelling or provisioning of a vessel;
(ii)   the loading, unloading, fuelling, repair and maintenance of an aircraft on a vessel,
being in either case a vessel which is engaged in pipeline works,

shall ensure that the address and telephone number of the office of the Executive for the sector in which the installation or well is situated, or the pipeline works, or activity described in sub-paragraph (d) above, is or are carried out, is known to or readily ascertainable by such person.

16.   Health surveillance.—(1) An employer of a person engaged in work on an offshore installation shall ensure that he is provided with such health surveillance as is appropriate to the health and safety risks incurred in the work; and, where that person is assigned to the work after the coming into force of these Regulations (apart from regulation 23(2)), the health surveillance shall be commenced before he is so assigned.

(2)   In this regulation "appropriate" means appropriate having regard to the nature and magnitude of the risks to the safety and health of the employee created by the relevant work.

17.   Drinking water. The duty holder shall ensure that—
(a)   an adequate supply of clean, wholesome drinking water is available at suitable locations on the offshore installation; and
(b)   such locations are clearly marked to show that drinking water is there.

18.   Provisions. The duty holder shall ensure that all provisions for consumption by persons on the offshore installation are fit for human consumption, palatable and of good quality.

19.   Identification of the offshore installation. Save where the nature of the structure makes it impracticable to do so, the duty holder shall ensure that the offshore installation—
(a)   displays its name or other designation in such a manner as to make the installation readily identifiable on approach by sea or air; and
(b)   displays no name, letters or figures likely to be confused with the name or other designation of another offshore installation.

20.   Certificates of exemption.—(1) Subject to paragraph (2) and to any of the provisions imposed by the Communities in respect of the encouragement of improvements in the safety and health of workers at work, the Executive may, by a certificate in writing, exempt any person, offshore installation or class of persons or offshore installations from any requirement or prohibition imposed by these Regulations and any such exemption may be granted subject to conditions and with or without limit of time and may be revoked by a certificate in writing at any time.

(2)   The Executive shall not grant any such exemption unless, having regard to the circumstances of the case and, in particular, to—

(a)   the conditions, if any, which it proposes to attach to the exemption; and

(b)   any other requirements imposed by or under any enactments which apply to the case,

it is satisfied that the health and safety of persons who are likely to be affected by the exemption will not be prejudiced in consequence of it.

21.   Application of the Employers' Liability (Compulsory Insurance) Act 1969.—(1) The 1969 Act shall apply to employers of relevant employees employed for work on or from offshore installations, or on or from associated structures in the course of activities undertaken on or in connection with such installations, subject to such modifications and extensions as are hereafter in this regulation prescribed.

(2)   In section 1 of the 1969 Act applied as aforesaid—

(a)   in subsection (1) the words "carrying on any business in Great Britain" shall be omitted and, for the words from "his employees" to the end of the subsection, there shall be substituted the words "those of his relevant employees who are employed by him for work on or from an offshore installation, or on or from an associated structure in the course of an activity undertaken on or in connection with an offshore installation, and arising out of and in the course of their employment for that work"; and

(b)   at the end of paragraph (d) of subsection (3) there shall be added the following paragraph—

"(e)   any expression to which a meaning is given by the Offshore Installations and Pipeline Works (Management and Administration) Regulations 1995, and to which a meaning is not given by this Act, shall have the same meaning in this Act."

(3)   Section 2(2)(b) of the 1969 Act applied as aforesaid shall have no effect.

(4)   In section 4(2)(a) of the 1969 Act applied as aforesaid, after the word "insurance" there shall be inserted the words "or make arrangements to secure the maintenance of such copies on offshore installations or associated structures".

(5)   After section 5 of the 1969 Act applied as aforesaid there shall be inserted the following sections—

"Liability of owners of offshore installations.

5A.—(1) In respect of any offshore installation, it shall be the duty of the owner of the installation to ensure that requirements imposed by or under this Act are complied with and where, in respect of that installation—

(a)   any employer is on any day not insured in accordance with this Act, the owner of the installation shall be guilty of an offence and liable on summary conviction to a fine not exceeding level 3 on the standard scale; or

(b)   any person fails to comply with a requirement imposed by or under section 4 of this Act, the owner of the installation shall be guilty of an offence and liable on summary conviction to a fine not exceeding level 2 on the standard scale.

(2)   In proceedings against the owner of an installation for an offence under this section it shall be a defence for the accused to prove—

    (a)   that he has used all due diligence to prevent the commission of the offence; and

    (b)   that any relevant contravention was committed without his consent, connivance or wilful default.

(3)   Section 37 of the Health and Safety at Work etc Act 1974 shall apply in relation to an offence under this section as if it were an offence under that Act.

(4)   In proceedings for an offence under this section an averment in any process of the fact that anything was done or situated within relevant waters shall, until the contrary is proved, be sufficient evidence of that fact as stated in the averment.

(5)   Proceedings for any offence under this section may be taken, and the offence may for all incidental purposes be treated as having been committed, in any place in Great Britain.

(6)   References in this section to "the owner", in relation to an offshore installation, are to the person who controls the operation of the installation.

5B.   No proceedings shall be instituted in England and Wales for any offence under this Act in respect of an offshore installation except by the Secretary of State or by a person authorised in that behalf by the Secretary of State".

22.   Repeals and modifications of the 1971 Act.—(1) The provisions of the 1971 Act specified in column 1 of Part I of Schedule 1 are repealed to the extent specified in the corresponding entry in column 3 of that Part.

(2)   Section 12(1) of the 1971 Act shall have effect subject to the modifications specified in Part II of Schedule 1.

23.   Revocation and modification of instruments.—(1) The instruments specified in column 1 of Part I of Schedule 2 shall be revoked to the extent specified in column 3 of that Part.

(2)   Regulation 29 of the Offshore Installations (Operational Safety, Health and Welfare) Regulations 1976 shall be revoked.

(3)   The instruments specified in Part II of Schedule 2 shall have effect subject to the modifications specified in that Part.

SCHEDULE 1

Regulation 22

Repeals and Modifications of the 1971 Act

Part I
Repeals

Column 1 Provision	Column 2 Description	Column 3 Extent of repeal
Section 1	Application of Act	The whole section.
Section 3	Construction and survey regulations for offshore installations	In sub-section (4) the words "and of the installation manager, and of every person who, in relation to the installation, is a concession owner"; where they next occur, the words "the installation manager and every person who, in relation to the installation, is a concession owner"; and the word "each".
Section 4	Managers of offshore installations	The whole section.
Section 5	Managers of offshore installations, further provisions	The whole section.
Section 9	Offences: general provisions	In sub-section (3) the words "section 4 or section 5".
Section 11	Civil liability for breach of statutory duty	Sub-sections (5) and (6).
Section 12	Interpretation	In sub-section (1), the definitions of "designated area" and "foreign sector of the continental shelf"; and sub-sections (2) and (3).

Part II
Amendments to Section 12(1)

1. Before the definition of "controlled waters" there shall be inserted the following definition:

> "'the 1995 Regulations' means the Offshore Installations and Pipeline Works (Management and Administration) Regulations 1995;".

2. For the definition of "controlled waters" there shall be substituted the following definition:

> "'controlled waters' means—
>   (a) tidal waters and parts of the sea in or adjacent to Great Britain up to the seaward limits of territorial waters; and
>   (b) any area designated by order under section 1(7) of the Continental Shelf Act 1964;".

3. For the definition of "installation manager" there shall be substituted the following definition:

> "'installation manager' has the meaning given by regulation 2(1) of the 1995 Regulations;".

4. For the definition of "offshore installation" there shall be substituted the following definition:

> "'offshore installation' has the same meaning as in regulation 3 of the 1995 Regulations;".

5. For the definition of "owner" there shall be substituted the following definition:

> "'owner', in relation to an offshore installation, means the person who is, in relation to the installation, the duty holder as defined by regulation 2(1) of the 1995 Regulations in relation to that installation;".

SCHEDULE 2

Regulation 23

PART I
REVOCATIONS OF INSTRUMENTS

1 *Title*	2 *Reference*	3 *Extent of revocation*
The Offshore Installations (Registration) Regulations 1972	S.I. 1972/702 amended by S.I. 1991/679	The whole Regulations.
The Offshore Installations (Managers) Regulations 1972	S.I. 1972/703 amended by S.I. 1991/679	The whole Regulations.
The Offshore Installations (Logbooks and Registration of Death) Regulations 1972	S.I. 1972/1542 amended by S.I. 1991/679	Regulations 1(2) and 2 to 7; in regulation 12(1) the words "2(1)" to "or"; in regulation 12(2) the words "2(1)" to "7"; and regulation 12(3) to (5).
The Offshore Installations (Inspectors and Casualties) Regulations 1973	S.I. 1973/1842 amended by S.I. 1991/679	In regulation 1(2) the definition of "manager"; in regulation 5(1) the words "or manager"; regulation 8(1); regulation 9(b); in regulation 12(2) the words in sub-paragraph (a) "excluding therefrom" to the end of that sub-paragraph; and the words "a reference" to "logbook and".
The Offshore Installations (Application of the Employers' Liability (Compulsory Insurance) Act 1969) Regulations 1975	S.I. 1975/1289	The whole Regulations.

1 Title	2 Reference	3 Extent of revocation
The Offshore Installations (Operational Safety, Health and Welfare) Regulations 1976	S.I. 1976/1019 amended by S.I. 1984/419, 1989/1672 and 1992/2932	In regulation 1(2) the definition of "installation manager"; regulation 3; in regulation 5(3) the words "and 25(2)"; in regulation 5(4) the words "who shall read" to "logbook"; regulations 7 to 9, 16, 17(2), 18 to 26, and 30; in regulation 32(1) the words "the installation manager, and of" and "and of the concession owner,"; regulation 32(3) to (7); and in regulation 34(1) the words "the installation manager, the concession owner and" and "each"; and Schedule 2.
The Offshore Installations (Well Control) Regulations 1980	S.I. 1980/1759 amended by S.I. 1991/308	In regulation 1(2) the definition of "installation manager"; in regulation 3(1) the words "the installation manager, the concession owner and"; and the word "each".
The Diving Operations at Work Regulations 1981	S.I. 1981/399 amended by S.I. 1990/996 and 1992/608	Regulation 4(1)(b)(ii).
The Offshore Installations (Safety Representatives and Safety Committees) Regulations 1989	S.I. 1989/971 amended by S.I. 1992/2885 and 1993/1823	In regulation 2 the definitions of "installation logbook" and "installation manager"; and in regulation 13(b) the words "the installation manager shall record those facts in the installation logbook and".
The Offshore Installations (Included Apparatus or Works) Order 1989	S.I. 1989/978	The whole Order.
The Offshore Installations (Emergency Pipe-line Valve) Regulations 1989	S.I. 1989/1029	In regulation 2 the definitions of "controlled waters" and of "manager".
The Offshore Installations (Amendment) Regulations 1991	S.I. 1991/679	Regulations 2 to 4.

PART II
MODIFICATIONS OF INSTRUMENTS

The Offshore Installations (Operational Safety, Health and Welfare) Regulations 1976

1. In regulation 1(2) (definitions) of the Offshore Installations (Operational Safety, Health and Welfare) Regulations 1976 there shall be substituted, for the definition of "responsible person", the following definition:

> "'responsible person' means a competent person authorised by or on behalf of the owner;".

The Offshore Installations (Well Control) Regulations 1980

2. In regulation 1(2) (definitions) of the Offshore Installations (Well Control) Regulations 1980 there shall be substituted for the definition of "responsible person" the following definition:

> "'responsible person' means a competent person authorised by or on behalf of the owner;".

The Diving Operations at Work Regulations 1981

3. In regulation 2(1) (definitions) of the Diving Operations at Work Regulations 1981 ("the 1981 Regulations") there shall be added, after the definition of "offshore installation" the following definition:

> "'owner', in relation to an offshore installation, means the person who is, in relation to the installation, the duty holder as defined by regulation 2(1) of the Offshore Installations and Pipeline Works (Management and Administration) Regulations 1995 in relation to that installation;".

4. In regulation 5(4)(b) of the 1981 Regulations there shall be substituted for paragraph (i) and (ii) the following paragraph:

> "(i) from or in connection with an offshore installation, the owner".

The Offshore Installations (Safety Representatives and Safety Committees) Regulations 1989

5. In regulation 2 (interpretation) of the Offshore Installations (Safety Representatives and Safety Committees) Regulations 1989 ("the 1989 Regulations"):
   (a) after the definition of "the 1974 Act" there shall be inserted the following definition:

> "'the 1995 Regulations' means the Offshore Installations and Pipeline Works (Management and Administration) Regulations 1995";

   (b) after the definition of "appropriate languages" there shall be inserted the following definition:

> "'duty holder' in relation to an offshore installation means the person who is the duty holder within the meaning of regulation 2(1) of the 1995 Regulations for the purpose of those Regulations"; and

   (c) for the definition of "installation manager" there shall be substituted the following definition:

> "'installation manager' has the meaning given by regulation 2(1) of the 1995 Regulations;".

6.   For regulation 3 (application) of the 1989 Regulations there shall be substituted the following regulation:

> "3.   These Regulations shall apply to an offshore installation at a working station in controlled waters which normally has persons on board;".

7.   In regulations 11, 17, 20, 22, 24, 25 and 28 of the 1989 Regulations, in place of the words "installation owner" wherever they occur, there shall be substituted the words "duty holder".

8.   In regulation 19 of the 1989 Regulations, in place of the words "owner of an offshore installation" there shall be substituted the words "duty holder in relation to an offshore installation".

9.   In regulation 22 (safety committee—functions) of the 1989 Regulations, in paragraph (1)(c), in place of the word "employers" there shall be substituted the words "duty holder".

10.   For regulation 23 (duties of installation owners and installation managers) of the 1989 Regulations there shall be substituted the following regulation:

> **"23.   Duties of installation operators and owners, and employers.—**
> (1) The provisions of this regulation shall apply to every offshore installation served by a safety committee.
> (2) It shall be the duty of the duty holder—
>
> (a)   to facilitate the exercise by the committee of its functions and by the safety representatives of their functions and powers in respect of the installation under these Regulations, and for that purpose to make available the necessary accommodation, facilities for communication and office equipment supplies;
>
> (b)   to consult safety representatives with a view to the making and maintenance of arrangements which will enable them and the workforce to co-operate effectively in promoting and developing measures to ensure the health and safety of persons working on or from the installation, and in checking the effectiveness of such arrangements; and
>
> (c)   without prejudice to sub-paragraph (b) above, to consult safety representatives in good time with regard to—
>
> >   (i)   the preparation of a safety case relating to the installation under the Offshore Installations (Safety Case) Regulations 1992;
> >   (ii)   the introduction to the installation of any measure which may substantially affect the health and safety of the workforce; and
> >   (iii)   the health and safety consequences for the workforce of the introduction (including the planning thereof) to the installation of new technologies.
>
> (3) It shall be the duty of the duty holder and any employer of members of a workforce to consult safety representatives in good time with regard to—
>
> (a)   any health and safety information he is required to provide to members of a workforce by or under the relevant statutory provisions; and
>
> (b)   the planning and organisation of any health and safety training he is to provide to members of a workforce by or under the relevant statutory provisions.
>
> (4) It shall be the duty of every employer of members of a workforce to consult safety representatives in good time with regard to his arrangements for appointing persons in accordance with regulation 6(1) of the Management of Health and Safety at Work Regulations 1992".

11.   For regulation 27 (training) of the 1989 Regulations there shall be substituted the following regulation:

> **"27.   Training.** It shall be the duty of the duty holder to ensure that—
>
> (a)   a safety representative for the installation is provided with such training in aspects of the functions of a safety representative as are reasonable in all the circumstances; and

(b) any costs associated with such training, including travel and subsistence costs, are not borne by the safety representative".

The Offshore Installations (Emergency Pipe-line Valve) Regulations 1989

12. In regulation 2 (interpretation) of the Offshore Installations (Emergency Pipe-line Valve) Regulations 1989—
    (a) before the definition of "associated installation" there shall be inserted the following definition:

        "'the 1995 Regulations' means the Offshore Installations and Pipeline Works (Management and Administration) Regulations 1995";

    (b) for the definition of "installation manager" there shall be substituted the following definition:

        "'installation manager' means, in relation to an associated installation, the person appointed for the purposes of regulation 6(1)(a) of the 1995 Regulations who is for the time being in charge of it";

    (c) for the definition of "offshore installation" there shall be substituted the following definition:

        "'offshore installation' means an installation within the meaning of regulation 3 of the 1995 Regulations other than an installation which is—
            (a) used exclusively for flaring, or
            (b) used exclusively for the loading of substances into vessels or for their reception and storage prior to such loading and which normally has no persons on board"; and

    (d) for the definition of "owner" there shall be substituted the following definition:

        "'owner', in relation to—
            (a) an offshore installation, means the person who is, in relation to the installation, the duty holder as defined by regulation 2(1) of the 1995 Regulations in relation to that installation; and
            (b) a pipeline in respect of which no person has been designated as its owner in pursuance of section 33(3) of the 1975 Act, means the person in whom the pipeline is vested;".

The Offshore Installations and Pipeline Works (First-Aid) Regulations 1989

13. In regulation 2 (interpretation) of the Offshore Installations and Pipeline Works (First-Aid) Regulations 1989—
    (a) the definition of "the 1971 Act" shall be revoked;
    (b) after the definition of "the 1989 Order" there shall be inserted the following definition:

        "'the 1995 Regulations' means the Offshore Installations and Pipeline Works (Management and Administration) Regulations 1995;";

    (c) for the definition of "offshore installation" there shall be substituted the following definition:

        "'offshore installation' has the same meaning as in regulation 3 of the 1995 Regulations";

    (d) for paragraph (a) of the definition of "person in control" there shall be substituted the following paragraph:

        "(a) in relation to an offshore installation, the person who is the duty holder as defined by regulation 2(1) of the 1995 Regulations for the purposes of those Regulations;";

(e)   for paragraph (c) of the definition of "person in control" there shall be substituted the following paragraph:

> "(c) in relation to an activity in connection with an offshore installation—
> > (i)   the person who is, in relation to the installation, the duty holder as defined by regulation 2(1) of the 1995 Regulations for the purposes of those Regulations; and
> > (ii)   the employer of persons engaged in that activity;".

The Offshore Installations (Safety Case) Regulations 1992

14.   In regulation 2 (interpretation) of the Offshore Installations (Safety Case) Regulations 1992 ("the 1992 Regulations")—

(a)   in paragraph (1) (definitions)—
> (i) for the definition of "the 1971 Act" there shall be substituted the following definition:
>
> > "'the 1995 Regulations' means the Offshore Installations and Pipeline Works (Management and Administration) Regulations 1995;";
>
> (ii) for the definition of "the 1989 Order" there shall be substituted the following definition:
>
> > "'the 1995 Order' means the Health and Safety at Work etc Act 1974 (Application outside Great Britain) Order 1995";
>
> (iii) for the definition of "concession owner" there shall be substituted the following definition:
>
> > "'concession owner' in relation to an installation has the same meaning as in regulation 2(1) of the 1995 Regulations";
>
> (iv) for the definition of "installation" there shall be substituted the following definition:
>
> > "'installation' means an offshore installation within the meaning of regulation 3 of the 1995 Regulations"; and
>
> (v) for paragraph (a) of the definition of "owner" there shall be substituted the following paragraph:
>
> > "(a) a mobile installation means the person who controls the operation of the installation";

(b)   in paragraph (5) (reference to operating an installation) for the words from "carrying" to the end there shall be substituted the words—

> "using the installation for any of the purposes described in regulation 3(1) of the 1995 Regulations"; and

(c)   in paragraph (8) (reference to an activity in connection with an installation) for the words "article 4(1)(b) of the 1989 Order" there shall be substituted the following words:

> "sub-paragraph (b) of paragraph (1) of article 4 of the 1995 Order, other than an activity specified in paragraph (i) or (ii) of that sub-paragraph".

15.   In regulation 14 of the 1992 Regulations (co-operation) in paragraph (2)—
(a)   after sub-paragraph (f) the word "and" shall be omitted; and
(b)   after sub-paragraph (g) there shall be added the words—

> "and (h) the manager of the first-mentioned installation".

16.   In Schedule 3 to the 1992 Regulations (particulars to be included in a safety case for a mobile installation) in paragraph 1, after the word "name" there shall be added the words "and address".

THE OFFSHORE INSTALLATIONS (PREVENTION OF FIRE AND EXPLOSION, AND EMERGENCY RESPONSE) REGULATIONS 1995

(S.I. 1995 No. 743)

General note. These Regulations, which came into force on 20 June 1995, contain requirements for measures for the protection of persons on offshore oil and gas installations from fire and explosion, and for securing effective "emergency response". The Regulations give effect, in relation to offshore installations in territorial waters adjacent to Great Britain or in the UK sector of the continental shelf, to certain provisions of Council Directive 92/91/EEC concerning the minimum requirements for improving the safety and health protection of workers in the mineral-extracting industries through drilling. The Regulations also give effect to Art. 11.2 of Council Directive 89/391/EEC on the introduction of measures to encourage improvements in the safety and health of workers at work (in part). Breach of a duty under these Regulations gives rise to civil liability; see the Health and Safety at Work etc. Act 1974, s. 47(2).

ARRANGEMENT OF REGULATIONS

The Secretary of State, in exercise of the powers conferred on him by sections 15(1), (2), (3)(a), and (5)(b), and 82(3)(a) of, and paragraphs 1(2), 8, 9, 11, 12, 13(1) and (3), 14, 15(1), 16, 18 and 20 of Schedule 3 to, the Health and Safety at Work etc Act 1974 ("the 1974 Act") and of all other powers enabling him in that behalf and for the purpose of giving effect without modifications to proposals submitted to him by the Health and Safety Commission under section 11(2)(d) of the 1974 Act after the carrying out by the said Commission of consultations in accordance with section 50(3) of that Act, hereby makes the following Regulations:

1. Citation and commencement. These Regulations may be cited as the Offshore Installations (Prevention of Fire and Explosion, and Emergency Response) Regulations 1995 and shall come into force on 20th June 1995.

2. Interpretation.—(1) In these Regulations, unless the context otherwise requires—

"the 1995 Order" means the Health and Safety at Work etc Act 1974 (Application outside Great Britain) Order 1995;

"the 1974 Regulations" means the Offshore Installations (Construction and Survey) Regulations 1974;

"the 1995 Regulations" means the Offshore Installations and Pipeline Works (Management and Administration) Regulations 1995;

"acoustic signal" means a coded sound signal which is released and transmitted by a device designed for that purpose, without the use of a human or artificial voice;

"concession owner" in relation to a fixed installation has the same meaning as in regulation 2(1) of the 1995 Regulations;

"duty holder" means—

(a) in relation to a fixed installation, the operator; and

(b) in relation to a mobile installation, the owner;

"emergency" means an emergency of a kind which can require evacuation, escape or rescue;

"emergency response" means action to safeguard the health and safety of persons on or near an installation in an emergency;

"evacuation" means the leaving of an installation and its vicinity, in an emergency, in a systematic manner and without directly entering the sea;

"the Executive" means the Health and Safety Executive;

"explosion" means unplanned explosion;

"fire" means unplanned or uncontrolled fire;

"fixed installation" means an installation other than a mobile installation;

"illuminated sign" means a sign produced by a device made of transparent or translucent materials which are illuminated from the inside or the rear in such a way as to give the appearance of a luminous surface;

"installation" means an offshore installation within the meaning of regulation 3 of the 1995 Regulations;

"major accident" has the same meaning as in regulation 2(1) of the Offshore Installations (Safety Case) Regulations 1992;

"mobile installation" means an installation (other than a floating production platform) which can be moved from place to place without major dismantling or modification, whether or not it has its own motive power;

"muster areas" shall be construed in accordance with regulation 14(1)(a);

"operator" in relation to—

(a) a fixed installation means the person appointed by a concession owner to execute any function of organising and supervising any operation to be carried out by such installation or, where no such person has been appointed, the concession owner; and

(b) a mobile installation means the person for whom the owner has agreed to carry out the operation concerned or, where no such person has been appointed, the concession owner;

"owner" in relation to a mobile installation means the person who controls the operation of the installation; and

"personal protective equipment" has the same meaning as in regulation 2(1) of the Personal Protective Equipment at Work Regulations 1992.

(2) Unless the context otherwise requires, any reference in these Regulations to—

(a) a numbered regulation is a reference to the regulation in these Regulations so numbered;

(b) a numbered paragraph is a reference to the paragraph so numbered in the regulation in which the reference appears.

3.   Application.—(1) These Regulations shall apply—

(a) in Great Britain, and

(b) to and in relation to installations and activities outside Great Britain to which sections 1 to 59 and 80 to 82 of the 1974 Act apply by virtue of articles 4(1) and (2)(b), 5 and 6 of the 1995 Order.

(2) Regulations 4 to 22 shall not apply in relation to an installation which is in transit to or from a station; and an installation is not in transit to or from a station while it is being manoeuvred at the station.

4.   General duty.—(1) The duty holder shall take appropriate measures with a view to—

(a) protecting persons on the installation from fire and explosion; and

(b) securing effective emergency response.

(2) Any more detailed requirement in regulations 6 to 21 for the purposes referred to in paragraph (1) shall be without prejudice to the generality of paragraph (1).

5.   Assessment.—(1) The duty holder shall perform, and thereafter repeat as often as may be appropriate a process (in this regulation called "an assessment") described in paragraph (2) in relation to the installation.

(2) An assessment shall consist of—

(a) the identification of the various events which could give rise to—

(i) a major accident involving fire or explosion; or

(ii) the need (whether or not by reason of fire or explosion) for evacuation, escape or rescue to avoid or minimise a major accident;

(b) the evaluation of the likelihood and consequences of such events;

(c) the establishment of appropriate standards of performance to be attained by anything provided by measures for—

(i) ensuring effective evacuation, escape, recovery and rescue to avoid or minimise a major accident; and

(ii) otherwise protecting persons from a major accident involving fire or explosion; and

(d) the selection of appropriate measures.

(3)   The duty holder shall—
    (a)   record the assessment (including each repetition of it);
    (b)   keep the record at an address in Great Britain; and
    (c)   notify the Executive of such address.

6.   Preparation for emergencies.—(1) The duty holder shall establish such appropriate organisation and arrangements as are to have effect in, or in anticipation of, an emergency and which shall include arrangements—
    (a)   for command by competent persons which can be maintained, so far as is practicable, throughout an emergency;
    (b)   for there to be a sufficient number of persons on the installation competent to undertake emergency duties and operate relevant equipment;
    (c)   in the case of an installation on which personnel are present, for a sufficient number of such persons to be in attendance at the helicopter landing area during helicopter movements; and
    (d)   for lists of persons referred to in sub-paragraphs (a), (b) and (c) above to be posted at suitable locations on the installation when persons are present.

(2)   The duty holder shall ensure that every person on the installation—
    (a)   is provided with adequate instruction and training in the appropriate action to take in an emergency; and
    (b)   can consult written information on the use of emergency plant.

7.   Equipment for helicopter emergencies. The duty holder shall ensure that there is kept available near the helicopter landing area equipment necessary for use in the event of an accident involving a helicopter.

8.   Emergency response plan.—(1) The duty holder shall, after consulting persons who are likely to become involved in emergency response, prepare and, as often as is appropriate, revise a document (in this regulation called "the emergency response plan") containing sufficient information, for the guidance of such persons, on—
    (a)   the organisation and arrangements which are to have effect in an emergency; and
    (b)   procedures by way of emergency response to be followed in different circumstances.

(2)   The duty holder shall ensure that—
    (a)   the emergency response plan is available to all persons on the installation; and
    (b)   each person on the installation, and each person who may be called upon to assist in implementing the emergency response plan, are given such notification of its contents as is sufficient for them.

(3)   The duty holder shall ensure that the organisation, arrangements and procedures referred to in paragraph (1) are tested, by practice and otherwise, as often as may be appropriate.

(4)   Every person on the installation shall, in an emergency, so far as is practicable, conform to the appropriate procedure in the plan.

9.   Prevention of fire and explosion.—(1) The duty holder shall take appropriate measures with a view to preventing fire and explosion, including such measures to—
    (a)   ensure the safe production, processing, use, storage, handling, treatment, movement and other dealings with flammable and explosive substances;
    (b)   prevent the uncontrolled release of flammable or explosive substances;

(c)   prevent the unwanted or unnecessary accumulation of combustible, flammable or explosive substances and atmospheres; and

(d)   prevent the ignition of such substances and atmospheres.

(2)   The measures to prevent ignition referred to in paragraph (1) shall include—

(a)   identifying and designating areas in which there is a risk of a flammable or explosive atmosphere occurring;

(b)   controlling the carrying on of hazardous activities in such areas;

(c)   ensuring that, save under procedures pursuant to sub-paragraph (b) above, no plant is used in such areas unless suitable for use within them; and

(d)   controlling the placing or use in such areas of electrical fixtures or other sources of ignition.

10.   Detection of incidents. The duty holder shall take appropriate measures—

(a)   with a view to detecting fire and other events which may require emergency response, including the provision of means for—

(i)   detecting and recording accumulations of flammable or toxic gases; and

(ii)   identifying leakages of flammable liquids; and

(b)   with a view to enabling information regarding such incidents to be conveyed forthwith to places from which control action can be instigated.

11.   Communication.—(1) The duty holder shall make appropriate arrangements—

(a)   for giving warning of an emergency, by audible and, where necessary, visual alarm systems, to all persons on the installation; and

(b)   for the purpose of emergency response, for communication between—

(i)   persons on the installation;

(ii)   the installation and persons not on it and engaged in activities in connection with it; and

(iii)   the installation and persons beyond it;

and shall ensure that, so far as is reasonably practicable, the arrangements are capable of remaining effective in an emergency.

(2)   Subject to paragraph (3), the duty holder shall ensure that—

(a)   an illuminated sign provided pursuant to paragraph (1)(a) is—

(i)   in the case of a warning of toxic gas, a red flashing sign; and

(ii)   in all other cases, a yellow flashing sign; and

(b)   an acoustic signal provided pursuant to paragraph (1)(a) is—

(i)   in the case of a warning to prepare for evacuation, a continuous signal of variable frequency;

(ii)   in the case of a warning of toxic gas, a continuous signal of a constant frequency; and

(iii)   in all other cases, an intermittent signal of a constant frequency.

(3)   Where an illuminated sign or acoustic signal is in lawful use immediately before the date of coming into force of these Regulations, but it does not meet the requirements of paragraph (2), it shall be sufficient compliance with that paragraph if a change to a sign or signal so complying is made before 20th December 1997.

12.   Control of emergencies. The duty holder shall—

(a)   take appropriate measures with a view to limiting the extent of an emergency, including such measures to combat fire and explosion; and

(b)   shall ensure that—

(i)   where appropriate, those measures include provision for the remote operation of plant; and

(ii) so far as is reasonably practicable, any arrangements made and plant provided pursuant to this regulation are capable of remaining effective in an emergency.

13. Mitigation of fire and explosion. The duty holder shall—

(a) take appropriate measures with a view to protecting persons on the installation during an emergency from the effects of fire and explosion; and

(b) ensure that, so far as is reasonably practicable, any arrangements made and plant provided pursuant to this regulation are capable of remaining effective in an emergency.

14. Muster areas etc.—(1) The duty holder shall make appropriate provision for—

(a) areas for persons to muster safely in an emergency (in these Regulations referred to as "muster areas");

(b) safe egress from accommodation and work areas, and safe access to muster areas, temporary refuge, and evacuation and escape points; and

(c) safe evacuation and escape points.

(2) The duty holder shall ensure that the muster areas, egress, access and evacuation and escape points referred to in paragraph (1)—

(a) are kept unobstructed;

(b) are provided with adequate emergency lighting; and

(c) are marked by suitable signs,

and shall take appropriate measures to ensure that, so far as is reasonably practicable, the egress and access remain passable in an emergency.

(3) The duty holder shall ensure that—

(a) doors for use in an emergency—

(i)   open in the appropriate direction or, if this is not possible, are sliding doors; and

(ii) are not so fastened that they cannot readily be opened by any person who may require to use them in an emergency; and

(b) accommodation areas are provided at each level with at least two means of egress situated a proper distance apart.

(4) The duty holder shall—

(a) ensure that—

(i)   each person on the installation is assigned to a muster area; and

(ii) for each muster area a list of names of persons assigned to it is kept up-to-date and displayed; and

(b) establish procedures—

(i)   for mustering at such areas; and

(ii) for accounting for persons.

15. Arrangements for evacuation. The duty holder shall ensure that such arrangements are made which include, to the extent necessary—

(a) the provision of plant on the installation; and

(b) such arrangements with suitable persons beyond the installation, as will ensure, so far as is reasonably practicable, the safe evacuation of all persons and their being taken to a place of safety, or to a place from which they can be recovered and taken to a place of safety under arrangements made pursuant to regulation 17.

16. Means of escape. The duty holder shall provide such means as will ensure, so far as is reasonably practicable, the safe escape of all persons from the installation in case arrangements for evacuation fail.

17. Arrangements for recovery and rescue. The duty holder shall ensure that effective arrangements are made, which include such arrangements with suitable persons beyond the installation, for—

    (a) recovery of persons following their evacuation or escape from the installation; and

    (b) rescue of persons near the installation; and

    (c) taking such persons to a place of safety,

and for the purposes of this regulation arrangements shall be regarded as being effective if they secure a good prospect of those persons being recovered, rescued, and taken to a place of safety.

18. Suitability of personal protective equipment for use in an emergency.—(1) In relation to personal protective equipment which protects a person in an emergency against risks to his health and safety—

    (a) in conditions of fire, heat, smoke, fumes or toxic gas; or

    (b) in the event of his immersion in the sea,

the duty holder shall, for the purposes of the Personal Protective Equipment at Work Regulations 1992, be treated as the only employer of all persons on the installation, and such persons shall be treated as only employed by him.

(2) The duty holder shall ensure that there is prepared and operated a written scheme for the systematic examination and, where appropriate, testing, by a competent person, of the equipment referred to in paragraph (1) and for recording the results thereof.

19. Suitability and condition of plant.—(1) The duty holder shall ensure that all plant on the installation provided in compliance with these Regulations (other than aircraft, or equipment to which regulation 18 applies)—

    (a) is so constructed or adapted as to be suitable for the purpose for which it is used or provided; and

    (b) is maintained in an efficient state, in efficient working order and in good repair.

(2) Without prejudice to the generality of paragraph (1) and subject to paragraph (3), the duty holder shall ensure that there is prepared and operated a suitable written scheme for the systematic examination, by a competent and independent person, of plant (other than aircraft, or equipment to which regulation 18 applies), provided—

    (a) in compliance with regulations 11(1)(a), 13, 15 and 16;

    (b) as means required to be provided by regulation 10—

        (i) for detecting fire; and

        (ii) for detecting and recording accumulations of flammable gases; and

(c)   pursuant to the measures required by regulation 12 to combat fire and explosion,

and for recording results thereof.

(3)   A scheme prepared pursuant to paragraph (2) shall—
   (a)   specify the nature and frequency of examination;
   (b)   provide for an examination to be carried out, where appropriate, before plant is—
      (i)   first used on the installation; and
      (ii)   first used on the installation after modification or repairs (other than running repairs);

and it may make different provision for different plant or categories of plant.

(4)   In this regulation, reference to examination is reference to careful and critical scrutiny of plant, in or out of service as appropriate, using suitable techniques, including testing where appropriate—
   (a)   to assess its suitability for the purpose for which it is used or provided;
   (b)   to assess its actual condition; and
   (c)   to determine any remedial measures that should be taken.

(5)   Subject to paragraph (6), reference in paragraph (2) to the suitability of the scheme is reference to its suitability for the purpose of discharging the duties specified in paragraph (1).

(6)   The scheme referred to in paragraph (2) need not provide for the examination, while a Certificate of Fitness is in force in relation to the installation, of any equipment, which was attached to or formed part of the installation at the time of a survey, if—
   (a)   the equipment was included in the survey;
   (b)   the survey found that the installation complied with Schedule 2 of the 1974 Regulations; and
   (c)   a declaration of such survey was considered before the Certificate of Fitness was issued.

(7)   For the purpose of paragraph (2) a person is independent where, even though he may be employed by the duty holder, he is sufficiently independent of any other persons accountable to the duty holder for the discharge of his duties under these Regulations in respect of the installation to ensure that the discharge of his duty under the scheme will not be prejudiced.

(8)   In paragraph (6) "Certificate of Fitness", "equipment" and "survey" have the same meaning as in regulation 2(1) of the 1974 Regulations.

20.   Life-saving appliances. The duty holder shall ensure that survival craft, life-rafts, life-buoys, life-jackets and plant for like purposes—
   (a)   are of such colour as will make them conspicuous when in use;
   (b)   are (where applicable) suitably equipped; and
   (c)   are kept available for immediate use in sufficient numbers.

21.   Information regarding plant. The duty holder shall ensure that information, giving the location of—
   (a)   areas in which there is a risk of a flammable or explosive atmosphere occurring;

    (b)   non-automatic plant for fighting fire; and
    (c)   plant to which regulations 18(1) and 20 apply (other than plant issued to
          particular persons),

is available to all persons on the installation.

22. Certificates of exemption.—(1) Subject to paragraph (2) and to any of
the provisions imposed by the Communities in respect of the encouragement of
improvements in the safety and health of workers at work, the Executive may, by a
certificate in writing, exempt any person, installation or class of persons or
installations from any requirement or prohibition imposed by these Regulations and
any such exemption may be granted subject to conditions and with or without limit
of time and may be revoked by a certificate in writing at any time.

(2) The Executive shall not grant any such exemption unless, having regard to the
circumstances of the case and, in particular, to—
    (a)   the conditions, if any, which it proposes to attach to the exemption; and
    (b)   any other requirements imposed by or under any enactments which apply
          .to the case,

it is satisfied that the health and safety of persons who are likely to be affected by the
exemption will not be prejudiced in consequence of it.

**23. Amendment of the Offshore Installations (Safety Representatives
and Safety Committees) Regulations 1989.** Regulation 23(2)(c) of the
Offshore Installations (Safety Representatives and Safety Committees)
Regulations 1989 shall be amended—
    (a)   by deleting the word "and" after paragraph (ii); and
    (b)   by adding the following paragraph:

        "and (iv) the arrangements for the appointment of persons referred to in
            regulation 6(1) of the Offshore Installations (Prevention of Fire and
            Explosion, and Emergency Response) Regulations 1995".

**24. Amendment of the Offshore Installations (Safety Case)
Regulations 1992.**—Regulation 8 of the Offshore Installations (Safety Case)
Regulations 1992 shall be amended by adding, after paragraph (1), the following
paragraph:

        "(1A) The particulars required by paragraph (1) shall include a summary of
        the record kept pursuant to regulation 5(3) of the Offshore Installations
        (Prevention of Fire and Explosion, and Emergency Response)
        Regulations 1995".

25. Revocation. The instruments specified in column 1 of the Schedule hereto
are hereby revoked to the extent specified in column 3 of the Schedule.

SCHEDULE

Regulation 25

(1) Title	(2) Reference	(3) Extent of revocation
The Offshore Installations (Operational Safety, Health and Welfare) Regulations 1976	S.I. 1976/1019	Regulations 2(1), 4(6) and 18(4)
The Offshore Installations (Emergency Procedures) Regulations 1976	S.I. 1976/1542	The whole Regulations
The Offshore Installations (Life-saving Appliances) Regulations 1977	S.I. 1977/486	The whole Regulations
The Offshore Installations (Fire-fighting Equipment) Regulations 1978	S.I. 1978/611	The whole Regulations
The Health and Safety (Fees) Regulations 1993	S.I. 1993/1321	Regulation 2

THE HEALTH AND SAFETY (FEES) REGULATIONS 1995

(S.I. 1995 No. 2646)

General note. These Regulations, which came into force on 3 November 1995, update and replace the Health and Safety (Fees) Regulations 1994 (S.I.1994 No. 1397).

ARRANGEMENT OF REGULATIONS

Schedule 6. Fees for examination or surveillance by an employment medical adviser.

Schedule 7. Fees for medical surveillance by an employment medical adviser under the Control of Lead at Work Regulations 1980.

Schedule 8. Fees for applications for approval or reassessment of approval of dosimetry services and for type approval of radiation generators or apparatus containing radioactive substances under the Ionising Radiations Regulations 1985.

Schedule 9. Fees payable under the Explosives Act 1875 and instruments made thereunder, under the Petroleum (Consolidation) Act 1928 and the Petroleum (Transfer of Licences) Act 1936.

Schedule 10. Fees for application for the grant or alteration of the terms of an explosives licence under Part IX of the Dangerous Substances in Harbour Areas Regulations 1987.

Schedule 11. Vocational training certificates under the Road Traffic (Training of Drivers of Vehicles Carrying Dangerous Goods) Regulations 1992.

Schedule 12. Fees for notifications under the Genetically Modified Organisms (Contained Use) Regulations 1992.

Schedule 13.` Fees for notifications and applications under the Notification of New Substances Regulations 1993.

Schedule 14. Revocations.

The Secretary of State, in exercise of the powers conferred on him by sections 43(2), (4), (5) and (6) and 82(3)(a) of the Health and Safety at Work etc Act 1974 ("the 1974 Act") and of all other powers enabling him in that behalf and for the purpose of giving effect without modifications to proposals submitted to him by the Health and Safety Commission under section 11(2)(d) of the 1974 Act, hereby makes the following Regulations:

1. Citation, commencement and interpretation.— (1) These Regulations may be cited as the Health and Safety (Fees) Regulations 1995 and shall come into force on 3rd November 1995.

(2) In these Regulations, unless the context otherwise requires—

"approval" includes the amendment of an approval, and "amendment of an approval" includes the issue of a new approval replacing the original incorporating an amendment;

"employment medical adviser" means an employment medical adviser appointed under section 56(1) of the 1974 Act;

"the Executive" means the Health and Safety Executive;

"the mines and quarries provisions" means such of the relevant statutory provisions as relate exclusively to—

(a) mines and quarries within the meaning of section 180 of the Mines and Quarries Act 1954

(b) tips within the meaning of section 2(1) of the Mines and Quarries (Tips) Act 1969;

and includes regulations, rules and orders relating to a particular mine (whether they are continued in force by regulation 7(3) of the Mines and Quarries Acts 1954 to 1971 (Repeals and Modifications) Regulations 1974 or are health and safety regulations);

"original approval" and "original authority" do not include an amendment of an approval or an amendment of an authority;

"renewal of approval" or "renewal of licence" means respectively the granting of an approval or licence to follow a previous approval or licence without any amendment or gap in time;

"respiratory protective equipment" includes any respirator and any breathing apparatus.

(3) Unless the context otherwise requires, any reference in these Regulations to—

(a) a numbered regulation or Schedule is a reference to the regulation or Schedule in these Regulations so numbered;

(b) a numbered paragraph is a reference to the paragraph so numbered in the regulation in which the reference appears.

2. Fees payable under the mines and quarries provisions.— (1) A fee shall be payable by the applicant to the Executive on each application for an original approval, an amendment of approval or a renewal of approval under any of the mines and quarries provisions.

(2) The fee payable under paragraph (1) on application for such approval as is mentioned in column 1 of Part I of Schedule 1 shall be respectively that specified in the corresponding entry in column 2, 3 or 4 of that Part and shall be payable on making the application for approval, or, where any such entry specifies a fee as an amount per hour worked, the fee so calculated shall be payable prior to the notification of the result of the application.

(3) Where the Executive requires testing to be carried out by its staff to decide whether approval can be granted, a fee shall be payable to the Executive by the applicant prior to the notification of the result of the application for the approval as described below—

(a) in the case of explosives and detonators, for each test specified in column 1 of Part II of Schedule 1, the fee shall be that specified in the corresponding entry in column 2 of that Part;

(b) in any other case, the fee shall be determined under Part III of Schedule 1.

3. Fees for applications for approval of respiratory protective equipment.— (1) A fee shall be payable by the applicant to the Executive on each application for approval of respiratory protective equipment—

(a) under the Factories Act 1961, or any regulations made or having effect as if made under that Act;

(b) under the Control of Lead at Work Regulations 1980;

(c) under the Ionising Radiations Regulations 1985;

(d) under the Control of Asbestos at Work Regulations 1987; and

(e) under the Control of Substances Hazardous to Health Regulations 1994.

(2) The fee payable on application for approval of respiratory protective equipment shall be that specified in column 2 of Schedule 2 and the fee so calculated shall be payable prior to the notification of the result of the application for approval.

(3) For the purposes of Schedule 2, the number of hours worked shall include time spent by the Executive's staff carrying out any testing to determine whether approval can be granted.

4. Fees payable under the Agriculture (Tractor Cabs) Regulations 1974.— (1) A fee shall be payable by the applicant to the Executive on each application for approval of plant and equipment under the Agriculture (Tractor Cabs) Regulations 1974.

(2)   The fee payable on application for such an approval or revision of an approval as is described in column 1 of Schedule 3 shall be that specified in the corresponding entry in column 2 of that Schedule.

5. Fee payable under the Freight Containers (Safety Convention) Regulations 1984.—(1) A fee shall be payable by the applicant to the Executive on each application for approval of a scheme or programme for examination of freight containers under the Freight Containers (Safety Convention) Regulations 1984.

(2)   The fee payable on application for the approval described in column 1 of Schedule 4 shall be that specified in column 2 of that Schedule.

6. Fee for application for a licence under the Asbestos (Licensing) Regulations 1983.—(1) A fee shall be payable by the applicant to the Executive on each application for a licence under the Asbestos (Licensing) Regulations 1983.

(2)   The fee payable on application for a licence described in column 1 of Schedule 5 shall be that specified in column 2 of that Schedule.

7. Fees for examination or surveillance by an employment medical adviser.— (1) A fee shall be payable to the Executive by an employer in respect of a medical examination or medical surveillance of each of his employees by an employment medical adviser for the purposes of any provision specified in column 1 of Schedule 6.

(2)   The fee payable under paragraph (1) shall be a basic fee for each examination or on each occasion when surveillance is carried out together with additional fees for X-rays and laboratory tests where these are taken or carried out in connection with the examination; and for each provision specified in column 1 of Schedule 6—

   (a)   the basic fee shall be the amount specified in column 3 of that Schedule for that provision;
   (b)   the additional fee for X-rays shall be the amount specified in column 4 of that Schedule for that provision and shall cover all X-rays taken in connection with any one examination;
   (c)   the additional fee for laboratory tests shall be the amount specified in column 5 of that Schedule for that provision and shall cover all such tests carried out in connection with any one examination.

(3)   Where an employment medical adviser carries out a medical examination of a self-employed person for the purposes of the Control of Asbestos at Work Regulations 1987, that self-employed person shall pay to the Executive fees ascertained in accordance with paragraph (2).

8. Fees for medical surveillance by an employment medical adviser under the Control of Lead at Work Regulations 1980.— (1) A fee shall be payable to the Executive by an employer in respect of medical surveillance of any of his employees by an employment medical adviser for the purposes of the Control of Lead at Work Regulations 1980.

(2)   The fee payable for each item described in column 1 of Schedule 7 shall be that specified in the corresponding entry in column 2 of that Schedule.

9. Fees for applications for approval or reassessment of approval of dosimetry services and for type approval of radiation generators or apparatus containing radioactive substances under the Ionising Radiations Regulations 1985.— (1) A fee shall be payable by the applicant to the Executive on each application for an approval of dosimetry services or for the reassessment of an approval of dosimetry services previously granted for the purposes of the Ionising Radiations Regulations 1985.

(2)   A fee shall be payable by the applicant to the Executive on each application for the type approval of a radiation generator or an apparatus containing a radioactive substance.

(3)   The fee payable for approval or reassessment or type approval in respect of each matter described in column 1 of Schedule 8 shall be that specified in the corresponding entry in column 2 of that Schedule.

(4)   A fee shall be payable by the applicant to the Executive where the Executive requires any work to be carried out by its nuclear or other specialist inspectors in connection with any application in respect of which a fee is payable by virtue of paragraph (1) or (2) and the fee for work in connection with each such matter described in column 1 of Schedule 8 shall be that specified in the corresponding entry in column 3 of that Schedule for each hour or part of an hour worked.

(5)   Where the Executive requires an inspection to be carried out in connection with any application mentioned in this regulation, a fee shall be payable by the applicant to the Executive of an amount equal to the reasonable cost of travelling and subsistence of any member of the Executive's staff in connection with the inspection.

(6)   Any fee payable under paragraph (4) or (5) shall be payable prior to notification of the result of the application.

10. Fees payable under the Explosives Act 1875 and instruments made thereunder, under the Petroleum (Consolidation) Act 1928, the Petroleum (Transfer of Licences) Act 1936 and the Classification and Labelling of Explosives Regulations 1983.—(1) Where any application in relation to a provision specified in column 1 of Part I of Schedule 9 is made for a purpose specified in column 2 of that Part, the fee specified in the corresponding entry in column 3 of that Part shall be payable by the applicant to the Executive.

(2)   The fee or maximum fee payable under each provision specified in column 1 of Part II of Schedule 9 for the purpose described in the corresponding entry in column 2 shall be that specified in the corresponding entry in column 3 of that Part.

(3)   A fee shall be payable to the Executive where the Executive requires any work to be carried out by its specialist inspectors in connection with any application in respect of which a fee is payable by virtue of paragraph (1) for any purpose specified in column 2 of Part I of Schedule 9 for which there is a corresponding entry in column 4 of that Part, and the fee for work in connection with each such purpose shall be that specified in the corresponding entry in column 4 of that Part for each hour or part of an hour worked and such fee shall be payable prior to notification of the result of the application.

(4)   A fee shall be payable by the applicant to the Executive on each application being made for each purpose specified in column 1 of each of Parts III, IV, and V of Schedule 9, and the fee for each such purpose shall be that specified in the corresponding entry in column 2 in the respective part.

(5) A fee shall be payable to the Executive where the Executive requires any work to be carried out by its specialist inspectors in connection with any application in respect of which a fee is payable by virtue of paragraph (4) for any purpose specified in column 1 of each of Parts III, IV and V of Schedule 9 for which there is a corresponding entry in column 3 of the respective Part, and the fee for work in connection with each such purpose shall be that specified in the corresponding entry in column 3 of that Part for each hour or part of an hour worked and such fee shall be payable prior to notification of the result of the application.

(6) A fee shall be payable to the Executive where the Executive requires any testing to be carried out in connection with any purpose specified in column 1 of Part VI of Schedule 9, and the fee for testing in connection with each such purpose shall be that specified in the corresponding entry in column 2 of that Part for each hour or part of an hour worked in respect of such testing and such fee shall be payable prior to notification of the result of the application.

(7) Where the Executive requires an inspection of premises to be carried out in connection with an application for—
  (a) a factory or magazine licence, or any amendment to such a licence, or
  (b) the original approval of premises in which acetylene is to be manufactured or kept, or any amendment to such an approval, or
  (c) the original approval of premises in which acetylene is compressed, or any amendment to such an approval,

a fee shall be payable by the applicant to the Executive of an amount equal to the reasonable cost of travelling and subsistence of any member of the Executive's staff in connection with the inspection.

11. Date from which fees are payable under the Petroleum (Consolidation) Act 1928 and the Petroleum (Transfer of Licences) Act 1936. Notwithstanding the provisions of section 4 of the Petroleum (Consolidation) Act 1928 or section 1(4) of the Petroleum (Transfer of Licences) Act 1936 the fees in respect of applications for petroleum licences prescribed by these Regulations shall be payable for any licence first having effect or any transfer or renewal of a licence first taking effect on or after the coming into force of these Regulations irrespective of the date of the application for that licence, transfer or renewal.

12. Fees for applications for explosive licences under Part IX of the Dangerous Substances in Harbour Areas Regulations 1987.—(1) A fee shall be payable by the applicant to the Executive on each application for an explosives licence or for any alteration in the terms of an existing licence under Part IX of the Dangerous Substances in Harbour Areas Regulations 1987.

(2) The fee on an application for each purpose specified in column 1 of Schedule 10 shall be that specified in column 2 of that Schedule and where the fee is determined as an amount per hour, the fee so calculated shall be payable prior to notification of the result of the application.

13. Vocational training certificates under the Road Traffic (Training of Drivers of Vehicles Carrying Dangerous Goods) Regulations 1992.— (1) A driver may only be issued with a vocational training certificate in accordance with paragraph (1) of regulation 5 of the Road Traffic (Training of Drivers of Vehicles Carrying Dangerous Goods) Regulations 1992 where a fee of the sum specified in Schedule 11 has been paid to the Secretary of State.

(2) The validity of a vocational training certificate may only be extended in accordance with paragraph (5) of regulation 5 of the Road Traffic (Training of Drivers of Vehicles Carrying Dangerous Goods) Regulations 1992 where, within the period of 12 months which precede the expiry of the original certificate or any extension of it granted in accordance with that paragraph, a fee of the sum specified in Schedule 11 has been paid to the Secretary of State.

(3) Nothing in this regulation shall be construed as making a fee payable by a person in any of the capacities specified in section 43(4) of the 1974 Act.

14. Calculation of hours worked. In calculating the number of hours worked for the purpose of determining the amount of a fee payable under regulation 2(2), 2(3)(b), 3(2) or 10(6) no account shall be taken of any typing, messenger or ancillary work (for which no further charge shall be payable).

15. Fees for notifications under the Genetically Modified Organisms (Contained Use) Regulations 1992.—(1) A fee shall be payable by a notifier to the Executive on each notification of the intention to use premises for activities involving genetic modification for the first time and of individual activities involving genetic modification under the Genetically Modified Organisms (Contained Use) Regulations 1992.

(2) The fee payable for each notification described in column 1 of Schedule 12 shall be that specified in the corresponding entry in column 2 of that Schedule.

16. Fees for notifications under the Notification of New Substances Regulations 1993.—(1) The fee fixed by column 2 of Schedule 13 shall be payable by a notifier to the Executive on each such notification or application under the Notification of New Substances Regulations 1993 as is referred to in the corresponding entry in column 1 of that Schedule.

(2) The Executive shall repay to the notifier the amount of any rebate due to the notifier in the circumstances described in Schedule 13.

17. Revocations. The instruments specified in column 1 of Schedule 14 are hereby revoked to the extent specified in the corresponding entry in column 3 of that Schedule.

18. Northern Ireland. These Regulations shall not apply to Northern Ireland.

SCHEDULE 1

Regulation 2

FEES PAYABLE UNDER THE MINES AND QUARRIES PROVISIONS

PART I
FEES FOR APPLICATIONS FOR APPROVAL OF PLANT, APPARATUS OR SUBSTANCE UNDER THE MINES AND QUARRIES PROVISIONS

1 *Subject matter of approval*	2 *Fee for an original approval*	3 *Fee for amendment of approval*	4 *Fee for renewal of approval*
(a) Approval of breathing apparatus	£1,041	£521	£55

1	2	3	4
Subject matter of approval	*Fee for an original approval*	*Fee for amendment of approval*	*Fee for renewal of approval*
(b) Approval of dust respirators	£70 per hour worked	£70 per hour worked	£70 per hour worked
(c) Approval of explosives	£194	£134	£55
(d) Approval of locomotive or other vehicle	£2,069	£541	£55
(e) Approval of electrical equipment for use in potentially gassy zones	£640	£419	£55
(f) Approval of methanometers	£308	£197	£55
(g) Approval of electric safety lamps	£308	£197	£55
(h) Approval of other types of apparatus	£156	£156	£55

Part II
Fees for Testing Explosives and Detonators Under the Mines and Quarries Provisions

1 *Test*	2 *Fee for test*
(a) Ballistic pendulum shot	£43
(b) Break test shot	£51.25
(c) Deflagration shot	£35
(d) Detonator test (per 100 shots)	£380
(e) Detonator delay time test (per 100 shots)	£232
(f) Gallery shot	£87
(g) Mortar shot	£41
(h) Velocity of detonation test (per 3 shots)	£73

Part III
Fees for Other Testing

The fee for any testing not fixed by Part II of this Schedule shall be £70 per hour worked in the testing.

SCHEDULE 2

Regulation 3

Fee for Application For Approval of Respiratory Protective Equipment

1 *Subject matter of approval*	2 *Fee*
Approval of respiratory protective equipment	£70 per hour worked

SCHEDULE 3

Regulation 4

FEES FOR APPLICATIONS FOR APPROVAL UNDER THE AGRICULTURE (TRACTOR CABS) REGULATIONS 1974

1 *Subject matter of approval*	2 *Fee*
(a) Original approval of tractor cab	£244
(b) Revision of an existing approval of a tractor cab	£136

SCHEDULE 4

Regulation 5

FEE FOR APPLICATION FOR APPROVAL UNDER THE FREIGHT CONTAINERS (SAFETY CONVENTION) REGULATIONS 1984

1 *Subject matter of approval*	2 *Fee*
Approval of scheme or programme for examination of freight containers	£75

SCHEDULE 5

Regulation 6

FEE FOR APPLICATION FOR A LICENCE UNDER THE ASBESTOS (LICENSING) REGULATIONS 1983

1 *Subject matter of licence*	2 *Fee*
Licence for work with asbestos insulation or asbestos coating or renewal of original licence	£505

SCHEDULE 6

Regulation 7

FEES FOR EXAMINATION OR SURVEILLANCE BY AN EMPLOYMENT MEDICAL ADVISER

1 *Provision*	2 *Reference*	3 *Basic Fee*	4 *Additional fees where appropriate* *Fee for X-Rays*	5 *Fee for Laboratory tests*
(a) The Work in Compressed Air Special Regulations 1958	S.I. 1958/61 (relevant amending instrument is S.I. 1973/36)	£42.13	£45.23	£27.17

1	2	3	4	5
Provision	Reference	Basic Fee	Additional fees where appropriate	
			Fee for X-Rays	Fee for Laboratory tests
(b) The Ionising Radiations Regulations 1985	S.I. 1985/1333	£19.90 where surveillance is confined to examination of, and making entries in, records £39 in other cases	£45.23	£27.17
(c) The Control of Asbestos at Work Regulations 1987	S.I. 1987/2115	£43	£45.23	£27.17
(d) The Control of Substances Hazardous to Health Regulations 1994	S.I. 1994/3246	£40	£45.23	£27.17

SCHEDULE 7

Regulation 8

FEES FOR MEDICAL SURVEILLANCE BY AN EMPLOYMENT MEDICAL ADVISER UNDER THE CONTROL OF LEAD AT WORK REGULATIONS 1980

1 Item	2 Fee
(a) On the first assessment of an employee (including any clinical medical examination and laboratory tests in connection with the assessment)	£45.70
(b) On each subsequent assessment of an employee—	
(i) for laboratory tests where these are carried out	£27.17
(ii) for a clinical medical examination where this is carried out	£28

SCHEDULE 8

Regulation 9

FEES FOR APPLICATIONS FOR APPROVAL OR REASSESSMENT OF APPROVAL OF DOSIMETRY SERVICES AND FOR TYPE APPROVAL OF RADIATION GENERATORS OR APPARATUS CONTAINING RADIOACTIVE SUBSTANCES UNDER THE IONISING RADIATIONS REGULATIONS 1985

1 *Description*	2 *Fee*	3 *Fee for work by Nuclear or Specialist Inspector*
Approval or reassessment of approval of Dosimetry Services granted under regulation 15 of the Ionising Radiations Regulations 1985		
Group I		
Dose record keeping		
(a) Where the application is solely in respect of Group I functions	£59.40	£38.15 per hour worked
(b) Where the application for Group I functions is linked to an application in respect of functions in another group		£38.15 per hour worked
Group II		
External dosimetry	£59.40	£38.15 per hour worked
(a) Whole body (beta, gamma, thermal neutrons) film		
(b) Whole body (beta, gamma, thermal neutrons) thermoluminescent dosimeter (TLD)		
(c) Whole body (neutron), other than sub-groups (a) or (b)		
(d) Whole body, other than sub-groups (a), (b), or (c)		
(e) Extremity monitoring		
(f) Accident dosimetry, other than in the previous sub-groups		
Group III		
Internal Dosimetry		
(a) Bio-assay, in-vivo monitoring or air sampling	£59.40	£38.15 per hour worked
(b) for each additional one of the above techniques		£38.15 per hour worked
Type approval of a radiation generator or an apparatus containing a radioactive substance under sub-paragraph (f) or (g) respectively of Schedule 3 to the Ionising Radiations Regulations 1985 (which excepts such type approved radiation generators or apparatus containing radioactive substances from the notification requirements of regulation 5 of those Regulations)	£95	

SCHEDULE 9

FEES PAYABLE UNDER THE EXPLOSIVES ACT 1875 AND INSTRUMENTS MADE THEREUNDER, UNDER THE PETROLEUM (CONSOLIDATION) ACT 1928 AND THE PETROLEUM (TRANSFER OF LICENCES) ACT 1936

PART I

APPLICATIONS FOR FACTORY LICENCES, MAGAZINE LICENCES AND IMPORTATION LICENCES AND AMENDING LICENCES UNDER SECTIONS 6, 12 AND 40(9) OF THE EXPLOSIVES ACT AND REPLACEMENT OF SUCH LICENCES

1 *Provision under which a licence is granted*	2 *Purpose of application*	3 *Fee*	4 *Fee for work by Specialist Inspector*
Explosives Act 1875 c. 17			
Section 6 (as applied to explosives other than gunpowder by sections 39 and 40)	Factory licence	£428	£36.72 per hour worked
	Magazine licence	£428	£36.72 per hour worked
	Replacement of one of the above licences if lost	£23	
Section 12 (as applied to explosives other than gunpowder by sections 39 and 40)	Factory amending licence	£123	£36.72 per hour worked
	Magazine amending licence	£132	£36.72 per hour worked
	Replacement of one of the above licences if lost	£23	
Section 40(9) as applied to compressed acetylene by The Compressed Acetylene (Importation) Regulations 1978	Licence for importation of compressed acetylene	£16	£36.72 per hour worked
	Replacement of the above licence if lost	£16	£36.72 per hour worked
	Amendment to an existing licence	£16	£36.72 per hour worked

PART II

FEE OR MAXIMUM FEE PAYABLE IN RESPECT OF APPLICATIONS FOR THE GRANTING AND RENEWAL OF AN EXPLOSIVES STORE LICENCE, THE REGISTRATION OR RENEWAL OF REGISTRATION OF PREMISES USED FOR KEEPING EXPLOSIVES AND THE GRANTING AND TRANSFER OF PETROLEUM-SPIRIT LICENCES

1 *Provision under which a fee or maximum fee is payable*	2 *Purpose of application*	3 *Fee or maximum fee*
Explosives Act 1875 c. 17		
Section 15 (see note 1)	A store licence	£60

1 *Provision under which a fee or maximum fee is payable*	2 *Purpose of application*	3 *Fee or maximum fee*
Section 18 (see note 1)	Renewal of a store licence	£60
Section 21 (see note 1)	Registration and renewal of registration of premises for the keeping of explosives with a local authority	£10.20
Petroleum (Consolidation) Act 1928 c. 32		
Section 4 (see notes 2 and 3)	Licence to keep petroleum-spirit of a quantity—	
	not exceeding 2,500 litres	£28.55 for each year of licence
	exceeding 2,500 litres but not exceeding 50,000 litres	£42.15 for each year of licence
	exceeding 50,000 litres	£83 for each year of licence
Petroleum (Transfer of Licences) Act 1936 c. 27		
Section 1(4)	Transfer of petroleum-spirit licence	£7

Note:

1. Part 1 of the Explosives Act 1875 (which includes sections 15, 18 and 21) is applied to explosives other than gunpowder by sections 39 and 40 of that Act.

2. In the case of a solid substance for which by virtue of an Order in Council made under section 19 of the Petroleum (Consolidation) Act 1928 a licence is required, the fee payable under this Schedule shall be calculated as if one kilogram of the substance were equivalent to one litre.

3. The fee payable for a licence of more or less than one year's duration shall be the fee set out above increased or decreased, as the case may be, proportionately according to the duration of the period for which the licence is granted or renewed.

PART III
APPLICATIONS UNDER PARAGRAPH (1) OF THE PROVISO TO ORDER IN COUNCIL (NO 30) OF 2ND FEBRUARY 1937 FOR APPROVALS OF PREMISES AND APPARATUS IN WHICH ACETYLENE IS TO BE MANUFACTURED OR KEPT

1 *Purpose of application*	2 *Fee*	3 *Fee for work by Specialist Inspector*
(a) Original approval of premises in which acetylene is to be manufactured or kept	£16.05	£36.72 per hour worked
(b) Amendment of an approval of premises in which acetylene is to be manufactured or kept	£16.05	£36.72 per hour worked
(c) Approval of apparatus in which acetylene is to be manufactured or kept	£16.05	£36.72 per hour worked

PART IV
APPLICATIONS FOR COMPARISONS AND APPROVALS IN RESPECT OF CONDITIONS (1) AND (8) IN THE ORDER OF THE SECRETARY OF STATE (No 9) OF 23RD JUNE 1919

1 *Purpose of application*	2 *Fee*	3 *Fee for work by Specialist Inspector*
(a) Comparison of a porous substance with a sample porous substance	£27.54	
(b) Original approval of premises in which acetylene is compressed	£16.05	£36.72 per hour worked
(c) Amendment of an approval of premises in which acetylene is compressed	£16.05	£36.72 per hour worked

PART V
MISCELLANEOUS APPLICATIONS

1 *Purpose of application*	2 *Fee*	3 *Fee for work by Specialist Inspector*
(a) Classification of an explosive under the Classification and Labelling of Explosives Regulations 1983, or authorisation of an explosive under section 40(9) of the Explosives Act 1875	£53.50	£36.72 per hour worked
(b) Grant of an ammonium nitrate mixtures licence under article 3 of the Ammonium Nitrate Mixtures Exemption Order 1967	£139	£36.72 per hour worked

PART VI
FURTHER FEES PAYABLE IN RESPECT OF CERTAIN TESTING REQUIRED BY THE HEALTH AND SAFETY EXECUTIVE

1 *Purpose of application*	2 *Fee*
(a) Application for a licence for the importation of compressed acetylene (Part I above)	£70 per hour worked
(b) Approval of apparatus in which acetylene is to be manufactured or kept (Part III above)	£70 per hour worked
(c) Comparison of a porous substance with a sample porous substance (Part IV above)	£70 per hour worked
(d) Classification of an explosive under the Classification and Labelling of Explosives Regulations 1983 or authorisation of an explosive under section 40(9) of the Explosives Act 1875 (Part V above)	£70 per hour worked
(e) Application for a licence to manufacture explosive in pursuance of the Ammonium Nitrate Mixtures Exemption Order 1967 (Part V above)	£70 per hour worked

SCHEDULE 10

Regulation 12

FEES FOR APPLICATIONS FOR THE GRANT OR ALTERATION OF THE TERMS OF AN
EXPLOSIVES LICENCE UNDER PART IX OF THE DANGEROUS SUBSTANCES IN HARBOUR
AREAS REGULATIONS 1987

1 Purpose of application	2 Fee
Grant of an explosives licence or alteration of the terms of an existing explosives licence	£268+ £36.72 per hour worked

SCHEDULE 11

Regulation 13

VOCATIONAL TRAINING CERTIFICATES UNDER THE ROAD TRAFFIC (TRAINING OF
DRIVERS OF VEHICLES CARRYING DANGEROUS GOODS) REGULATIONS 1992

1 Description	2 Fee
Issue or extension of vocational training certificate	£2.70

SCHEDULE 12

Regulation 15

FEES FOR NOTIFICATION UNDER THE GENETICALLY MODIFIED ORGANISMS (CONTAINED
USE) REGULATIONS 1992

	1 Description	2 Fee
(a)	Notification of intention to use premises for activities involving genetic modification for the first time under regulation 8 other than a case where a consent is required under regulation 8(3).	£70.15
(b)	Notification of the intention to use premises for activities involving genetic modification for the first time, where a consent is required under regulation 8(3).	£87.15
(c)	Notification of individual activities involving genetic modification under regulation 9, other than a case where a consent is required under regulation 9(5).	£106.65
(d)	Notification of individual activities involving genetic modification where a consent is required under regulation 9(5).	£217.25

SCHEDULE 13

Regulation 16

FEES FOR NOTIFICATIONS AND APPLICATIONS UNDER THE NOTIFICATION OF NEW SUBSTANCES REGULATIONS 1993

1 *Subject matter*	2 *Fees*
For the evaluation of a notification under regulation 4 ("base set") (see note 1)	£6,090 (+£350 VAT)
For the evaluation of a notification under regulation 5(1)(a) (> 10 tonnes per year)	£2,000
For the evaluation of a notification under regulation 5(1)(b) (> 100 tonnes per year)	£4,200
For the evaluation of a notification under regulation 5(1)(c) (> 1000 tonnes per year)	£3,500
For a notification under regulation 6 (see note 2)—	
(a) quantity of the new substance equal to or more than 100 kg (regulation 6(1))	£1,170 (+£87.50 VAT)
(b) quantity of the new substance up to 100 kg (regulation 6(2))	£915 (+£87.50 VAT)
For an application made by a notifier for an exemption relating to him under regulation 23	£2,000
Note 1 Rebate where an adequate draft risk assessment is included	£2,000 (+£350 VAT)
Note 2 Rebate where an adequate draft risk assessment is included	£500 (+£87.50 VAT)

SCHEDULE 14

Regulation 17

REVOCATIONS

1 *Description of Instrument*	2 *Reference*	3 *Extent of revocation*
The Genetically Modified Organisms (Contained Use) Regulations 1992	S.I. 1992/3217	Regulation 22
The Notification of New Substances Regulations 1992	S.I. 1993/3050	Regulation 24 and Schedule 4
The Health and Safety (Fees) Regulations 1994	S.I. 1994/397	The whole Regulations